CASES

DECIDED

IN THE SUPREME COURT

OF THE

CAPE OF GOOD HOPE,

DURING THE YEAR

1873,

WITH TABLE OF CASES AND ALPHABETICAL INDEX.

VOL. III.

REPORTED BY

EBEN. J. BUCHANAN,

OF THE INNER TEMPLE, BARRISTER-AT-LAW

J. C. JUTA & CO.,

CAPETOWN. | JOHANNESBURG.

1891.

JUDGES OF THE SUPREME COURT

DURING THE YEAR

1873.

BELL, C. J. [sat for last time, before retiring, on the 7th August].

DE VILLIERS, C.J.: [Appointed 8th December].

DENYSSEN, J.

FITZPATRICK, J.

Attorney-General: J. H. DE VILLIERS [Appointed Chief Justice 8th December, 1873].

      „   „   S. JACOBS [Appointed 24th December, 1873].

CASES REPORTED IN THIS VOLUME.

INDEX TO THE VOLUME.

SUPREME COURT REPORTS.

1873.

PART I.

J. M. Scheepers, Appellant, *vs.* C. F. Scheepers' Executrix, Respondent.

Survivor.   Second Marriage.   Collation.

An Executrix, survivor of a second marriage, can not, in her own right, in taking an account of the first wife's estate, require collation to be made by a child of the first marriage, such claim having been waived by the acts of the deceased spouse.

1872.
Nov. 26.
1873.
February 1.

J. M. Scheepers
vs.
C. F. Scheepers'
Executrix.

This was an action brought by Johannes Marthinus Scheepers for the payment of the maternal inheritance due him from the estate of his mother, the first wife of the late Coenraad Fredrik Scheepers, against Jacomina Aletta Scheepers, the widow of his father, the said C. F. Scheepers, by a second marriage, and his executrix testamentary. The facts of the case will be found fully stated in the judgments given below.

The cause came before the Eastern Districts Court on the 22nd and 23rd February, 1872, when after hearing the evidence it was declared the plaintiff was entitled to such sum, if any, as should appear to be due to him upon certain accounts and inquiries being taken and made. Afterwards, on the 27th of the same month, the case having been set down by the plaintiff for final judgment, the plaintiff's counsel declining to go into the accounts ordered, the Eastern Districts Court gave judgment for defendant with costs.

An appeal was noted, and the case argued before the Supreme Court (November 26, 1872) by *Jacobs, Acting*

B

1872.
Nov. 26.
1873.
February 1.

J. M. Scheepers
vs.
C. F. Scheepers'
Executrix.

A.G. (with him *Hodges*) for the plaintiff and appellant, and by *Cole* (with him *De Villiers*) for the defendant and respondent.

Postea (February 1).—The Court reversed the decision of the Court below, and gave judgment for plaintiff for the amount claimed, with costs.

BELL, C.J.—This was an appeal from a decision of the Eastern Districts Court, pronounced in an action brought by the son of the first marriage, against the widow and executrix testamentary of his father by a second marriage for payment of £247 15s. 11d., as his share of his *maternal inheritance* derived from his mother, the wife of the first marriage.

The declaration states that the plaintiff is one of eleven children of Coenraad F. Scheepers by Elsie Elizabetha, his first wife, to whom he was married in community of property, and also one of the heirs under the last will of the spouses, bearing date the 15th of December, 1857. That his mother died in or about the year 1858, leaving her husband her surviving, who, by the will, was appointed executor of her estate, and who duly acted as such. The declaration further says that afterwards the said Coenraad F. Scheepers caused to be made a liquidation and distribution account of the estate of the said spouses, whereby the balance of the estate for distribution was shown to be £5,451 11s., and whereby the portion due to the plaintiff as his maternal inheritance was shown to be £247 15s. 11d. That afterwards, the said Coenraad F. Scheepers intermarried with the defendant, and died in or about 1870, leaving the defendant him surviving, who, on the 24th of September in that year, received letters of administration as executrix testamentary of the estate of Coenraad F. Scheepers. That although the said Coenraad F. Scheepers during his lifetime, and the defendant since his death, have been so requested, neither of them has paid to the plaintiff any part of his maternal inheritance; wherefore he prays that the defendant may be adjudged to pay him such inheritance, to wit, the sum of £247 15s. 11d.

To this the defendant pleaded the general issue, and specially that during the subsistence of the marriage of Coenraad F. Scheepers and Elsie Elizabetha, the plaintiff, together with several of his brothers, purchased from the said Coenraad F. Scheepers certain farms belonging to the said Coenraad F. Scheepers, situated in the field-cornetcy of Olifantshoek, for the nominal sum of £1,500 or thereabouts, and that when the abovementioned sales were effected, " it was mutually agreed by and between them, the several parties thereto, including the plaintiff, that such sale should be in lieu and stead of the *legitimate portion* to which any of the parties, and amongst them the plaintiff, would be entitled, on the death of the first dying of their parents, and that, in consideration of the premises, no purchase money was passed by the plaintiff in payment of the share in the said property which was subsequently transferred to him."

1872.
Nov. 26.
1873.
February 1.

J. M. Scheepers
vs.
C. F. Scheepers'
Executrix.

As the action was brought for the payment of the plaintiff's maternal inheritance, and the special plea is to a claim for his legitimate portion, which was not in question, the plea does not in fact meet the case, and the defence rests entirely upon the general issue.

Such being the state of the pleadings, I shall now state the history of the case, as it appears from the evidence, oral and documentary.

The father seems, at one time, to have been possessed of considerable landed property. In the year 1850, during the subsistence of the first marriage, the spouses being minded to remove their residence to another part of the country from where they had hitherto resided, the husband, to relieve himself of the burden of his landed estate, and, possibly, in anticipation of its descent to his children at his death, went through the form of a sale of his different farms to his children, of whom there were eleven, and regularly executed a deed of transfer in their favour, sixty pounds (£60) being stated to be the purchase money. But in the declaration of purchase made by the children in order to satisfy the transfer duty payable on a sale, the price was declared to be £1,000.

Why the form of a deed of gift was not adopted does not appear, for it was not pretended that £1,000 or any other sum was paid by the children to the father.

At the time of this transaction the spouses had been already married at least upwards of thirty-two years, as there was produced a will executed by them in September, 1818, and, as before observed, they had had eleven children born to them.

After having made the gift to their children, the spouses removed to an erf which they had at Hertzog, in the district of Fort Beaufort, their former residence having been in Olifantshoek, and they lived at Hertzog till the close of their lives—the children, so far as appears, possessing, cultivating, reaping, and enjoying the produce of the farms in Olifantshoek which their father had transferred to them.

On the 15th September, 1857, the spouses executed a will by which they revoked all prior ones. They bequeathed by

1872.
Nov. 26.
1873.
February 1.

J. M. Scheepers
vs.
C. F. Scheepers'
Executrix.

it to the survivor "a complete bullock-wagon with two boxes, 12 oxen, 2 cows with calves, a riding horse with saddle and bridle, a gun, a complete bed, 2 tables and 6 chairs, besides the erf situated at Hertzog, at present occupied by us; all which are to be entered upon and possessed as free and unencumbered property."

By this will the spouses instituted the survivor of them, together with the children procreated in this their marriage, heirs in all their property, nothing excepted, *except what has already been disposed of*, and the whole was directed to be "realized by public auction by the survivor, within three months of the first dying, so as to be better able to ascertain and distribute the portions of our heirs." This will appointed "the survivor of us as executor or executrix of this our will, and also administrator or administratrix of our estate and effects."

I think it reasonable to suppose that the exception in this will, from the inheritance of "what has already been disposed of," referred to the bullock-wagon and other things bequeathed to the survivor at the outset of the will, and had not any reference to the farms which had already been given away to the children.

Some time in the year 1858 the wife died, being survived by the husband, who took out letters of administration as her executor. So far as appears, he does not seem to have turned the estate into money, or "ascertained and distributed the portions of our heirs," as directed by the mutual will. Three or four months after the death of his wife the husband married the present defendant.

In the year 1860 the husband, whom I shall henceforth call the father, accompanied by one of his sons, waited upon Campbell, a notary in Graham's Town, and expressed a wish that an account should be made out of the first wife's property. Campbell, at the dictation of the father, made out an account entitled "in the joint estate of Elsie Elizabetha Scheepers, born Landmann, and surviving husband Coenraad Fredrik Scheepers: liquidation account."

On the debit side of this account, there are only two items—"valuation of property movable, £2,431 10s.," and "valuation of property immovable, £3,100, making together £5,531 10s." On the credit side there are several items of disbursements connected with the administration, amounting to £79 19s.; there being deducted from the debit side, the "balance as per distribution" is stated to be £5,431 11s.

There is another account entitled "distribution account." To the debit of this account is placed £5,451 11s., and to the credit side there are entries to the surviving spouse of £2,725 15s. 6d., being the half of £5,451 11s., and eleven entries of £247 15s. 11d. to each of the eleven children by name, making together £2,725 15s. 6d., the other half of £5,451 11s.

1872.
Nov. 26;
1873.
February 1.

J. M. Scheepers
vs.
C. F. Scheepers'
Executrix.

Another document produced bore the title, " In the joint estate of Elsie Elizabetha Scheepers, born Landmann, and surviving husband, Coenraad Frederick Scheepers; inventory of property and valuation thereof." There then follow nineteen entries of property, immovable and movable, with the values, amounting in all to £5,531 10s., the sum entered to the debit of "liquidation account."

None of these accounts have the signature of the father, or anything on the face of them to show that they were either known or assented to by him; indeed, Campbell swears the account was not signed by testator, and he adds the accounts were made out "from dictation of the father, of which a minute was made, the account was submitted to him and approved, the value was put down and is fair. It was mutually agreed upon by father and son. The account puts it at £5,531 10s. I can't remember he said it was the estate in lifetime of his former wife. The two sons," Coenraad and a younger one, "assisted the father in making out the inventory. I made out the valuation from a statement of the two sons and the father. I did not see the property."

Eleven separate papers for each of the children, saying he or she had examined and approved the liquidation account, and acknowledged that he or she had received £247 16s., the sum awarded by it, all dated the 31st day of July, 1860, but not one of them signed by anybody, are among the documentary evidence, but by whom they are produced, and for what purpose, does not appear.

Campbell swears " he directed me to draw up promissory notes. I made out the promissory notes before the date they bear, but they were to bear date from the time mentioned." Whether by "he " the father was intended or the son Coenraad, whose name is last mentioned, does not appear, neither is it explained what the promissory notes were for, nor by whom they were to be signed, nor what was meant by their "bearing date from the time mentioned."

The plaintiff in his evidence says he had a conversation with his father three or four months after the death of his mother, and before the second marriage. He brought up the estate in conversation. Coenraad was with him. He said, " Stoffel and Coenraad have annoyed me very much. They would not sign the paper that they had received their mother's portion. I did not see the paper. He asked me if I would sign it. I said I have not had it and I won't sign it. He said, Where is the ground you got? It is more

1872.
Nov. 26.
1873.
February 1.

J. M. Scheepers
vs.
C. F. Scheepers'
Executrix.

worth than I have got. I said I won't summon you for the estate, but at your death I will have every penny of it— use it all your life as much as you please."

As the mother of plaintiff died in 1857, and his father married his second wife three or four months after the death of his first wife, and the plaintiff says the conversation he here speaks of occurred before the second marriage, the paper which Stoffel, Coenraad, and the plaintiff refused to sign could not have been the papers made out after Campbell's interview and preparation of the accounts, because that took place in 1860, and it does not appear what the paper was.

The plaintiff in a subsequent passage of his evidence says:—"At the time my father had been with Campbell he spoke to me about it I said, Don't speak to me about the estate; you insulted me about it last time. He said, But now I have altered my mind. I intend to give you your portion. He said he had instructed Campbell, and that he had appointed Coenraad on my side, and that together they had made a proper valuation. I saw him again at Christmas, 1869. He said he had a will made after my mother's death. He said Coenraad had £155 and Fuller £100. He said, I intend paying you all out as money comes in. He said he would give the next £100 to the next, and so on until he had settled."

This evidence so far confirms that of Campbell, as it obviously refers to the valuation and accounts prepared by Campbell. There was produced for the plaintiff a letter written by the father to his son Coenraad. That letter is dated 5th May, 1863. "My son, C. F. S.,—You and I, your father, have appraised the estate, and you know that there are goods which are bequeathed to me, your father, by testament, also taken into account, and should these be deducted I think you will not have to get out as much as you have, through your agent, demanded of me, £155 sterling. You could, without having employed your agent, have asked me, and I should not have withheld that which was due to you. I have thus sent the £155 sterling to Mr. F. Carlisle, at Graham's Town, where you can receive that sum on the 10th of this month. Please send me the inventory or liquidation account of the estate, in order that I may myself see how much each heir must be paid out; then I will pay out to every one his portion without being asked by them."

There was produced with this letter a promissory note bearing date Hertzog, 1st April, 1863, signed by the father, whereby he promised to pay his son Coenraad £155, "being in full payment of his maternal inheritance due to him by me."

There is also another letter from the father to the same son, dated Hertzog, 17th June, 1863, in which the father says, "I have heard that you will not or would not receive £155 unless I give the £100 in addition. I am willing to do so, but I am at this moment not in money."

1872.
Nov. 26.
1873.
February 1.

J. M. Scheepers
vs.
C. F. Scheepers'
Executrix.

This action is not for administration of the joint estate of the first marriage; if it had been, there might have been ground to hesitate whether there should not be a new valuation of the estate, for looking at Campbell's valuation, made without seeing the items of property valued, and taking the property and its value to be as stated by Coenraad, the son, I should not have considered that that valuation could have concluded any one entitled to dispute it, more especially when I look at the details of the valuation with the light thrown on them by Meurant, a witness for the defendant.

But the action is for payment of the plaintiff's share of that valuation, and is directed against the executors of the father. It is impossible to read the evidence of Campbell and the plaintiff, and the letters of the father to the son Coenraad, without feeling assured that the father had assented to the valuation sworn to by Campbell, and to the distribution account of the estate made by that gentleman, and that he meant to pay according to it so soon as he could find means to do so.

The plea of the defendant to the action was that the sale to the children of the farms in Olifantshoek was pretended; and that, in truth, the farms were accepted in lieu and stead of the legitimate portions to which they would be entitled on the death of their mother. It is sufficient to say that, in support of this defence, reading it as applicable to the claim for maternal inheritance instead of for the legitimate portion, not a tittle of evidence is to be found in the proceedings below.

Though not pleaded, it was argued before us (whether it was argued in the Court below I do not know) that the plaintiff was not entitled to have a share of his mother's inheritance, without bringing into collation his share of the farms which he received from his father in his lifetime. It is evident from the father's observation to Coenraad, when speaking of his unreasonableness in not signing the paper, whatever it was, " Where is the ground you got ? It is more worth than I have got," and his remark to the same son in his letter of 5th May, 1863, " You know that there are goods which are bequeathed to me, your father, by the testament, also taken into account," that the gift of the farms had not been reckoned in the liquidation and distribution account, although the father's legacy had been, and yet that he was willing to pay upon that footing.

1872.
Nov. 26.
1873.
February 1.

J. M. Scheepers
vs.
C. F. Scheepers'
Executrix.

I do not know that this would have concluded the father from seeking the benefit of collation of these farms, in taking the account of his first wife's estate, had he insisted upon it in his lifetime, but he did not do so. He left the matter upon the liquidation account framed by Campbell, which he adopted, and he expressed his intention to pay according to the distribution account framed by the same gentleman. He did nothing in his lifetime to show a wish to depart from that, and now collation is asked by his executrix, not in assertion of any claim made by him, but apparently in her own right, as survivor of the second marriage. It is sufficient to say that no authority was shown to us, nor am I aware of any that will support a claim for collation, by a party standing in the relation the defendant does to those interested in the estate of the first marriage. An interlocutory judgment of the Court below found that the plaintiff was entitled to such sum, if any, as should appear to be due to him upon the following accounts and inquiries :—

1. An account of the estate of the first wife at the time of her death.

2. An inquiry what children were entitled to legitimate portions out of it, and the value of such portions.

3. An account of the estate transferred by the spouses to the plaintiff, and in taking such account the defendant, as representing the father, to have credit for the value of the portion transferred as aforesaid to the plaintiff at the time of such transfer.

It is obvious from the evidence I have read that the first of the accounts was unnecessary ; it had already been taken and assented to by the father.

The second inquiry, as to number of children, was unnecessary, because it was admitted that there were eleven, as was the inquiry in regard to title to legitimate portions, as none such was raised by the action.

The account in the third branch of the judgment could only be applicable to a case where collation was in question. None such was raised by the pleading ; and if it had, it could not have been maintained by the defendant.

The plaintiff declined to go into the account and inquiries directed, and thereupon the Court gave judgment for the defendant with costs.

I am of opinion that the Court below miscarried in directing these accounts and inquiries, as the evidence showed that they were rendered unnecessary by what the father had done in his lifetime; and I am also of opinion that the judgment of the Court below was erroneous, and ought to be reversed, plaintiff having proved his claim, and that our judgment ought to be for the plaintiff for the sum claimed by his declaration, with costs here and in the Court below.

1872.
Nov. 26.
1873
February 11.

J. M. Scheepers
vs.
C. F. Scheepers'
Executrix.

DENYSSEN, J.—The petitioner is one of eleven children of Coenraad F. Scheepers and Elsie Elizabetha Scheepers. His mother died in 1858, leaving her husband surviving, who, in terms of a joint will made in 1857, took out letters of administration as executor testamentary of the joint estate. An inventory and valuation of the joint estate, as well as the liquidation and distribution account, were made, specifying the half share due to the husband, it having been a marriage in communion, and also the portion due to the children as their maternal inheritance. The father married the defendant in this suit, when does not exactly appear, but he died in 1870, leaving her surviving, and she then took out letters of administration as executrix testamentary in terms and by virtue of a will made by her and her deceased husband. The petitioner claims from her, as such executrix, the amount of maternal inheritance due to him out of his mother's estate, under and by virtue of the liquidation and distribution account above mentioned; and the defence to this claim is, first, a general denial, and secondly, that during the lifetime of his father and mother certain farms were sold and transferred to him and their other children at a nominal price, and under an agreement that such sales should be in lieu and stead of a legitimate portion to which any of the parties, and among them the petitioner, should be entitled at the death of the first dying of the parents, and that in consideration thereof the purchase price was not paid. At the trial the petitioner put in the inventory and valuation of the so joint estate, the liquidation and distribution account, which, although informal in certain respects, was proved to have been made out at the instance of the father and executor, to have been adopted and acted upon by him, but not a particle of evidence was led to establish the defence raised by defendant. The Eastern Districts Court declared after hearing the evidence and argument that the petitioner was entitled to such sum, if any, as should appear to be due to him upon the following accounts and inquiries being taken and made, that is to say:—1. An account of the estate of Mrs. Elsie Elizabetha Scheepers at the time of her decease. 2. An inquiry what children were entitled to legitimate portions out of the said estate, and the value of such portions. 3. An account of the estate transferred by Coenraad Fredrik Scheepers, the elder, and his predeceased wife, to the petitioner, and in taking such account the defendant, as representing the estate of the deceased Scheepers, the elder, is to have credit for the value of the portion of the estate transferred as

1872.
Nov. 26.
1873.
February 1.

J. M. Scheepers
vs.
C. F. Scheepers'
Executrix.

aforesaid to the petitioner at the time of such transfer; and the said Court ordered the question of costs to stand over. The counsel for the petitioner having declined to go into such accounts, the Eastern Districts Court on a subsequent occasion, and in the absence of any such accounts as above mentioned, gave judgment for the defendant with costs. From this judgment the petitioner appeals to this Court. I agree with my brother Dwyer, of the Eastern Districts Court, in his remarks appended to the judgment, that the question of collation is out of the case, although I do not comprehend the object of the account required by the order of the Court. If the parties thought they could and intended to raise that question, it should have been done by a special plea. Nor has any issue been raised upon the pleadings in respect of the inventory and valuation of the joint estate of Scheepers and his first wife, or of the liquidation and distribution account, which the Court must assume, therefore, for the purposes of this action, as correct; the only defence upon which the defendant relied being that the farms alluded to were given or sold and transferred to the petitioner and the other children, upon the understanding and agreement entered into between the said children and their parents during the lifetime of the latter, that they were so given or sold and transferred in lieu of any legitimate portion due to them at the decease of the first dying of their parents. There is not a particle of evidence to support that defence, and it therefore wholly failed. The evidence of the petitioner being complete, I think there should have been a judgment in his favour, with costs, and I concur, therefore, in the judgment just delivered.

FITZPATRICK, J., concurred.

[Appellant's Attorneys, FAIRBRIDGE & ARDERNE.
  Respondents' Attorneys, REID & NEPHEW.]

TRUSTEES OF WRIGHT *vs.* EXECUTORS OF WRIGHT.

Legacy: interest on. Interest: rate of.

Interest which has accrued on a Legacy after the time it should be paid over belongs to the Legatee. The rate of interest depends on the amount of profits earned.

February 26.
" 28.

Trustees of
Wright *vs.* Exrs.
of Wright.

It appeared that the late Mrs. Rosa Wright did, on the 19th June, 1866, at Graham's Town, make and execute her last will and testament, in which among other matters she directed that her executors should, so soon as conveniently may be after her deceace, pay over and transfer a sum of £7,000 to certain trustees named in the will, in trust to build and endow a church at Oatlands, near Graham's Town, and for other purposes. Testatrix died in February, 1867. Letters of administration were issued by the Master to the executors under the will on the 16th March, 1867. On the 31st August, 1870, the executors paid to the trustees a sum of £6,089 1s. 6d., which together with a piece of land transferred to them made up the amount of the legacy.

1873.
February 2. 6.
„ 28
——
Trustees of
Wright *vs.* Exrs.
of Wright.

The trustees, the plaintiffs in this action, now claimed that in addition to such capital sum they are, as such trustees, entitled to receive interest on the same at the rate of six per cent. per annum from the 17th September, 1867, being the day upon which the said executors were by law bound to file their liquidation account of the estate (*i.e.*, six months after the date of the letters of administration), to the said 31st August, 1870, the day upon which the said capital sum was in fact paid to them.

The defendants, the executors, pleaded the general issue; and then, specially, that interest was not claimable, because so soon as conveniently could be after the decease of the testatrix, to wit, in the month of August, 1870, they paid and transferred, and the plaintiffs accepted and received, the amount of the legacy; further, that so soon as conveniently could be after the decease of the said testatrix, to wit, at the end of the year 1868, and at divers times afterwards, and before the said 31st August, 1870, they tendered and offered to pay the said capital sum, but the plaintiffs refused to receive it; further, that no deed of settlement or of trusts has been executed in accordance with the requirements of the will; and lastly *plene administravit*.

The plaintiffs' replication was, firstly, general; and then, specially, admitting the trust mentioned in the defendants' plea to be binding on the plaintiffs, it was and is impossible to have such trust deed as was referred to prepared and executed until the interest is paid over or declared not to be claimable. And as to the last plea, plaintiffs say defendants before administration had full notice of the claim and of plaintiffs' intention of enforcing it.

Cole (with him *Maasdorp*) appeared for the plaintiffs, and *De Villiers, A.G.* (with him *Reitz*) for the defendants. After hearing evidence in support of the pleas and the arguments at Bar,

Cur. adv. vult.

Postea (February 28),

BELL, C.J., in delivering judgment, said:—The sole question involved here is one of interest. The action is brought for payment of £1,065 18s., being the interest from the 17th of September, 1867, to the 31st of August, 1870, and the question was supposed to depend upon three grounds which were raised; the first being, Was the legacy payable till a certain trust deed was executed? secondly, Did the interest belong to the trustees or to the general estate? and thirdly, From what date did the interest commence? An authority was quoted from the *Code* to the effect that interest could only be claimed after *litis contestatio*, whatever period that was; and the argument assumed from that was, that whatever period might intervene between the death of the testator and the *litis contestatio* raised by the heirs, the interest would go, not to the legatee, but to the estate. But that, as I observed at the time, would lead to the strange conclusion that the executors might conceal from the persons entitled under the will, not only the existence of the will itself, but their rights under it, whereby there might be a gain to the estate but an injury to the legatee, who would be a loser of any interest or *fructus* that would accrue in the meantime,—*fructus* and *usurius* being used conjunctively in the authority. This, however, would be an apparent hardship, which it would not be in the power of the legatee to correct, for he could not recoup himself in any way. He might be absent from the Colony, or otherwise ignorant of the existence of the will, and have no inducement to raise any *litis contestatio*. *Voet* lays it down distinctly that both interest and *fructus* accrue to the legatee from the death of the legator; and then goes on to say that there are commentators some of whom take one view, and some another. I am disposed, however, to adopt the opinion of so great an authority as *Voet*, which is always recognised in this Colony as a supreme authority, and think that the interest which accrued—not from the death of the testator, but from the time which, under the terms of the will, it was convenient for the money to be paid, to wit, the end of December, 1867—that interest from that time accrued to the legatee. That being the case, the remaining question need not be disposed of, except in so far as it trenches upon the question of costs. The first question raised was, Was the legacy payable until the trust deed was executed? Now, according to the will, the bequest is almost in the nature of a specific legacy, which according to the law of England, and as far as I can see is the law here, bears interest from the beginning. After sundry minor legacies, this £7,000 is given to those persons in trust for a certain charity, and having done so, the testatrix goes on to put her estate under the management of executors. It seems to me that these executors had a very proper duty to discharge in requesting that the trustees should prepare and execute the trust deed. The will set forth the terms of the trust and the conditions upon which the trustees were to accept the money from the executors. The will makes them bound and obliged to prepare this deed as soon as possible after testatrix's death, and their duty manifestly was to do so as speedily as they could. The executors, I think, were perfectly justified in saying "It would be dangerous for us to part with this money until we see by what hands it is to be held." I take it that the object of the testatrix in the selection of the executors as trustees was to secure the money, so that it should not be lost, which might be the case if the fund was handed over without protection. The safety of the money was to be guaranteed by the execution of the deed before the former was handed over, which was properly withheld up to the date when it was paid, after which there should be no question. The whole matter that is prayed for by the declaration is this right to £1,065 18s. interest, the defendants maintaining that they were entitled to take that interest and put it into the estate, dividing it among the other legatees; but having failed in proving that, it seems to me that judgment ought to be for the plaintiffs, with costs.

DENYSSEN, J.—I am of the same opinion. It appears to me that the will contemplated that the trust deed should be executed during the testatrix's lifetime, and that all the rules and regulations had been specified and stipulated by which the trustees were appointed and constituted. The trust deed having been executed, the executors were to pay over to the trustees under that deed, whenever it was convenient, the legacy of £7,000. It was provided for in the will that in case the deed should not be executed during Mrs. Wright's lifetime, it should be executed immediately after her death, and, consequently, it appears to me that she, by these different provisions in the will, intended that the trust deed should first be executed before the executors were bound or authorized to pay over to the trustees under that deed the amount of the legacy. In my opinion, the executors would have been fully justified under the provisions of the will to have withheld the amount of the legacy, as well as any interest due, until such trust deed should have been executed. The next question that arises is with reference to the interest. It is quite clear, according to the Roman and Dutch law, that the legatee is *dominus* of the legacy. There is a great difference of opinion as to the date from which this interest should be made payable; but here I think that question does not arise, because in the last will it is provided that, as soon as

1873.
February 26.
„ 28.

Trustees of
Wright *vs.* Exrs.
of Wright.

1873.
February 26.
„ 28.
Trustees of
Wright vs. Exrs.
of Wright.

convenient, the executors (meaning after the execution of the trust deed) should pay over to the trustees the amount of the legacy so given to them. According to the evidence and the books produced, it was convenient for the executors to have paid over the money at the end of December, 1867; and if they had then paid it there cannot be the least doubt that the interest which accrued upon that amount of £7,000 would then have belonged to the trustees for the benefit of the trust. This the executors failed to do. They kept the money, and, of course, the interest accruing upon it. I therefore fully agree with what has fallen from the Chief Justice, that they should be held liable to pay not only the amount of the legacy, but also interest thereon from the time that it was convenient to them to do so, viz., the first of January, 1868.

FITZPATRICK, J.—I also concur; but as it is unnecessary to decide who was right or wrong in the controversy as to the payment of the legacy before the completion of the deed, I do not desire on such a short notice to express any decided opinion as to whether the executors were bound to pay the money before the execution of the deed, or not. I concur with the judgment of the Court, that the defendants are liable for the interest and costs also.

BELL, C.J.—It seems to have been assumed that interest was claimable, or rather that the executors were liable for the interest, from six months after the death of the testatrix; but that is not so. The executors are bound to produce their account, in order to show to those interested in the estate that they are accurate in their administration. The law is very vague on that point, and according to the law of the Colony there is no time fixed. In England a year is allowed to executors to look round, realize the estate, and ascertain the proportions the several persons interested are entitled to; but even there, if the executors can show that no interest had accrued to the estate, the legatee would not be entitled to it. In the present case, if it were not regulated by the will, there would not be any absolute rule as to the time an executor is to pay over. Each case depends upon its own circumstances.

De Villiers, A.G., inquired what the rate of interest was to be.

Cole:—Our claim is for six per cent.

BELL, C.J., thought the trustees should only get the interest which had been actually earned.

After further argument, the Court made an order as follows:—Finding that the legacy was in the hands of the defendants from the first of January, 1868, and that the plaintiffs are entitled to the interest or profits thereof from that date, the matter be referred to Mr. Holland, Registrar and Master of the Eastern Districts Court, to ascertain how the money was employed or invested, and the interest or profits earned, the enquiry to embrace the period between the 1st of January, 1868, and the 31st of August, 1870, when the money was paid.

1873.
February 26.
„   28.

Trustees of
Wright *vs.* Exrs.
of Wright.

BELL, C.J., said, as the majority of the Court thought that the executors were justified in withholding the money, and as every one must be of opinion it could not take three years to prepare the trust deed, they would not give costs on either side. Each party must pay their own.

[Plaintiffs' Attorneys, FAIRBRIDGE & ARDERNE.]
[Defendants' Attorney, VAN ZYL.]

MAGISTRATES' REVIEWED CASES.

MASTERS AND SERVANTS ACT, No. 15 OF 1856, CH. V., SECS. 3 AND 4.

1873.
January 13.

Masters and Servants Act, No. 15 of 1856, Ch. V., Secs. 3 and 4.

BELL, C.J., called attention to a case which had come before him as Judge of the week, in which a lad had been tried under the Masters and Servants Act, No. 15, 1856, chapter 5, section 3, sub-section 3. The prisoner had been found guilty, and the magistrate had sentenced him to three months' imprisonment with hard labour. This was a second conviction. Under section 3, it was competent to the magistrate to sentence a prisoner to imprisonment with or without hard labour for any period not exceeding one month. By section 4 the magistrate was empowered, in case of a second conviction within the space of six months next after any former conviction, to extend the term of imprisonment to a period of six weeks. In the present instance the magistrate had exceeded his authority, and the sentence must accordingly be reduced to six weeks' imprisonment with hard labour.

ACT No. 20, 1856, SEC. 47.

The request of a Prisoner to receive his punishment at once must be recorded, signed by the Prisoner, and also witnessed.

January 13.

Act No. 20, 1856, Sec. 47.

DENYSSEN, J., said he had, as Judge of the week, a case before him, where certain coloured prisoners were charged with theft, and having pleaded guilty, they requested that the punishment awarded might be inflicted at once. The 47th section of Act 20 of 1856 expressly required that where parties desired to be punished at once, such desire should be recorded and signed by the prisoners, and the record duly witnessed. In this case there was no record of the prisoners' desire to be punished at once, and therefore there could be no witnessing. Then, with regard to the merits of the case, the evidence might be satisfactory as to some of the prisoners, but it was certainly unsatisfactory as to others. He thought the matter was one of which notice should be taken by being referred to the Government.

FITZPATRICK, J.—Under the circumstances, the record must be sent to the Attorney-General.

1873.
January 13.

BELL, C.J.—According to my experience, the natives very often pleaded guilty, and afterwards it was proved that they were not so. In the present case the punishment had been inflicted in an irregular and unjustifiable way. That could not, of course, be recalled, but the record should be transmitted to the proper authority.

Act No. 20, 1856,
Sec. 47.

Ordered accordingly.

PROCEDURE.

Sentence of imprisonment and an order to find security to keep the peace ought to be kept distinct.

FITZPATRICK, J., said a case had come before him wherein the magistrate, in addition to sentencing the prisoner to imprisonment with spare diet, called upon him to find sureties, himself in £25 and two others in £50 sterling, that he would keep the peace for the next twelve months after the expiration of the sentence. He was not aware that the magistrate had any authority for that in addition to the punishment, and he would therefore refer the matter to the Attorney-General to see if the magistrate's decision could be sustained.

February 1.
„   18.

Postea (February 18).

De Villiers, A.G., appeared in support of the sentence; and *Cole*, at the request of the Court, argued *contra* on behalf of the prisoner.

It appeared that the prisoner had been charged with brutally ill-treating his wife by beating and kicking her. In the course of the trial before the magistrate it was elicited that he had threatened to kill his wife if he were sent to prison for beating her. The magistrate sentenced the prisoner to three months' hard labour for beating his wife, and bound him over to keep the peace towards her in future. The doubt as to the legality of the sentence arose from the two things being joined together. The imprisonment was inflicted by the magistrate in his capacity as such, and the binding over to keep the peace in his capacity as justice of the peace, there being separate statutes conferring jurisdiction in each case.

The Court held that while it would have been more formal to have had the two things kept distinct, the judgment ought to be sustained.

ORD. NO. 9, 1851, SECS. 46 AND 47.

*Sentences pronounced the same day all regarded as first
convictions.*

BELL, C.J., said a conviction had come before him as
Judge of the week, in which there were three charges all
tried upon the same day against the same person, which all
appeared to have arisen out of one case. He referred the
papers to the Attorney-General to see whether the convictions could be sustained. In the first of these cases, the
accused was fined £6 13s. 4d. Under what authority this
fine was imposed he did not know, for the Ordinance fixed
the fine for the first offence at £10. In the second case
the magistrate imposed a fine of £10, while the Ordinance
fixed it at £20, and in the third case he imposed a fine of
£20. It appeared to him that the whole of these cases had
arisen out of one case.

De Villiers, A.G., pointed out that the 47th section of the
Ordinance gave the magistrate the power to mitigate the
fine.

BELL, C.J., said he had not noticed the section mentioned.
But the three sentences having been pronounced on the same
day, the two last could not be regarded as second and third
convictions.

Postea (March 1).

De Villiers, A.G., said that he had looked into the
papers. He thought the decision could not be supported
with regard to the last penalty of £20. The magistrate
had first fined the man £6 13s. 4d., which was two-thirds
of the fine of £10, but by the 47th section it was competent
for him to modify the penalty. The magistrate had next
inflicted a fine of £10. That was justified by the Act.
The third fine of £20 could not be sustained, and he submitted it should be reduced to £10. In his opinion, they
were all first convictions.

FITZPATRICK, J., could not regard it as a second conviction
where there was no time intervening between the first and
second convictions to allow of the first punishment operating
on the man's mind.

BELL, C.J., thought the construction which the magistrate appeared to have put on the matter was never
contemplated by the Act. As, however, the man had
paid the fine, and there seemed to be some little doubt
as to the sale, the Court would grant the usual certificate
for the two first penalties, and reduce the third from £20
to £10.

SUPREME COURT REPORTS.

1873.

PART II.

IN RE THE WIDOW OF J. J. PIENAAR.

Minors, immovable property of. Ord. No. 105, Sec. 24.

Transfer of his portion to one part owner of a farm, on division, not an alienation of the property of minors, owners of another undivided share in the same farm.

The deceased, Jacobus Johannes Pienaar, one Oosthuysen, and others, were owners of a farm in undivided shares. During the life of Pienaar an apportionment of the farm. was agreed upon, but it had not been carried into effect. By last will Pienaar bequeathed his share to his children, minors. It was now sought by the co-proprietors to give transfer in accordance with the apportionment to Oosthuysen of his share.

De Villiers, A.G., for Adriana Petronella Joubert, widow and executrix testamentary of the said late J. J. Pienaar, and guardian of the minor children, prayed an order on the Registrar of Deeds to accept and pass the transfer by applicant and the other part owners to Oosthuysen. The Registrar of Deeds had grounded his refusal to pass the transfer on section 24 of Ordinance No. 105, which provides that the immovable property of minors shall not be alienated without the sanction of the Court.

BELL, C.J., said there was no necessity in this case for the authority of the Court. The Registrar would intimate this to the Registrar of Deeds.

[Applicant's Attorney, C. C. DE VILLIERS.]

C 2

OTTO *vs.* OTTO.

Divorce. Malicious desertion. Evidence.

Service of order of Court in an action for divorce, on the ground of malicious desertion, should, the defendant being in default, be proved like any other fact in the case, and not by affidavit.

This was an action on the part of the husband for a divorce on the ground of malicious desertion, the wife having been previously ordered by the Court to return to her husband. The wife was in contempt, and did not appear.

The order of Court, and an affidavit of "due service" thereof on defendant personally by one De Vos, an agent residing at Worcester, at which place the defendant had also been residing, was put in.

The Court refused, in an action of this serious nature, to receive the affidavit as a proof of the due service of the order of Court. Service must be proved by the best evidence, like any other material fact in the case. An affidavit was not such evidence.

De Villiers, A.G., for the plaintiff, relied on the general practice among the side-bar, and quoted *Van Blerk vs. Naudé*, 1 *Menz.*, 257, where affidavits had been received to prove service of certain notices.

FITZPATRICK, J.—The question in that case was on another point. The concluding paragraph of the report throws a doubt on the proposition that affidavits were considered sufficient proof.

Postea (same day).—De Vos was put in the box, and proved personal service of the order of Court on the defendant, and also the statement of defendant that she would not return to her husband.

After hearing all the evidence, the Court granted the decree as prayed.

[Plaintiff's Attorney, C. C. DE VILLIERS.]

⎯⎯⎯⎯⎯⎯

LAUBSCHER *vs.* VIGORS AND FRYER.

Lis pendens, effect of plea of. Tender. Waiver of production of the money. Sheriff, duty of.

Where plaintiff said to the Deputy Sheriff, "Do not attach my things; I will pay you immediately" ("net nu"), but no money was produced, though it was given in evidence there was sufficient money in the house to satisfy the writ, and the defendant, the Deputy Sheriff, replied, " Unless you sign this power of attorney, I cannot receive the money," and plaintiff refused to sign, and an attachment was made, held to be a tender sufficient to found an action for malicious seizure.

This was an action for £500 damages, alleged to have been sustained by reason of a wrongful, unlawful, and malicious seizure of goods in execution.

1873.
May 20.
„ 27.
„ 29.

Laubscher *vs.*
Vigors & Fryer

The plaintiff, Gerhardus Jacobus Laubscher, is a farmer residing at Zandberg, in the division of Clanwilliam. The first-named defendant, Percy Vigors, is the Sheriff of the Colony, and the second-named (defendant by intervention), Charles Montagu Fryer, his deputy for the division of Clanwilliam.

The plaintiff and others and one Richard Walter Fryer were co-proprietors in undivided shares of the farms Hollebakstrandfontein and Platklip, situate in the aforesaid division of Clanwilliam. These co-proprietors executed a deed of submission on the 4th July, 1870, agreeing to submit the arbitrament of differences which had arisen between them, and the division of the property, to the award of the second-named defendant (brother to the said R. W. Fryer) and Josias Andries Engelbrecht. The arbitrators made an award. Plaintiff and several of the co-proprietors were dissatisfied with it; but it was, in default of their appearance, on the 12th October, 1870, duly made a rule of Court. R. W. Fryer instituted proceedings to compel transfer to him of his share in terms of the award, and, the other co-proprietors being again in default, obtained judgment on the 29th August, 1871. The plaintiff and the other co-proprietors, feeling themselves aggrieved, commenced an action to set aside the rule of Court confirming the award. This action was unsuccessful. Meanwhile, a writ of execution was issued, dated 27th October, 1871, upon the judgment obtained by R. W. Fryer. It was upon the execution of this writ, which was in the following terms, that the present cause of action arose :—

" We command you,—first, that you call upon Gerhardus Jacobus Laubscher and Jacobus Adriaan Louw, of Zandberg, and Pieter Joachim Wilhelm Slabbert, of Elandsfontein, all of the district of Clanwilliam, and demand them forthwith to comply with a certain order or judgment of the Honourable the Supreme Court, bearing date the 29th day of August, 1871, and given in the case wherein Richard Walter Fryer was plaintiff and they were the defendants, and by which order or judgment they were compelled to comply with the

1873.
May 20.
„ 27.
„ 29.

Laubscher *vs.*
Vigors & Fryer.

terms of a certain award between them and one Petrus Andries Louw and the said plaintiff, and which award was made a rule of Court on the 12th day of October, 1870, and by which award, rule, or order of Court or judgment, they, the said G. J. Laubscher, J. A. Louw, and P. J. W. Slabbert, were ordered jointly as well as severally, and condemned to join the said P. A. Louw and the said R. W. Fryer, as co-proprietors in the farms commonly known as Hollebak-strandfontein and Platklip, *alias* Lot No. 825, situate in the district of Clanwilliam, in giving mutual transfers of the said farms, in terms of the said award and rule or order of Court and judgment, and as delineated in the plan referred to in the said award and rule or order of Court and judgment, copies of which have been duly served upon the defendants.

"Secondly,—We command you that of the goods and chattels of the said G. J. Laubscher, J. A. Louw, and P. J. W. Slabbert you cause to be made the sum of £78 7s. 3d. sterling, of lawful money, being the taxed costs and charges of the said R. W. Fryer, incurred by him in and about a certain notice of motion made on behalf of the said defendants as applicants against the said plaintiff as respondent, to have the said award set aside, which said costs of the said respondent in and about opposing the motion the said applicants, as defendants, were by order of the Honourable the Supreme Court bearing date the 30th day of August last condemned to pay, less the sum of £35 sterling received on account.

"And have you then and there this writ," &c.

The Sheriff's return on this writ was as follows:—

"The defendant P. J. W. Slabbert was, on the 31st of October, 1871, called on by the deputy sheriff of Clanwilliam to give the transfer commanded by this writ, which he refused to do; and the defendants G. J. Laubscher and J. A. Louw were on the first day of November, 1871, called on by the said deputy sheriff to give like transfer as herein commanded, which they refused to do; and the goods and chattels of the said defendants were thereupon duly attached, as commanded hereby, and were subsequently released from attachment upon payment made of the costs named herein.

"PERCY VIGORS, High Sheriff.

"6th June, 1872."

The declaration complained that on or about the 31st October, 1871, when C. M. Fryer, as deputy sheriff, came to plaintiff's farm, Zandberg, and produced the writ, plaintiff tendered and offered to pay to the said C. M. Fryer the full amount specified in the writ, together with all costs legally payable, and in all other respects was prepared to satisfy the exigency of the said process; but the said C. M. Fryer, as deputy sheriff, refused to accept any money, and proceeded wrongfully, unlawfully, and maliciously to make a seizure, and attached certain articles; by reason of which the plaintiff sustained damages in the sum of £500 sterling.

1873.
May 20.
„ 27.
„ 29.

Laubscher vs.
Vigors & Fryer.

The summons in this action was dated the 28th May, 1872. Previously, however, on the 22nd November, 1871, a similar summons had been issued; but in it the plaintiff, jointly with J. A. Louw and P. J. W. Slabbert, claimed from the first defendant, Vigors, £1,000 as damages arising from the same seizure. To this appearance had been entered, and a declaration was filed, but no further steps were taken.

To the present declaration defendant Vigors pleaded specially that the former action was still depending; was for the same identical causes of action; that the said G. J. Laubscher, the plaintiff in this action, was the same G. J. Laubscher who was one of the plaintiffs in the former action; that the defendant was the same defendant in both actions; and that the costs of the said former action had never been paid. And further, should the above be deemed insufficient, but not otherwise, the general issue. Defendant Fryer (who had intervened) pleaded generally.

The plaintiff's replication to defendant Vigors' special plea was that the former action had been duly withdrawn before the issuing of the summons in the present case; that due notice of such withdrawal had been given, and that the plaintiff had always been willing, and still was ready and willing, and hereby again tendered and offered, to pay defendant his duly taxed costs therein.

The defendants' rejoinder was general.

On the reading of the pleadings, and hearing *De Villiers, A.G.*, for the plaintiff, on the special plea in bar,

The Court ordered the case to stand over till the records had been purged of the former suit, with costs of the day against the plaintiff.

Postea (May 27).—The summons in the previous action having in the meantime been withdrawn, and costs paid, the case was again set down for argument of the exception and trial, when *Cole* (with him *E. J. Buchanan*), for the defendants, contended that the special plea of *lis pendens* was a good defence in the present case, and therefore the plaintiff should commence all proceedings *de novo*.

1873.
May 20.
,, 27.
,, 29.

Laubscher vs.
Vigors & Fryer.

The Court, as the grounds of the exception had been removed, ordered the trial to proceed on the merits, but allowed defendant the costs of the exception.

The evidence taken *viva voce* consisted of that of the plaintiff, who, through the interpreter, said *inter alia:*— " When Fryer came to me with the writ, I said, ' Do not attach my goods; I will pay you immediately.' Fryer replied, ' Even if you want to pay me £100, I have no right to receive the money.' I had upwards of £100 in the house, and £50 in my pocket."

P. A. Louw, residing on the same farm as plaintiff, and who was present at the seizure, corroborated. He said:— "Plaintiff asked Fryer, ' Why do you make an inventory? I will pay you immediately ' (*net nu*). Fryer said, even if plaintiff wished to pay £100, he could not receive the money; but if plaintiff would sign the power of attorney, he (Fryer) would not make an inventory. Plaintiff did say that the money had been sent to his attorney in town, but he said money was ready here also. He did not hold it out in his hand."

G. van Zyl, field-cornet, who accompanied Fryer to plaintiff's, gave similar evidence.

Defendant Fryer, on the other side, denied that any tender had been made, or that plaintiff had said he would pay. What plaintiff did say, he alleged, was, " Why have you come to attach my goods? I have sent the money to Mr. Tiran " (his attorney). After the seizure was made, plaintiff said he would not sign the power of attorney, but that the money was lying ready. He did not say where, or actually offer it.

De Villiers contended the evidence was clear that plaintiff had offered to pay, but the defendant Fryer would not accept the money without the power of attorney also was signed. This was a good tender, defendant having dispensed with the necessity of the production of the money. (*Harding vs. Davis*, 2 *C. and P.* 77; *Polyglass vs. Oliver*, 2 *C. and J.*, 15; *Douglas vs. Patrick*, 3, *T. R.*, 683.)

[FITZPATRICK, J.—You must give the very terms of the offer to bring this under the cases cited. In each of these cases the exact words used are given.]

The evidence was given in Dutch. The general sense of the evidence shows an offer of the money. We must take the general terms of the evidence. Plaintiff said, " I will pay you immediately." That was an offer to pay now, without any medium intervening.

Cole, for the defendants, replied. Admitting the words "the money lies ready " may have been used, that did not amount to a tender; so there could have been no waiver of the production of the money. To make a legal tender there must either be an actual offer of the money produced, or the production of it dispensed with. (*Saunders on Pleading*, vol. 2, 1,049; *Thomas vs. Evans*, 10, *E.*, 101.)

1873.
May 20.
„ 27.
„ 29.

Laubscher *vs.*
Vigors & Fryer.

De Villiers.—*Thomas vs. Evans* has since been over-ruled.

BELL, C.J.—Judgment must be for plaintiff. From the evidence, I think it clear Fryer did not go to plaintiff's to get this money, but with the intention, by pressure of execution, to compel the plaintiff and the other co-proprietors to sign the power of attorney. He abused his office of deputy sheriff. He was brother to R. W. Fryer, who wished to obtain a transfer in terms of an award the other co-proprietors considered unjust, and had then an action pending to set aside; and he had also been an arbitrator in the division of the farm. He did not do his duty as a public officer. When the plaintiff said he would not sign the power, but "the money lies ready," it was Fryer's duty to say, "Well, give me the money." He did not do this, but rather shirked his duty. Judgment will be for plaintiff, £50 damages, and costs.

DENYSSEN, J.—I concur. I think defendant Fryer went to these parties, not for the purpose of executing the writ, but for the purpose of forcing them to sign this power. A tender was made. Plaintiff said, "I will pay you immediately "—*net nu*—now.

FITZPATRICK, J., also concurred.

The Court allowed plaintiff his costs as a witness.

[Plaintiff's Attorney, TIRAN.
Defendants' Attorney, VAN ZYL.]

QUEEN *vs.* ANDRIES PIETER AND MALAGAS MAROON.

Act No. 15, 1864, Sec. 3.   Act No. 3, 1861, Sec. 8.

Rape.

Conviction of Common Assault held good on an indictment charging Rape only.

Andries Pieter and Malagas Maroon were tried at Piquetberg Circuit Court on the 13th April last, on the charge of rape. The jury returned a verdict of guilty of common assault, which verdict the presiding judge (DENYSSEN, J.) accepted, and passed sentence of three years' imprisonment with hard labour.

June 5.

Queen *vs.*
Andries Pieter
and Another.

1873.
June 5.

Queen vs.
Andries Pieter
and Another.

Maasdorp, for the prisoners, now submitted that such a conviction was irregular, incompetent, and contrary to law, and prayed that it might be set aside, and the judgment of the Circuit Court vacated. No direct authorities could be found in support of the application. By section 3 of Act No. 15, 1864, a prisoner tried on an indictment charging assault with intent to commit a rape may be found guilty of common assault. The Legislature then, having had the subject prominently before them, expressly limited the power of convicting on the lesser charge to an assault with intent, and had not extended it to the greater charge of rape itself. Act No. 3, 1861, section 8, provided that a prisoner charged with committing any offence may be convicted of attempting to commit such offence; but there was no enactment enabling a jury to convict of common assault when the charge laid in the indictment was that of rape. There had been a decision in England, arrived at after some doubt, that a prisoner acquitted upon an indictment for rape may be indicted for a common assault. (*R. vs. Dungey*, 4 *F. and F.*, 99. The case is also mentioned in *Archbold*, 17*th ed.*, 659, 707.)

De Villiers, A.G. (for the Crown).—The charge of rape necessarily includes that of assault. Act No. 15, 1864, lays stress on charging the intent, and does not refer to the crime itself. Verdicts of guilty of common assault have been taken on indictments charging rape. (*R. vs. McRue*, 1 *C. and P.*, 641; *R. vs. Williams*, 8 *C. and P.*, 286; *R. vs. Hallet*, 9 *C. and P.*, 748.)

Maasdorp.—The form of indictment in the English case is different from the form in use in this Colony. The English form, as given in *Archbold*, charges that the prisoner "violently and feloniously did make an assault, and her, the said A. N., then violently, and against her will, feloniously did ravish and carnally know," &c. In our form the prisoner is charged with being "guilty of the crime of rape;" and it is in the subsequent and descriptive part of the indictment that an assault is alleged.

BELL, C.J.—The cases show that under the English indictment a man acquitted of rape may on the same indictment be convicted of assault. The only thing against that is a *semble* which favours the argument that the offence of common assault is not included in the charge of rape. But this is not a decision; the book says "it seems." The indictment in this case does charge that the prisoners did "wrongfully and unlawfully assault," and afterwards goes on, that they "did ravish and carnally know." The sentence of the Circuit Court ought to be sustained.

FITZPATRICK, J.—My impression at first was altogether the other way; but seeing the decisions reported in *Carrington and Payne*, I feel compelled to follow those cases, and hold that assault is included in the charge of rape.

DENYSSEN, J.—I am glad the point has come for argument before the full Court. I had my doubts at the time when the verdict was returned whether it was a correct verdict or not, and thought judgment might have been reserved.

[Prisoners' Attorney, C. DE WET.]

1873.
June 5.
Queen *vs.*
Andries Pieter and Another.

SOUTH AFRICAN ASSOCIATION *vs.* MOSTERT.

(See Buchanan's Reports, 1869, p. 231; and Appendix to this part.)

Cole, for the S. A. Association, moved that execution issue for the amount of the judgment of the Privy Council, with interest, and the taxed costs on appeal.

Mostert appeared in person, and having said it was a matter of account,

The Court directed a reference to the Master to ascertain if the account of money claimed to be due was in accordance with the judgment of the Privy Council.

This matter was not again mentioned, as defendant's estate was afterwards, on another claim, compulsorily sequestrated.

June 5.
South African Association *vs.* Mostert.

STANDEN *vs.* CLARK.

Arrest. Provisional sentence. Procedure.

Provisional sentence granted and arrest confirmed on the return day of the writ.

Maasdorp applied for provisional sentence and for confirmation of arrest upon the following summons, directed to the Sheriff:—

June 12.
Standen *vs.* Clark.

"We command you that you take Edward Clark," &c., "and safely keep him so that you have him before our Justices of our Supreme Court of our said Colony, at Cape Town, on the 12th day of June, 1873, at ten o'clock in the forenoon, then and there to answer Charles Standen, of Cape Town, hotel-keeper, wherefore he hath not paid to the said Charles Standen the sum of £68 8s. 9d. sterling of lawful money, together with interest thereon *a tempore moræ*, which he owes to and unjustly detains from the said Charles Standen upon and by virtue of a certain promissory note, bearing date the 1st day of May, 1873, payable on demand, made and signed by the said Edward Clark to and in favour of the said Charles Standen or order, and whereof the latter is still the legal holder, as it is said: and unless he shall do so, then summon the said Edward Clark, that he acknowledge or deny his signature affixed to the said promissory note or the validity of the said debt.

"And also summon the said Edward Clark then and there to plead to the provisional claim of the said Charles Standen for payment thereof," &c.

The affidavit upon which the arrest had been issued stated that Clark " is making preparations, and is about to remove from this Colony."

The defendant had been arrested, and was brought into Court in custody of the Sheriff's officer. He acknowledged the debt, but stated he had no means to pay it. He was awaiting remittances, and on receiving them would pay the bill. He had no intention of leaving the Colony until he had done so.

The Court granted provisional sentence, and confirmed the arrest.

The defendant left the Court in custody.

[Plaintiff's Attorneys, CHRISTIE & FORD.]

IN RE INSOLVENT ESTATE OF MASKELL.

Arrest. Contempt.

Personal attachment issued against a Trustee for not complying with order of Court to file liquidation and distribution account.

Ella, trustee of Maskell's insolvent estate, had been ordered, upon motion made on behalf of Scanlen, a creditor, to file the account and plan of distribution in the estate, before the 12th May, 1872. The order had not been complied with.

Maasdorp now moved on behalf of the creditor, upon notice given to the trustee, for a decree of personal attachment for contempt.

The trustee did not appear.

The Court desired an explanation why so long time had been allowed to elapse between the making of the order and the present motion. The application stood over to obtain this information.

1873.
June 12.
„ 14.
In re Insolvent
Estate of
Maskell.

Postea (June 14).—Affidavit and letters were read, showing that the trustee had requested indulgence, and that applicant had been on a visit to England. Since applicant's return, the trustee had in February last desired to have a " short time longer " allowed him, but had not yet filed any account.

The Court granted the decree.

[Applicant's Attorneys, FAIRBRIDGE & ARDERNE.]

IN RE DR. P. J. A. VAN BREDA.

Jurisdiction over criminal lunatic ordered to be detained during the pleasure of the Crown.

In July, 1871, Dr. Pieter Johannes Albertus van Breda was tried in the Eastern Districts Court on the charge of murder. After hearing the evidence the jury returned a verdict of " Not guilty on the ground of insanity." The presiding Judge thereupon ordered the prisoner to be detained in custody during the Governor's pleasure. Dr. Breda was placed in the lunatic asylum at Robben Island, where he now is. It was alleged that since his confinement Dr. Breda had been restored to sanity. A petition for his release, supported by medical certificates, was forwarded to His Excellency the Governor. Correspondence ensued, which resulted in Dr. Breda's attorneys being informed that the Government did not feel justified in ordering his release unless it should be decided by the Supreme Court that his further detention was not, under all the circumstances of his case, authorized by law.

E. J. Buchanan now applied, on the petition of Dr. Breda's mother, for an order directing the production of the person of Dr. Breda before the Court, at such time as to the Court should seem meet ; and that pending the application about to be made to the Court for his release, Dr. Breda be placed in restraint in some suitable place in Cape Town, with liberty to see and consult with his legal advisers.

[BELL, C.J.—What jurisdiction has the Court in this matter ?]

July 1.
In re Dr. P. J.
A. van Breda.

1873.
July 1.

In re Dr. P. J.
A. van Breda.

The Governor has referred us to the Supreme Court. There is no statute here, as in England, giving the custody of criminal lunatics to the Crown. The Governor in this instance derived his authority from the order of Court; and the Court, as the upper guardians of lunatics, had jurisdiction.

De Villiers, A.G. (for the Crown) did not object to Dr. Breda being brought over to the mainland for the purposes named in the petition.

BELL, C.J.—This is not a case for any relaxation of the strictest forms of law. You must get up the case the best way you can. If you can find any authority giving us jurisdiction, we will hear it. There are hard cases, but this is not one of them.

Application refused.

[Applicant's Attorneys, FAIRBRIDGE & ARDERNE.]

APPENDIX.

SECRETARY S. A. ASSOCIATION *vs.* MOSTERT.

[The following is the report of this case on appeal before the Judicial Committee of the Privy Council. For the proceedings in the Court below, *vide Buchanan's Rep.*, 1869, p. 231.]

June 6.
―――
Secretary S. A.
Association *vs.*
Mostert.

On appeal from the Supreme Court of the Cape of Good Hope.

[Law J. Rep. (N.S.), P. C., p. 41.]

ABRAHAM DENYSSEN, APPELLANT, *vs.* SYBRAND JACOBUS MOSTERT, RESPONDENT.

Cape of Good Hope.—Roman Dutch Law.—Husband and Wife.—Community of Goods.—Mutual Will.—Death of Husband.—Revocation by Wife.—Reception of Benefits.

By the Roman Dutch law the mutual will of a husband and wife, notwithstanding its form, is to be read as the separate will of each. The dispositions of each spouse are to be treated as applicable to his or her half of the joint property. Each is at liberty to revoke his or her part of the will during the co-testator's lifetime, with or without communication with the co-testator, and after the co-testator's death; but where a spouse who first dies has bequeathed any benefit in favour of the survivor, and has afterwards limited the disposal of the property in general after the death of such survivor, then such survivor, if he or she accepts such benefits, may not afterwards dispose of his or her share in any manner at variance with the will of the deceased spouse.

1872.
June 6.

Secretary S. A.
Association vs.
Mostert.

This was an appeal from a judgment of the Supreme Court of the Cape of Good Hope, in an action wherein the appellant, as secretary of the South African Association for the Administration and Settlement of Estates, was plaintiff, and the respondent was defendant.

The action was brought to recover the amount of a mortgage bond bearing date the 11th of November, 1859, executed by the respondent in favour of one Cornelis Mostert, for securing payment of the sum of £3,750.

Cornelis Mostert, the mortgagee in the mortgage bond, was the husband of Elizabeth Jacoba Mostert, to whom he was married in community of property. He was the owner of a farm near Cape Town, called " Valkenberg," which he sold to the respondent, who was his nephew and son-in-law, and for securing the purchase money the respondent executed in favour of Cornelis Mostert the mortgage bond sued upon by the appellant. By this bond the respondent hypothecated the farm " Valkenberg " for securing the sum of £3,750 and for interest thereon.

On the 31st August, 1860, Cornelis Mostert and Elizabeth Jacoba, his wife, made together, in the manner customary in the Colony of the Cape of Good Hope, a "mutual will." Cornelis Mostert died on the 15th of December, 1862. On the 23rd of December, 1862, letters of administration were granted to the widow and the South African Association.

On the 21st January, 1863, the widow intimated to the appellant her intention to reject all benefits under her deceased husband's will, and to claim as a surviving spouse her own free half of the joint estate. The appellant then instituted the action now under appeal.

The declaration set out the mortgage bond and the cession of it to the Association, and prayed for the balance due on the bond and interest.

The respondent pleaded amongst others a special plea, submitting that the mortgage bond sued on by the appellant constituted a debt which, according to the meaning and intent of the will aforesaid, could not be legally claimed from the respondent, and prayed that the claim of the appellant might be rejected with costs.

By the replication, the appellant submitted that the widow of Cornelis Mostert, after she became free from the marital power and influence of her husband, rejected all benefits under the will, and elected to claim her half of the joint estate as her own free property.

The cause was heard and the judgment of the Court was as follows:—That the widow was not entitled to claim a right to take and receive a free half of the joint estate which had been in community between herself and her deceased husband ; but, on the contrary, that she was bound and obliged, as regarded her half of the joint estate, to give effect to the stipulations contained in the mutual will of the 31st of August, 1860.

From this judgment the present appeal was brought.

Sir *R. Palmer*, Mr. *Rigby*, and Mr. *Myburg*, for the appellant. The respondent by his acquiescence in the acts of the widow after he had the means of ascertaining his own rights, is estopped from setting up those rights. The Association would not have taken the mortgage bond until the respondent's rights had been disposed of, if the respondent had given them notice of the same. Even if the respondent is not estopped by acquiescence, and if the effect of the will aforesaid, regarded as the will of the testator, Cornelis Mostert, amounted to a discharge of so much of the testator's half of the debt as should prove to be in excess of the paternal inheritance of the respondent's wife, the Association are in the place of the surviving widow, and are entitled to her rights in regard to the debt. By the Roman-Dutch law in force in the Colony of the Cape of Good Hope, the surviving widow was entitled to assert her right to one half of the estate which had belonged in community to her husband and herself, and, as part of the estate, to one half of the mortgage debt due by the respondent. The widow was by law entitled to repudiate the will, provided her acts and conduct after the death of her husband did not amount to adiation or election by her to be bound by the will. There is no evidence that the widow elected to adopt the will of her husband. They referred to *Institutes of the Laws of Holland* (1); *Grotius* (2); *Dutch Consultations, Cons. pt.* 275; *Van der Berg's Advys Boek, Cons.* 210; *Oosthuysen vs. Oosthuysen* (3); *Van der Keessel, Th.* 25; *These Boel ad Loenium,* 137; *Schorer on Grotius, b.* 2, *ch.* 15, *s.* 9; *Voet, l.* 28, *s.* 11; *Van Leeuwen, b.* 3, *c.* 11; *Burge Col. Law, b.* 4, *p.* 405; *Hofmeyr vs. De Wet* (4); *Sande's Decisiones, Fris. b.* 2, *Def.* 2; *Cape Ordinances, No.* 104.

Sir *J. Karslake* and Mr. *Busk* for the respondent. The will was binding upon the widow after the husband's death. The widow, in fact, elected to adopt the will of her husband. She proved the will and acted on it. The husband and wife by their joint will in effect consolidated their estates, so far, at all events, as to render their joint estates incapable

(1) Van der Linden, Henry's Trans. p. 129.
(2) Herbert's Trans., b. 1, c. 5, s. 25, and b. 2, c. 17, s. 24.
(3) Buch., Cape Rep., 1868, p. 51.
(4) Buch., Cape Rep., 1868, p 317.

1872.
June 6.

Secretary S. A.
Association vs.
Mostert.

of separation the one from the other. After the death of her husband, the widow, though she had full power to dispose of the share given to her as one of the universal heirs under the joint will, and to accept or not as she might think fit her conditional fore-legacy, could not alter the dispositions of the joint will in favour of third persons; she had no power to alter the family arrangement made or assented to by the testator's regulating the disposition of the property of each for the benefit of their children. The joint will and codicil were not only a reciprocal and mutual disposition, but they contained dispositions in favour of third persons, and were only revocable during the joint lives of both testators. They referred to *Van der Linden, pp.* 147, 148.; *Van der Keessel* (5); *Britz vs. Britz* (6); *Van der Berg's Advys Boek, vol.* 1, *Cons.* 32, *p.* 56.; *Cons.* 210, *p.* 500.; *Coren's Obser.* 12, *p.* 54; *Dufaur vs. Pereira* (7); *Williams on Executors, 3rd ed., vol.* 1, *p.* 90; *Scorey vs. Scorey* (8); *Walpole vs. Lord Orford* (9); *Censura Forensis (Van Leeuwen)* 3, 11, 7; *Peckius, Rodenburg, ed.* 1653, *tit.* 2, *c.* 4, *p.* 281.

Sir ROBERT P. COLLIER delivered the judgment of their Lordships (10). This was an action of debt on a bond brought by the plaintiff as acting executor of the late Cornelis Mostert, against the defendant for the recovery of the sum of £3,750. Among other pleas, not now material to notice, the defendant pleaded that he had been released from this obligation by the terms of the mutual will of Cornelis Mostert, deceased, and his surviving wife. The plaintiff replied by a general denial, and further that the defendant was at all events liable for half the amount of the bond, the share of the surviving spouse, who had repudiated the mutual will. Judgment was given for the defendant by the Chief Justice and Mr. Justice Fitzpatrick, the majority of the Court—Mr. Justice Denyssen dissenting. The appellant now contends that he is entitled to judgment for one half, but only one half, of the amount of the bond.

The facts material for the decision of this case are as follows :—

The bond was executed by the defendant on the 11th of November, 1859, in favour of Cornelis Mostert, whose nephew he was, and whose daughter he had married, to secure the purchase-money of a farm which Cornelis

(5) Thes. 283.
(6) Buch., Cape Rep., 1868, p. 312.
(7) 1 Dick. 219 ; s. c. 2, Harg. Jur. Cas. 101.
(8) Menzies' Rep., p. 231.
(9) 4 Ves. 404.
(10) Sir J. W. Colville, Sir Montague Smith, and Sir R. P. Collier.

Mostert had sold to him. Cornelis Mostert had been married to Elizabeth Jacoba his wife in community of goods. On the 31st of August, 1860, Cornelis Mostert and his wife, made what is commonly called "a mutual will," in the manner customary in the Colony.

The provisions of that will, as far as they are material to the present case, were these :—

An estate, together with the fixtures, furniture, &c., was left as a pre-legacy to the survivor, on condition of the survivor paying £3,000 to the estate of the predeceaser.

Certain specific legacies were given to some of the children and grandchildren, to be paid after the death of the survivor of the testators. Certain "sole and universal heirs" were nominated, being the survivor of the testators, and their children and grandchildren, mentioned by name, in the whole to the number of ten, all of whom were to take equal shares; and "in case of the predecease of one or more of them their lawful descendants by representation *per stirpes*," subject to the following among other stipulations, to wit :—

"1st. That in computation with the inheritance of each of the instituted heirs being children or grandchildren of the testators shall have to be brought all that he or she respectively shall be found to be indebted to the estate of the testators.

"2ndly. That when and where such debts should happen to exceed the amount of the inheritance from the estate of the first dying, the heir or heirs whom it may concern shall not need to bring up (pay) the excess directly, but that it shall be sufficient for them to remain indebted to the survivor for such excess above inheritance from the estate of the first dying, to be afterwards at the death of the survivor of the testators brought into computation with his, her, or their inheritance from the estate of the latter.

"3rdly. That in so far as the inheritance from the estate of the first dying falling to the share of one or more of the instituted heirs might exceed the amount of his, her, or their debts *to the estate*, the excess of inheritance above debts may and shall be paid out to him, her, or them respectively, free and unburdened.

"4thly. That all that shall fall to the share of the aforesaid instituted heirs of the testators as inheritance from the estate of the survivor of the testators (and in case and in so far as the said heirs may have remained indebted to the survivor of the testators for surplus of debts above the inheritance from the first dying, then after deduction of such debts) shall be and remain, as the same is hereby, burdened with the entail of *fidei commissum*, in such manner that only the interest or usufruct thereof shall be enjoyed by the heirs of the testators and their surviving spouses, the latter so long as they remain unmarried, whilst the capitals themselves shall devolve and go over, after their death, undiminished and unburdened, to their lawful descendants *per stirpes*. And the testators did further declare that they have made this *fidei-commissary* disposition in order to insure to their aforesaid heirs, as also to their children and spouses (the latter so long as they remain unmarried), maintenance and the means of living in case of misfortune, going backwards in pecuniary circumstances or mercantile affairs, insolvency or bankruptcy, or other accidents; and especially in so far as they may at present be insolvent."

1872,
June 6.

Secretary S. A.
Association vs.
Mostert.

And other provisious follow which are not so material to the present case.

"5thly. If, however, it should come to pass that one or more of the aforesaid instituted heirs of the testators is or are indebted to the estate of the survivor of the testators more than the amount falling to his, her, or their share as inheritance therefrom, it is in such case the will and desire of the testators that any excess of debts above the inheritance falling to the share of such heir or heirs *shall be remitted* to him, her, or them, as the same is hereby remitted to him, her, or them, *nunc pro tunc,* and that such excess of debts above inheritance shall not be allowed to be taken in the computation *of the inheritance of the respective heirs,* as *it is not the* desire of the testators that the same shall be *considered as forming* any part of the estate, but that, on the contrary, the inheritances of the respective heirs shall be decreased equally in proportion to the joint amount of the excess of debt above inheritance remitted in manner aforesaid."

Then follows the appointment of executors in these terms :—

"And the testators declared to nominate and appoint as executors testamentary, administrators of the estate, and guardians of the minor and *fidei-commissary* heirs, to wit: the testator, his wife, the present testatrix, together with the South African Association for the Administration and Settlement of Estates, and the testatrix declares to nominate and appoint her husband the present testator alone."

Cornelis Mostert died on the 15th of December, 1862.

On the 23rd of December, 1862, a certificate was duly granted by the proper authority to the widow of Cornelis Mostert and to the South African Association, appointing them executors testamentary of the will of Cornelis Mostert. On the 21st January, 1863, the widow wrote the following letter to the Association :—

"To the Board of Directors of the South African
            Association for the Administration and
            Settlement of Estates, Cape Town.

                                    "Cape Town, 21st January, 1863.

"Gentlemen,—With reference to the will of my late husband, Mr. C. Mostert, senior, I hereby declare that I do not accept the pre-legacy made to me of the garden or estate called Welgedaan, situated at the upper end of St. John's-street, with all the movable property, trinkets, and cattle which are therein, and request you to sell the same publicly, for account of the estate, in the month of March. I shall supply you with a list of some articles which I wish to keep out for myself.

"With respect to the piece of land with the buildings thereon, situated in Breda-street, now occupied by Mr. J. J. Meintjes, I desire that the same be without delay transferred to my daughter, Jacoba Anna Mostert, married without community of property to the said Meintjes, to whom the same was sold by my late husband for £1,500, when a mortgage bond must be passed by my said daughter for the full amount of the purchase money, £1,500, bearing interest from ——————, *in favour of the estate of my husband.* All the expenses of this transfer, and of the mortgage bond to be passed by my daughter, also transfer dues, expenses of diagram, and all other expenses in connection with the said transfer and mortgage bond, must be paid out of the estate of my husband.

" With regard to the different shares in companies which have been found in the estate, and are set forth on the inventory, it is my desire that the same be sold as advantageously as possible for the estate; with the exception, however, of one share in your Association, with regard to which my desire is that the same may be taken over by my son, Jan Fredrik Mostert, at the value now set upon it in the books, without any premium ; and as it will be necessary to take the opinion of the members of the Association on this subject, I request you will employ your influence as much as possible to have this my wish gratified.

" I am, your servant,

" WIDOW C. MOSTERT (born LOUW.)"

On the 28th August, 1863, she executed the following document :—

" I, the undersigned, Elizabeth Jacoba Louw, widow of the late Mr. Cornelis Mostert, senior, in my capacity as co-executrix testamentary with the South African Association, &c., of my aforesaid husband, Cornelis Mostert, senior, do hereby declare to ratify and approve of everything which has already been done and performed by the said Association in the administration of the estate of the said Cornelis Mostert, senior, and which shall hereafter be done and performed; and also hereby to grant full power and authority to the said Association, in their own name, and also (as acting for me) in my name to make transfer and conveyance to the respective purchasers of immovable property from said estate, and such transfer shall be considered by me as having been made with my concurrence and knowledge, under obligation of my person and property, according to law.

" E. MOSTERT.

"Cape Town, 28th August, 1863."

On the 18th September, 1863, the Widow Mostert wrote the following letter :—

" To the Board of Directors of the South African
          Association for the Administration and
          Settlement of Estates.

" Cape Town, 18th September, 1863.

" Gentlemen,—I have resolved to claim only the net half of the joint estate of my late husband and myself, and which, by virtue of the community of property which has existed between us, belongs to me by law, and to forego all legacies, and also the child's portion bequeathed to me by my late husband. I now kindly request you, as the administering executors of the said estate, to liquidate the same as speedily as possible, and to pay me the half share due to me, in cash, as I am not inclined to take in payment any bonds due by my children.

" I am, your obedient servant,

" E. MOSTERT."

1872.
June 6.

Secretary S. A.
Association vs.
Mostert.

The Association proceeded to administer the estate, and filed accounts headed as follows:—

"Liquidation and distribution account of the joint estate of the late Cornelis Mostert (sole and surviving spouse, Elizabeth Jacoba Louw, as relinquished by him), according to mutual will, which accordingly is framed by the said Elizabeth Jacoba Louw and the South African Association, in their capacity as executors testamentary, pursuant to letters of administration of the 23rd December, 1862."

And they received the ordinary commission as executors.

Subsequently, the executors relinquished all their interest to the plaintiff, who instituted this suit.

It was contended on behalf of the appellant, that, under these circumstances, the widow had a right to revoke the will as far as it dealt with her own property, and to claim that half of the joint estate of her late husband and herself to which she would have been entitled if she had made no will; that, consequently, she could sue the defendant for half of the debt owing by him to the joint estate, and transfer the power of suing for it to the plaintiff.

On the part of the respondent, it was contended that she had no power to revoke any part of the will, and that consequently the debt could not be sued for.

The main questions which arise in the case are these:—

(1.) Could the Widow Mostert revoke the will, as far as it affected her share of the property, if she took or elected to take the benefit of its provisions in her favour?

(2.) Could she revoke it if she did not take or elect to take such benefit?

(3.) Did she or did she not take or elect to take such benefit?

The views of the Judges of the Supreme Court of the Colony may be shortly stated thus:—

The Chief Justice inclined to the opinion that she had so elected, but held that, even if she had not, she could not revoke the will. Mr. J. Fitzpatrick held the latter proposition.

Mr. Justice Denyssen held that she had not so elected, and, that being so, that she had the power of revoking the will.

It is not to be expected that much light will be thrown upon the questions which arise in this case by the very scanty authority to be found on the construction of documents in the nature of mutual wills in this country, where they are of rare occurrence, and where the laws regulating the relations of husband and wife are in many respects different from those of the Colony.

It may be enough to observe that in the case of *Dufaur vs. Pereira* (7), Lord Camden held that a husband and wife, having made a mutual will, and that the wife, after her husband's death, having possessed all his personal estate, and enjoyed the interest thereof during his life, by that act bound her assets to make good all her bequests in the mutual will, and that her subsequent will, so far as it broke in upon the mutual will, was void. And that, in the case of *Walpole vs. Lord Orford* (9), Lord Loughborough refused to confirm the compact of a mutual will, under circumstances which are thus stated in Mr. Justice Williams' book on Executors, 6th edition, vol. 1., p. 122:—

1872.
June 6.

Secretary S. A.
Association *vs.*
Mostert.

"The will of George, Earl of Orford, made in 1756, and Horace Lord Walpole's codicil of the same date, made in concert, constituted, in effect, a mutual will. Horace Lord Walpole died in 1757, without revoking his part of the mutual will, viz., the codicil of 1756. George, Earl of Orford, died in 1791, when it appeared that he had made a codicil in 1776; and this, by reason of a reference to his last will, bearing date in 1752, was construed a revocation on his part of the mutual will, viz., the will of 1756.. A case was then raised in Equity, that the mutual will of 1756 became irrevocable on the death of Lord Walpole in 1757, though it was admitted to be revocable by either during the joint lives of Lord Walpole and Lord Orford, with notice to the other. And the judgment of Lord Camden in *Dufaur vs. Pereira* (7) was mainly relied upon in defence of that position. Lord Loughborough, however, refused to enforce the compact of the mutual will; but this was chiefly, it seems, by reason of the uncertainty, and, in some sense, unfairness of the compact; so that it leaves the principle of Lord Camden's decision in *Dufaur vs. Pereira* (7) wholly unshaken."

The solution of the questions in this cause must be found in the authorities on the Roman-Dutch law in use in the Colony.

By the Roman law the property of husband and wife was separate, and each was entitled to dispose of it at pleasure, either during life or by will.

The customs of the Dutch introduced community of goods between husband and wife, the husband being the administrator of the property, and holding the relation of curator or guardian to the wife; and this community of goods was enforced and preserved by a strict prohibition of all contracts relating to property between husband and wife. On the death of either, the survivor took half of the property; the other half, in the absence of testamentary disposition, going to the heirs of the deceased.

Both husband and wife retained the power of disposing of their respective shares by will, and any agreement renouncing this power was void (11). By custom, the form of mutual wills was introduced, which, sometimes adopted by persons not related to each other, became the common form of testamentary disposition by husband and wife. Much authority (as was to be expected) is to be found bearing upon wills of this description, and the following general rules of law may be treated as clearly established :—

1. That such wills, notwithstanding their form, are to be read as separate wills, the dispositions of each spouse being treated as applicable to his or her half of the joint property.

2. That each is at liberty to revoke his or her part of the will during the co-testator's lifetime, with or without communication with the co-testator, and after the co-testator's death.

In support of these general rules of law may be cited *Grotius' Introduction to Dutch Jurisprudence, b.* 1, *c.* 5, *s.* 25; *b.* 2, *c.* 17, *s.* 24 *and notes; Bynkershoek, Questiones Juris Privati, l.* 3, *c.* 7; *Huber's Heden Daaghe Reghtsgeleerheid, b.* 2, *c.* 12; *Schorer on Grotius, b.* 2, *c.* 15, *s.* 9; *Van der Keessel, Thes.* 298; *Van der Linden, Institutes of the Laws of Holland, p.* 129, and other authorities referred to in the judgment of Mr. Justice Denyssen.

The general rule being established, it next becomes necessary to ascertain the exceptions to it. They are thus stated by *Grotius, b.* 2, *c.* 15, *s.* 9 (translated by Mr. Herbert) :—

"When the spouse who dies first has bequeathed any benefit in favour of the survivor, and has afterwards limited the disposal of the property in general after the death of such survivor, then such survivor, if he accepts such benefits, may not afterwards dispose of his or her share by last will in any manner at variance with the will of the deceased."

The substance of this doctrine, though expressed in varying terms, is to be found in the leading authorities from the time of Grotius to the present day.

Van Leeuwen, in his *Censura Forensis,* a book of high authority, after stating the general rule, thus describes the exception :—

"Quæ tamen regula limitatur (præsertim inter conjuges) casu quo duo simul testantes, alter alterum herædem instituit, sub eâ conditione atque onere; ut omnia ea bona quæ post mortem ultimi morientis, ex mutuâ hereditate supererunt, relinquantur hinc aut illi. Quo facto super-

(11) Voet ad Pandectas, lib. xxviii, tit. 3, s. 10 : "Ambulatoria est hominis voluntas ad extremum vitæ halitum . . . ideo revocationem testamenti a jure concessum impedire nequit pactum de non revocandâ vol mutandâ voluntate interpositum.

vivens, *postquam hereditatem primi morientis adierit*, pro suâ etiam parte aliter, aut contra voluntatem mutuam de novo disponere haud potest, mutuo quasi consensu, eorumdem patrimonio consolidato, et ad unicum patrimonium reducto."

A passage to the same effect is to be found in *Van Leeuwen's Commentaries on the Roman-Dutch Law, b.* 2, *c.* 3, *s.* 8.

Their Lordships understand the expression, "postquam hereditatem primi morientis adierit"—" after he has *adiated* the inheritance of the predeceaser."—as equivalent to the " acceptance of benefits" spoken of by Grotius. " Adiation" is a term well known to the Roman-Dutch law, and although Mr. Justice Connor, in the case of *Oosthuysen vs. Oosthuysen,* may be correct in saying that its technical sense, as applicable to the institution of an heir, may have become obsolete, it appears to be used by *Van Leeuwen* and other writers, when applied to the survivor of two co-testators under a mutual will, in a sense equivalent to the adoption and confirmation of the will by the acceptance of benefits under it.

Many extracts from the *Hollandsche Consultatien*, translations of which, certified by the Registrar of the Supreme Court of the Colony, have been sent to us, are in accordance with these doctrines (among them may be cited vol. i. Consultation 50; vol. ii. Consultation 53; vol. iii. Consultation 3; vol. iv. Consultation 43). To the same effect are extracts translated and certified in the like manner from *Van der Berg's Advys Boek.*

The circumstances of the case referred to in Consultation 210 of the second book of this work very much resemble those of the present.

There the husband made a will to which the wife gave her written assent (the effect of which is stated to be equivalent to her having been a party to a mutual will), whereby the property of both was given to the wife for life, with remainder on her death if she should survive and die unmarried, to the blood relations of both in the proportion of two-thirds to those on the side of the testator, one-third to those on the side of the testatrix. There was also a provision " that the testing parties concurred in giving to the testator's brother all that he was in any way indebted to the estate, not wishing that he should be called upon to pay it."

The widow, for four years after the death of her husband, remained in possession of the common estate; nevertheless, it was held that she could revoke the will as far as it related to her half of the joint property, and that she could sue the testator's brother for her half of the debt due by him to the

1872.
June 6.

Secretary S. A.
Association vs.
Mostert.

estate. It was said, "there is no difficulty in the way of the widow now repudiating the testament and retaining the half of the common estate by virtue of the community that she has for four years remained in possession of the common estate, for such continuance in possession is not an act from which it can be understood that she wishes to renounce her right of community and take under the will, for, as survivor, she was entitled to remain in possession until such time as she was called upon to make partition."

Other extracts from *Van der Berg's Advys Boek*, some from the *Consultations of Utrecht*, and others from *Coren's Decisiones et Concilia*, support the doctrine laid down by *Grotius*.

These authorities have been recognised and confirmed by three cases decided in the Supreme Court of the Colony: viz., *Britz vs. Britz* (6), *Hofmeyr vs. De Wet* (4), and *Oosthuysen vs. Oosthuysen* (3), to be found in Mr. Buchanan's *Reports of Decisions of the Supreme Court of the Cape Colony*.

In *Hofmeyr vs. De Wet* (4), Sir John Wylde, then the Chief Justice, thus lays down the law : " A husband and wife may both make their testament in one and the same paper writing, but the paper is considered to contain two separate testaments, which each of them may always alter separately, and without the knowledge of the other, before as well as after the death of either of them ; but if they have benefited each other reciprocally, and directed how the common estate is to go after the death of the survivor, if the latter has enjoyed or wishes to enjoy the benefit of it, such survivor can make no other last will or testamentary disposition of his or her share, unless he or she had rejected the benefit made and ceded the same. In *Oosthuysen vs. Oosthuysen* (3), Sir William Hodges, then Chief Justice, says: " If the joint spouses have benefited each other, and have jointly and by common consent directed how the estate shall go after the death of the survivor, such survivor cannot, after the adiation of the estate and the enjoyment of the benefit, make another testament of his or her share of the joint estate."

Much on the same principle it was decided by the Supreme Court of the Colony that an express renunciation by the wife during her husband's life of her right to a half of the joint property, and an agreement to accept in lieu thereof the provisions of his will, were not binding upon her after his death, but that the right of election remained (12).

It may be added that Mr. Burge, in his *Commentaries on Colonial Law*, vol. 4, p. 405, lays down the same doctrine.

(12) Scorey *v.* Scorey, Menz. p. 231.

1872.
June 6.

Secretary S. A.
Association vs.
Mostert.

These authorities (to which more might be added) establish that power which a surviving spouse generally has to revoke a mutual will as far as it affects half of the property is taken away on the concurrence of two conditions—

1. That the will disposes of the joint property on the death of the survivor, or, as it is sometimes expressed, where the property is consolidated into one mass for the purpose of a joint disposition of it.

2. That the survivor has accepted some benefit under the will.

It may be observed that these conditions appear to apply as much to a will made by one spouse with the authority of the other, as to a mutual will in the strict sense of the word, i.e., a will executed by both.

It next becomes necessary to inquire what authority there is for rejecting the second condition, and holding that a mutual will " consolidating into a mass " the joint property is absolutely irrevocable and unalterable by the survivor.

The main authority cited in support of this proposition appears to be a passage in *Peckius, l.* 1, *c.* 43, which is as follows :—

"Quoniam verò est alterius loci inquirere, quomodo in universum testamenta sunt revocabilia, quibusque in hoc cautionibus utendum sit : supersedebo illis omnibus huc extra ordinem congerendis, si illud unum addidero cosultum quoque esse ad impediendam revocationem, ut alter conjugum cum consensu alterius, de utriusque bonis et eorum parte ad communium utilitatem liberorum solus testetur. Tunc enim dispositio, licet revocabilis sit ex parte testantis, tamen ex parte consentientis transit in contractum et sit irrevocabilis."

It is to be observed that the authorities which *Peckius* cites in support of this proposition are not by his own statement of them directly in point, inasmuch as they do not refer to wills of husband and wife, and, further, that it is not easy to conceive a testamentary *contract* by which one party is bound while the other is left free.

This doctrine, however, of *Peckius* is controverted by *Huber* in his *Prelectiones* (*lib.* 28, *tit.* 3), who contends with much force that it is opposed to the law which prohibits contracts between husband and wife for prescribing the manner and extent to which the common property shall be enjoyed by the survivor, and observes : "Verius tamen videtur, non obstante tali pacto, testamentum posterius factum valere : quià contractus et ultimæ voluntates sunt res ita separatæ, ut hæ per illos impediri non debeant, neque possint, adeo ut ne quidem pactis dotalibus de futurâ successione, testamenti factio cuiquam adimatur."

1872.
June 6.
——
Secretary S. A.
Association vs.
Mostert.

A passage from *Coren's Obser.*, 12, *p.* 54, cited by the Chief Justice in his judgment, confirms the view of *Huber.* After stating a case of a mutual will and adiation by the surviving wife, *Coren* proceeds, " she had given her consent to the husband's disposing as he did, and then, *by adiating her husband's inheritance*, she bound herself by a *quasi* contract to the observance of his will." The *quasi* contract arose not upon her consent being given to the making of the will (as the Chief Justice appears to read the passage), but on her election to accept the benefit of it after her husband's death.

It is to be observed, however, that *Van Leeuwen,* in the extract above quoted from his *Censura Forensis*, in which he lays down " adiation" as one of the conditions necessary to deprive a surviving spouse of the power of revocation, refers to the above cited passage in *Peckius* as an authority for his position, from which it would seem probable that, reading the passage in connection with the context, he understood this condition to be implied. It is further to be observed that *Groenewegen* would appear to take this view, for in his note to the passage of *Grotius* above quoted, he also cites the same passage in *Peckius* as supporting the doctrine laid down in the text. If the passage is to be read with this qualification, it is consistent with all the authorities. Their Lordships have not found any other passage than the above in *Peckius*, in which a gift over of the joint property to children is suggested to be less revocable than such a gift to other relations, or indeed strangers.

A passage from *Voet De Pactis Dotalibus* (*lib.* 28, *tit.* 4. *s.* 63) has been read, in which he does not mention " adiation" as necessary to deprive a surviving spouse of the power of revocation; but inasmuch as he cites the extract above given from the *Censura Forensis*, it cannot be assumed that he intends to controvert its authority.

A celebrated cause to which the will of Philip, Duke of Arshot, and Johanna Van Halewyn, his consort, gave rise, wherein it was decided that the mutual will was irrevocable by the survivor, was cited on behalf of the respondents from *Decker* (*Dissert. Jur.*, *lib. i. c.* 1), who reports his own argument at great length, but the decision somewhat shortly. Whether or not the survivor in that case had " adiated" does not appear very clearly from *Decker's* report, but " adiation" may be inferred from the reference to the case in *Van Leeuwen's Roman-Dutch Law* (*b.* 3, *c.* 3, *s.* 8), which is as follows:—" When two married persons have reciprocally benefited each other, and directed how the goods of the common estate should devolve after the death of the survivor of them, such *survivor having enjoyed* the *benefit*, cannot dispose of his or her share by such rule; and so it was adjudged in the causes upon a will between Philip, Duke of Arshot, and Mrs. Johanna Van Halewyn, his consort, by the High Court of Mechlin."

On the whole, their Lordships are of opinion that the great preponderance of authority (to say the least of it) supports the doctrine laid down by *Grotius*, and re-affirmed but a few years since by two successive Chief Justices of the Colony, whereby "adiation," or reception of benefits, is treated as one of the conditions without which a surviving spouse is not deprived of the power of revocation.

It remains to apply the law to the facts of the present case.

It has been argued that the joint disposition of the property after the death of the survivor in the present case applies only to part of it, that some provisions of the will indicate an intention that the dispositions of the respective testators should apply only to their own shares, and that in this case even "adiation" would not deprive the widow of the power of revoking the instrument as far as it applies to her share of the property.

Their Lordships, however, are of opinion that the will so deals with the joint estate that the widow would not have had the power to revoke any part of it if she had "adiated" in the sense before explained.

On the 18th of September, 1863, she wrote a letter expressly repudiating any benefit under the will, and declaring her election to take her share of the inheritance to which she would have been entitled if no will had been made. Their Lordships are unable to concur with the Chief Justice that before this she had declared her election to adopt the will. They do not infer this election from her letter of the 21st of January, 1863, in which she renounces the pre-legacy of the farm, at the same time expressing to her co-executors her desires with respect to the administration of portions of the property; nor from her acceptance of commission, even if that commission were more than she might be strictly entitled to as executrix of her husband's will; nor from the form of the accounts made out by the Association, which were certainly intended to be prepared on the footing of the letter of the 18th of September, whereby she renounced the will. Their Lordships, therefore, find upon the evidence, concurring herein with Mr. Justice Denyssen, that the widow Mostert did not "adiate" or adopt the will, in the sense of electing to receive the benefits to which she would have been entitled under it, and that being so, they are of opinion that she had by law a right to revoke it as far as it affected her property, and to claim her half of the inheritance.

The Chief Justice expresses his opinion that "it is much more consistent with justice and fair dealing, and much more conducive to confidence and good feeling between spouses, to hold that the survivor has made his or her election in the lifetime of the predeceaser, than that the survivor, having given the predeceaser every reason to believe that the arrangement between them would be operative after his or her death, may after the death of the predeceaser altogether upset it by resorting to his or her rights."

This reasoning applies with equal force to the power of revocation during the life of a co-testator without communication with him, a power which appears to be placed beyond doubt by the authorities. If the question were to be discussed upon principle independently of authority, it should be borne in mind that, while the power of revocation may be in some cases open to the objections urged by the Chief Justice, yet that, to limit it as his judgment would do, might enable husbands disposed unduly to exercise their marital authority and influence to coerce their wives into renouncing irrevocably those rights of inheritance which it appears the especial policy of the law of the Colony to protect. But these considerations are for the Legislature. *Bynkershoek* indeed speaks with strong disapprobation of abuses of the law, not infrequent in his time, whereby one co-testator, whose testamentary dispositions had been the consideration of those of the other, revoked his part of the will without communication with his co-testator: but *Bynkershoek* treats the right to do this by law as clear, nor can it be doubted that that great judge and jurist would have deemed himself bound to give effect to the law as he had laid it down, whatever may have been his opinion of its policy.

Their Lordships have but one duty—to declare what they deem to be the law: and for the reasons they have given will humbly advise Her Majesty to reverse the judgment of the Supreme Court of the Colony, and to order that judgment be entered for the plaintiff for one moiety of the bond with interest, credit being given for any payments in account which have been made.

The appellant will have the costs of this appeal.

SUPREME COURT REPORTS.

1873.

PART III.

EXECUTORS OF CERFONTEYN *vs.* O'HAIRE.

Codicil—Mental capacity to execute— Undue Clerical Influence
—Reservatory Clause.

A Codicil made at the instance of a Roman Catholic Priest,
and signed shortly before death on the day of the decease
of testatrix, the testatrix having for some time previously
been suffering from pulmonary consumption, and in the
habit of taking opiates, set aside on the grounds of in-
capacity arising from bodily disease and mental debility,
and of undue clerical influence on the part of the priest,
the spiritual adviser of the testatrix.

The Rev. James O'Haire, priest of the Roman Catholic
Church of St. Mary's, Cape Town, was summoned to answer
the plaintiffs, George William Steytler and Charles Aiken
Fairbridge, in their capacity as the executors testamentary
of the late Johanna Magdalena Cerfonteyn, in an action to
have a certain codicil, alleged to have been executed by the
said J. M. Cerfonteyn, on or about the 16th April, 1873, set
aside and declared null and void for the reasons hereinafter
set forth.

The declaration stated that the late J. M. Cerfonteyn
did on or about the 8th January, 1872, make and execute
her last will and testament, whereby, amongst other things,
she declared to nominate the plaintiffs as joint executors of
her will, administrators of her estate and effects, and tutors
and guardians of her minor children, with the usual powers
of assumption, substitution, and surrogation. That on the
24th December, 1872, testatrix executed a codicil, in which
she amended the manner of disposition of her property

1873.
June 12.
„ 20.
„ 30.
July 1.
August 1.

Executors Cer-
fonteyn vs.
O'Haire.

E

1873.
June 12.
„ 20.
„ 30.
July 1.
August 1.

Executors Cer-
fonteyn vs.
O'Haire.

among her children, but in no other way altered or revoked the will as to the appointment of plaintiffs. That the testatrix died on the 16th April, 1873. That on the 2nd of May letters of administration were issued, confirming the plaintiffs as executors testamentary of the estate of the testatrix. That the defendant alleges the said J. M. Cerfonteyn did, on the day of her death, make and execute a certain other codicil, dated the 16th April, 1873, in which, by virtue of the reservatory clause contained in her will, she revoked the appointment of plaintiffs as tutors and guardians of her minor children, and in their place and stead appointed the defendant as such tutor and guardian, with all such power and authority as was required by law; in all other respects confirming her before-mentioned will and codicil. That if such alleged codicil of the 16th April was really signed and executed by the said J. M. Cerfonteyn, the same was done by her at a time when she was incapable from bodily disease and mental debility of knowing what she was doing; or otherwise, that if when the said J. M. Cerfonteyn signed such codicil she was capable of knowing what she was doing, then that she was induced to sign through the undue clerical influence and pressure brought to bear upon her by the defendant during her dying moments, and not through her own free will and desire. Wherefore the plaintiffs prayed judgment, declaring the said alleged codicil null and void, and that plaintiffs were entitled to exercise their office as tutors and guardians of the minor children.

The defendant pleaded first the general issue, and then specially that the codicil of the 16th April was executed in a due, proper, and legal manner; and that it was signed and executed at a time when testatrix was legally competent to sign the same, and that she did so voluntarily and of her own free will; and in reconvention defendant claimed that the said codicil is good and binding in law, and that he is thereby duly and legally appointed tutor and guardian of the minor children.

The replication was general.

De Villiers, A.-G. (with him *E. J. Buchanan*), appeared for the plaintiffs; and *Reitz* (with him *Maasdorp*) for the defendant.

For the plaintiffs the following evidence was called :—

Charles Aiken Fairbridge, who stated :—I am one of the plaintiffs, but am not the attorney in this case. I knew the late J. M. Cerfonteyn, and had known her for twenty years. I was legal adviser both of herself and Kannemeyer. I took the instructions for the will of 8th January, 1872, and had it prepared in my office. She wished me to accept

the office of guardian to the minors. I objected. She was
very much distressed at my refusal, and said I knew her
affairs so thoroughly, and knew the children, and that she
would not rest satisfied unless I accepted the appointment,
as she had no confidence in any one but myself. I said,
that being the case, I would accept, provided one of the
public companies was appointed guardian with me, and
therefore she appointed the Colonial Orphan Chamber. I
saw her frequently during her last illness. She had been
in a very ailing state for three years. I saw her more frequently six months before her death. She frequently had
conversations with me about her children and their prospects.
On the 24th March last she was obviously fast sinking.
She sent me a message that she wished to see me. I
went, and saw her in her parlour. The conversation
commenced with reference to a bond which we were
arranging for her. She then said to me she could not
sleep at night without taking opiates, but that sometimes
they had the contrary effect, and she was dizzy and stupid
in consequence, and hardly knew what she was saying, or
that she could hardly speak—that her mind was not clear,
at all events. She said, " Yesterday, Father O'Haire called,
and wants to know if I have made any provision for the
guardianship of the children. I was in a stupid state, and
I told him that I didn't recollect. However, this morning
I am better, and have looked at the will, and I find it all
right. I want you particularly to recollect this." In consequence of her having mentioned Father O'Haire's name,
I said to her, " Do you then still consider yourself a member
of the Catholic Church ?" She looked on the ground for
a little while, and then said, " Well, in a way, yes." I
said, " Then, I suppose you wish to speak to me about the
future religious education of the children ?" She said,
" Yes." I asked what her wish was. She said, " They
have all been brought up in the Protestant Church—in the
Church of England—which they attend, and it is their
wish to continue to attend that Church, and not to be
Catholics. They are all agreed upon this, even the little
ones." I asked her what was the age of these little ones.
She said, " Eddy is seven, Charley and James are twelve
and thirteen." I said, " Surely, children of that tender
age can't have much judgment in a question of this nature."
She said, " Oh, yes, they are very sharp, very intelligent,
all of them. We have often talked the matter over together
in the family. Besides, it is my wish that the children
should be brought up in the faith of their father. You
now know my wishes, and I hope you will attend to them."
She then got into conversation about the abilities of the
children, and the conversation went off to affairs con-

1873.
June 12.
„ 20.
„ 30.
July 1.
August 1.

Executors Cer-
fonteyn vs.
O'Haire.

1873.
June 12.
„ 20.
„ 30.
July 1.
August 1.

Executors Cer-
lonteyn vs.
O'Haire.

nected with the estate. I went to my office and made a minute of our conversation, which I put with the other papers connected with her estate. I produce the minute (put in). I saw her again on the next Saturday. She was very feeble, sitting in an arm-chair, and looking very bad indeed. We first spoke about some money affairs. I then said to her, "Mrs. Kannemeyer, I have been thinking a good deal over our last conversation and your instructions. When I agreed to be guardian I hardly bargained for getting into a very unpleasant question which I see is likely to arise. I have a great horror of the idea of getting into a religious controversy, either with my own Catholic friends and relatives—for I happen to possess both—or with Father O'Haire. I have made a note of your wishes, but it will be a very great satisfaction to myself if you will state them yourself in writing. A very few lines will do." She put her hands on the side of the chair, but sank back again, as she was very feeble, and said, "It is not necessary. There will be no one to interfere with you, and you know my wishes." She remained silent for a few minutes, and then said, "Do you know I could see quite plain that Father O'Haire wants me to make him guardian of the children; in fact, he told me so himself, not in any way to interfere with your management of the estate, but that he might look after the children who are so young." I said, "Very well, what are your wishes?" She said, "I want you to advise me." I said, "This is a matter upon which you should judge for yourself." She said, "No, Mr. Fairbridge, you must advise me. I have consulted you in everything, and you know I would not do anything against your advice." I said, "Well, Mrs. Kannemeyer, if you put it in that way to me, then I must say I do not see the necessity of appointing a Roman Catholic clergyman, however respectable, to the task of bringing up a lot of little girls and boys as Protestants." She looked down for a minute or two, and then said, "Quite right, quite right; leave it so." After another pause she said, "But I am terribly bothered by this Father O'Haire." I said, "Mrs. Kannemeyer, be open, be frank. Do you or do you not wish to appoint Father O'Haire guardian to those children? If you do, I will add a codicil to your will at once." She said, "No, no, no." I then said to her, "I really wish you would give me a few lines, however short, stating your wishes about the children." She said quite fretfully, "It is not necessary. There will be no one to interfere with you, and you know all I want." We then talked about other matters. That was the Saturday, the 29th of March, I think. I saw her two or three times after that,—the last time, to the best of my memory, the day before Good

Friday. She spoke to me about having an inventory of her property made while she was alive, as she felt her end was not far off. I called at her house on Easter Tuesday. She died on Easter Wednesday. I did not see her. I was asked by her sister, Mrs. Miller, to see her, but thought I had better not trouble her. As I was leaving, Mrs. Miller said to me, "Father O'Haire says I am to ask you if you do not think it would be better, seeing how much work you have to attend to, to appoint some one with you to look after the children." I am not certain, but I think she said some clergyman ought to be appointed. I said, "I could always assume a co-guardian, and there was the Colonial Orphan Chamber; and you tell Father O'Haire, with my compliments, I do not see the necessity of appointing a Catholic clergyman to bring up children as Protestants." I then left. I did not see deceased again.

1873.
June 12.
  " 20.
  " 30.
July 1.
August 1.

Executors Cerfonteyn vs. O'Haire.

Cross-examined:—I never heard of deceased using the expression, "I am terribly bothered by the Attorney Fairbridge." She expressed a great respect for me. I am not aware she stood in fear of me. I am not aware, or have the slightest cause to suppose, she stood in mental fear of me. I am not aware that I used to speak to her in a brisk or brusque manner. I may deny that I did so. The morning I alluded to, when she spoke about opiates, she was better. I had seen her in the state I described, suffering from the effect of medicine which had not given her sleep,—dull, and heavy, and depressed. When I saw her in this depressed state, her mind was clear. I do not know in what state of mind she was when she made the last codicil. I had no opportunity of knowing. I should not have thought her insane if she had happened to change her mind after she saw me. She pressed me to become both executor and guardian to look after the children, not to become executor only. She was more anxious about my being guardian than about the executorship, and I was anxious to escape it, as it is a thankless and profitless undertaking. She gave as a reason she had more confidence in me than in any one else she knew.

Antonio Lorenzo Chiappini stated:—I am a Doctor of Medicine, practising in Cape Town. I attended the deceased Cerfonteyn in her last illness. She was suffering from pulmonary consumption. She died on the 16th April. I was present when she died. It was about three o'clock in the afternoon. I had been attending her for about two months before. Latterly I attended her daily; sometimes twice, and the last few days three times a day. I had been there between ten minutes and a quarter of an hour before she died. She was sinking when I first came. There was no mental capacity at all, the brain was gone. She was

1873.
June 12.
„ 20.
„ 30.
July 1.
August 1.

Executors Cer-
fonteyn vs.
O'Haire.

sleeping. I was there between nine and ten that morning. She was beginning to sink then. She was very restless, and was taking opiates all through her illness. She had a cough mixture which she was constantly using; there was opium in it. I think I did not prescribe for her that morning. A very small quantity of opium affected her. There was a small quantity in the prescription. I was there at two o'clock that morning. She was then delirious. Between nine and ten she had rallied a little. It is difficult to say what her mental condition was an hour before her death, but I should not think she could have had much of a mind then.

Cross-examined :—If deceased was told an hour before her death the contents of her will, that a certain codicil was then read to her, that she was asked. " Do you understand it ? " and she said " Yes," and signed the document,—would you say that that was impossible ?—It is not impossible, but it is highly improbable.

Mrs. Wilhelmina Barendina Miller stated:—I am a sister of the late Miss Cerfonteyn. We often spoke to one another about the children. We often spoke about domestic duties and religion, but I never interfered. I am a Roman Catholic. One day Father O'Haire told my sister it was her duty to bring up her children in the Roman Catholic faith. This was about a week before her death. She said she never did anything against the advice of Mr. Fairbridge, and she would consult him. After Father O'Haire left she asked my advice. I would not advise her in any way. The children were all christened in the Church of England. My sister said she had promised Mr. Kannemeyer on his death-bed she would never take the children away from the church they had been brought up in. As far as I remember, I saw Father O'Haire at my sister's during her illness about three times. I went to him to ask him to come, because I knew my sister was in a dying state, and she was a Roman Catholic. I was not in when he came. He administered the holy communion to my sister on the Monday or Tuesday before her death. She died on the Wednesday. When I came my sister was speechless. She died at about ten minutes past three. I had seen my sister at twelve o'clock that day. She did not then speak to me. I do not know if she was able to speak; she appeared very dull. I remember saying to her step-daughter how very strange she was looking. She was very weak. I was up with her all the night previous, when she was very bad. She spoke during the night, but very little. I mean by saying she looked strange at twelve o'clock that she was in a dying state. I had left her at eight o'clock that morning. She was very weak. She did not speak to me. I don't remember speaking to her. I was not there when deceased spoke to her daughter that morning. During the night she took a sleeping draught. I saw Mr. Fairbridge there one day, when I delivered a message to him from Father O'Haire. I think this was the Tuesday, the day before her death. My sister would not agree to sign any document until she had seen Mr. Fairbridge; consequently Father O'Haire told me to tell Mr. Fairbridge he would accept the guardianship of the children, and that he was perfectly satisfied with the way the will was made. He merely wished to be appointed guardian, as he was the guardian of all the minor children belonging to our family. I delivered this message. Mr. Fairbridge said he did not think there was any occasion for it, as there were already two appointed, and if he saw it was necessary he could appoint one. My sister was not afraid of Mr. Fairbridge. My sister never expressed any desire to appoint Father O'Haire guardian of the children.

Cross-examined :—I do not think my sister was afraid of Father O'Haire. He visited her during her illness as her spiritual director. My sister never adhered to her Church until after I arrived here, which is two years ago. My father was a Roman Catholic. I always was one. I was present when Father O'Haire told my sister a week before her death that it was her duty to bring up her children in the same faith. My sister asked me my advice after Father O'Haire left. I am aware none of the children ever belonged to the Roman Catholic Church. One of the girls went to the St. Mary's Convent, but did not like it. I don't think she was there more than a few days; it may have been a week. My sister wished her to finish her education there. The children were refused admittance at the convent. My sister was always in the habit of taking a sleeping draught. I have seen her after she has had a sleep in consequence of such a draught. She was very stupid afterwards. I could not tell how long she remained very stupid, because I did not stay with her always.

By the Court:—Father O'Haire was appointed guardian over my brother's children, but not over my father's children, for they were all of age. My sister attended the Roman Catholic Church during the last two years. Latterly, within the last three months, we had two sittings there, one for my sister and one for me.

Eliza Johnson stated :—I am a sick nurse. I remember nursing the late Miss Cerfonteyn during her illness, from the 27th March to the 12th April. On several occasions Father O'Haire visited deceased, but I only saw him there once. This was during the last week I was there. I left on the 12th, and Miss Cerfonteyn died on the 16th. Deceased

1873.
June 12.
„ 20.
„ 30.
July 1.
August 1.

Executors Cerfonteyn vs. O'Haire.

1873.
June 12.
  „   20.
  „   30.
July 1.
August 1.

Executors Cer-
fonteyn vs.
O'Haire.

was in the drawing-room, and Dr. Chiappini was with her. I answered a knock at the front door. Father O'Haire was there. I told him he could not see deceased, as the doctor was with her. He waited a few minutes. Dr. Chiappini came out soon after, and said to Father O'Haire, "You are the very one I wanted to see." What passed I don't know, for I went back into the room deceased was in. I told her Father O'Haire was there. She said, " Oh, why did you not tell him I am too ill to be seen? for he is bothering my life out to be guardian over the children. How can I make him guardian, although he is my priest? My children are Protestants, and he is a Catholic, and I promised their father on his dying-bed that I should not make them turn. Mr. Fairbridge has all my affairs in hand, and I never do anything without consulting him first." Father O'Haire came into the room, and I went out. I can't say how long they were together. I have seen Mr. Fairbridge there, but did not speak to him.

Annie Antoinette Kaunemeyer stated :—The deceased was my step-mother. I remember the day of her death. I saw Father O'Haire at deceased's house on the day of her death. He came at half-past two. Deceased was upstairs in her bed-room. I was upstairs. After the documents were made downstairs, Father O'Haire and Mr. Reid came upstairs. Neither of them had been in the sick room before that. I am not quite sure if Father O'Haire had been there that morning. Mr. Reid had not. I was in the sick-room when they came in. I was sent out of the room by deceased. She said I was to go out of the room so long. Deceased was in bed. I went into the next room, leaving Father O'Haire and Mr. Reid alone with the deceased. The door was open. A document was read. I heard some one say "Read louder." I can't say who spoke. Deceased did not speak at all. They went downstairs, and I went again into the room. Deceased wished to go downstairs, and I carried her down. She died very soon after. I dressed her, that is I put on her morning wrapper. It was about a quarter to three when I brought her down, and she died about three. It was her wish to go downstairs, and she died downstairs. I gave her her medicine at eleven o'clock that morning. I asked her then how she felt. She said the whole left side of her face was very queer, and she said she was sinking very fast. I could not say how long Father O'Haire and Mr. Reid were in the room together.

Cross-examined :—I did not help to support deceased while Father O'Haire and Mr. Reid were there. She was sitting up all the morning. When Father O'Haire and Mr. Reid came in I was in the room alone. They went and fetched Kearns afterwards. I do not know who went. Father O'Haire and Mr. Reid were still in the room when Kearns was there. I am not certain whether Kearns came after or before the document was read. I think he came after. They all went downstairs together,—Father O'Haire, Mr. Reid, and Mr. Kearns. These three only were in the room. Father O'Haire was sent for again afterwards when deceased was dying. This was after we had taken her downstairs. I am quite positive Eliza was not in the room when the document was read. I went out of the room because deceased sent me. She also desired me to take her downstairs.

1873.
June 12.
  „   20.
  „   30.
July 1.
August 1.
———
Executors Cer,
fonteyn vs.
O'Haire.

The Rev. Frederick Wood Bindley stated:—I am a clergyman of the Church of England, and precentor of St. George's Cathedral. I know the children of deceased very well. When I came here, two years and six months ago, I found one of the boys in the Cathedral choir, and I noticed the Misses Kannemeyer and a little boy, in fact, two little boys, constantly at church during the week-day services. I have seen the late Mrs. Kannemeyer, and talked with her about five times. The subject of our conversation was always her children. About the girls her conversation was general. She was glad they were good girls, and regular at Church, and so on, and took a part in church work. About the little boys it was more special. At the first conversation I had with her she said she was anxious they should come to the Cathedral grammar-school I was then about to open. They did not come to my school then, but attended regularly the church services. They were some of the most regular boys in the choir, and were catechised on Sunday afternoons. Several times when the boys had been irregular in their attendance I spoke to their mother, and after that they were more regular. All the girls are communicants.

By the Court:—The boys at this moment are still in the Cathedral choir. I saw them last Wednesday. I did not know then that the mother was a Roman Catholic, and I should never have imagined it.

John Howard Cosnett stated:—I knew the late Mrs. Kannemeyer, otherwise called Miss Cerfonteyn. I frequently had conversation with her about Mr. Fairbridge. The last occasion was on Good Friday. On that day, while we were alone, she took occasion to speak of Mr. Fairbridge's kindness to her. She had often spoken to me of his kindness before. She spoke very feelingly, and said she did not know how she would have got on without his assistance and advice.

De Villiers, A.-G., put in the original of the will and codicil, and closed the case for the plaintiffs.

1873.
June 12.
„ 20.
„ 30.
July 1.
August 1.

Executors Cer-
fonteyn vs.
O'Haire.

Reitz, for the defence, called

The Rev. James O'Haire, who stated:—I am a priest of the Catholic Church. I arrived in this Colony in July, 1863. I am now officiating at St. Mary's, Cape Town, where I have been for the last four years. As a priest I knew deceased. I first knew her about September, 1863. I went to her to get her separated from Mr. Kannemeyer. I spoke to her about the children. I said she was bound to bring them up in the Roman Catholic faith. This was in the presence of Kannemeyer. My visit had no effect. She did not state she would or would not. They did not answer me. They were both silent. After the death of Kannemeyer I called on deceased, some three or four years ago, and reminded her of her obligation to bring up the children in the Roman Catholic faith. She authorized me to make an application to St. Mary's Convent to admit the two girls. Her expressions showed her willingness to have the children brought up as Roman Catholics. The two girls were not admitted to the convent. From time to time from the death of her husband, but regularly for the last six months, deceased attended at St. Mary's. She did not attend before the death of her husband. On several occasions I expressed to deceased my belief it was her duty to bring up her children in the Roman Catholic faith. She was anxious to have the children brought up so, but was disconcerted. She asked how could she do so when the nuns would not receive them? She spoke on several occasions to me about Mr. Fairbridge, and always seemed to be in very great dread of him. She used some such words as that Mr. Fairbridge had always been very kind to her in her affairs, and she did not wish to displease him, and she knew it would displease him to bring up her children as Roman Catholics. Especially throughout the month previous to her death, I urged upon her the necessity of providing for the religious education of the children. I did not go to see her especially with that object in view. Mine were pastoral visits, and I admonished her on this duty. I am colonial chaplain, chaplain to the military, and hospital chaplain. The mother made an arrangement with me for the children to come together about this matter of their religious education, about ten days before her death, on the subject of the guardianship. This I should say was in consequence of my reminding her of her obligations. This arrangement was not carried out, because on the evening appointed I had too many sick calls to make. I had no thought she would have died so soon, and my duties kept me morning, night, and day : that was why the codicil was only made so shortly before her death. On the morning of her death, 16th April, I called at the house, and was told

by her daughter Eliza that deceased was very ill. I then
asked Eliza what about the guardianship, for I had spoken
to Eliza on the subject before, as she had always been
willing I should become guardian. Eliza is the eldest
daughter, and one of the objects of my care. She said she
had spoken to Mr. Fairbridge on the subject, and he would
not allow it. Then it was I determined to see to it, not
that I thought Mrs. Kannemeyer was in immediate danger,
but feeling that Mr. Fairbridge's interference was undue.
I called upon an eminent lawyer, a barrister, Mr. Porter,
and stated the case to him. I acted upon the advice he
gave me by calling upon Mr. Reid. I did not go direct
from Mr. Porter to Mr. Reid. I returned to deceased, and
told her Mr. Porter's advice. After having spoken to the
sick woman about her spiritual interests, I then alluded
again to the subject of the guardianship. I told her what
Eliza had said to me. She said she knew it was correct
that Mr. Fairbridge objected to my appointment, and had
it not been for the public holidays she would have sent for
Mr. Fairbridge and remonstrated with him on the subject.
I said, "What then are you prepared to do?" She said,
"To make you the guardian of my children." I said, "I
must consult a lawyer before anything is done, so that the
act may be valid, for Mr. Fairbridge himself being an
attorney would try and upset the codicil." She then said,
"Go, consult a lawyer." I did so, and returned alone to
deceased for the purpose of examining whether there was a
reservatory clause in the will. I went to deceased's bed-
room and told her of the legal instructions I had received.
She then directed Mrs. Pope that Eliza should be called.
Mrs. Pope was in the room all this time. Eliza came, and
deceased handed her a bunch of keys, first selecting one
key, and saying to Eliza, "Go, open the drawer," giving
the description of a drawer downstairs. "In the drawer you
will find a box; bring that box to me." Eliza went, and
returned in a few moments without the box, saying, "I
can't find it, it is not in that drawer." Eliza handed her
back the keys, and her mother said, "You stupid girl, you
tried the wrong drawer; this is it," presenting her with the
proper key. Eliza left again, and came back with the box,
which she gave, with the keys, to her mother. Her mother
opened the box, and took from it a book, and out of the
book took the will, which was in a large envelope. She
presented the will to me. Deceased was in bed at this
time. Her daughter Eliza was present all the time.
Deceased, said, "See if it contains what you require." I
examined the will, and found it contained the reservatory
clause, and handed back the will to deceased. I told her,
"It's all right." She said, "Very well, get some one to

1873.
June 12.
  „   20.
  „   30.
July   1.
August 1.

Executors Cer-
fonteyn vs.
O'Haire.

1873.
June 12.
   „ 20.
   „ 30.
July 1.
August 1.

Executors Cer-
fonteyn vs.
O'Haire.

draw the codicil." I went to Mr. Reid. This was about
twelve o'clock, I should say. I stated the matter to Mr.
Reid. It might have been half-past twelve. Mr. Reid
accompanied me to the house from his own office. This
was about one o'clock. Eliza opened the door and received
us in the hall, and supplied pens and ink and the will, that
Mr. Reid might write the codicil. Eliza remained while
Mr. Reid was writing the codicil, and heard it read by Mr.
Reid to me. Then he asked Eliza if we could go upstairs.
She said yes. Mr. Reid and myself and George Kearns,
who was driving my carriage, went up to the bed-room.
Kearns is sacristan of St. Mary's Cathedral. There was
some woman in the room. I was under the impression it
was the daughter. She lifted her mother that she might
sit up properly. Mr. Reid read the codicil. I did not
think he read loud enough, so I said to him, "Read in a
louder tone," and he did so. After having read it he
asked, "Did you understand it?" She said, "Yes," and
then it was signed. She asked where she was to put her
name, "here or here," pointing to two places. She then
signed her name. Afterwards she folded the will herself,
and I took it from her hand to put it in the box, when she
said, "No, put it in the envelope." I then put it in the
envelope, and she placed it in the box. Mr. Reid and Mr.
Kearns then left the room. I remained for a moment. I
said, "I am sure you're happy now this has been executed."
She said, "Yes, I am." I may have said other things at
the time. I then left the room, and did not see her alive
again. I administered to her all the sacraments on the day
previous. I administered the sacrament of the holy communion, which, according to the rubric of the Roman
Catholic Church, cannot be administered to a person of
whose mental capacity to receive it the priest can have a
doubt. On this occasion I had not the slightest doubt—
not the shadow of a doubt. I had administered the sacrament about ten o'clock on the day before. When I went
with Mr. Reid, with the codicil, I did not notice any difference between her mental state then and on the day previous. I did not threaten to withhold the sacrament if she
did not sign the codicil. I would have been bound to withhold it if she had been unwilling to do so, as she was a
Roman Catholic. I did not use that pressure because I
knew she was thoroughly willing to provide for the Catholic
education of her children. I can fix the time the codicil
was executed. After it was executed I went to my own
house and made certain domestic arrangements, and went
from there to the military hospital. I cannot swear I did
not call at other houses on my way; it is probable I did. I
made a regular visitation of the hospital; there are two

distinct wings in the hospital, and there were about fifty Roman Catholics in the wards—about the usual number. I visited all, and then signed the book of the hospital; according to that book my visitation had been made at 2.45. It usually takes me three quarters of an hour, or perhaps half-an-hour, to make the hospital visitation. The time is nearly always put down at the close of the visitation. I very rarely sign it at the beginning of the visitation. I put down the hour myself. I never saw the deceased in a delirious or in a semi-delirious state. I never saw her weak-minded, except you mean heavy, as sick persons will be. Her mind was sufficiently strong to execute that codicil.

1873.
June 12.
  „   20.
  „   30.
July 1.
August 1.

Executors Cer-
fontevn vs.
O'Haire.

Cross-examined:—I stated I called on the deceased several times, and reminded her of her obligations. I cannot remember the exact words I used, but I said in effect, "You are bound as a Roman Catholic to bring up your children in the Catholic faith; and you now have an opportunity of doing so." I meant that Mr. Kannemeyer was then dead. As far as I can remember, her answer was, "I prefer commencing with the girls, but I fear it will be difficult to manage Eliza and Annie, and therefore I will place them in the convent school if the nuns will admit them, so that, their prejudices being removed, I may be able to manage the others the more easily." Protestant as well as Catholic children are educated in the convent school. Deceased told me they were very much prejudiced against the Catholic religion. I do not remember deceased telling me on the above occasion she had promised Kannemeyer not to bring up the children in any other faith than the Protestant. On another occasion she said to me, "I have some scruples in consequence of a promise I made to Mr. Kannemeyer that I would bring up the children in his faith." I replied, "Kannemeyer was not your husband, and even had he been, Catholics are prohibited from marrying with Protestants, unless such Protestants will previously sign a written agreement that the issue of the marriage, whether male or female, will be educated as members of the Roman Catholic Church. From this you can see the nature and extent of your obligation." She said then, "I fear Mr. Fairbridge also. I know he will not agree to it. He has been very kind to me. I wish I could gain him over on the matter." I replied, "When you appear before the tribunal of Almighty God, even though Fairbridge could accompany you, he could not plead your cause with God." This conversation was immediately before the meeting was arranged, and about a week or ten days before her death. It was then arranged that I was to meet her and her children together, so that she might notify to them

1873.
June 12.
" 20.
" 30.
July 1.
August 1.

Executors Cer-
fonteyn vs.
O'Haire.

that I was to be their guardian. She positively stated that was to be the object of the meeting. I don't think deceased said her promise to Kannemeyer was made on his death-bed. The conversation I have spoken of took place in the parlour downstairs; nobody else was present. It was during a pastoral visit, and no one would be permitted to be present. I went that morning to hear deceased's confession. That finished, and temporal matters being discussed, anyone could then be present. She did not confess that day. I postponed her confession for reasons known to myself. I have a right to withhold my reasons. I refuse to give them. She had confessed to me once. before this conversation, and twice afterwards. It was for reasons known to myself that I took her confession on the previous occasion and postponed taking it on this. I am not allowed to state my reasons. She confessed to me about a week or ten days before this conversation. It is impossible for me to answer whether the reasons which induced me to postpone the confession were removed when I heard the subsequent confession. I could not give her absolution if the reasons were not removed. I could hear the confession, but could not give her absolution. I decline to answer if I gave her absolution. I often take a confession without giving absolution. One of the subsequent confessions was made three or four days before her death, and the other the day immediately preceding her death. I usually called about eleven o'clock. The day before her death the confession was made about half-past nine o'clock, and she had communion about ten o'clock. The day before her death I was alone at confession with deceased. The day before her death I do not remember that I reminded deceased of her duty to bring up her children in the Roman Catholic faith. I did not think it necessary, as it had all been previously arranged. The meeting with the children never did take place, through my fault, or rather through my duty calling me elsewhere. On the day of her death I saw her three times. The first time I spoke about her spiritual interests. I should say I did not then speak of the guardianship of her children. I do include that among her spiritual interests. It was my having told deceased she was bound to provide for the Catholic education of her children that led her to say, " I have some scruples because of the promise I gave to Kannemeyer." She wished me to regulate her mind whether or not this promise was binding on her conscience. I had told her she was bound to bring up her children as Roman Catholics, and she had promised to do so, but the refusal of the nuns to admit the girls prevented her carrying out her desire. She said ten days before her death she had appointed Mr. Fairbridge,

and I think she also mentioned Mr. Steytler's name, of the
Colonial Orphan Chamber. I cannot say I frequently
urged her duty upon her, as I felt very much disconcerted
at the nuns' refusal, and I really felt delicate about pressing
the matter upon deceased. On the day of her death my
first call was before twelve; perhaps about half-past eleven.
I remained with deceased about ten minutes. It was about
ten or twenty minutes after twelve. I am almost certain
it was not past one o'clock. I gave the instructions for
the codicil to Mr. Reid. Mr. Reid did not take any instructions from the deceased, but from me as her agent.
I do not think Mr. Reid explained the codicil. He read it
half through, and I said, " Read louder," and he commenced
again, and when he had done he said, " Do you understand
it ? " I said to Mr. Reid, " Read louder," principally because he stood at the foot of the bed to get light, and I
thought deceased was a little deaf. I did not notice
deceased was quite paralysed on one side. As deceased
had expressed a wish for me to give instructions for the
codicil, I did not think there was any need to send Mr. Reid
in to take instructions from her. I did not tell Mr. Reid
not to go to her. I told Mr. Reid I was commissioned to
have the codicil drawn. On the day of the second confession I do not think I spoke about the guardianship of
the children. Deceased never spoke to me about the
occupation or profession of the children. I am aware they
have been brought up in the Protestant faith. My object
in wishing to be guardian is most decidedly to bring them
up in the Roman Catholic faith. I remonstrated with
deceased against having her children brought up as Protestants. I did not know her children were then attending
a Church of England school.

By the Court :—I administered the communion to the
deceased only once, and that was the day before her death.
In the course of the month before her death, I paid deceased
some seven or eight visits. On about three occasions I
spoke to her about the children. On every occasion the
answer was favourable, but she was afraid of Mr. Fairbridge
—that is, she was afraid of displeasing him. I have had
conversations with Eliza about this matter several times.
Eliza always exhibited a willingness that I should be the
guardian.

Henry Reid stated :—I am an attorney of this Court.
On 16th April defendant came to me at my office. He
said Mrs. Kannemeyer, as she was usually called, was very
ill, and wished to make a codicil to her will, appointing
him guardian of her children in the place of those named in
the will. He said he had consulted Mr. Porter, who said
it could be done. He asked me to go with him to the house

1873.
June 12.
  „   20.
  „   30.
July   1.
August 1.

Executors Cer-
fonteyn vs.
O'Haire.

1873.
June 12.
" 26.
" 30.
July 1.
August 1.

Executors Cer-
fonteyn vs.
O'Haire.

to prepare the codicil. I did so. When we arrived there we were shown into the parlour by Eliza, I believe. Eliza immediately brought the will without my asking for it. I looked at it, and found it contained the reservatory clause, and I then wrote the codicil. I read it over to myself, and asked if we could go upstairs. Eliza said yes, and we went up with Kearns. Eliza did not go up with us. Deceased was lying in bed. I did not know her, but I might have seen her before. Nobody spoke, but deceased returned my salute. I began reading the codicil. Defendant then said. "Read a little louder," and I commenced again. I asked deceased, "Do you understand it?" She moved her head and said "Yes." I placed the codicil before deceased on a small desk which Eliza brought, and she then signed it. She signed without any assistance. I went downstairs with the codicil, and Kearns and I witnessed it in the parlour. I took the will down. I then gave the will and codicil to the daughter Eliza. The deceased remained in bed. I believe this was between one and two o'clock. We were in the house about a quarter of an hour altogether. When I saw testatrix she appeared to be perfectly capable of executing the codicil.

Cross-examined:—The codicil was not written in any great hurry. I thought deceased was perfectly capable of executing the codicil from her appearance, from the answer she gave to me, and from the way in which she signed the document. I don't think I had ever spoken to deceased before. All she said to me was "Yes." She was weak, but I had not the least doubt that she was quite capable, and knew well what she was doing. I was in her room about five to seven minutes. While signing I believed deceased sat herself, without assistance, though she was helped to rise. She used the pen like a person who was capable of knowing what she was doing. Before reading the codicil to her I did not say anything. No one else said anything. I considered it was *bonâ fide*. I don't remember her asking me where to sign. She might have done so. Defendant remained behind. I waited downstairs about a minute for him, and we all left together. Kearns was present when deceased signed, and also when I witnessed the codicil.

By the Court:—Deceased appeared to be a willing signer of the codicil. I am not the general attorney of the deceased. I was her attorney for this purpose. I merely acted as any other attorney who might have been called in would have done.

George Kearns stated:—I am the sacristan of St. Mary's Cathedral. I witnessed a codicil on the 16th April last at Mrs. Kannemeyer's. It was read in my presence to the deceased. Father O'Haire, Mr. Reid, and myself were present. I cannot remember whether any one else was in the room. I stood at the bedside, and Mr. Reid read the codicil, and Father O'Haire stopped him, telling him to read louder. Mr. Reid asked deceased if she understood it, and she said, "Yes, yes." She bowed her head twice also. Deceased then signed the codicil, and it was brought downstairs by, I believe, Mr. Reid. I then witnessed it. Deceased appeared to know what she was doing.

Cross-examined:—She appeared to be in her senses, judging from her appearance and her manner. She was quite strong in signing the document. I do not know what the time was.

By the Court:—Before she signed she asked Father O'Haire, "Where am I to sign?" and he showed her. Before going to the house I had no conversation with defendant about deceased. Some weeks before she died, Father O'Haire told me she was very weak and in a dying state, and also that she wished him to become guardian of her children. I always believed Mrs. Kannemeyer to be in her full senses all along. I became acquainted with her about two months prior to her death.

Mary Ann Pope stated:—I am a nurse. Mrs. Miller called at my house the Monday before Mrs. Kannemeyer's death, and said her sister was very ill, and asked me to go and see her. She asked me to stop the night with her, and I did so. Towards morning she seemed very ill, and I thought she was dying. She sent for the doctor and her clergyman. The doctor came between three and four o'clock, and afterwards she rallied a little. She was a great deal better, and began to talk. Mrs. Miller was present. I asked her if she had settled all her affairs, and told her it was better she did so. She said, "Yes, I have settled all my affairs, all but the guardianship of my own children. I wish Father O'Haire to be the guardian of my own children." I said, "And why not?" Mrs. Miller replied, "Oh, she wishes it very much, but it is no use her thinking of it. Mr. Fairbridge will not allow it." I said, "Do the children wish it themselves?" and Mrs. Miller replied, "Oh, yes, but there is no use speaking of it; Mr. Fairbridge will not hear of it." Deceased appeared much distressed while this was going on. Between seven and eight o'clock in the morning I prepared to go home; but as deceased pressed me to stay, I remained with her. Mrs. Miller said her sister had often been as bad before; if she got worse they could send for her. Mrs. Miller then left. I was sitting by her bedside, and heard deceased saying, "I wish I had settled it about my poor children before." She said she wished to see Father O'Haire about being

1873.
June 12.
„ 20
„ 30.
July 1.
August 1.
Executors Cer-
fonteyn vs.
O'Haire.

F

1873.
June 12.
" 20.
" 30.
July 1.
August 1.

Executors Cerfonteyn vs. O'Haire.

guardian to her children. I asked, "Does not Father O'Haire come to see you every day?" She said, "Yes; but I do not know what time, and I feel I am sinking very fast." I had to go to Grave-street, and deceased said, "Do come back soon, for I want to have it settled about my children; and I wish Father O'Haire for their guardian." When I returned I met Father O'Haire just going into the bed-room. I told him that deceased was very anxious to see him about the guardianship, and if he had not come I would have sent for him. This was all said in the bed-room. Father O'Haire asked Mrs. Kannemeyer, "What is it you want, and what are you prepared to do?" She replied, "I want you to be the guardian of my children." Father O'Haire turned round to me and said, "We have often spoken about the matter, but it had never been decided." Mrs. Kannemeyer said, "I wish it decided now." Father O'Haire said he must consult a lawyer as to whether she could make the alteration she wished, and deceased told him to do so. Father O'Haire returned shortly after, saying he had seen Mr. Porter, who said she could make the alteration. He said he must go and get witnesses. He went out again, and returned with Mr. Reid and Mr. Kearns. I was not in the room when the will was signed. After it was over, and Mr. Reid and Mr. Kearns gone, I went up to deceased's room and found Father O'Haire there. I asked Mrs. Kannemeyer if she had everything done as she wished. She replied she had, and turned to Father O'Haire, and said, "Thank you very much." Father O'Haire left the room, and told me if she changed for the worse to send for him. She looked very cheerful, sitting against her pillows. I asked her if she felt well enough for me to go down and make her something warm for the evening. She said she was well enough. I went down, and stayed down about a quarter of an hour or twenty minutes, and then went back and sat by the bedside. After some conversation, she asked if I would not take her downstairs. I said I thought it would do her no good. She said the doctor said she might go down. I said, "Very well, we will have the door downstairs shut, and warm the house, and then I will take you down." I took her down about two hours after she had signed the codicil. I think it must have been about three o'clock before I took her down. I asked her where I could get anything warm to put upon her, and she told me where I could find her dressing-gown. Annie was in the room, and helped me to put it upon her. She would not let me carry her, but said there were two men at the stables who knew how to take her down, by putting her in an easy-chair and carrying her

1873.
June 12.
„ 20.
„ 30.
July 1.
August 1.
———
Executors Cer-
fontwyn vs.
O'Haire.

with her back to the stairs, and in that way she did not get
giddy. The two men carried her down, her daughter,
Annie, holding her feet. I wanted to put her in the bed
made for her in the sitting-room. She said, "No, Mrs.
Pope; do not be in a hurry; let me rest." About ten
minutes after, she said, "Now you may put me to bed." I
put her on the bed, and saw she was sinking fast. She
asked to see the doctor; and he was sent for, as also was
Father O'Haire. She did not speak at all after she was
put on the bed. I sent for her sister, Mrs. Miller. She
was very low when the doctor came. I mean by "very
low" dying. She died shortly after he came. This must
have been between three and four o'clock. When Mrs.
Kannemeyer thanked Father O'Haire, he said, "Well,
Mrs. Kannemeyer, I have done as you wished. I shall
receive no benefit, but I shall do my best for your children."
After the codicil had been signed, I asked her if she
would like Mr. Fairbridge to be sent for and made
acquainted with what had been done. She said, "No, it is
no use. It is hard to get at Mr. Fairbridge. He loses
nothing by it. It is my own wish, and I can do as I wish
myself." When they wanted to get the will, the deceased
said, "Mrs. Pope, please call Eliza." I did so. She asked
Eliza if she knew where the will was. She said, "Yes."
Mrs. Kannemeyer took a bunch of keys from under her
pillow, selected the key of the box in which the will was,
and gave it to Eliza. Eliza returned and said she could
not find it. The deceased said, "What a stupid girl you
are! Give me the keys." She took them and selected a key
and returned it to Eliza. Eliza returned with the little
box. Mrs. Kannemeyer opened it, and gave the will to
Father O'Haire, who looked at it, and said the alteration
could be made. Mrs. Kannemeyer was perfectly sensible.

Cross-examined:—Annie Kannemeyer was not in the
bed-room of the deceased the whole night previous to her
death. She was not there when deceased said she wished
Father O'Haire to be guardian of her children. It must
have been between three and four o'clock in the morning.
There were only Mrs. Miller and myself in the room at
that time. Annie was in and out afterwards. The first
time I saw Father O'Haire that day was between nine and
ten o'clock. We went into the bed-room together. I did
not hear Father O'Haire speak about spiritual matters to
her. I am quite sure Father O'Haire first said to deceased,
"Well, what do you want?" He stayed in the room about
ten minutes after Mr. Reid had gone. I have read the
evidence in the newspapers. I am a member of Father
O'Haire's congregation. I had no conversation whatever
with any one about this case. I did not tell Father

F 2

1873.
June 12.
„ 20.
„ 30.
July 1.
August 1.

Executors Cer-
fonteyn vs.
O'Haire.

O'Haire what my evidence would be. Mr. Reid took my evidence some time ago. I am certain that Mrs. Miller was in the room when the conversation I spoke of took place. Between twelve and one o'clock I could not see deceased was dying, but I thought she would not live very long. I thought she might live over the night. When Father O'Haire came to look at the will Mrs. Miller was not there.

Defendant closed his case.

De Villiers, A.-G., submitted he was entitled to recall Mrs. Miller to disprove this evidence, as she had not been cross-examined on the conversation alleged by the last witness to have taken place. Also, that the plaintiffs had the right to call rebutting evidence generally.

Reitz did not resist.

Mrs. Miller recalled :—I remember the night previous to my sister's death. I sat up with her till twelve o'clock ; then I laid down for an hour in the next room, and subsequently Annie Kannemeyer woke me. Till twelve o'clock Annie, one of her brothers, one of the younger ones, Mrs. Pope, and myself were there. Annie came for me at one o'clock. My sister had then taken a change for the worse. Mrs. Pope was in the room. We sent for the doctor. After the doctor had been I never recollect any conversation between my sister and Mrs. Pope about the guardianship of the children. She was far too ill. She could not have said anything without my hearing it. As to the conversation Mrs. Pope spoke of. I solemnly declare I never heard it. I will swear that I do not remember ever saying, " It is no use talking about it ; Mr. Fairbridge will not hear of it." My sister was a woman of very few words ; she scarcely spoke that night.

Mr. Porter stated :—Mr. O'Haire left me on the day in question at about five minutes past one o'clock ; it might be a minute more or a minute less.

Dr. Chiappini, recalled by the Court :—I remember the conversation mentioned by the nurse Johnson on the occasion I met Father O'Haire and said to him, " You are just the man I want." It was not on the day of the death, but several days before. It was to tell Father O'Haire that deceased was near her death, that she would die very soon. I told him she had not long to live. We afterwards spoke on general topics, and I left.

De Villiers, A.-G., for the plaintiffs, argued the deceased was not of sound and disposing mind when the codicil of the 16th of April was executed, and that undue clerical influence was brought to bear upon her by the defendant. It is not necessary to prove actual insanity. It is sufficient if it be shown a dominion was acquired over the testatrix, though otherwise she was sufficiently sound in mind for general purposes. If such dominion had been acquired so as to prevent thought, judgment, and discretion, it invalidated the bequest. Again, dispositions in favour of persons standing in particular relations to a testator, among others the relation of a penitent to her confessor, are presumed without proof to have been the effect of suggestion. 4, *Burge Com. on Col. Laws, pp. 339-347; Mountain* vs. *Brunett*, 1 *Cox's C.* 353.

[FITZPATRICK, J.—Here there is no pecuniary benefit conferred.]

The law gives it. Under the Ordinance No. 104, a guardian is entitled to his commission. In cases of weakness arising from the near approach of death, strong proof is required that the contents of the will are known, and that it is the testator's own spontaneous desire. The burden of proof lies on the beneficiary. He should in extreme cases take every precaution. 1, *Jarman*, 2nd ed., p. 27; *Dufaur* vs. *Croft*, 3 *Moore's P.C.C.*, 136; *Harwood* vs. *Baker*, 2 *Moore's P.C.C.*, 282; *Tennant's Notary's Manual*, p. 142. In this case no instructions for drawing the codicil were given by the testatrix, and when it was signed it was simply read over, and no explanation made by any one. The defendant was guilty of undue influence. He gave the instructions for the codicil, and was present at its execution. As long as the testatrix possessed thought, judgment, and discretion, she resisted his efforts to be appointed guardian, and it was only on the day of her death, after being weakened both bodily and mentally by disease, and after she had made her last confession and had received the sacrament, that she yielded to his importunity. The codicil could not have been signed more than an hour before her death, and defendant took no precautions such as were stated in *Harwood* vs. *Baker* ought to be taken.

The Court directed the attention of counsel to the manner in which the codicil had been executed. The witnesses did not attest in the presence of the testator.

Reitz, for the defendant:—The codicil, there being a reservatory clause in the will, does not need to be witnessed. Under the reservatory clause the codicil becomes part and parcel of the testament, and must be taken as if it was written above the signature, and therefore it is attested because the will is attested. The effect of the reservatory clause was discussed in Sir John Wylde's case, *Haynes and*

1873.
June 12.
" 20.
" 30.
July 1.
August 1.
———
Executors Cerfonteyn *vs.* O'Haire.

1873.
June 12.
„ 20.
„ 30.
July 1.
August 1.

Executors Cer-
fontein vs.
O'Haire.

Jarman's Concise Forms of Wills, p. 549.[*] The Ordinance
No. 105, 1845, does not affect this case. See also *V. d
Keesel, Th. 337 ; Bynkershoek, Quæs. Juris Privati, b. 3,
ch. 4, p. 393, ch. 5, p. 395.*

De Villiers, A.-G., admits the authorities are in support
of the validity of an unwitnessed codicil made under a
reservatory clause. See *Lybreghts Red. Vertoog, vol. 1, p. 323 ;
Bynkershoek, vol. 1, p. 500.*

The Court directed the argument to continue on the
merits, and they would dispose of the whole case together.

Reitz went on to contend plaintiffs had failed to prove
their case. The evidence did not show undue pressure on
the part of defendant. Deceased was of sound disposing
mind when the codicil was executed, and all that was
legally necessary to be done to give validity to that instrument had been done.

De Villiers, A.-G., replied.

Cur. adv. vult.

Postea (August 1).—Judgment was given by majority of
the Court (BELL, C. J., DENYSSEN, J.; FITZPATRICK, J.,
dissenting) for plaintiffs with costs.

BELL, C. J., after stating the cause of action, and
summarising and commenting on the evidence, continued :—
The evidence, that is to say so much of it as deserves
credit, satisfies my mind in coming to the conclusion that, as
to the preparation of this codicil and its execution, though
aware perhaps of the words in which it was expressed and
possessing sufficient capacity to answer "Yes," when asked
if she understood it, and to go through the acts necessary
for its execution, the testatrix did not, in her expiring condition, possess sufficient thought, memory, and understanding
to consider all the antecedents which had induced her to
appoint Fairbridge and Steytler guardians by her will,
made in January, 1872, confirmed by codicil in December,
1872, and which had induced her, notwithstanding the importunities of the defendant, continued till shortly before
the hour of death, to refrain from making this codicil re-
calling what she had done by her will ; she was as much a
passive instrument in the hands of the defendant as was
Mr. Reid, whom he brought there to do and who did nothing
but his bidding.

If the evidence of the defendant were credible in the
particulars, in respect of which in my opinion it is incredible,

[*] *Et vide* Appendix.

the most that could be said is that the defendant had
succeeded in making the deceased waver between her faith-
fulness to Mr. Kannemeyer and the injunctions of the
defendant, and that, at last, in the weakness, bodily and
mental, of her dying moments, his importunities prevailed.

1873.
June 12
„ 20.
„ 30.
July 1.
August 1.

Executors Cer-
fonteyn vs.
O'Haire.

"Quod si non coactus sed persuasus est testator cessat
poena." *Poth. ad Pand.* 29, 6, 5. If the testatrix had, in
making this codicil, been persuaded by the voice of reason,
of affection, or of religion, the act would not be challenged;
but in the language of another commentator: "Continuis
precibus, flagitationibus et persuasionibus testatorem ita
fatigata fuit ut illa tandem per œsa atque a molestiis libera-
tura faciat."

I am of opinion that the plaintiff has established the first
alternative prayer of his declaration that it should be found
that the deceased was incapable from bodily disease and
mental debility of knowing what she was doing.

In the case of *Higginson* vs. *Colcot*, 1 *Lee*, 138, the plaintiff was a creditor of the deceased, against whom the testator,
Hibberd, had a great aversion, expressed on more occasions
than one. On the 15th May, Higginson and Platt came to
the house of the testator, whom they found ill in bed.
Higginson asked how he was. He answered, better than he
had been. Higginson said he had brought a will according
to his desire, and produced it ready written, and asked if
he should read it. The deceased assented, it was read, and
the deceased approved of it, signed and published it, and
then desired Higginson "to remember his wife and family
after he had satisfied his own debt." The Court set aside
this will "as not being the free and voluntary act of the
deceased."

In the case of *Lamkin* vs. *Babb*, 1 *Lee* 1, Cutlove, who
had been sent for, said to the testator he had come to make
his will. Deceased said he would "make his will with all
his heart," and directed his estate to be divided equally
between his wife and two children. The will was then read
and approved. The deceased was lying in bed, and on his
moving some one asked him what he was going to do. "To
write my name," he answered. "What to?" "To my
will," he replied. At this stage his wife exclaimed to
Bristow, one of the executors who had come into the room,
"They have persuaded my husband to make a will," and
asked him to do what he could for her, and altogether made
such a noise that she was desired to go downstairs. The
testator then put his mark to the will, the disturbance
having upset him. This was on the 28th May. Next day,
29th May, Allen visited the deceased, when the wife asked
him to make his will. The deceased said, "Yes." Allen
then asked him if he was willing to make his will to his

1873.
June 12.
" 20.
" 30.
July 1.
August 1.

Executors Cer-
fonteyn vs.
O'Haire.

wife. He said, " Yes." Allen then drew a will in her favour alone, which was approved and executed by the deceased, and delivered to the wife. Afterwards the deceased said to her, "Molly, if you are satisfied I am content." The judge, Sir G. Lee, said he was of opinion that the first will was agreeably to the deceased's intention when he was capable and approved of it, and that he would have executed it if the noise and disturbance his wife made had not thrown him into a sudden incapacity, and that the second will was made "merely by the pressure and importunity of his wife clandestinely, and at a time when it was at least very doubtful whether the deceased had sense enough to know what he did," and gave judgment for the first will.

The case of *Harwood* vs. *Baker*, 3 *Moore P.C.C.*, 282, was relied upon. The facts in that case are so far similar to those in the present case that the testator's illness had produced a settled torpor of mind in which he lay until roused, by some one. When roused he was apparently capable of exercising thought. This done, he relapsed into torpor until again roused. In the present case the testatrix was under the constant effect, lesser or greater, of opiates, which after being taken "rendered her dizzy and prevented her thinking," and, as she told Fairbridge, made her not recollect when asked by the defendant whether she had made provision for the guardianship.

The difference between this case and Harwood's is this: the torpor in Harwood's case was the effect of disease, and continued so long as the testator was not roused; whereas the state of the testatrix's mind in the present case was artificially produced by medicine, and therefore only occasional, lasting while the effect of the opiates was active.

On the other hand, in Harwood's case, the illness of the testator had been of short duration, without having produced much effect on his bodily health; whereas the testatrix here had been long wasting away with a fatal disease, and on the day the codicil was executed was languishing and expiring, in the opinion of those around her, and did expire before the day ended. Assuming sickness to have so reduced her bodily powers as consequently to have affected her mental capacity, the case of Harwood is useful as showing the amount of intelligence displayed by the testator at the time of executing his will, which, nevertheless, was not held to be sufficient to sustain it.

If the testatrix in the present case, parodying the words of this judgment, had, while in a state of health, considered the terms and effect of the codicil questioned, and had formed the deliberate purpose of executing it, but had omitted to carry that purpose into effect before the immediate attack of which she died within less than an hour of its execution, less evidence of capacity might have been sufficient to show that the codicil really did contain the expression of her will. But when we find that up to the day of her death, if she had not resisted the execution of the codicil, she had at least evaded or failed to execute it, though urged to importunity by the defendant, I am of opinion, as I said before, that the plaintiff has established that the codicil was not an expression of the testatrix's deliberate uncontrolled will.

1873.
June 12.
,,   20.
,,   30.
July   1.
August 1.

Executors Cer-
fonteyn vs.
O'Haire.

A later case than that I have just been considering is *Jones* vs. *Goderich, 5 Moore, P.C.C., N.S.* There a will and codicil were challenged on the ground of incapacity. The Privy Council sustained the will notwithstanding acts by the testatrix's surgeon in whose favour it was made in regard to dealing with the property even before the death of the testatrix, which were characterized by the Court as highly reprehensible, because the evidence showed unmistakably that the testatrix had capacity when she executed the will, and had long before her death spoken of the will with approbation.

But the Privy Council disallowed the codicil reducing a legacy given by the will, and it did so under these circumstances. Lane, who drew the codicil, did so without communication with the deceased, from instructions given by Goderich, who was to benefit by the codicil. He had it fair copied, took it to the testatrix, and read it over, and she acquiesced in it, and signed it on a small table which stood beside the deceased.

At the same time, either immediately before or immediately after the signing of the codicil, Lane procured the execution by the testatrix of two instruments, one to transfer £1,200 consols, and the other to transfer £448 long annuities, in pursuance of an agreement, said by Goderich to have been made between him and the testatrix.

The application of these observations to this case, which is not the same altogether in its facts, is obvious, and requires no comment.

I am of opinion, after applying these cases to the evidence in this case, that the plaintiff has entitled himself to have it declared, according to the first prayer of his declaration, that the deceased was, at the time of executing the codicil, incapable from bodily disease, and consequent mental debility, not of knowing that she was signing a codicil and doing the things necessary for that purpose, but of apprehending the effect of the codicil, as interfering with her previous determination long persisted in.

The case might be rested here, but the alternative prayer of the plaintiffs' declaration to have it found that if the testatrix did understand what she was doing she was induced

1873.
June 12.
„ 20.
„ 30.
July 1.
August 1.

Executors Cer-
fonteyn vs.
O'Haire.

to sign the codicil by undue clerical influence and pressure, during her dying moments, and not through her own will and desire, remains to be considered.

Where a deed to take effect in the life of the parties to it is questioned, as giving an undue benefit by the one to the other, the parties standing to each other in the relation of minor and guardian, trustee and *cestui que trust*, attorney and client, confessor and penitent, the law presumes against the deed influence upon the party subject to the influence arising from these respective relations, and casts upon the party defending the deed the burden of proving that it was executed free from any such influence, and as fairly as if the parties had been strangers to each other. In doing this the law only calls upon the party to explain the part he took in bringing about the execution of the deed, in which, *ex facie* of it, he was an active party; and that the other party subject to the influence, necessarily arising from their relation to each other, was in a position that enabled him to form free and unfettered judgment as to the terms and effect of the deed challenged.

But where a will, or codicil, or a bequest under them is challenged, the law is the reverse—the burden of proving the ground of challenge is thrown upon the party challenging the instrument; the presumption of law being that the will or codicil has been made by a competent and willing testator. Until the contrary be proved, and that the influence used by the persons beforenamed as a guardian over his ward—a trustee over his *cestui que trust*—has only been the natural influence arising from these relations, affection, or attachment, that presumption is to be got the better of only by evidence that the will or codicil was made not as the result of natural affection or social estimation, but under the effects of importunity of force and coercion, destroying free agency; for this there is authority in many cases, but most prominently in the case of *Parfitt and Lawless, 2 Law Reports*, 462.

In that case a will was challenged upon the sole ground that it had been made in favour of the confessor of the testatrix, without an allegation even, or the slightest attempt to prove, that influence had been used by the confessor, duly or unduly, to procure it; the party challenging the will assuming that the mere relation of confessor raised a presumption against the will, and threw upon the party proposing the will the burden of proving that it had been duly made.

The Court of Probate had no difficulty in disallowing this ground of challenge and sustaining the will. Lord Penzance, by whom the judgment was delivered, drew the distinctions I have alluded to between the presumptions arising from relative positions in the case of deeds and of will*, in stating the evidence which would have been required to sustain the challenge of the will; he used these observations, which I quote as peculiarly applicable to the present case. "The propositions, which the defendant was bound to give reasonable evidence to establish, were that the plaintiff had interfered in the making of the will; that he had procured the gift of the residue to himself, and that he had brought this about, not by persuasion and advice, for that would be perfectly legal, but by some coercion or dominion exercised over the testatrix against her will, or by importunity so strong that it could not be resisted." Other authorities to the same effect will be found in *Williams on Executors*, v. 1, p. 39.

1873.
June 12.
  „ 20.
  „ 30.
July 1.
August 1.

Executors Cerfonteyn *vs.* O'Haire.

The nature or quality of the object sought to be attained by the use of the influence does not guide the decision of the Court. The "undueness" (if I may make use of the expression) of the influence is in the use of it, having respect to the condition, bodily and mental, of the person over whom it has been used, and to the extent to which it has been used by the person using it, having regard to the relation in which the parties stood to each other.

The defendant in pressing the deceased from time to time to bring up her children in the Roman Catholic faith; in representing to the deceased the omission to do it as a sin against which, when she appeared "before the tribunal of Almighty God," Mr. Fairbridge could not plead for her; in postponing on occasion her confession and absolution; in "determining" on the morning of her death "to see to" the procuring of the codicil in question, and carrying out that determination within one hour before her death, no doubt did it in the full strength of his zeal for his Church, and perhaps in the full depth of priestly regard for the soul of the deceased and for the souls of her progeny; though persons looking at the matter from a different point of view may differ perhaps from him in this; yet the question which the Court has to decide is, whatever may have been the object which the defendant had in view—meritorious or otherwise—was the deceased, who had failed, if she had not refused, up to the morning of the day on which she died, to do what the defendant that morning determined to get her to do and did accomplish, doing what she did in a state of strength of mind and body sufficient to weigh the arguments used by the defendant when speaking of her spiritual interest, in which he was forced to admit that he had included the question of her children's religious education, against the father of the children's reasons for bringing them up in the Protestant faith and her promise to him on his death-bed so to bring them up?

1873.
June 12.
„ 20.
„ 30.
July 1
August 1.

Executors Cer-
fonteyn vs.
O'Haire.

The evidence satisfies my mind that the testatrix was not in such a state of strength, mental or bodily, as would justify the Court in saying the execution of the codicil in question was not brought about by religious persuasion and advice. In my opinion it was brought about by the persistent importunity of the defendant, continued for years and culminating on the morning of the death, as I feel bound to infer from the nature of the defendant's evidence, in suggestions, if not threats, of terrors after death should she " appear before the tribunal of Almighty God " without having done what he was requiring her to do.

The judgment must be for the plaintiff in terms of his declaration, and the defendant must pay the costs of the action.

DENYSSEN, J., as to the mental capacity of the testatrix, said :—For the purpose of establishing legal incompetency, it is not necessary to prove that the testatrix was out of her mind, or that she wholly failed to understand what she was doing, nor was this the case here ; what the law requires is proof that, in consequence of the state of body and mind, from illness or other causes, she did not and could not exercise that thought, reflection, and judgment, which are absolutely and essentially necessary to enable her to form and express her real and true desire ; and it is for the Court to determine, upon the evidence adduced, whether she possessed, at the time she passed the deed, those qualifications or otherwise.

In cases of lunacy, intervals occur when a person recovers his mind, and no Court will question any testamentary act or deed passed during such lucid intervals. But is such the present case ? Let us refer to the evidence. The deceased had been in an ailing state three years before her death ; she was suffering from pulmonary consumption. On the 24th March, 1873, she was sinking. On the 29th March, according to Mr. Fairbridge, she was very feeble. On the morning of the 16th April, the day of her death, between one and two o'clock, she was delirious. At eight o'clock very weak, but had rallied a little. Between nine and ten, according to Dr. Chiappini, she was beginning to sink. Between eleven and twelve she said herself she felt very queer, and was beginning to sink very fast, that her left side was quite faint. At about twelve o'clock she was dull and speechless, and half-an-hour after she looked very queer. Dr. Chiappini, who saw her in the morning, says that, considering she was sinking between nine and ten, she could not have much of a mind an hour before her death, and if told that an hour before her death she sent for her will, and a certain codicil being read to her, was asked, " Do you understand it or not?" and she said "Yes," that he would think it not impossible, but highly improbable. She died about three o'clock the same day.

I am aware that in his evidence the defendant gives a conversation which took place in his presence about midday between the deceased and her step-daughter, Eliza Kannemeyer, about a box in which the will was, which the defendant wished to examine for the purpose of ascertaining whether it contained the reservatory clause so as to admit of his being appointed the guardian of the minor children under a codicil—which evidence is supported by Mrs. Pope, the sick nurse; but Mrs. Pope had prepared herself to give that evidence by reading over the evidence of the defendant as published in the newspapers, and as she is, moreover, contradicted in certain important particulars by Mrs. Miller, whose evidence I fully believe, I cannot attach any weight to her statements; besides which her account of what took place on that occasion is to some extent contradicted by Reid and Kearns, the attesting witnesses of the codicil; and the fact of the testatrix being able to enter into that conversation is so inconsistent with the professional evidence of Dr. Chiappini as to the state of her mind, and of the other witnesses, that it does not satisfy me. But does not the absence of Eliza Kannemeyer upon a point of such importance cast more than a suspicion upon the truth of that evidence? The person with whom the conversation is said to have been held is kept out of the witness-box—why? Nor do I lose sight of the statements of Mr. Reid and of Kearns, that in their opinion the testatrix knew what she was about in passing the codicil, judging from her appearance; the one answer of "Yes" which she gave, and the manner in which she signed it; also of Annie Kannemeyer about the request to be carried down; but these opinions and statements are equally unsatisfactory in the face of the important facts given by the other witnesses. A request to be carried down requires no thought, reflection, or judgment; an alteration of a testamentary disposition made by the will, and not altered by the codicil of 1872, does.

From nine, if not from two, of the morning of the 19th April she was sinking; at midday she became dull and speechless; after that, faint or paralysed on one side, lost her mental capacity, and died, and within an hour before her death the document in question was passed. This was not a case of lunacy with lucid intervals, it was a gradual sinking from morning until death, from which at no time on the 16th had she sufficiently recovered as to possess those qualities which are necessary to render her capable to alter her duly made will and codicil of 1872. *   *   *

[On the question whether the testatrix signed the codicil

1873.
June 12,
"   20,
"   30.
July   1.
August 1.

Executors Car-
fonteyn vs.
O'Haire.

1873.
June 12.
„ 20.
„ 30.
July 1.
August 1.

Executors Cer-
tonteyn vs.
O'Haire.

voluntarily and of her own free will, or whether she was
induced to sign it through the undue clerical influence
and pressure brought to bear upon her by the defendant
during her dying moments; after referring to the evidence,
His Lordship continued]:—In a case recently decided in
the Probate and Divorce Court in England, Lord Penzance
laid down the following propositions which, if proved,
vitiated deeds of this and similar descriptions, and the
principles therein contained I entirely adopt:

1. If it can be proved that the party (the defendant in
this case) had interfered in the making of the will (here the
codicil).

2. If he had procured the gift (in the case referred to by
Lord Penzance of the residue of an estate, in this case of
the beneficial appointment as guardian of minor children)
to himself.

3. That this had been brought about not by persuasion
and advice, but by some coercion or dominion exercised
over the testatrix against her will, or by importunity so
strong that it could not be resisted.

In *Burge*, v. 4, p. 347, the same principles are laid down,
and also in the cases therein referred to.

The influence to vitiate an act must amount to force and
coercion destroying free agency; it must not be the influence of affection and attachment; it must not be the
mere desire of gratifying the wishes of another; there must
be proof that the act was obtained by coercion, by importunity which could not be resisted, that it was done merely
for the sake of peace so that the motive was tantamount to
force and fear.

Now it cannot be disputed that as long as the deceased
was in a fair state of health she did not and would not dis-
obey the dying request of the person who, although not
married to her according to law, was the father of her
children, and for whom she evidently felt much respect and
esteem; and I cannot admire the reference of the defendant
in her dying moments to this unfortunate circumstance, not
for the purpose of bringing to her notice the sin she had
committed and to induce her to repent, but to justify her in
violating her promise and to promote his own interests;
and the allusion to Fairbridge, as not being able to plead
her cause before God Almighty, in my own opinion ill
accords with the character of a priest. The object was to
destroy the confidence the deceased had in him, and gain a
benefit for his Church as well as for himself individually.
Nor can it be doubted that she did not wish the children
to forsake the faith of their father and to adopt that of
the priest. Mrs. Miller, her sister, and herself a Roman
Catholic, denies it: and why did the children remain in a

Protestant school? Why allow the children to be catechised every Sunday by the Rev. Mr. Bindley if her wishes
were otherwise? It was during her last moments when
very feeble, occasionally delirious, speechless, having little
or no mind, that the defendant procured and instructed Mr.
Reid (not her friend Mr. Fairbridge or after a personal
interview with the testatrix) to frame this codicil, to appoint himself the guardian of the minor children. And how
was this benefit to be obtained,—by persuasion and advice?
No; by delaying upon her confession, absolution, and the
sacrament of the Church until he (the priest) had been appointed as the guardian so as to force the children to
renounce the faith of their father.

She resisted till the last moment, for—"How about the
guardianship?"—such was the exclamation of the defendant the morning of her death, when Eliza Kannemeyer told
him she was very ill; and "What do you want? What are
you prepared to do?" were the questions put to the dying
woman. And it was then, and not until then, when thought,
reflection, and judgment could no longer be exercised,
when importunity could no longer be resisted, against her
will, and for the sake of peace, that the dying woman
signed the codicil in question.

I am of opinion, therefore, that there should be judgment
for the plaintiffs with costs.

FITZPATRICK, J., after stating the facts, and noticing
the importance of this case as regards the character and
reputation of the parties affected, proceeded to discuss the
two issues raised in the order in which they appeared in the
declaration, namely, was there legal incapacity in the testatrix at the time of her executing this codicil? or if not, was
it executed under the undue influence of the defendant?
He said:—It will be convenient first to state what the undisputed law is as to each of these questions in their order,
and then to test the evidence by the standard of that law:—
First as to incapacity—"If a party impeach the validity of
a will on account of a supposed incapacity of mind in the
testator, it will be incumbent on such party to establish
such incapacity by the clearest and most satisfactory proofs.
*The burthen of proof rests upon the person attempting to
invalidate what on its face purports to be a legal act.
Sanity must be presumed till the contrary is shown.* Hence
if there is no evidence of insanity at the time of giving instructions for a will, the commission of suicide three days
after" will not invalidate the instrument, by raising an inference of previous derangement. *Williams on Executors,*
p. 18, v. 1, and cases there cited. "A mad or lunatic person cannot, during the insanity of his mind, make a testa-

1873.
June 12.
"   20.
"   30.
July 1.
August 1.

Executors Cer-
fonteyn vs.
O'Haire.

ment of his land or goods; but if during a lucid interval he makes a testament, it is good." *Jarman on Wills*, v. 1, p. 26. "The court does not depend on the opinion of the witnesses, but on the facts to which they deposed." "The strongest and best proof that can arise as to a lucid interval is that which arises from the act itself of making a will. That I look upon as the thing to be first examined, and if it can be proved and established that it is a *rational act, and rationally done*, the whole case is proved." "If you can establish that the party habitually affected by a malady of the mind has intermissions, and if there was an intermission of the disorder at the time of the act, that, being proved, is sufficient; and the general insanity will not affect it." Sir W. Wynne, in *Carthright* vs. *Carthright; 1 Phill.*, 90; *Williams on Executors*, v. 1, p. 21. [His Lordship then commented on the evidence as to the capacity of the testatrix, and compared it with the principles laid down in the authorities quoted. His Lordship came to the conclusion that the evidence clearly proved that testatrix was in full possession of all her mental faculties at the time the testament was signed.]

On the question of undue influence, his Lordship said: I will first state a few undisputed principles of law on the subject. "The influence which will set aside a will," says Mr. Justice Williams, "must amount to force and coercion, destroying free-will agency. It must not be the influence of affection or attachment, it must not be the mere desire of gratifying the wishes of another, for that would be a very strong ground in support of a testamentary act. Further, there must be proof that the act was obtained by this coercion, by importunity that could not be resisted, that it was done merely for the sake of peace, so that the motive was tantamount to force and fear." *Williams on Executors*, v. 1, p. 44. With respect to a will obtained by influence, it is not unlawful for a man, by honest intercession and persuasion, to procure a will in favour of himself or another person. *Williams on Executors*, v. 1, p. 43. "It is not part of the testamentary law of this country that the making of a will must originate with the testator, nor is it required that proof should be given of the commencement of such a transaction, provided it be proved that the deceased completely understood, adopted, and sanctioned the disposition proposed to him, and that the instrument itself embodied such disposition." (Sir John Nicholl in *Constable* vs. *Terfrick,* 4 *Hagg*, 477, affirmed on appeal.) In *Boyce* vs. *Colclough,* Lord Lyndhurst says:—"With respect to undue influence, I am prepared to say that influence, in order to be undue within the meaning of any rule of law, which would make it sufficient to vitiate a will, must be an influence exercised either by coercion or by fraud." Further on he says :— "One point, however, is beyond dispute, and that is, that when once it has been proved that a will has been enacted with due solemnities by a person of competent understanding and apparently a free agent, the burthen of proving that it was executed under undue influence is on the party who alleges it. *Undue influence cannot be presumed.*" " No amount of persuasion or advice, whether founded on feelings of regard or religious sentiment, would avail, according to the existing law, to set aside this will so long as the free volition of the testatrix to accept or reject that advice was not invaded." (*Parfit* vs. *Lawless*, L.R., v. 2, p. 474). [After going through the evidence bearing on this point, his Lordship continued]:—I have searched every law book to which I have access, and have not been able to find one case like the present, where the person charged with having exercised undue influence to procure the execution of a will had not a personal interest of one shilling in the transaction, and did not gain one farthing as the result of his influence. There are, however, several cases in which large pecuniary advantages were gained by the person exercising the influence charged to be undue, in which the wills have been sustained. I have already alluded to two remarkable cases, *Boyce* and *Colclough*, where the wife was charged with exercising undue influence over her husband, whereby she induced him to make a will in her favour, to the exclusion of all his own relations, under which she inherited £60,000 and £7,000 a year ; and *Parfit* and *Lawless*, in which the domestic chaplain and confessor of a lady received under the will some £70,000 to the exclusion of testatrix's relatives. I will mention one other case, that of *Jones* and *Gooderich*, before the Privy Council, and reported 6, *H. L. C.*, p. 16. The judges present were Lord Langdale, Mr. Baron Parke, the Right Hon. Dr. Lushington, and the Right Hon. T. Pemberton Leigh. In that case the testatrix was a spinster, aged eighty-six years. She had resided for three years before her death in the house of her medical adviser, and whilst there executed a testament and codicil whereby she revoked two wills which she previously made, substantially set aside the objects of her bounty under those wills, her own friends and relations, and secured to her medical attendant the bulk of her property, some £10,000 or £12,000. Certain acts were done by this legatee, the medical attendant, of which the judgment thus speaks:— " These are acts which any court of justice must view with suspicion, and some of which are deserving of the severest disapprobation ; these are acts by which Gooderich has directly benefited, and by which before the death of the deceased he obtained the control of nearly all her property."

1873.
June 12.
„ 20.
„ 30.
July 1.
August 1.

Executors Cer-
fouteyn vs.
O'Haire.

1873.
June 12.
„ 20.
„ 30.
July 1.
August 1.

Executors Cer-
fonteyn vs.
O'Haire.

And yet this will and codicil were sustained by the great judges before whom this appeal was heard, because, although the testatrix was old and feeble, no incapacity was proved, and because, although her medical attendant had acquired such influence over her as to obtain the control of nearly all her property, there was no evidence of coercion. And was there coercion in the present case? The learned counsel for the plaintiff does not say there was evidence of it; but he says there must have been coercion in fact, because her spiritual adviser was unsuccessful until she was near death and weakened by disease. But he had obtained her promises, and she had striven to fulfil them long before that. Even if she had given no signs of compliance with his counsel before the very day of her death, I would not attribute her adopting of it then to coercion. I would rather say that reflection, stimulated by the sense of approaching death, caused her mind to be accessible to the counsel to which she had hitherto lent a dull and unwilling ear. However this may be, it is evidence—not suppositions or probability—that is wanted. In the expressive language of Lord Lyndhurst, you must prove either force or fraud.

There is only one other fact in the case which has been much dwelt upon, and which I have not yet noticed—perhaps to many minds the most important fact of all, namely, that the defendant was confessor to the testatrix. "As her confessor," said the Attorney-General, "the deceased was, so to speak, quite in his power; and under all the circumstances, the most powerful-minded woman would have been unable to resist his influence." One would suppose that this confession was some mysterious and cabalistic rite, which confers on the initiated supernatural and unholy powers, and paramount and undue influence over the human mind, such as you read of in the dark ages; and yet St. James says:—" Confess therefore your sins one to another; and pray for one another that you may be saved." And the Right Rev. Jeremy Taylor says in his Holy Dying, page 474 of the 14th volume of his works:—" In all cases of receiving confessions of sick men and the assisting to the advancement of repentance, the minister is to apportion to every kind of sin such spiritual remedies which are apt to mortify and cure the sinner—restitution of moneys, satisfaction of injuries." Still it is solemnly submitted to the Court as a fact from which the existence of irresistible power and the exercises of undue influence must be inferred. But it is not upon such suspicious fears and phantoms, but upon evidence, that a high court of judicature must administer impartial justice. By a curious coincidence, it so happened that a volume of re-

ports reached my hands by the steamer which arrived a few
days after the hearing of this case. In it the case of
Parfitt and *Lawless* is reported. In that case a Roman
Catholic priest had resided for many years with a Roman
Catholic lady, and for the greater part of the time, and at
the time the will was made, had been the lady's confessor.
After her husband's death, this lady bequeathed to her confessor property to the amount of £70,000, subject to life
annuities to the amount of £3,000. This will was impugned
under the plea, as in the present case, of undue influence.
The case was tried before Lord Penzance and a special
jury. The facts I have stated were proved, and the judge
decided that there was no evidence to go to the jury on
the plea of undue influence, and directed the jury to find
a verdict for the plaintiff, the chaplain and confessor.
Subsequently an application was made for a new trial on the
ground of misdirection by the learned judge who tried the
case. The question was urged before Lord Penzance,
Baron Pigott, and Justice Brett. The ruling of the judge
was unanimously affirmed, and in pronouncing the judgment of the Court, Lord Penzance used these words:—
" Again, it was argued that there were certain facts in this
case calculated to give rise to serious suspicions, and it
seemed to be contended that any conclusions which might
suggest themselves by way of suspicions merely, however
vague, might properly. if the jury pleased to indulge in
them, form the basis of a verdict; and consequently that if
facts were proved calculated to generate such suspicions,
enough had been done to make a case fit to go to the jury.
If this proposition were correct, it would follow that the
defendant had nothing more to do in a case like the present
than to prove that the plaintiff was a Catholic priest, that
he was the confessor of the testatrix, and that she had made
him her residuary legatee. For, upon this basis of fact,
suspicion freely indulged and directed by eloquent comment
might easily build up the fabric of undue influence, or even
fraud." (*Parfitt* and *Lawless*, 2, *L.R.*, v. 2, p. 474). These
are the views which present themselves to my mind, and,
having given the entire case my best attention, I am of
opinion that judgment should be for defendant with costs.

> Plaintiffs' Attorney, MOORE.
> Defendant's Attorneys, REID & NEPHEW.

1873.
June 12.
„ 20.
„ 30
July 1.
August 1.

Executors Cer-
fonteyn *vs.*
O'Haire.

Van Wyk *vs.* Van Wyk.

Costs.

The plaintiff, in a successful action to compel transfer, entitled to deduct his costs from the purchase money.

The plaintiff, William Robertson Van Wyk, brought an action against the executor testamentary of his mother, the late Mary Ann Van Wyk, to obtain transfer of a certain farm sold to him by his mother during her life-time for £500. At the trial the plaintiff obtained judgment in his favour with costs. The matter came before the Court on several occasions, when ultimately it was ordered that the plaintiff pay the purchase price of the farm as follows, namely, the sum of £200 to the Master for the benefit of the minor children of one Leopold Van Wyk, and the sum of £300 to the executor testamentary of the estate of the late Mary Ann Van Wyk, the defendant; and that on these payments being made the said executor do give transfer.

The plaintiff paid the £200 to the Master, and tendered to defendant the sum of £300 less the sum of £153 11s. 6d., being his (the plaintiff's) taxed costs in the principal action. This tender the plaintiff refused, and issued execution for the full sum of £300. Plaintiff's attorney had applied for payment of his costs, but had been informed that defendant, as executor, had no funds, and was contemplating surrendering deceased's estate as insolvent.

Cole, for the plaintiff, moved that the writ of execution be set aside, and the defendant ordered to accept the £300 less the said sum of £153 11s. 6d.

De Villiers, A.-G., for the defendant, opposed.

The Court ordered that the £300 claimed by the defendant be reduced by the amount of the plaintiff's costs in the former action, the costs of the writ, and the costs of this motion, and on payment of the balance the writ to be set aside.

[Plaintiff's Attorney, Van Zyl.]
[Defendant's Attorney, Tiran.]

Thornton *vs.* Brook.

" Good-for." Provisional Sentence.

Provisional sentence refused for the balance due on a " good-for," the defence being that the money was given for the purposes of a joint speculation in diamonds, which speculation had partially failed, and the defendant had paid to the plaintiff his share of the loss.

Provisional sentence was claimed for £111 2s. 3d., being the balance of a " good-for " for £500, made and signed by defendant, dated the 13th December, 1871. The sum of £388 17s. 9d. had been paid by the defendant to the plaintiff on the 25th January, 1873, leaving the balance now claimed.

E. J. Buchanan, for the defendant, produced an affidavit setting forth that the £500 in the "good-for" mentioned had been given to the defendant by the plaintiff to purchase diamonds, upon the understanding that the profits arising from such purchase should be equally divided between plaintiff and defendant. That diamonds were purchased; but the venture resulting in a loss, the defendant had paid the plaintiff the sum of £388 17s. 9d., being the amount realised by the sale of the diamonds, and his (the defendant's) share of the loss suffered.

De Villiers, A.-G., for the plaintiff, read an answering affidavit, but

The Court refused provisional sentence, costs to be costs in the cause.

[Plaintiff's Attorneys, REID & NEPHEW.
Defendant's Attorneys, BERRANGE & DE VILLIERS.]

STRYDOM *vs.* TIRAN.

Exceptions. Co-proprietors. Non-joinder.

Exceptions to declaration, that the plaintiff and defendant are co-proprietors in undivided shares of a farm, and that all the co-proprietors have not joined in suing, overruled, in an action for damages sustained by reason of defendant's trespass on a defined portion of the farm occupied by the plaintiff.

The declaration stated that Camille Frederick Tiran, the defendant, had been summoned to answer Elsie Johanna Strydom, widow, and executor testamentary of the late J. P. Strydom, in an action for damages sustained by reason of the defendant having wrongfully and unlawfully destroyed, broken down, and removed certain buildings, walls, and fences, situate on a certain portion of the farm "Krakeel River." That the late J. P. Strydom was, and the plaintiff in her said capacity still is, the proprietor in undivided shares of one-thirtieth share of the said farm. That J. P. Strydom in his lifetime did, and plaintiff in her said capacity still does, occupy a defined portion of the said farm, with the consent of the remaining co-proprietors thereof. That plaintiff let to defendant her share so defined for a period of five years. That before the expiration of the said period defendant became the proprietor of one-sixtieth part of the said farm, which was not divided or partitioned from the remaining portion, but was likewise a defined part thereof. That at the expiration of the lease aforesaid, plaintiff allowed defendant to occupy her portion aforesaid for a further period, in order to enable him to complete a certain house he was then building upon his sixtieth portion of the said farm. That while so occupying plaintiff's portion defendant committed the acts complained of, whereby the plaintiff suffered damages.

To this the defendant excepted—first, that according to the declaration the defendant and the plaintiff are co-proprietors in certain undivided shares of the said farm; second, that from the declaration it appears that at the time of the alleged commission of the acts complained of, the plaintiff was not possessed of or interested in the said farm, except jointly and undividedly with certain other parties still living and within the jurisdiction of the Court, not particularly named in the plaintiff's declaration, but who are well known to the plaintiff.

The exceptions were this day set down for argument, when

Cole (with him *Hodges*), for the defendant, appeared to support the exceptions. All partners, or joint-tenants, or tenants in common, must join in suing. (*Sanders*, 2nd ed., v. 2, p. 536, and the cases there referred to.) Non-joinder may be taken advantage of in a plea in abatement. If all the co-proprietors did not join, the defendant would be liable to an action by each. The plaintiff was not without remedy, for she might obtain partition of the farm.

De Villiers, A.-G., for the plaintiff, *contra.* There is no joint tenancy in this Colony. Our tenancy is tenancy in common; though tenants in common may join in suing for an injury to the land, they should in general sever. (*Chitty on Pleading*, 4th ed., v. 1, p. 55; *Addison on Tort*, 3rd ed., p. 275.) By the Roman-Dutch law there can be no doubt one tenant in common may be liable to another; for instance, if he alter the nature of the land, as turning pasture into arable land. How can this be done except by action? As to the general right of owners in undivided shares, see *Voet*, 10, 3, 7.

Cole having replied,

The Court considered that, as the plaintiff might be able to establish damage done to the portion of the property in her occupancy, they could not say that no action at all would lie. Exceptions therefore overruled with costs.

[Plaintiff's Attorney, C. C. DE VILLIERS.]
[Defendant's Attorney, TIRAN.]

KROHN vs. NURSE.

Bill of Lading. Liability of Ship-owner.

Damages.

*Where the defendant, a ship-master, received a quantity of
iron in good order, to be delivered to the plaintiff in like
good order, and signed bills of lading in which liability
for damage arising from rust was specially excepted,
and on delivery of the iron it was found to be unmerchantable from rust, and the plaintiff brought an
action for damages, the Court gave absolution from the
instance on the ground that the damage was not proved to
have arisen from the negligence of the defendant or of his
servants.*

John Nurse, master of the ship *Lizzie Waters*, defendant,
was summoned to answer Peter Frederick Krohn, of East
London, the plaintiff in this suit, in an action for damages.
In that the defendant, by a bill of lading, dated 25th
November, 1872, acknowledged two hundred and fifty
bundles of iron to have been shipped in good order and
condition in the ship *Lizzie Waters*, then in the river
Thames, and thereby promised to deliver the same in
like good order and condition to the plaintiff or his assigns
at East London, the usual dangers and accidents of navigation excepted, and the defendant not to be accountable
for "leakage, breakage, or *rust*." That no loss or damage
to the said goods arose by any of the perils, dangers, or
causes so excepted as aforesaid, yet the defendant did not
deliver the said goods at East London in the like good
order and condition in which they were shipped; but, on
the contrary, by reason of the negligent and improper
conduct of the defendant in and about the stowage or
conveyance of the said goods or otherwise, delivered the
same to the plaintiff in a damaged and unmerchantable
state, and, by reason of the premises, of no use or value to
the plaintiff, whereby he has sustained and been put to
expense and damage in the sum of £137 10s. 1d., for which
he prays judgment, &c.

1873.
August 22.
„ 26.
Krohn vs. Nurse.

The defendant pleaded the general issue.

The case was set down for trial before the Eastern Districts
Court on the 10th June, 1873, and after hearing the evidence
and arguments of counsel, the Court (DWYER and SMITH, J.J.)
was unable to agree as to what ought to be the judgment;
whereupon, it was ordered, the parties consenting, that the
case, together with the record of proceedings therein, be
removed for trial to the Supreme Court.

This day (August 22) the case was heard by the Supreme Court, when

De Villiers, A.-G., appeared for the plaintiff, and *Cole* (with him *Tennant*) for the defendant.

The records taken below were read. The plaintiff said: —"I saw the iron in my store after it was taken out of the ship. It was very much rusted. The rust was dry on it, but it was a damp day. I had a survey held on it. The weather was damp, but not showery, when the iron was landed. It got no wet in the landing. A large portion of the salt [part of the vessel's cargo] was landed before the iron. If the salt was uppermost and got damp, the water from the salt would get to the iron.

W. H. Townsend:—I was formerly master of a vessel. The iron was dry but rusty. I never saw iron arrive in the same condition as this without salt water or salt itself getting near it. I surveyed the iron the morning after it was landed with Mr. Gately. If the iron had been properly stowed it should not have presented that appearance. When the iron was landed I could see the salt glistening on it. No damp on the day the iron was landed would account for the rust.

John Gately :—From the state of the iron when landed it was impossible that it could have received the damage going from the vessel to the shore.

John E. Wood :—Even having salted hides in the same building with iron would cause it to rust away. I have seen iron in that state delivered from on board ship. It is quite unmerchantable.

For the defence was called—

John Nurse, defendant :—I am part owner of the *Lizzie Waters*. I received the iron some time before signing the bill of lading. No provision was made as to what cargo we were to take. A stevedore stowed the vessel. Part of the cargo consisted of 500 or 600 bags of salt. All the salt was in bags. The iron was stowed before the main-mast in the centre of the vessel. All the salt was in the after-hold. The nighest salt to the iron would be five or six feet. Between were different kinds of dry goods. I had very heavy weather for three or four days in the Bay of Biscay; none after. The vessel shipped large quantities of water; none got to the cargo. It was damp, hazy weather when the cargo was put on board ship. I have been at sea seventeen years. I attribute the rust on the iron to the sweating of the ship and to the dripping of the ship's deck. The salt was in no ways damaged. The salt did not come in contact with the iron. No bulkheads are in the stowage part. My ship does not sweat more than ordinary. Sweat of a ship is more or less salt. No other goods were damaged except two bales of cotton blankets, for which I paid 25s. damages; and some galvanized buckets. The goods were protected from contact with the salt. The division was as complete as if there had been a wooden bulkhead. I can't say that wet might not have got from the salt to the iron.

1873.
August 22.
,, 26.
Krohn *vs.* Nurse.

James Crome :—I am mate of the *Lizzie Waters*. The iron was stowed before the main-mast athwartships. There were about forty tons of small coal ; next to coal we received salt : we put the salt in the after-hatchway. None of the salt got to the main-hatch.

William Pigott :—I was boatswain. The iron was more or less rusty. Salt could not have touched it. The salt was in good condition.

George Walker:—I am Harbour Master at East London. I saw the hatches taken off, and everything was in good condition. It is not usual in vessels of this tonnage to have bulkheads. It is common to bring salt and iron in the same vessel, only one is kept away from the other as much as possible.

Plaintiff was allowed to give further evidence, and called

William James :—I am an ironmonger. I have examined the iron here; it is unmerchantable. I have seen iron before in that condition, from being in the bottom of the ship and getting bilge water on it. Ordinary rust we would not consider of any importance. This is eaten away. The iron appears to be injured by salt water. It is evident that it has been wetted by salt water. I say so from the peculiar look of the rust.

R. W. Nelson :—I have had ten or eleven years' experience in hoop iron. I have seen the samples. The iron is badly damaged by salt or salt water. There is crystallization on the iron which might arise from salt or salt water getting on it and being damp.

In their report Gately and Townsend, who held a survey on the iron, state:—" All which we find more or less damaged by salt water, * * and entirely unmerchantable."

De Villiers, A.-G., for the plaintiff, contended that it must be taken as admitted by the bill of lading that the iron was received on board in good order. From the evidence there can be no doubt that it was taken out of the vessel in an unmerchantable and worthless condition. Therefore the defendant would be liable for the damage unless he could show it had arisen from perils of the sea, or some other cause, sufficient to relieve him from liability. He had not pleaded or shown any such cause. The master of a vessel is responsible for the stowage of the cargo,

1873.
August 22.
"   26.,
Krohn vs. Nurse.
unless this duty was done by stevedores hired by the shipper; and if damage occur to the cargo, the master or owner is liable therefor, without proof of personal negligence. *McLachlan on Merchant Shipping*, p. 350. The bill of lading excepted liability from rust. Where there is an exception of that nature and damage ensues, the onus of negligence which would otherwise rest on the master is thrown on the plaintiff. It is not necessary to prove gross negligence to entitle the plaintiff to recovery; it is sufficient to show a cause from which the damage might have ensued without proving it actually did ensue from such cause. *Czech* vs. *Gen. Steam Nav. Co.*, 3, *L.R.*, *C.P.*, 14; *Orhoff* vs. *Briscall*, 1, *L.R.*, *P.C.*, 231; *The Figlia Maggiori*, 2, *L.R.*, *Adm.*, 106. As to the way salt ought to be stowed, and the necessity of bulkheads to prevent it damaging other cargo, especially iron, *vide Stevens on Stowage*, p. 478. The master must use the greatest diligence. *Dig.* 19, 2, 25, 7.

Cole, for the defendant, argued *contra.* There was not much difference of opinion on the principles of law on which this case ought to be decided, but only in the way of applying those principles. The passage cited from the *Digest* referred to common carriers, and it had been laid down that a ship master was not a common carrier. *The Duero,* 2 *L.R.*, *Adm.*, 393. The principle was admitted that, where there is an exception made in a bill of lading and damage ensues, the onus of proof of negligence on the part of the carrier rests on the person complaining. In this particular case, what is charged is that defendant has delivered the iron in a condition unmerchantable from rust. The bill of lading expressly guards against liability in regard to rust. Plaintiff has not proved any negligence. The surveyor's report states that the iron was damaged by salt water. If the injury has arisen from salt water and not from the salt, that is a peril of the sea, for which defendant is not liable. There is no proof at all that the injury has been done by the salt. Even if it could be said that the probabilities are that it was, there is no proof that it was due to defendant's default. In *Czech's* case the evidence showed that the damage could have arisen in no other way than in that alleged. So also in *Orhoff's* case the negligence of the defendant was clear.

De Villiers, A.-G., replied. If the damage had been done by perils of the sea, the captain ought to have protested. There was no sea protest against such damage.

Cur. adv. vult.

Postea (August 26), the Court [BELL, C. J., absent] gave absolution from the instance, with costs.

DENYSSEN, J., having stated the facts of the case, and summarised the evidence, said :—The question to be decided is, Has the plaintiff succeeded in satisfying the Court that the damage caused to the iron must be ascribed to the negligence of the master of the *Lizzie Waters* or of his servants ? If so, although his bill of lading exempts him from liability in respect of ordinary rust, he is chargeable for the damage, but not otherwise. It was not necessary to prove *gross* negligence, but as negligence cannot be presumed, some satisfactory evidence must be led to establish it, and in my opinion the plaintiff has failed to do so. Salt from its moisture is usually divided by bulkheads, to prevent it coming in contact with other goods; vessels, however, of the description of the *Lizzie Waters* do not carry bulkheads; and every precaution was therefore taken to stow the cargo in such a way as not to admit of the salt coming in contact with the iron. It was stowed in the after-hatchway, while the iron was stowed before the mast, and the intervening space so filled up as to preclude the possibility of their coming together. No evidence whatever was given to satisfy me that the cargo was not properly stowed, nor was the competency of the stevedore employed on the occasion called in question. But the theory for the defence is that the damage to the iron must be ascribed to the evaporation of the salt. According to *Stevens on Stowage,* evaporation settles against the under part of the deck of a vessel, and when it falls may be injurious to some description of goods below, such as iron and machinery; but there is no evidence of such settlement here. On the contrary, with the exception of the witness Townsend, who saw salt glistening on the iron, and Nelson, who says the damage may arise from salt water or salt, all the other witnesses ascribe it to salt water, of which there is no proof that any touched the iron. In the two cases referred to by the counsel for the defence, the judge was satisfied that negligence had been proved, in the one case by the manner of stowing tobacco and oil-cake, both generating heat, and in consequence of which the oil-cake, which was stowed round and above the tobacco, was damaged; and as regards the leakage of oil in the other case; but there is nothing of this sort in the case before us. The salt was stowed at a considerable distance from the iron; it was taken out perfectly dry from the hold of the ship; and no satisfactory evidence having been produced that the damage was caused by the evaporation of the salt, I am of opinion there must be absolution from the instance with costs.

FITZPATRICK, J., agreed that there should be absolution from the instance with costs. This was a very important

1873.
August 22.
" 26.
Krohn vs. Nurse.

commercial question, and the evidence should have been more complete and satisfactory than was the case in the present instance to warrant the Court in deciding a matter of this kind. It had been said that it was not necessary to prove gross negligence; in fact, it was very difficult to define what gross negligence was. Lord Cranworth defined it as being nothing but ordinary negligence, with a vituperative epithet attached to it; and another very eminent judge, Chief Justice Erle, said that a great mistake was made in speaking of negligence as a positive act when it was a simple omission. It was not an act of commission, but of omission. Negligence simply meant a neglect to do what in the ordinary and proper discharge of duty should have been done. According to *Stevens on Stowage* some persons might consider that it was an act of negligence not to have bulkheads, for that was the only fact in this case on which an insinuation of negligence could be founded at all. But the vessel was of such a nature that bulkheads were not or could not be used, and those persons who employed such vessels knew very well how they were constructed. I do not consider the Court would be entitled to set that fact down as negligence. Then, it must also be remembered that the salt was not stowed in bulk, but it was all in bags, and there was, as had been described, a space of five feet wide well filled with an iron tank, bales of goods, and so on, between the salt and the iron. The opinions expressed by the persons on shore who examined the iron did not seem to be opinions entitled to much weight, or the opinions of experts. They were not persons much acquainted with cargo, except Mr. John Wood. It was stated that it looked like salt or salt water, and one person said he thought he saw the salt glistening on the iron. Mr. Wood's evidence was rather bare, for he said he often saw iron of this kind landed in an unmerchantable state. He did not say that the cargo he saw landed might be considered to be damaged by the negligence of the master of the vessel, and that, therefore, the owners ought to be made responsible. It might follow quite naturally from what he said, that it was very often the necessary result of sending iron hoops in such a vessel as the *Lizzie Waters*. On the whole, it was a prudent and proper decision to arrive at, that there should be absolution from the instance, so that this case would not be considered as laying down the law as to the stowage of iron hoops. The parties, if they thought they had neglected opportunities they might have availed themselves of to get more satisfactory evidence, could do so. It was a very important and nice question to decide where negligence really did take place.

[Plaintiff's Attorneys, FAIRBRIDGE & ARDERNE.]
[Defendant's Attorney, VAN ZYL.]

In re Hartzenberg.

Admission of Attorney. Rule of Court, No. 149.

An articled clerk must serve the whole of his time within the Colony to qualify for admission as attorney of the Supreme Court.

De Villiers, A.-G., applied for the admission as attorney of this Court of William Geddes Hartzenberg, under the following circumstances. Applicant was duly articled to Mr. Foster, an enrolled attorney of this Court, then practising in the Colony. About eighteen months afterwards, Mr. Foster removed to Griqualand West, where he has since been practising, and where Hartzenberg accompanied him. Having now served the stipulated time he applied for admission here. The 149th Rule of Court required that an articled clerk shall, during the whole of his time of service, have continued to be actually employed within this Colony. When he removed, Griqualand West had not been created a separate Colony.

1873.
August 28.

In re Hartzenberg.

The Court [Bell, C.J., absent] refused the application.

Applicant's Attorney, Van Zyl.]

In re Widow of A. J. Swart.

Rehabilitation of joint estate of husband and wife granted on the application of the widow, the executrix and surviving spouse, without filing the usual accounts.

De Villiers, A.-G., moved for the rehabilitation of the estate of A. J. Swart, deceased, and of his widow, the surviving spouse. He produced an affidavit sworn to by the widow, in which she stated that on her husband's death, finding his estate insolvent, she, as executrix, had surrendered the same; and that, being ignorant of her husband's dealings, she was now unable to file the accounts required.
There was no opposition.

1873.
August 28.

In re Widow of A. J. Swart.

The Court [Bell, C.J., absent] granted the rehabilitation.

[Applicant's Attorney, C. C. de Villiers.]

IN RE INSOLVENT ESTATE OF J. H. STANDEN.

Ord. No. 6, 1843, sec. 33.

Interest on a mortgage bond accruing after sequestration allowed at the rate stipulated for in the bond.

1873.
July 1.
August 28.

In re Insolvent
Estate of
J. H. Standen.

Objection was taken to the plan of distribution in the above estate, on the ground that the trustee had awarded to W. B. Biddulph, the first mortgagee, preference for interest at the rate of twelve per cent. per annum from date of the order of sequestration to the date of the filing of the account. There was a second objection that preference should only be given for the interest of one year and the current year, but this objection was not pressed, as the interest in dispute had accrued since the surrender of the estate. It appeared that in January, 1868, the insolvent passed a bond in favour of Biddulph for £300, bearing interest at the rate of twelve per cent. per annum, to be reckoned from the 1st July, 1868. He subsequently passed a second bond, bearing interest at the same rate, in favour of Pulvermacher. In October of the same year the estate was surrendered. A first liquidation and distribution account had been filed and confirmed, and the proceeds then for distribution had been awarded to the first mortgagee. The second account was the one now objected to. By awarding preference to Biddulph for the balance of his bond and interest at twelve per cent., the second mortgagee was awarded only a portion of his principal.

E. J. Buchanan, for Pulvermacher, the objecting creditor, submit ed that, after sequestration, interest at six per cent. only should be allowed, that being the rate of interest recognised by the Insolvent Ordinance.

De Villiers, A.-G., for the trustee, relied on sec. 33 of Ord. No. 6, 1843, as entitling the mortgagee to the same preference for interest accruing subsequent to the surrender as he was entitled to prior thereto.

The Court ordered the matter to stand over to allow it to be ascertained from the Master what had been the practice hitherto in cases where bonds bore a higher rate of interest than 6 per cent.

Postea (August 28), the Master's report was read, stating that in accounts filed in the insolvent estates of R. P. Meeding and J. J. Durant, interest had been awarded at the rate of ten and twelve per cent. after the date of the sequestration. The master also reported he found it the usual practice to allow interest on bonds after the order of sequestration at the rate stipulated for in the bonds.

The Court [BELL, C.J., absent] ordered the objections to be expunged, with costs, and the account to be confirmed as filed.

1873.
July 1.
August 28.

In re Insolvent
Estate of
J. H. Standen.

[Attorneys for the Trustee, FAIRBRIDGE & ARDERNE.]
[Attorney for Pulvermacher, TREDGOLD.   ]

RYAN *vs.* ABRAMS.

Arrest : Civil, confirmation of.   Costs, security for.

Where the defendant, on being arrested, paid the amount claimed into the hands of the Sheriff as security, and was released, and entered appearance to defend, it is not necessary for the plaintiff, on the return day of the writ, to move for the confirmation of the arrest.

Plaintiff and defendant being peregrini, plaintiff ordered to find security for costs or the arrest to be discharged.

The defendant, Frederick Abrams, had been arrested at the suit of the plaintiff, Martin Ryan, upon a writ returnable this day. The sheriff made his return that "the defendant was duly arrested and was subsequently released upon handing over as security the full amount of the writ, with costs and fees of capture." Defendant had subsequently entered appearance to defend the claim of the plaintiff.

1873.
August 1
„ 28.

Ryan *vs*
Abrams.

E. J. Buchanan, for the plaintiff, moved for a confirmation of the arrest.

De Villiers, A.-G., for the defendant, objected.

The Court held that it was unnecessary to make any order. Costs to be costs in the cause.*

Postea (August 28).—Application was made on behalf of the defendant to have the arrest set aside, as the plaintiff had failed either to give security for costs according to his undertaking, or to file his declaration. Plaintiff and defendant were both domiciled at the Diamond-fields in Griqualand West, and were but temporarily in this Colony.

Plaintiff denied the undertaking to give security, and had filed his declaration the day notice of this application had been given. Counsel further contended that, as defendant had not himself given security for costs, but only for the amount claimed, he was not in a position to entitle him to demand security from the plaintiff. (*Pothier, Des Personnes,* part 1, tit. 1, sec. 2 ; *et vide Voet.,* 2, 8, 10.)

* But *vide James vs. Webb,* 1 Roscoe, 106.

1873.
August 1.
" 28.

Ryan vs.
Abrams.

The Court [BELL, C.J., absent] ordered the plaintiff to find security by the last day of term, or the arrest to be discharged.

[Plaintiff's Attorney, BUCHANAN.
Defendant's Attorneys, FAIRBRIDGE & ARDERNE.]

STUTTAFORD & CO. vs. BARROW.

Damages recovered for breach of contract entered into in England for service within this Colony.

1873.
August 30.

Stuttaford & Co.
vs. Barrow.

The defendant was summoned for £50 damages arising from breach of contract. The plaintiffs, on the 14th April, 1873, through their agents in London, entered into a written agreement whereby the defendant, amongst other things, undertook and agreed to proceed from London by the steamer *European*, sailing from Southampton on the 15th April, 1873, and for a period of three years, computed from his arrival in Cape Town, to serve the said plaintiffs in the capacity of assistant or salesman in their business at Cape Town ; and the plaintiffs undertook to pay for the defendant's passage to Cape Town, and to pay a certain salary to the defendant for his services during the three years. The defendant left England as agreed, and the plaintiffs paid for his passage. On the 14th May, 1873, the defendant commenced his duties in plaintiffs' service in terms of the said agreement. On the 30th June following, the defendant, by letter, informed the plaintiffs he was dissatisfied with his situation and tendered his resignation, and thereafter, on the 2nd July, 1873, defendant left plaintiffs' service, in breach of the terms of the agreement aforesaid.

De Villiers, A.-G., for the plaintiffs, proved the facts as above stated.

Defendant was in default.

The Court [BELL, C.J., absent] gave judgment for plaintiffs for £25 damages and costs.

[On the same day, the Court gave judgment for plaintiffs for the same amount, in the case of *Stuttaford & Co.* vs. *Telbart,* an action arising out of similar circumstances.]

[Plaintiffs' Attorneys, REID & NEPHEW.]

SUPREME COURT REPORTS.

1873.

PART IV.

TAUTE vs. EXECUTORS OF VAN RENSBURG.

Pleading. Non-joinder.

Exception to plea that both executors (defendants) had not joined in the defence overruled.

This was an action against Wehmeyer and Swemmer in their capacity as executors of Van Rensburg. To the declaration Wehmeyer only had pleaded, Swemmer making default. Plaintiff excepted to Wehmeyer's plea, on the ground that he was sued jointly with his co-executor, and it was therefore not competent for him to answer alone, and that he did not profess to defend for himself and co-executor.

Cole (with him *Maasdorp*), for the plaintiff, appeared in support of the exception. The defendants being co-executors, to be effectual judgment must be against both, and, under the course adopted, the anomaly might arise of one executor confessing judgment while the other was successful in his defence.

De Villiers, A.-G., for the defendant, admitted that judgment against one executor would only bind that one; but there was nothing to prevent the case being tried against both executors simultaneously. The declaration had actually been filed of default as against Swemmer, and the Court would give the same judgment against him as they would against Wehmeyer.

Cole, in reply: If the case was the other way, Wehmeyer could not bring the action alone, and therefore he could not defend alone.

Exception overruled with costs.

[Plaintiff's Attorney, Du Preez.
Defendants' Attorney, De Korte.]

H

In re Esterhuysen.

An executor dative removed, on motion, from his office, on the ground of his having become of unsound mind and totally incapable of attending to any business whatever.

Affidavits received in proof of allegation of unsound mind.

1873.
Nov. 27.
—
In re Ester-
huysen.

De Villiers, A.-G., moved, on the petition of Mrs. J. A. Louw, one of the children and heirs of the late Charl Johannes Esterhuysen, for an order removing her husband, J. A. Louw, from his office as one of the executors dative of the estate of the said C. J. Esterhuysen, by reason of his having become of unsound mind and totally incapable of managing his affairs or attending to any business whatever. It was necessary for the interests of the estate that there should be some one to perform the duties of executor. There was an affidavit verifying the petition, as also one from Dr. Zeederberg, describing the unsound state of mind and body in which Mr. Louw was at present, and stating that there was not the least hope of his bodily or mental faculties being in any way restored.

The Court (DENYSSEN, J., and FITZPATRICK, J.) granted the order for the removal of Mr. Louw from his office, and directed that the Master publish the necessary edict for the appointment of another executor in his place.

[Applicant's Attorney, J. HORAK DE VILLIERS.]

SWEMMER, TRUSTEE OF HEYNS, *vs.* WEHMEYER.

Resident Magistrate's Jurisdiction. Taxed Bill of Costs, liquidity of. Act No. 20, 1856, sec. 8.

Where a Trustee of an insolvent estate sought to recover in the Resident Magistrate's Court, from one of the creditors, a sum of £28, being part of a taxed Bill of Costs paid by the Trustee to his Attorney on account of an action brought in the Circuit Court against the estate, HELD,—*not to be a claim on such a "written acknow-ledgment of debt commonly called a liquid document," as to be within the Magistrate's jurisdiction, under sec. 8, of Act No. 20, of 1856.*

Nov. 27.
—
Swemmer,
Trustee of
Heyns, vs.
Wehmeyer.

The estate of one Heyns had been surrendered as insolvent. Biddulph was duly appointed trustee, realized part of the estate, and distributed the proceeds. He subsequently died, and Swemmer was appointed trustee in his stead. Sauer, who had purchased from Biddulph part of Heyns' landed property, sued for transfer. Swemmer thereupon called a meeting of Heyns' creditors, which meeting Wehmeyer and Prietsch only attended. There were no assets remaining in the estate, but the trustee was at this meeting instructed to defend the action instituted by Sauer. The action was tried at the Circuit Court of George on the 17th of March, 1873, when judgment was given for defendant, each party to pay their own costs. The attorney for the estate made out his bill of costs, and had it duly taxed. The trustee paid the amount of the bill so taxed, namely, £57 7s. 11d., out of his own funds, and then demanded half the amount thereof from Wehmeyer and Prietsch respectively. Prietsch paid his half, but Wehmeyer refused to pay his. Swemmer thereupon sued Wehmeyer for the same, the amount being £28 13s. 11d., in the Court of the Resident Magistrate at George. On the hearing of this case defendant took several exceptions, one of which was that the amount sued for was beyond the jurisdiction of the magistrate. After hearing the evidence, the magistrate overruled the exceptions, and gave judgment for plaintiff for the amount claimed, with costs. From this judgment the defendant appealed.

De Villiers, A.-G., for the appellant, argued in support of the exception taken in the Court below. The Act No. 20, of 1856, sec. 8, gave the Resident Magistrate jurisdiction to the extent of £40, on any bill of exchange, promissory note, good-for, "or other written acknowledgment of debt commonly called a liquid document"; in all other cases he had jurisdiction only to the extent of £20. A bill of costs was not such a written acknowledgment of debt as to be within the Act.

E. J. Buchanan, for the respondent, replied that a taxed bill of costs was a liquid document, as appeared from the fact that provisional sentence could be obtained thereon in the Supreme Court. (*Sequestrator* vs. *Vos*, 1 *Menz.*, 290; *De Wet* vs. *Meyer*, 1 *Menz.*, 59.) The liquidity of a taxed bill of costs being established, the magistrate would have jurisdiction to the extent of £40. The amount sued for was only £28, and therefore within the limit of the magistrate's jurisdiction.

The Court (DENYSSEN, J., and FITZPATRICK, J.) upheld the exception, and allowed the appeal, with costs.

[Appellant's Attorney, DE KORTE.
Respondent's Attorney, C. C. DE VILLIERS.]

1873.
Nov. 27.

Swemmer, Trustee of Heyns, *vs.* Wehmeyer.

Graham, N.O., *vs.* Levi,

Act No. 10, 1872, Sec. 67.

Costs, security for. Rule of Court, No. 125. Defence in formâ pauperis.

In an action to obtain the condemnation of goods seized by the Customs and for penalties, the owner of the goods must, under section 67, of Act No. 10, 1872, before he can be admitted to defend such action, find security for costs in the sum of £100 sterling.

The defendant in this case, applying for leave to defend in formâ pauperis, his petition was referred to counsel for report as to whether he had probable cause of defence.

Nov. 20.
„ 27.
Dec. 9.
————
Graham, N.O.,
vs. Levi.

The defendant applied for leave to defend the above action *in formâ pauperis*, and in support of his application submitted affidavits showing that he was not possessed of property of the value of £10 besides his wearing apparel and the goods in the hands of the Customs authorities sought to be confiscated. He also prayed that he might be allowed £100 out of the goods seized, for the purpose of producing the attendance of necessary witnesses now living at Port Elizabeth.

De Villiers, A.-G., for the plaintiff objected. The action was for the condemnation of goods and for the penalties prescribed by law for attempted smuggling. By sec. 67, of Act No. 10, of 1872, it was enacted that, " No owner or other lawful claimant shall be admitted to enter a claim in the Vice-Admiralty Court aforesaid, or to defend any action, suit, or proceeding in any other court as aforesaid, in regard to anything seized in pursuance of any Act relating to the Customs, until sufficient security shall have been given in the court where such proceedings shall have been instituted, in a penalty not exceeding £100 sterling, to answer and pay such costs as may be awarded against the party giving such security." The defendant cannot be admitted even to appear until he found the security required.

Cole, for the defendant, asked that the application might stand over till he decided on what course to adopt.

Postea (November 27).— *Cole* said he had nothing further to advance, and as the Court were opposed to the motion, with permission he withdrew the application.

Postea (December 9).—The case was put down for trial by default, when

Cole moved that the petition of the defendant to sue in *formâ pauperis*, presented on the previous occasion, be referred to an advocate for report. He had omitted on the previous occasion to point out that, under the 125th Rule of Court, on any person applying for leave to sue or defend as a pauper, his application "*shall* be referred to an advocate" for report. The section of the Customs Act referred to a different stage of the proceedings. The defendant, he submitted, was entitled now to have his petition referred, and then, should the advocate report thereupon that there was a good cause of defence, exception could be taken that he must find security. In the meantime he asked that the trial of the case be postponed.

Reitz, for the plaintiff, was taken by surprise by this application. The motion to defend in *formâ pauperis* was refused on the previous occasion. If their Lordships, however, were of opinion that the petition should be referred to counsel, let it be so.

The Court (DENYSSEN and FITZPATRICK, J.J.) granted the application, and referred the petition to *Cole* for report.*

[Plaintiff's Attorneys, REID & NEPHEWS.
Defendant's Attorneys, FAIRBRIDGE & ARDERNE.]

1873.
Nov. 20.
„ 27.
Dec. 9.

Graham, N.O.,
vs. Levi.

IN RE LAWS.

A Clerk articled to an Attorney, a member of a firm, who had, after the departure from the Colony of the partner to whom he was articled, continued to serve in the office of the remaining partners, allowed, without fresh articles, to qualify for admission as an attorney, by reckoning the time so served towards the period of service required by the Rules of Court.

Cole presented a petition from H. W. F. Laws, praying for admission as an attorney of this Court. The petitioner had been articled to Mr. Appleby, of the firm of Messrs. Reid & Nephews, on the 28th October, 1868. Mr. Appleby had, after the date of the articles, left the Colony for England, and was expected to return shortly, but had not done so. In the meantime petitioner, as appeared from the affidavit of Mr. Henry Reid, had served and been employed continuously during the full term of five years in the office of Messrs. Reid & Nephews, just as he would have served had Mr. Appleby been in the Colony. Counsel submitted that the rules in England were similar to those in force here, and in *Chitty's General Practice of the Law*, vol. II.,

1873.
Dec. 11.
„ 18.

In re Laws.

* See *Graham, N.O., vs. Levi*, Buch. S. C. Rep., 1874, p. 8.

p. 11a, 3rd ed., it appeared that a clerk articled to one partner may comply with the statute by serving all in their joint capacity.

[DE VILLIERS, C.J.—Is Appleby a member of the firm?]

He has not been gazetted out of it.

[DENYSSEN, J.—Was Appleby a partner when the petitioner was articled?]

Yes. On the following page of *Chitty* to that quoted *supra*, the author says that if there has been *bonâ fide* actual service the Courts will not be too astute in construing the rule. A case was there given where a clerk, who had served part of his time with an agent with the consent of his master, was admitted.

The application was ordered to stand over for further information, and this day (December 18) *Cole* read an affidavit made by Mr. J. H. Reid, corroborating that of his partner, as to the continuous service by petitioner. He, moreover, stated that when the articles were entered into petitioner's guardian wished the name of the firm to be inserted, but as each of the other partners had clerks articled to them individually, the name of Mr. Appleby was inserted in these articles. When Mr. Appleby left, no fresh articles were entered into, as he was expected shortly to return. As a matter of fact he was still a member of the firm.

DE VILLIERS, C.J., said, under the peculiar circumstances the Court would grant the application. It seemed from the affidavits that Mr. Appleby was always expected back, and still appeared to be a member of the firm, and for that reason no fresh articles had been entered into. At the same time, the profession should bear in mind the proper course would have been to enter into fresh articles. If this had been done no difficulty would have arisen. But this case was not likely to become a precedent; and the application would be granted.

Mr. Laws was thereupon admitted.

IN RE GOODRICKE.

An application made on behalf of an Advocate and Attorney of the Supreme Court of Natal, praying for a Rule of Court under the 46th sec. of the Charter of Justice, by which he might be admitted an attorney of this Court, refused. The Court ought not to make a general rule to meet a special case.

Cole appeared in support of a petition from J. R. Goodricke, praying for the promulgation of a Rule of Court under sec. 46 of the Charter of Justice, for his admission to 1873.
Dec. 18.
In re Goodricke. practise as an attorney of the Supreme Court of this Colony. Petitioner stated he was an admitted advocate and attorney of the Supreme Court of the Colony of Natal, a Court having the same jurisdiction as this Court has under sec. 30 of the Charter of Justice, and administering the same or similar laws. Petitioner was admitted an advocate and attorney of the then District Court of Natal on the 3rd September, 1850, which said Court was erected by Ordinance of the Cape Legislature, No. 14, 1845, and its business conducted under rules enacted under Cape Ordinance No. 32, 1846, with right of appeal to this Court, for which purpose, by section 31, of said Ordinance No. 14, 1845, the said District Court was considered and deemed and taken to be a Circuit Court of the Colony of the Cape of Good Hope, with all and singular the provisions of sections 41, 42, and 43, of the Charter of Justice, applying to and regulating the proceedings of the said District and Supreme Courts respectively. In 1857 the District of Natal was by Royal Charter created a separate Colony, and a Supreme Court of the Colony of Natal was formed, but with right of appeal direct to the Privy Council. Petitioner was admitted an advocate and attorney of said Supreme Court, and has up to the present time continued to practise as such in Natal. By the 15th and 18th sections of the Natal Law, No. 10, 1857, barristers, advocates, and attorneys of the Supreme Court of the Cape of Good Hope are admissible to practise as such in the Supreme Court of Natal. Petitioner has, during his practice as an advocate and attorney, been concerned in one or other capacity in most of the important trials which have taken place in Natal, and has otherwise enjoyed a large practice, but is now desirous of removing to the Cape Colony on account of ill-health. By the rules of the Privy Council, the Court of Appeal for both Colonies, petitioner is on application entitled to act as agent in the Privy Council in appeal cases from Natal, and is in this respect on equal footing in the Privy Council with Cape attorneys. The 46th section of the Charter of Justice, referred to in the petition, authorized the Supreme Court "by any Rules or Orders of Court to be by them from time to time for that purpose made and published, to frame, constitute, and establish such Rules, Orders, and Regulations as to them shall seem meet," concerning the admission of barristers, advocates, attorneys, &c. The Court had power, therefore, to make a rule for the admission of the petitioner.

[FITZPATRICK, J.:—You wish us to make a general rule to meet this special case?]

Yes.

FITZPATRICK, J.:—The Court has over and over again refused to make such rules. A rule had been refused when Mr. Buyskes, a talented and efficient agent in the Graaff-Reinet Court, applied to be admitted as an attorney. The Court should not make rules for special cases.

DE VILLIERS, C.J.:—The Legislature could deal far better than the Court with an application of this kind, for then the profession could express their opinions thereon by means of petition. It would be better if Mr. Goodricke applied to the Parliament for a general law relating to this matter. Besides the case just mentioned, an application was made some time since on behalf of Mr. Coetzee, who applied to be admitted as a Circuit Court attorney on the ground of having served his articles of apprenticeship to Mr. Aspeling. There was no rule of Court to meet his particular case, and his application was refused. The same objection applied there as in Mr. Goodricke's case. The Court had power to make general rules to meet general cases, but it ought not to exercise the power of making general rules to meet special cases.

Application refused.

[Applicant's Attorney, FAIRBRIDGE.]

CANE, APPLICANT, *vs.* BERGH AND MADER, RESPON-
DENTS.

Act No 4, 1865. Member of Divisional Council, qualification of. Civil Commissioner, duty of.

Registration as a Voter under the Constitution Ordinance necessary to qualify a person to become a member of a Divisional Council.

The Civil Commissioner is not authorized, under the Divisional Councils Act, to inquire into and determine an objection to the qualification, on the ground of non-registration as a voter, of a candidate nominated for election or elected a member of a Divisional Council.

The Court was this day moved on behalf of the above applicant, on notice calling on the respondents to show cause,—first, why the first named respondent, Bergh, should not by order of Court be disqualified from taking his seat, or from participating in the proceedings of the Divisional Council of Clanwilliam, as a member declared by notice in the *Gazette* to have been elected for the Districts Nos. 2 and 6 in the said division, by reason of the illegality of such election, upon the ground that the said Bergh was not

1873.
Dec. 18.

Cane, Appli-
cant, vs. Bergh
and Mader
Respondents.

a registered voter as required by section 13, of Act No. 4, 1865; and why the name of the applicant should not be substituted in lieu and in stead as a member for District No. 2; and secondly, why the second named respondent, who was Civil Commissioner of the district, should not be condemned, jointly with the said Bergh, to pay the costs of this motion by reason of his refusal to institute an investigation, in terms of the provisions of said Act No. 4, 1865, into the complaint made by the applicant against the election of the said Bergh.

An affidavit made by applicant in support of the motion set forth that deponent was eligible to be elected as a member of the Divisional Council of Clanwilliam. That deponent was at the recent election duly nominated as a candidate for District No. 2 of said division. That respondent Bergh and two others were also nominated as candidates for the said district. That Bergh not being a registered voter, deponent had entered an objection with the second named respondent, Mader; but, notwithstanding this objection, the respondent, Bergh, did contest the election, and was returned by a majority of one vote over deponent as member for District No. 2. That the respondent, Mader, took no notice of the objection, whereas it was his duty as Civil Commissioner to investigate the same under the provisions contained in sections 37, 38, and 39 of Act No. 4, 1865; and, lastly, that the respondent, Mader, as Civil Commissioner, has declared the respondent Bergh duly elected.

For the respondents was put in an affidavit made by Bergh, setting forth that the said Bergh stands registered as a voter for District No. 2, on the list for the years 1865, 1866, 1867, 1868, 1869, and up to November, 1870; and that from the time he was first registered he had never become disqualified, or parted with any of his property. That he had now become aware that the Field-cornet for Ward No. 2 struck off his name from the list of voters published in 1871, under the mistaken impression that deponent's property was situated in Ward No. 6, instead of in Ward No. 2. Further, that deponent has been a member of the Divisional Council for Clanwilliam from the month of November, 1869, to the present time. Also, a corroborating affidavit made by J. P. Crowly, the Field-cornet of Ward No. 2.

Cole, for the applicant, referred to section 13, of Act No. 4, 1865, which enacted that "every person *registered* as a voter" shall, with certain exceptions specified in the succeeding section, be eligible to be elected. Actual registration at the date of election was, therefore, necessary to the qualification of a member of the Divisional Council, in

1873.
Dec. 18.

Cane, Appli-
cant, vs. Bergh
and Mader,
Respondents.
this respect differing from the qualification of a member of the House of Assembly, the Constitution Ordinance in such a case requiring only that the member was qualified to be registered, and not necessarily actually registered. The respondent, Bergh, might formerly have been a registered voter, but it was clear his name was not now on the list, and, consequently, he was not qualified to be elected. The respondent, Mader, ought to have investigated the objection made by applicant, and, not having done so, it had been sought to make him liable for costs. This, however, was not pressed.

E. J. Buchanan, for the respondents, asked for Mr. Mader's costs against the applicant. The Civil Commissioner had no right to inquire into objections, except under such authority as was given him by Act No. 4, 1865, and the authority so given extended only to objections connected with any irregularity fallen into at the poll, or to objections to qualification on the grounds specified in the 14th section of the Act. The Civil Commissioner would, therefore, have exceeded his duty had he investigated the complaint made by the applicant. As to the respondent Bergh's qualification, he had been a registered voter, and had not in any way become disqualified. In fact, he was actually a member of the Council up to the time of the fresh election. His name, as appeared from the affidavits, had been removed from the list through mistake.

[FITZPATRICK, J.—We cannot go behind the voters' roll now.]

There was nothing in the Act to prevent the respondent, Bergh, from taking his seat, having been duly elected. The 13th section of the Act merely provided that persons registered as voters shall be eligible, but it did not disqualify unregistered persons. The 14th section mentions the grounds of disqualification, and non-registration is not there enumerated.

The Court (DENYSSEN and FITZPATRICK, J.J.) granted the application so far as to declare the respondent Bergh's election to be void, but did not declare the applicant to be elected. Costs, with the exception of those incurred by respondent, Mader, which were to be paid by applicant, given against respondent Bergh.

[Applicant's Attorney, TIRAN.
Respondents' Attorney, VAN ZYL.]

J. H. Steyn *vs.* Trustee of J. G. Steyn.

Effect of antenuptial contract, excluding communio bonorum between the spouses, on communio quæstuum.

Placaat of 5th October, 1840.* Dowry. Purchase made by one spouse from the other stante matrimonio.

This case was tried in the Circuit Court at Swellendam, before BELL, C.J., on the 10th March last, and, after hearing the evidence, was remitted to the Supreme Court for argument and decision.

John Joseph Barry, sole trustee in the insolvent estate of Jan Gysbert Steyn, M.'s son, the defendant in this suit, was summoned to answer Johanna Hillegonda Steyn (born De Jongh), the plaintiff in this suit, duly assisted by her husband, the said Jan Gysbert Steyn, M.'s son, in an action to have plaintiff's ownership in certain goods and chattels declared, and for other purposes.

The summons, which stood as the declaration, stated that on the 14th May, 1867, the plaintiff was married to the said J. G. Steyn, M.'s son, now insolvent. That before the said marriage was solemnized, namely on the 13th May, 1867, an antenuptial contract was duly entered into, whereby community of goods between the parties was excluded; and the said J. G. Steyn, M.'s son, being then perfectly solvent, made over and settled on the plaintiff a life policy for £1,000, and certain other movable property, described in schedule marked A. Further, that at the time of the marriage plaintiff was the owner of certain property described in schedule marked B. That, after her said marriage, plaintiff was entitled to receive as and for her inheritance, out of the estate of her deceased mother, the sum of £273, with which said sum she purchased from her husband the said insolvent, *stante matrimonio*, divers goods and chattels described in schedule C, the purchase price thereof, namely, £272, being paid out of the amount of the said inheritance. That thereafter the plaintiff became the owner by exchange of certain lambs, progeny of stock belonging to her, of certain cattle described in schedule marked D. That thereafter she received a donation from her father of certain cattle, described in schedule marked E. That thereafter she purchased out of her own money certain cattle described in schedule marked F. Further, that she received a donation from her father of certain 2J0 sheep, that have now increased to the number of 330; and that at divers times thereafter she became owner of divers other goods and

———
* Sixth section of Placaat repealed by Act No. 21, 1875, sec. 1.

chattels, all of which, including the said 330 sheep, are described in schedule marked G. That the estate of plaintiff's husband was sequestrated as insolvent on the 13th December, 1872, and defendant was appointed sole trustee thereof on the 20th January, 1873. That at the third meeting of creditors, it was resolved that all the movable property claimed by plaintiff, with the exception of the property contained in the inventory attached to the antenuptial contract (schedule B), be disposed of for the benefit of the insolvent estate. That plaintiff obtained an interdict restraining such sale until the issue of this action. And the plaintiff now prayed that it be declared that the goods and chattels specified in the said schedules marked A, B, C, D, E, F, and G, respectively, are her lawful property, and do not form part of the assets of the insolvent estate; and that defendant, in his capacity as trustee of such estate, be interdicted from selling the same, and be ordered to deliver to plaintiff such of them as are in his possession; and for such further and other relief as to the Court shall seem meet, with costs of suit.

The defendant pleaded, first, the general issue; then specially, that although the antenuptial contract excluded the *communio bonorum* as between the insolvent and plaintiff, it did not exclude the *communio quæstuum*, which last-mentioned community, therefore, took place upon their intermarriage. That, by virtue of such last-mentioned community, the plaintiff and her property were liable for all debts incurred by the husband, the said insolvent, *stante matrimonio*, anything in the said antenuptial contract to the contrary notwithstanding. Further, that the debts of the several creditors were debts incurred during the existence and subsistence of the marriage between the said insolvent and the said plaintiff. Further, that the life policy and movables, set forth in schedule marked A, were a dowry, gift, or benefit, constituted by the said insolvent from and out of his own property, in favour of his wife, and that the said plaintiff is not by law, and more especially by certain provisions of the *Placaat* of Charles V., dated 5th October, 1540, entitled to claim the said policy, or movables, or any part of either of them, until all the creditors of the said insolvent shall first be paid and satisfied; and after the said policy and said movables shall have been realized, and the value, together with the rest of the estate applied to the payment of debts, there will remain a large deficiency still due and owing to the creditors in the insolvent estate. And as to the property alleged to have been purchased by the plaintiff from her husband, set forth in schedule C, the defendant said that by the sixth clause of the antenuptial contract, the insolvent had, during the sub-

1873.
July 8.
Dec. 18.

J. H. Steyn *vs.*
Trustee of
J. G. Steyn.

sistence of the marriage, the sole and exclusive administration of all the plaintiff's property, estate and effects; and the defendant submitted that, even if the plaintiff might, had she by the antenuptial contract reserved to herself the free administration of her property, estate and effects, have purchased property from her husband, and received from him valid delivery thereof, yet that, under the said sixth clause, the plaintiff could not make a valid purchase from the insolvent during the subsistence of the marriage, or receive a valid delivery from him. And, for a claim in reconvention, the defendant said he is the same John Joseph Barry who is in the said antenuptial contract mentioned, and therein made a trustee for certain purposes connected with the life policy before mentioned; and that he did, in his capacity as such trustee, submit himself to the judgment of this honourable Court in regard to the disposal of the said policy. And he prayed that it be declared that the said plaintiff is not, against or in competition with the creditors of the insolvent, entitled to the said policy, or interest therein, or benefit therefrom; and that it may be declared that the said policy shall belong to and be administered by the defendant in his capacity as trustee of the insolvent estate. And the defendant further prayed, in case this honourable Court shall be of opinion that the property of the plaintiff is liable for all debts incurred by her husband *stante matrimonio,* but shall also be of opinion that the ownership of her property is not vested in defendant in his capacity as trustee of the insolvent estate, that he may be authorized and empowered to realize, for the benefit of the insolvent estate, all such assets, matters, and things now in his possession as shall be found and adjudged to belong to the plaintiff, or that the plaintiff may be condemned to pay to the defendant in his said capacity the value of all such assets, matters and things; and that the defendant may have further and other relief; the defendant waiving and giving up, in pursuance of a resolution to that effect of the creditors, all claim against the articles, matters, and things set forth in schedule marked B, consenting that the same shall remain or become the property of the plaintiff.

The plaintiff's replication and plea to the claims in reconvention were general.

The antenuptial contract above referred to stipulated:—

1. That there shall be no community of property between the said intended consorts, but that he or she shall respectively retain or possess all his or her estate and effects, movable or immovable, in possession, reversion, expectancy, or contingency, or to which he or she has or may have any eventual right or title, as fully and effectually to all intents

and purposes, as he or she might or could do or have done if the said intended marriage did not take place.

2. That the one of them shall not be answerable, or in any wise liable for the debts, engagements, or responsibilities of the other of them, contracted either before, during, or after the said intended marriage, but that each shall be liable for his or her own debts, engagements, and responsibilities, and no more.

3. That all inheritances, legacies, gifts, donations, *inter vivos* or *mortis causá*, or bequests, which may have been, or may hereafter be devised, bequeathed, or given, or made to either of the said intended consorts, or which may devolve upon either of them by succession *ab intestato*, shall be the sole, separate, and exclusive property of him or her upon whom or to whom the same shall devolve, or have been devised, bequeathed, or given.

4. That each of the said intended consorts shall be at full and free liberty to dispose of his or her property, estate, and effects, whether in possession, reversion, remainder, or expectancy, and wheresoever situate, nothing excepted, by last will, codicil, or other testamentary disposition, in such manner, and to such person or persons, and in such shares and proportions, and upon such terms and conditions as he or she respectively may think fit, without any restriction, any laws or ordinances now or then in force in the said Colony to the contrary notwithstanding.

5. That each of the said intended consorts shall have the full rights, power, and privilege, at any time or times after the solemnization of the said intended marriage, to benefit the other with a gift or settlement of property, money, or effects, to any amount, either by formal donation or otherwise.

6. That the said appearer of the first part shall, during the existence of the said intended marriage, have the sole and exclusive administration of all the property, estate, and effects of his said intended consort, as well as his own, for the purpose of the support of the said intended marriage, to which purpose he may at all times appropriate the interest and usufruct thereof, but so, however, that he shall not acquire any other right or power over the property of his intended consort (or over the policy of life assurance hereinafter mentioned), and shall not encumber, mortgage, or alienate or sell, or otherwise dispose of the same or any part thereof, unless with the special written consent of his said intended consort, signed and inscribed by herself, and by and in the presence of two competent witnesses.

7. And the said Jan Gysbert Steyn, Marth.'s son, doth further agree to give and deliver unto the said Johanna Hillegonda de Jongh, as a marriage gift, the articles of

furniture now in his dwelling-house at Rotterdam, division of Swellendam, as stated in the list annexed hereto, and hereby declares to have delivered the said articles of furniture unto the said Johanna Hillegonda de Jongh, who accepts the same as her own free and absolute property.

1873.
July 8.
Dec. 18.

J. H. Steyn vs.
Trustee of
J. G. Steyn.

8. It is further agreed, in consideration of the said intended marriage, the said Jan Gysbert Steyn, Marth.'s son, shall settle the policy of insurance, No. 972, effected by him on his life, in the Mutual Life Assurance Society of the Cape of Good Hope, for the sum of £1,000 sterling, upon the trustee hereinafter named, in manner and upon the trusts and for the interests and purpose hereinafter expressed and declared of and concerning the same, &c., &c.

The evidence taken on circuit having been read,

De Villiers, A.G. (with him *Cole*), for the plaintiff, argued that the antenuptial contract expressly excluded the wife from liability for the debts, engagements, and responsibilities of the husband now insolvent. This contract was not disputed. The pleader must have overlooked the first three clauses of the antenuptial contract, for it could not be maintained in the face of those clauses that the *communio quæstuum*, or community of profit and loss, was not excluded. (*Et vide Grotius*, 2, 12, 11.) The *Placaat* of Charles V. applied only to merchants. A translation of the *Placaat* is to be found in *Buchanan's Reports*, 1869, p. 111. The latter part of the section also excludes the creditors from claiming the wife's own property and such as she may have acquired. In *Chiappini's case* (*Buchanan's Reports*, 1869, p. 143), there was a dictum of Mr. Justice Watermeyer's, that this placaat applied to others besides merchants, but Chiappini himself being a merchant, it was not necessary for the decision of the case to show it had that effect. Then there is nothing to prevent a husband contracting with his wife. (*Voet*, 23, 2, 63.) As to the delivery, there was no proof or allegation of *mala fides.*

Cole, on the same side, cited *Van Leeuwen, Cens. For.*, 1, 12, 18, that where the contract related to profit and nothing was said about loss, it shall be taken to include loss, and *vice versa.*

Reitz, for the defendant, argued, as to the movables described in schedule A, that the placaat gave the creditors of insolvent preference over the wife, as decided in *Paterson's* and *Chiappini's cases.* The general law of Holland made no distinction between merchants and others in this respect. (*V. D. Keessel, Th.* 262; *Neostad, de Pact. Ant.*, *Obs.* 10, and 21; *Voet*, 24, 3, 25.) Besides, in the evidence the insolvent admitted he was a trader. The articles

1873.
July 8.
Dec. 18.

J. H. Steyn *vs.*
Trustee of
J. G. Steyn.

enumerated in schedule B were given up. As to schedule C, goods bought from the husband with money coming to the wife, the husband having under the antenuptial contract the sole control of the wife's property, there could be no valid sale and no valid delivery. The articles in schedules D. and F came under the placaat; and also as there had been no exclusion of community of gain, this community existed. The exclusion of community of goods was not sufficient. It was necessary there should be express exclusion of community both of profit and of loss. (*Van Leeuwen, Cens. For.* 4, 11, 5.) The law of community being the general law, every particular community sought to be excluded must be expressly stated. The wife is liable to the extent of one half on all contracts of the husband, unless the community *both* of profit *and* loss has been excluded. (*V. D. Keessel, Th.* 93; *et vide Van Leeuwen, Cens. For.,* 1, 12, *sec.* 10; *Neostad, Obs.* 4; *Voet,* 23, 4, 28; *Coren's Dec. et Cons., Obs.* 30.)

[DENYSSEN :—As to what is included under *quæstus* see *Burge,* 1, p. 283.]

To secure preference to the property named in schedules E and G, it should have been kept distinct from the husband's property. If there was community of profits between the spouses, the trustee of the insolvent was entitled, at any rate, to half of this profit.

De Villiers, A.G., replied. As to the delivery, the transaction was *bonâ fide.* It was not necessary there should be manual possession. Possession by the husband, *qua* husband, was possession for the wife.

Cur. adv. vult.

Postea (December 18).—BELL, C.J., having retired from office, it was intimated that, as a difference of opinion had existed, their Lordships would require the case to be re-argued.

MAGISTRATES' REVIEWED CASES.

—————•—————

Procedure. Evidence.

A prisoner pleading guilty must be sentenced before he is admissible as a witness in the same case against any remaining prisoners.

DENYSSEN, J., mentioned a case where three men were charged before a Resident Magistrate with the crime of theft. The first pleaded not guilty, the second guilty, and the other not guilty. The last mentioned prisoner, a lad of about thirteen years of age, was the son of the first prisoner. Two of the prisoners were sentenced to eight months' imprisonment, and the lad to receive a private whipping. The evidence was not satisfactory, and the Magistrate's judgment must be reversed. There was, moreover, another irregularity in reference to the proceedings, for the prisoner who pleaded guilty had been admitted as a witness against the others before he had been sentenced.

1873.
Nov. 20.

———————————————

Act No. 5, 1866-67, sec. 3.

Conspiracy to escape from custody.

A prisoner cannot be guilty of conspiracy or confederating with another prisoner to escape from custody unless such other prisoner consent and join in the conspiracy.

DE VILLIERS, C.J., said a case had come before him, as judge of the week, where one Klaas Hendricks, a convict, had been charged before the Resident Magistrate with contravening the third section of Act 5, of 1866-67, for the better maintenance of discipline among persons under sentence of imprisonment with hard labour. The charge against the prisoner was, that he conspired or confederated with another prisoner to make his escape from the custody of the constable. The only evidence against him was that

Dec. 18.

I

of the prisoner with whom he was alleged to have conspired. He was found guilty, and sentenced to receive thirty-five lashes. There could, however, be no conspiracy without the consent of the person who was conspired with; it was an attempt to induce another to run away, but not conspiracy. The sentence must therefore be quashed.

ACT No. 17, 1867.

Where a prisoner is sentenced to three months' imprisonment with hard labour, he cannot be also sentenced to spare diet more frequently than on two days in each week, on which days he is not to be put to hard labour.

Dec. 19. DE VILLIERS, C.J., said that, as judge of the week, a case had come before him where a Resident Magistrate seemed to have mistaken the meaning of the Government Circular relating to spare diet. Act 17, of 1867, gave the Magistrate larger jurisdiction in the case of thefts of cattle and stock, and it provided that, in regard to spare diet, the Magistrate should be regulated by the provisions which might from time to time be made by the Government. The last Government Circular was dated the 24th of August, 1869, and provided that a prisoner sentenced to imprisonment with hard labour for a term not exceeding three months might be sentenced to spare diet two days in each week, on which days he was not to be put to hard labour. The Magistrate had sentenced the prisoners to three months' hard labour, and during the last fortnight they were to be put every alternate day on spare diet. According to that, the prisoner might have in one week three days on spare diet, and in another week four days, which was quite contrary to the regulations. The sentence of the Magistrate was therefore irregular.

APPENDIX.

———

In re the late Sir John Wylde's Will.

(Cited in Executors of Cerfonteyn vs. O'Haire, *ante*, p. 47.)

Reservatory Clause, effect of. Ord. No. 15, 1845.

A reservatory clause has equal force whether in a notarial will or in an underhand or non-notarial will.

A codicil made under a reservatory clause is valid though signed by the testator only, and unattested.

By an underhand or non-notarial will, dated the 6th February, 1856, and duly attested, as required by Ordinance No. 15, 1845, the late Sir John Wylde had appointed the South African Association as executors of his estate, and guardian of his minor heirs. This will contained a reservatory clause, in the usual terms, as follows :—" Finally, I reserve to myself the right to make all such alterations in, and additions to, this my last will as I may think proper, either by separate writing or at the foot hereof, desiring that all such alterations and additions so made shall be equally valid as if they had been inserted herein." Under this clause the testator executed a codicil, dated 6th September, 1857, signed by the testator only, and unwitnessed, revoking the appointment of the South African Association, and in the place thereof appointing as executors the present applicants, the Hon. William Porter, C. T. Wylde, Esq., and E. T. Wylde, Esq.

Denyssen now moved for an order on the Master of the Supreme Court, requiring him to grant letters of administration to the executors named in the codicil. The South African Association had been served with notice, but did not appear.

The Master, in person, referred to Ordinance No. 104, of 1833, section 20, which states that, " If it shall appear to

1859.
Dec. 20.
„ 22.

In re the late Sir John Wylde's Will.

1859.
Dec. 20.
„ 22.

In re the late
Sir John
Wylde's Will.

the said Master, * * that any deed by virtue whereof any person or persons shall claim to be the testamentary executor or executors of any person deceased, is not in law sufficient to warrant and support such claim, then and in every such case letters of administration shall not be granted until the validity and legal effect of such deed shall have been determined by the judgment of some competent Court." He considered himself prohibited from granting letters of administration until the Court had decided the validity of the writing containing the appointment of the applicants.

[WATERMEYER, J.:—If that codicil, being without witnesses, had been a codicil to a notarial will, you would have no doubt or difficulty in granting letters of administration?]

It is customary to grant them in such cases.

[WATERMEYER, J.:—Then the question in your mind is, whether an underhand will can contain a reservatory clause or not, so as to make a codicil under that clause valid?]

It comes to that.

Denyssen, for the applicants, in support of the codicil, cited *V. D. Keessel Th.* 337; *Lybreght's Reden. Vert.*, vol. I., p. 323; *Hollandsche Consultatien*, 154.

At the request of the Court,

The Master undertook to instruct counsel to appear on his behalf.

Postea (December 22).—After hearing *Denyssen* for the applicants, and *Brand* for the Master,

HODGES, C.J., in delivering judgment, said:—This is a case of very considerable importance, and I think the Master has acted with great propriety in asking the opinion of the Court upon a matter which is attended with such weighty consequences, for I quite join in the remarks made in *Voet*, as to the great danger that may arise from the law permitting a will, executed in the presence of witnesses, to be subsequently altered by a codicil, which contains nothing more than the name of the party making it, without any witnesses whatever. But Mr. *Brand* admits that by the law of this Colony, previous to the passing of the statute 15, of 1845, codicils of this sort, having for their object the change of executors and the giving additional legacies, would be good, although not executed in the presence of any number of witnesses, either five or seven; and that being the state of the law, it certainly a little surprised me at first; but finding it to be so, it is only necessary then to see what effect the statute 15, of 1845, has in the matter. Now, I am quite clear that if the Legislature had intended that in all cases where there was a will executed and a codicil, that in all such cases of testamentary writings, not being writings entered into before a notary, two witnesses should be required, they would have used language quite different to that found in the third section. The third section does not say that all wills and other testamentary writings and powers of attorney shall be executed in the presence of two witnesses, but it restricts it to all wills and other testamentary writings which required to be witnessed by seven or some other competent number of witnesses; restricting the operation of that statute, therefore, to all testamentary writings which previously required to be executed in the presence of a certain number of witnesses. Well, that being so, there is an end of the matter, because it is admitted that a codicil of this kind, by the law of the Colony, did not require to be executed in the presence of any number of witnesses, in consequence of the insertion of the clause which I find at the end of the will:—"Finally, I reserve to myself the right to make all such alterations in, and additions to, this my last will as I may think proper, either by separate writing, or at the foot hereof, desiring that all such alterations in, and additions so made, shall be equally valid as if they had been inserted herein." Now, according to the law of the Colony existing previously to the passing of the statute, the executors may be changed and additional legacies given by mere writing, without witnesses. Under these circumstances, the doubt I at first entertained has been removed; and the result will be that the Master will have to grant letters of administration to the three executors named in the codicil. Whether the law should be changed or not is another matter, and one on which I express no opinion.

CLOETE, J.:—I entirely concur in the view taken by the Chief Justice of this case; but I think it may be fitting to make a few remarks on the only point urged on behalf of the Master by his counsel, who considered that by the constructions of the sections of Ordinances 1843, 1844, and continued in the 15th of 1845, there is, in some way or other, some different law applicable to a last will and testament executed before notaries, to the law applicable to those executed before seven witnesses, commonly called private wills. Now, I do not know that any such distinction in law is warranted. We all know, historically, that it was only in the sixteenth century, chiefly in Holland, Belgium, and those places, that the profession, you may call it, of notary sprung

1859.
Dec. 20.
„ 22.

In're the late Sir John Wylde's Will.

1859.
Dec. 20.
„ 22.

In re the late
Sir John
Wylde's Will.

up. Formerly, according to the Roman law, every will in which the testator meant to dispose of his property was nuncupative *coram* seven witnesses. Subsequently, when writing became more general, seven witnesses also were required to sign such testamentary papers; and then, at the date I have mentioned, there was introduced in Holland the profession of notaries, before whom it became a fixed custom to have last wills executed; for, strange to say, up to the present time such a general custom does not prevail in England. The law, then, by a legal fiction, considered that when a notary was called in he was supposed at once to be possessed of and clothed with the same kind of power in regard to the authenticity of attestation as any five witnesses by law. From this emerged the common custom in the Dutch law requiring a notary and two witnesses to attest all such documents. But we can very naturally understand that, though the testator declared his will before the notary, yet he frequently had certain little directions which he wished to keep to the very last moment of his existence within his own bosom, and which he did not wish at once to commit to writing, or declare before such a number of persons. From that principle originated the "reservatory clause," which the notary then introduced, such as we also find in this will of Sir John Wylde's, passed on the 5th of February, 1856. Consequently, it is manifest that where there is not the least suspicion or doubt as to the genuineness of the testator's own writing or signature on the codicil, which may be found at the foot of the will, or on another slip of paper attached to that document, that codicil, by virtue of this reservatory clause, becomes part and parcel of, and is of the same effect as if it had been inserted in the very body of the will itself. That is the principle laid down by the law: and although we find that *Voet*, and other authorities who touch upon the subject, were not favourable at all, and, I think, very properly, to such a plan being generally adopted, because it is calculated, as they consider, to open a door to very questionable dispositions, yet the authorities quoted by Mr. *Denyssen*, up to the latest date of the present century, entirely uphold the principle that where the testator by his last will has especially reserved to himself the right to make such a codicil, such a document shall be admitted as part and parcel of the will itself. Now, Mr. *Brand* has endeavoured ingeniously to make out that there is some difference in the interpretation of the law on account of this not having been a notarial document; but, as I have already stated, the law does not recognise any such nicety. No privilege is given to a notarial last will, except in regard to the lesser number of witnesses being required to attest it; and all the provisions to be found in the Ordinances of 1843, 1844, and 1845, applied specially to the malpractices which were creeping in very widely in this Colony at that time, by which underhand wills became frequently concocted, not subscribed by witnesses attesting them, nor following out the directions of the law as to number, and in some cases even attested by witnesses after the death of the testator. It was the desire of the Legislature to do away with all these malpractices which gave origin to this law. I am, therefore, of opinion, although it was very proper that the Master brought the subject under discussion before us, that a document of this kind, being genuine, should be admitted, and in all such future cases I think the Master will always feel himself justified, when he is satisfied by affidavit or otherwise of the authenticity of the testator's signature to such document, in granting letters of administration.

WATERMEYER, J.:—I quite concur that these letters of administration should be granted to the gentlemen named in the codicil. I put the question to the Master whether, if this had been an unattested codicil by virtue of the reservatory clause to a notarial will, he would have found any difficulty in granting these letters of administration? The reply was, that in that case he would not have felt any difficulty. It was because this is what is called an underhand will in our practice that he felt a difficulty. The question, then, appears to be whether, it being admitted that a notarial will can contain a reservatory clause, by virtue of which an underhand codicil would be valid, an underhand will can also contain such a clause? As has just been stated by my brother Cloete, there is no validity, force, or principle in the distinction between notarial wills and the underhand will attested by seven witnesses, as it used to be attested, or now by two witnesses, in accordance with the Ordinance of 1845. A notary and two witnesses are considered to be equivalent to the seven witnesses. The will with the seven witnesses is the will of the Roman law. The will with the notary and two witnesses is the will of the Dutch law. Indeed, a question of this nature having been raised before the Court, of which *Bynkershoek*, to whom reference has been made, was Chief Justice, there the inquiry was not whether in an underhand will with seven witnesses there could be a reservatory clause, but whether, while it was admitted there could be such a clause in that description of will, there could also be one in a notarial will; and the argument was this: It was argued that the will with seven witnesses of the Romans was a written will, in which the testator, himself in person, declared his desire after death. The notarial will, on the other hand, it was

1859.
Dec. 20.
„ 22.

In re the late
Sir John
Wylde's Will.

1859.
Dec. 20.
„ 22.

In re the late
Sir John
Wylde's Will.

contended, was a purely nuncupative will, in which the testator was brought before a notary, and by word of mouth told him what he wanted him to do for him. That, therefore, the notarial will, in one sense, was not a written will at all. It was nuncupative, reduced to writing by the notary; and although for the sake of security it was subscribed by the testator, yet in principle it was merely the words of the testator taken down as evidence by the notary. Therefore, it was said, to such a will there could not be, in principle, any addition for the purpose of supplying anything else the testator desired to do afterwards by way of private writing, because the notarial will, in the first instance, was no writing at all. That argument was answered very properly that, although in form a notarial will was simply the nuncupative will of the Romans, yet in fact it had become a more solemn kind of written will, and, therefore, what applied to written wills also applied to notarial wills. I merely mention this to show that the question raised in the Dutch Courts was not, "It being admitted that a notarial will could have a reservatory clause, could, therefore, an underhand will have such a clause also?" But it was, "It being admitted that an underhand will could have such a clause, could, therefore, a notarial will have such a power also?" As has been stated already, the will with seven witnesses has now, by the Ordinance 15, of 1845, become the will of two. What was done by the will of seven formerly can now be done in the will of two; and whereas such a clause would have validity in a will of seven, therefore such a clause, being properly attested in a will of two, would have the same power.

HODGES, C.J.:—The costs of the motion will come out of the estate, as the Court is unanimous in thinking the point a very proper one to be brought on for decision by the Master.

LONDON: PRINTED BY WILLIAM CLOWES AND SONS, LIMITED, STAMFORD STREET
AND CHARING CROSS.

CASES

DECIDED

IN THE SUPREME COURT

OF THE

CAPE OF GOOD HOPE,

DURING THE YEAR

1874,

WITH TABLE OF CASES AND ALPHABETICAL INDEX.

VOL. IV.

REPORTED BY

EBEN. J. BUCHANAN,

OF THE INNER TEMPLE, BARRISTER-AT-LAW.

J. C. JUTA & CO.,

CAPE TOWN. | JOHANNESBURG.

1891.

JUDGES OF THE SUPREME COURT

DURING THE YEAR 1874.

De Villiers, C.J.

Denyssen, J.

Fitzpatrick, J.

CASES REPORTED IN THIS VOLUME.

INDEX TO THE VOLUME.

SUPREME COURT REPORTS.

1874.

PART I.

In re Esterhuysen.

An Executor removed, after due notice, from his office, on the grounds of insolvency and absence from the Colony.

Josias Esterhuysen was one of the surviving executors dative of the estate of the late C. J. Esterhuysen, and sole surviving executor testamentary of the estate of the said C. J. Esterhuysen's deceased spouse. Application was made, on behalf of one of the children and heir in the estates, for an order to remove the said J. Esterhuysen from his offices as executor dative and executor testamentary respectively, on the ground that he had surrendered his estate as insolvent in October, 1870, and had shortly after proceeded to the Diamond-fields, where he was still residing. He had not appointed any one to represent him as such executor in this Colony, and he was still an unrehabilitated insolvent.

1873.
Nov. 27.
1874.
Jan. 12.

In re Esterhuysen.

The Court (November 27) granted a rule *nisi*, notice to be served on the said J. Esterhuysen.

This day (January 12) *Buchanan* prayed to make the rule absolute. There had been personal service on Esterhuysen at Kimberley, Griqualand West, of notice of this application, but he was in default.

The Court ordered the removal of J. Esterhuysen from his office of executor in both estates.

[Applicant's Attorney, J. Horak de Villiers.]

In re Estate of T. J. Campbell.

Rehabilitation.—Foreign Affidavits.

Affidavits sworn before Justices of the Peace of Foreign States must in future be verified by notarial certificate.

1874.
Feb. 2.

In re Estate of
T. J. Campbell.

This was an application for the rehabilitation of the above insolvent, formerly of Graham's Town, but now of Kimberley. The insolvent's schedules were sworn to by him before Mr. Wright, who signed himself as a Justice of the Peace for the province of Griqualand West.

The Court, there being no opposition, granted the order, but intimated that in future they would require an affidavit sworn to in a foreign state to be accompanied by a notarial certificate to the effect that the person before whom it purported to be sworn was a Justice of the Peace, or authorized to administer oaths.

[Applicant's Attorney, Moore.]
[Buchanan applied.]

Ex parte Johanna Hess.

Act 20, 1856, sec. 47.—Jurisdiction of Supreme Court over sentences of Resident Magistrates.

The Supreme Court has power to review decisions of Resident Magistrates, even though the sentences awarded are below the limit fixed by Act 20, 1856, sec. 47.

Feb. 2.

Ex parte Johanna Hess.

This was an *ex parte* application, on behalf of one Johanna Hess, for an order on the Resident Magistrate of Bredasdorp, to forward the records and proceedings in a case tried before him, in which Dirk Gysbert van Breda was charged with assault, to the Registrar of the Supreme Court, for the purpose of bringing the said case in review.

The petition and affidavit, on which the application was founded, set forth that in October last petitioner, Johanna Hess, was in the service of Breda, at Ratel River. That on the 27th October, Breda, without cause, committed a serious assault on petitioner's person, by striking her with his fist in her eye, seizing her by the throat, throwing her to the ground, and treading on her breast and leg, presenting a pistol to her stomach and threatening to shoot her, handcuffing her, putting a reim round her neck, pressing her to the ground with his knees behind her back, threatening to kill her, and other injuries. That on the 30th October, petitioner lodged her complaint with the Magistrate, whereupon the said Breda was summoned to trial before the Magistrate on the 10th November. That after hearing the evidence, the Magistrate found Breda guilty of the crime of handcuffing and fastening petitioner with the reim, and fined him only ten shillings, or ten days' imprisonment, a punishment wholly inadequate to the grave assault committed. Petitioner submitted that this judgment was not in accordance with the evidence, or with real and substantial justice. Further, that the Magistrate showed great partiality during the trial towards the said Breda.

1874.
Feb 2.
——
Ex parte Johanna Hess.

Buchanan, for the petitioner, in support of the jurisdiction of the Court, referred to the 32nd sec. of the Charter of Justice, which gave the Supreme Court full authority to review the proceedings of all inferior Courts within the Colony, with power to set aside or correct the same. Also to the similar provision contained in sec. 4, of Ord. No. 40, 1828. By sec. 42, of Act No. 20, 1856, it was enacted that the Resident Magistrates of the Colony should have jurisdiction, " without appeal or review in all cases of crimes and offences wherein any person may be accused of any crime or offence not punishable by death, transportation, or banishment." In sec. 47, there was a proviso that every sentence of imprisonment exceeding one month, or of a fine exceeding five pounds, should be laid before one of the Judges in Chambers for his consideration. But that the Court did not consider itself foreclosed by this Act from having jurisdiction even where the sentence imposed was less than that referred to in the 47th section was shown by the case of *Queen* v. *Smyth, Buch. Rep.*, 1869, *p.* 176.

DE VILLIERS, C.J.—That case was different from this, as there the Magistrate had not performed a part of his duty, in omitting to pass sentence altogether. There, too, the Attorney-General moved. It would be objectionable if any private person, not satisfied with the punishment inflicted by a Magistrate, could move for a review.

Jacobs, A.G., said that when the papers had come before him, as Attorney-General, he had at first thought a very serious assault had been committed. The proper course would have been for the Magistrate to have taken a preliminary examination. As far as he could judge, the Magistrate was wrong in simply fining the defendant ten shillings, for if the case was proved it was a serious one. The evidence was, however, very conflicting, and he was not prepared to say that the Magistrate would not have been perfectly justified in acquitting the man altogether. He did

1874.
Feb. 2.

Ex parte Johanna Hess.

not therefore feel called upon to take any action in the matter.

Buchanan said he had quoted the above case to show that the Court had exercised a control over Magistrates' sentences, even though such sentences were below the limit mentioned in the Act. There was another case of one Jacob Weihan, which was before the Court on the 20th and 28th Sept., 1870, in which the Magistrate had imposed a penalty of £5. This Court reviewed the case and set aside the sentence. That differed from the present case in being an application on the part of the prisoner; whilst this was an application made by the complainant. There had also been a case decided, in which the Court had held it had the power to increase the sentence of the Magistrate, and had actually done so.

DE VILLIERS, C.J., said that had been done in the case of Van Jaarsveld, in which the Court had increased the sentence of the Magistrate; but he would like to hear the point fully argued before he personally gave his assent to such a doctrine. He did not think the Court was foreclosed by Act No. 20 from reviewing the proceedings of a Magistrate in cases in which gross injustice had been done; but a clear case should be made out, and notice given to the Magistrate. In the present case it did not appear to him that the petition was sufficiently corroborated to authorize the Court to grant the application. If the petitioner could make out a stronger case, another application could be made, the Magistrate receiving notice.

DENYSSEN, J., was not prepared to ignore the right of the Court to enter into and review Magistrates' decisions, even though these decisions were under the limit prescribed by the Magistrates' Court Act. In the present case, although the affidavit was slight, the facts stated showed a serious assault. It also complained of partiality on the Magistrate's part. He would have preferred that the matter should be referred back for corroborative evidence, with an order to serve the Magistrate with a copy, and to call upon him to show cause why the records should not be sent to the Registrar.

FITZPATRICK, J., concurred with the Chief Justice that the Supreme Court was not foreclosed from reviewing and criticizing Magistrates' sentences, no matter how small the punishment awarded might be. But a very strong case would be required. That strong case had not been made out here.

Application accordingly refused.

[Applicant's Attorney, C. C. DE VILLIERS.]

Du Preez *vs.* Bobbins.

Cheque.

Provisional sentence granted, at the instance of an indorsee of a cheque, against the drawer.

1874.
Feb. 5

Du Preez *vs.*
Bobbins.

Reitz applied, at the instance of the indorsee of a cheque, for provisional sentence against the drawer. The cheque was in the following terms :—

"Cape Town, 17th January, 1874.
"London and South African Bank, Cape Town.

"Pay E. Goodall, Esq., or order, eighty-six pounds six shillings and sixpence sterling.
"£86 6s. 6d. "JOHN BOBBINS.

"(Indorsed) "E. Goodall."

He referred to the case of *Berrangé* vs. *De Villiers*, 1, *Menz.*, 12, which was overruled by *Rens* vs. *Smith*, 1, *Menz.*, 13.

The defendant did not appear.

Provisional sentence granted as prayed.

[Plaintiff's Attorney, CHRISTIE.]

COOPER *vs.* NIXON.

Injury, verbal.—General issue, evidence in mitigation of damages under.

In an action for slander, when only the general issue had been pleaded, it was held not to be competent for the defendant to give evidence, even in mitigation of damages, of conduct on the part of the plaintiff on a previous occasion, which might tend to justify the slander complained of.

Feb. 10.

Cooper *vs*
Nixon.

This was an action for damages for defamation of character, by reason of the defendant having made use of the following false, scandalous, malicious, and defamatory expressions towards and against the plaintiff, on the 26th December last, viz., "You (meaning the plaintiff) b—— rogue, thief, swindler, and gambler." The defendant pleaded the general issue.

Cole (with him *Buchanan*) for the plaintiff, called evidence to prove that the defendant had walked down the avenue at Rathfelder's Hotel, to where the plaintiff and others were playing skittles, and without any provocation had shaken his fist in plaintiff's face, and called him the defamatory appellations laid in the declaration, in the presence of about twenty people there assembled.

Jacobs, A.G. (with him *Purcell*), for the defendant, wished to cross-examine the plaintiff about expressions he had used regarding defendant, whether plaintiff had not, on a previous occasion, called defendant an atheist; and whether he had not been the means of defendant's being black-balled at one of the Lodges. He quoted the case of *Moodie* vs. *Fairbairn, Buch. Menz., vol. 3, p.* 14, in support of his right to give this evidence under the plea of the general issue, in mitigation of damages.

The Court ruled such evidence to be inadmissible.

FITZPATRICK, J., said evidence might be given generally that plaintiff and defendant were not on good terms; but the defendant was not entitled, under the pleadings in this case, to go into specific evidence of what had occurred on previous occasions, unconnected with the matter now in dispute.

Jacobs, A.G., in consequence of the ruling of the Court, did not call any witnesses for the defence, but submitted that the expressions made use of were merely a string of abusive epithets, from which the plaintiff had not shown that he had suffered damage. The defendant had lost his temper in consequence of what had occurred before, and had abused the plaintiff the first time of meeting him.

DE VILLIERS, C.J., said judgment must be for plaintiff; and in assessing damages he was not at all influenced by what had been said with regard to plaintiff having called defendant an atheist. Even if it had been clearly proved that the plaintiff had done so it would have made no difference in his judgment. It was said that the defendant was in a rage at the time he uttered the words complained of; but this rage was not occasioned by anything that had happened there and then, but by something alleged to have taken place on a previous occasion. This, to his mind, rather aggravated the complaint than otherwise. If there had been a quarrel, and the words had been used *in rixâ*, the defendant might have freed himself from damages, if, before pleading, he had withdrawn what he had said. *Voet,* 47, 10, 1, laid down the same doctrine as to words used when in a state of drunkenness. The same also applied when words were spoken in great anger, *ab iræ impetu*; but that only referred to the case where there was an immediate quarrel. Judgment would be for plaintiff for £50 damages and costs.

DENYSSEN, J., and FITZPATRICK, J., concurred.

[Plaintiff's Attorney, TREDGOLD.]
[Defendant's Attorney, ASCHEN.]

RAUBENHEIMER *vs.* CAMPHER.

Promissory Note.—Provisional Sentence.—Warranty.—Consideration.

Provisional sentence on a promissory note refused; the defence being that the note was given for the purchase price of an ostrich, warranted by the plaintiff to be a healthy bird, whereas in fact the bird was diseased, and had since died.

Provisional sentence was prayed on a promissory note made by defendant in favour of the plaintiff, for the sum of £50 sterling, dated 21st October, 1873, and payable three months after date.

Feb. 12.
Raubenheimer
vs. Campher.

Jacobs, A.G. (with him *Buchanan*), for the defendant, opposed, and submitted affidavits detailing the circumstances under which the note was given. The consideration therefor was a male ostrich, which plaintiff, in selling to defendant, had guaranteed and warranted to be a healthy pairing and hatch bird; whereas it was alleged the bird at the time of the sale was diseased, and had since died.

Cole, for the plaintiff, read answering affidavits, and contended that looking to the liquidity of the document on which the claim was founded, provision should be given, leaving the defendant to his redress in the principal case.

Jacobs, A.G., referred to the facts stated in the affidavits put in for the defendant, and which he maintained had not been satisfactorily answered, as showing sufficient grounds for refusing provision. He quoted the prefatory remarks on Provisional Sentence in *Menzies*, vol. I., p. 8, as showing the principle guiding the Court,—namely, that if they considered the allegations made, if duly proved in the principal case, would ensure a judgment for the defendant, and if they could not be answered or explained by the plaintiff, provisional sentence would not be granted.

The Court refused provision, the averments being so contradictory as not to allow the facts to be satisfactorily determined on affidavit. Costs to be costs in the cause.

[Plaintiff's Attorneys, FAIRBRIDGE, & ARDERNE.]
[Defendant's Attorney, C. C. DE VILLIERS.]

[NOTE.—The defendant subsequently was successful in the principal case.]

GRAHAM, N. O., *vs.* LEVI.

Customs Act, No. 10, 1872. Costs, security for. Defence in formâ pauperis.

The defendant to an action for the forfeiture of goods seized by the Customs, allowed to defend in formâ pauperis conditionally on his complying with sec. 67, of Act No. 10, 1872, requiring security in the sum of £100 for costs.

1874.
Feb. 17.

Graham, N. O.,
vs. Levi.

In this case (for previous application *vide Reports*, 1873, p. 98), counsel having reported that the defendant had probable cause of defence, *Cole* moved on his behalf for leave to defend in *formâ pauperis*.

Jacobs A.G. (with him *Reitz*), for the plaintiff, opposed relying on section 67, of Act No. 10, 1872, which provided, that security in the sum of £100 to answer any costs which may be awarded against him, must be found by the defendant before he could be allowed to enter any claim or defend any action in regard to anything seized in pursuance of that Act.

The Court [DENYSSEN, J., and FITZPATRICK, J.] granted the rule, conditionally on the defendant complying with the terms of the said 67th section of Act No. 10, 1872; security to be given by the 26th inst.

[The defendant failing to give security, the trial of this cause proceeded by default on the 26th of February, when judgment was given for plaintiff as prayed.]

⌈Plaintiff's Attorneys, REID & NEPHEW.
⌊Defendant's Attorneys, FAIRBRIDGE & ARDERNE.⌋

DE BRUYN *vs.* DE BRUYN.

Ord. No. 15, 1845, sec. 3. Will, attestation of. Ord. No. 104, sec. 26. Letters of Administration revoked.

The witnesses to a will must be present at one and the same time when the will is signed, or the signature of the testator is acknowledged by him.

Letters of administration granted under a will subsequently declared void, revoked.

Feb. 24.

De Bruyn *vs.*
De Bruyn.

Daniel de Bruyn, and his wife Maria Constantia de Bruyn, executed their joint will on the 15th February.

1873. Daniel de Bruyn died, leaving his wife him surviving, and his executrix under the joint will. Letters of administration were granted to Mrs. de Bruyn by the Master on the 23rd September, 1873. The plaintiffs, children of Daniel de Bruyn by a former marriage, now sought to set aside the will, on the ground that, though apparently properly executed, in fact and in truth the signatures of the testator and testatrix were not made or acknowledged by them in the presence of the attesting witnesses, when such witnesses were both present at the same time. Plaintiffs also prayed that the letters of administration granted by the Master under the will should be revoked. For the defendant, Mrs. de Bruyn, the executrix under the will, the general issue was pleaded.

Cole (with him *Maasdorp*), proved that the attesting witnesses had not been present at the same time when the will was signed; nor had they at any time both been present when the signatures to the will were acknowledged.

Jacobs, A.G. (with him *Buchanan*), for the defendant, did not lead any evidence.

Judgment for plaintiffs as prayed. Costs to come out of the estate.

[Plaintiffs' Attorney. Du Preez.
Defendant's Attorneys, Redelinghuys & Wessels.]

RATHFELDER vs. RATHFELDER.

Legacy.—Mortgages on property bequeathed.—Legatee.—Heir.

If a testator bequeath property, and there be mortgages thereon, should no intention to the contrary appear, it will be for the heir to redeem the property, and not for the legatee.

This was an action brought by the executors of the late J. G. Rathfelder against the curators of the person and estate of P. G. M. Rathfelder, a lunatic, to compel them to accept transfer of certain property, and to pay several sums of money, in all amounting to £3,675.

A paper of admissions and contentions was agreed to between the parties, from which it appeared that the late J. G. Rathfelder and his first wife executed a mutual will on the 7th March, 1846, by which they bequeathed to their only son, the said P. G. M. Rathfelder, the house and erf at Diep River, known as Rathfelder's Hotel, subject to the condition of his paying in the sum of £1,000 to the estate of the survivor. This bequest was not to take effect until after the death of the survivor. At the date of the will, the property was burdened with mortgages amounting to the sum of £925, which mortgages were still unpaid. The testatrix died on the 25th December, 1846. At the date of the death of the testatrix, the joint estate of herself and husband was barely, if solvent. The surviving husband being in credit and of industrious habits carried on the business, and ultimately paid off all the liabilities of the joint estate, the said bonds for £925 excepted. On the 10th December, 1848, the husband, J. G. Rathfelder, married a second time. On the 12th February, 1861, the son, P. G. M. Rathfelder, was judicially declared to be of unsound mind, and placed under the curatorship of his father and the defendants. On the 4th March, 1869, the hotel was burnt to the ground. The only insurance on the property was one policy for £1,000, which sum was paid over to J. G. Rathfelder. Application was made to the Court, on behalf of all concerned, for authority to take up on mortgage a sum of money sufficient to restore the buildings, and after reference to the Master, the Court, on the 17th May, 1869, authorized £1,000 to be so raised, which was done upon second mortgage. This sum, and about £750 in addition, was laid out by J. G. Rathfelder in rebuilding, improving, and extending the property. J. G. Rathfelder died on the first April, 1873, leaving his second wife and family him surviving. By his last will, dated 13th November, 1868, he confirmed the bequest of the premises, contained in the mutual will of himself and first wife, to his son P. G. M. Rathfelder. The plaintiffs, executors of J. G. Rathfelder, offered to transfer the property to the son on payment of the several sums of £1,000 for which the property was bequeathed, of £925 for which it was mortgaged when bequeathed and still owing, of £1,000 raised by order of Court and secured by second mortgage, and of £750 expended by J. G. Rathfelder in rebuilding, in addition to the sum raised by authority of the Court. The defendants, as curators of the son, P. G. M. Rathfelder, offered to pay the sum of £1,000 for which the property was bequeathed, but denied their liability to pay the other sums demanded.

Cole (with him *Maasdorp*), for the executors of J. G. Rathfelder, did not argue strongly in support of the last claim of £750, which he thought must be taken as an accretion to the property, to the benefit of which the legatee was entitled. As to the £925 mortgages, he contended the burden of releasing the property therefrom fell on the legatee and not on the heirs. *Grot.*, 2, 22, 16; *V.*

1874.
Feb. 25.

Rathfelder vs.
Rathfelder.

d. Keessel, Th. 325; *Neos., dec.* 11, *pt.* 2; *Voet,* 30, 27, " *et generaliter,*" &c.; *Groenewegen, ad d. l.* 6, *C. de fidei-comm.*

DE VILLIERS, C.J., referred counsel to *Grot., Dutch Consul., pt.* 3, *v.* 2, *con.* 190.

Cole then gave up the contention on this point. As to the £1,000 raised for rebuilding the property, on reference to the order, it appeared that the Court had authorized the curators of P. G. M. Rathfelder to take up the sum, so that it was necessarily a charge against him, and not against the estate of the late J. G. Rathfelder.

Jacobs, A.G. (with him *Buchanan*), for the curators, called attention to the fact that in the admission paper it was stated that this sum was raised " for the benefit of all concerned." The order of Court itself, however, was against the executors, and under these circumstances he submitted to judgment.

The Court declared the legatee, P. G. M. Rathfelder, entitled to the property on paying the £1,000 mentioned in the will, and the £1,000 raised by authority of the Court. The heirs to pay the mortgages which existed on the property prior to the death of the testatrix. Costs to come out of the estate.

[Plaintiffs' Attorneys, FAIRBRIDGE & ARDERNE.]
[Defendants' Attorney, DU PREEZ.]

[NOTE.—*Et vide* 2, *Burge,* 224, 269, 272; *Inst.,* 2, 20, 5; 2, 20, 12; *Dig.,* 30, 8; 30, 5, 7; *Voet,* 30, 27; *V. d. Linden,* 142; *Van Leuwen,* 267; *Domat, p.* 518, *sec.* 3541; 1, *Roper on Leg.* 629; *Wms. on Exrs.,* 1206. On Accretion, *vide Inst.,* 2, 20, 19; *Dig.* 31, 39; *Grot., p* 153.—ED.]

RIDDELSDELL *vs.* WILLIAMS.

Ejectment.— Lease.— Waiver.— Mistake.— Fraud.— Exceptions of want of privity and consideration.

In an action of ejectment brought by the plaintiff, the purchaser of certain property, against the defendant, the lessee thereof, the defendant having before the sale agreed with the agent of the vendor to vacate the premises, exceptions of want of privity between the plaintiff and defendant, and of want of consideration for the agreement, overruled.

*Where the defendant, a lessee of property, having a copy of
the lease in his possession, agreed in writing with the
agent of the lessor to vacate the premises held on lease;
and thereafter, on the faith of that agreement, the plaintiff
had purchased and taken transfer of the property,
HELD—to be no defence to an action of ejectment brought
by the purchaser, that the agreement was signed in error,
and under a mistaken belief as to the date the lease
would expire, although it was alleged that such error
and mistake were caused by the fraud and misrepresentation of the agent of the vendor; but of which fraud
and misrepresentation the purchaser had no notice.*

1874.
Feb. 19.
„ 26.
„ 27.

Riddelsdell vs.
Williams.

This was an action brought against W. F. Williams to
eject him from certain premises in Adderley-street, which
premises had been purchased by the plaintiff from the
General Estate and Orphan Chamber, acting as the agents
of C. A. W. Schmieterlouw, on the 12th July last, and of
which the plaintiff had become the duly registered owner.
The defendant pleaded that he was in just and lawful
occupation, under and by virtue of a written agreement of
lease entered into on the 9th September, 1869, between the
defendant and J. F. G. Pietersen (the Secretary of the
G. E. and O. Chamber), acting in his capacity as the duly
authorized agent of the said C. A. W. Schmieterlouw, which
lease did not expire until the 1st July, 1874. Plaintiff
replied that on the 10th July, 1873, the defendant promised
and undertook, in writing, to give up and quit possession
of the premises on the 1st October then next ensuing, as would
appear from a letter addressed by the defendant to the
Secretary of the General Estate and Orphan Chamber,
on the faith of which promise the plaintiff had purchased the premises. Defendant excepted to this, on
the grounds that the written promise and undertaking
referred to had been made with the Secretary of the General
Estate and Orphan Chamber, and not with the plaintiff; and that the plaintiff was not at any time either
a party or privy to the said promise and undertaking; and
that the plaintiff did not allege that he had given or promised any consideration for the said promise and undertaking. Defendant also rejoined that plaintiff was not a
party or privy to such promise and undertaking. Further,
that the defendant had made the said promise and undertaking in error, and under the mistaken belief and impression that his lease expired on the 1st July, 1873,
whereas it would only expire on the 1st July, 1874; and
that such error and mistake were caused and induced by
the fraud and misrepresentation of the aforesaid J. F. G.

1874.
Feb. 19.
„ 26.
„ 27.
Riddelsdell vs.
Williams.

Pietersen acting in his capacity aforesaid; and that defendant was induced to make the said promise and undertaking by said fraud and misrepresentation. The plaintiff denied this. The promise and undertaking above referred to, dated 10th July, 1873, was in the following terms :—" As I am informed you are about selling the property of Mr. Schmieterlouw, I have to request that you will kindly make it a condition whereby I may be allowed to remain in the occupation of the rooms and shop until the 1st October next, on which date I herewith beg to give you notice that I will vacate the premises."

This day (February 19), *Maasdorp* (with him *Hodges*), for the defendant, appeared to support the exceptions. He contended that the plaintiff had mistaken his action; he ought to have brought it against Pietersen for not having delivered free and unincumbered possession. The defendant had title to the premises under his lease; and the agreement on which plaintiff now relied had not been made by defendant with plaintiff, but by the defendant with Pietersen, There was no privity betweeen defendant and plaintiff; nor had any consideration passed from plaintiff to defendant. Privity and consideration were essential to enable plaintiff to sue on the contract or agreement alleged. *Pothier on Ob.*, *v.* 1., *p.* 146; *Dig.*, 27., *tit.* 4; *Broom on Com. Law, pp.* 317, 320, 322, 323; *Leake on Contracts, p.* 261; *Bullen & Leake, p.* 59.

The Court, without calling on plaintiff's counsel, held there was sufficient privity between the parties to enable the plaintiff to sue; and that the terms of defendant's letter showed consideration.

Exceptions overruled, with costs.

Posteà (February 26, 27), the trial of the case proceeded on the merits before DENYSSEN and FITZ-PATRICK, J.J., when

Cole (with him *Buchanan*), for the plaintiff, put in plaintiff's title deeds; the conditions of sale on which he bought the premises from Pietersen, wherein it was stated that possession was to be vacated by defendant on the 1st of October; and defendant's letter to Pietersen referred to in the pleadings.

Maasdorp (with him *Hodges*), for the defendant, put in the lease of the premises, showing defendant's tenancy to continue to the 1st July, 1874.

1874.
Feb. 19.
„ 26.
„ 27.

Riddelsdell vs.
Williams.

Evidence was also led, from which it appeared that early in July, 1873, plaintiff had had communications with Pietersen about purchasing the property. Pietersen produced defendant's lease to plaintiff. Plaintiff, seeing defendant's lease would not expire until July, 1874, declined to have anything more to do with the property, unless he could get immediate possession. Pietersen afterwards brought him the letter from defendant, given above, dated 10th July. On the faith of this letter, and it being made a condition of sale that plaintiff should have possession of the part of the premises occupied by defendant by the 1st October, plaintiff concluded the purchase, took transfer, and entered into possession of the remainder of the premises, and received rents from defendant and from tenants of another portion of the premises. Notice was given to defendant of the sale on the 12th July. On the 24th July, defendant's attorneys wrote to Pietersen, stating that defendant had been in error about his lease, and that this error had been induced by Pietersen, and therefore withdrawing his letter of the 10th July. This letter was forwarded by Pietersen to plaintiff, the purchase and transfer having been already completed. Pietersen denied any such misrepresentation on his part as was alleged. Defendant, in his evidence, maintained there had been misrepresentation by Pietersen; and that it was through such misrepresentation that he had signed the letter. He admitted having a copy of his lease in his possession; and it was on referring thereto, about ten days after signing the letter, that he had discovered his error. Plaintiff had had no communication whatever with defendant, and was in no way cognizant of any misrepresentations. The letter of the 10th July was written by Pietersen's clerk at Pietersen's dictation, and signed by defendant, without, as defendant deposed, his reading it. This, however, was contradicted.

Maasdorp, for the defendant, argued that the letter of the 10th July was signed in error, and that this was induced by the fraud of Pietersen; and whatever defence could have been had, if Pietersen had sued for ejectment, was good as against the plaintiff, who claimed through Pietersen; for Pietersen could not transfer greater rights than he himself possessed. *Dig.*, 50, 17, 54. Pietersen's right was tainted, and he could only transfer it so tainted. All contracts derived their validity from the mutual and free consent of the parties; and were not binding when made in error, as in this case. *V. d. Linden, p.* 188. It was possible for defendant to have discovered his mistake; but there was fraud in so far that Pietersen suppressed the knowledge that defendant's lease did not expire as soon as defendant had supposed; and the suppression of a fact, the knowledge of which would have induced defendant not to have contracted, was fatal to the contract. *Leake on Contracts, p.* 189. *Chitty's Eq. Index, vol.* I., *sec.* 13, *p.* 925. *Et vide Addison on Contracts, 6th ed., p.* 907.

1874.
Feb. 19.
„ 26.
„ 27.

Riddelsdell *vs.* Williams.

Cole, for the plaintiff, admitted the principle that fraud vitiated a contract; but in this case there was not such misrepresentation as to amount to fraud. There was a class of misrepresentations which did not affect a contract, as where it was a misrepresentation of a fact equally within the knowledge of both parties. Even if there had been misrepresentation between Pietersen and defendant, it could not affect the plaintiff, a third party, ignorant thereof. Defendant's own culpable neglect precluded his setting up the defence of error. His own act had induced plaintiff to purchase, and he could not now take advantage of his own wrong. If Pietersen had acted as the agent of either party in the matter, it had been as the agent of defendant, rather than as agent of plaintiff. There had been no fraud proved, and the misrepresentation shown was not sufficient. Even if there had been fraud, a third innocent party, if he could not profit from it, could not on the other hand be made to suffer by it. The repudiation of the letter of the 10th July came too late. *Addison, 4th ed., pp.* 126, 128; *Pichard* vs. *Sears,* 6 *A. & E.,* 475; and *Freeman* vs. *Cooke,* 2 *Exch.,* 654; *Smith's L. C., 6th ed.,* 769; *Story,* §§ 12 *a,* 13, 90, 91; *Burge, v.* 2, *p.* 499.

Maasdorp replied.

DENYSSEN, J., said judgment must be for plaintiff, with costs. Of what had taken place between defendant and Pietersen the plaintiff was ignorant, except that he was shown the letter of the 10th July, from which it appeared he could obtain possession on the 1st October. On this being made a condition of sale, the purchase was concluded, and transfer effected on the 12th July; and it was not until the 24th July that the letter of the 10th July was repudiated. Defendant had been guilty of culpable negligence in not ascertaining the terms of his lease before signing the letter. He had been the cause of the contract of sale being entered into between plaintiff and Pietersen, and he must suffer the consequences of it.

FITZPATRICK, J., concurred.

Judgment accordingly for plaintiff with costs.

[Plaintiff's Attorney, MOORE.
[Defendant's Attorneys, FAIRBRIDGE & ARDERNE.]

STEYN *vs.* TRUSTEE OF STEYN.

Antenuptial Contract.—Dowry.—Placaat of Chas. V., 1540.

An Antenuptial Contract cannot secure to the wife, in competition with creditors, any of the husband's property not at the time of the marriage vested in trustees, to be administered by them without any right of interference on the part of the husband.

The wife's own property can be secured to her against the husband's creditors by Antenuptial Contract.

The Placaat of Chas., V., 4th October, 1840, sec. 6,* applies to all marriage settlements, whether made by merchants or not.

1874.
Feb. 2.
„ 3.
„ 28.

Steyn *vs.* Trustee
of Steyn.

This case [for particulars of which *vide Reports*, 1873, p. 105], was re-argued before DENYSSEN and FITZPATRICK, J.J., by *Cole* (with him *Hodges*), for the plaintiff, and *Reitz* (with him *Maasdorp*), for the defendants. The following authorities were cited by them :— *Burge*, v. 1, p. 282; *Cen. For.*, 1, 12, 18; *Voet*, 23, 2, 63; *Rodenburg*, tit. 2, c. 4, *num.* 21; *Placaat of Chas. V., Buch. Repts.*, 1869, pp. 149, 150; *V. d. Keessel, Th.* 262; *Grot.*, 2, 12, 11; *Voet*, 24, 3, 25; *Regts. Obs., deel*, 3, *Obs.* 38; *V. d. Keessel, Ths.* 252, 254; *Voet*, 23, 4, 35; *Coren, Ob.*, 30; *Voet*, 23, 4, 28; *V. d. Linden*, p. 87; *Neostad, Ob.* 4; *Grot.*, 2, 12, 17; *Cen. For.*, 1, 12, 10; *Burge*, v. 1, 283, 288-9; *Christinæus*, v. 3, *dec.* 51, *num.* 2.

Cur. adv. vult.

Posteà (February 28),

DENYSSEN, J., in giving judgment, after reciting the pleadings, said :—The antenuptial contract and the evidence of the plaintiff herself, supported by the other witnesses, establish, beyond any dispute, these facts : That the policy of insurance, ceded to the plaintiff, and the articles in the schedule A mentioned, constitute a dowry, gift, or benefit, given by the insolvent to her by the antenuptial contract, or derived from or out of his estate before marriage ; and in whatever other way the articles, in the several other schedules mentioned, came into her possession, that the husband had the sole and entire management and control over the same, without any interference whatever on the part of the plaintiff or of any other person. Such being the case, the question becomes a very simple one, upon which I never entertained any doubt, it having been settled by the judgment of Mr.

* Now repealed by Act No. 21, 1875, sec. 6.

Justice Cloete and Mr. Justice Watermeyer, delivered by the last-mentioned judge *in re* the insolvent estate of Edward Lorenzo Chiappini, and I can see no reason whatever for disturbing that judgment. By that judgment the doctrine, as established by the *Placaat of Charles V.*, the law of the land, is, first, that no antenuptial contract can secure in favour of the wife any of the husband's property in competition with the creditors ; and, secondly, that the wife's own property can be secured against the husband's creditors by antenuptial contract. The authorities upon which these doctrines are founded are so fully set forth in that able judgment, that I do not deem it necessary to refer to them again. It may be a hardship that the wife should be deprived of what was given her by her husband when he was perfectly solvent, or during marriage by others, but such is the law, which, until altered, we are bound to administer. At the same time, it must not be supposed that provision cannot be made to secure the property of the wife if, by the antenuptial contract, besides excluding community of property and of profit and loss, trustees had been appointed in whom Mrs. Steyn's property, existing at the time of marriage, and what she acquired during marriage, had been vested for the purpose of administering the same without any right of interference on the part of the husband, the interest to be paid to her, and to her only. The creditors in the insolvent estate of her husband could never have touched it, or any part thereof ; but this provision, although in some cases observed, I very much fear is too often omitted. In this case, the wife's property was to all intents and purposes treated as if it belonged to the husband, who had the sole and entire management and control over the same, and so the wife herself declared, without any interference on her part. Under these circumstances, the judgment of the Court is, that, with the exception of the certain articles, matters, and things in schedule B mentioned, which remain the property of the plaintiff, all the articles, matters, and things in schedules A, C, D, E, F, and G, be declared part and parcel of the insolvent estate of Steyn ; that the trustee of that insolvent estate be empowered to administer and dispose of the same as such, as well as of the policy of insurance ceded by her husband to the plaintiff; and that, in case any of the said articles, matters, and things are now in the possession of the plaintiff, she do deliver the same or pay the value thereof to the said defendant. The costs to be paid out of the insolvent estate.

FITZPATRICK, J.: I concur with the judgment delivered by Mr. Justice Denyssen. There were two questions which presented themselves to my mind, first, whether the *Placaat*

Side note:

1874.
Feb. 2.
" 3.
" 28.

Steyn *vs.* Trustee of Steyn.

1874.
Feb. 2.
,, 3.
,, 28.

Steyn *vs.* Trustee
of Steyn.

of Charles V. applied to any one but merchants; and, secondly, whether the property claimed by the wife was kept sufficiently apart and distinct, so as to become private and individual property. With respect to the first question, if I were for the first time to interpret the *Placaat of Charles V.*, I should find great difficulty in extending it beyond merchants; but considering the high authority of Justices Cloete and Watermeyer, in the case of Chiappini, where although the question was not before them for decision, and their opinions were merely dicta, still they were very carefully considered and solemnly pronounced, I do not feel at liberty to go contrary to their opinions. Therefore, whatever my own individual interpretation of that *Placaat* would have been if I were the first person to construe it, I bow to the judgment of Justices Cloete and Watermeyer, and consider the *Placaat* applies generally, and not to merchants exclusively. On the other point I have no doubt at all. The property was not kept sufficiently apart by the wife as to become her property beyond the control of her husband and free from the claims and liabilities of her husband's creditors.

Judgment for the defendant; costs to be paid out of the insolvent estate.

[Plaintiff's Attorneys, BERRANGE & DE VILLIERS.]
[Defendant's Attorneys, REDELINGHUYS & WESSELS.]

BEUKES *vs.* STEYN.

Set-off. Promissory Note.

A defendant sued for a debt due by him individually cannot set off to such debt, or claim in reconvention in the same action, the amount of a promissory note owing by the plaintiff to a third party, which note had been by such third party indorsed in blank to the defendant without value, after it became due, for the purpose of recovery from the plaintiff.

Feb. 19.
,, 28.

Beukes *vs.* Steyn.

At the Circuit Court, held at Swellendam, on the 8th September last, before Mr. Justice Fitzpatrick, the plaintiff sued the defendant for the sum of £96, being the purchase price of certain ten oxen sold by the plaintiff and purchased by the defendant, on the 20th May, 1873. It was agreed that the price should be paid in cash on the delivery of the oxen. The oxen were duly delivered by the plaintiff, but the defendant had neglected or refused to pay the purchase price.

1874.
Feb. 19.
,, 28.
Beukes vs.Steyn.

To this claim, after the general issue, the defendant pleaded as a set off a promissory note, dated 23rd November, 1865, made and signed by the defendant in favour of one J. J. P. le Grange, for the sum of £67 10s. sterling payable two months after date, and the interest thereon from the due date to the said 20th May, 1873, amounting to the sum of £29 14s. sterling, making in all the sum of £97 4s. sterling, which said note was by the said Le Grange indorsed in blank, and whereof the defendant was the legal holder. In reconvention defendant prayed judgment on the said note and interest.

The plaintiff replied generally.

Evidence was led, in which the plaintiff stated that he had given a promissory note to Le Grange for some sheep and goats he had bought from him; that this note was unpaid; that he had gone to the Free State in 1867, and returned in 1873. He, however, denied that the note sued on was the note in question. Defendant admitted the sale of the oxen at the price claimed, and that they had not been paid for. Further, that the promissory note had been endorsed to him by Le Grange without value, after it was due, on the condition that he could keep half of what he recovered on it.

Judgment was given for the plaintiff on the claim in convention with costs. Leave was reserved to the defendant (plaintiff in reconvention) to move the full Court on his claim in reconvention, all objections as to the date of the note and its being made by the plaintiff being waived, as also all questions as to the statute of limitations.

This day (February 19) the Supreme Court was moved to enter judgment for defendant on the claim in reconvention.

Reitz (with him *Maasdorp*), for the plaintiff in the original action, opposed. He contended that from the evidence it was clear defendant held this note only as agent for Le Grange, and he could not set off a debt due to him as agent to a debt due by him personally. *V. d. Linden,* b. 1, § 6. The same rule was laid down in *Executors of Naude* vs. *Executors of Ziervogel,* 3, *Buch. Menzies, p.* 358. Defendant was not *bonâ fide* holder of the note. There was not such a delivery as was required by *Voet* 41, 1, 35, to transfer the ownership of the note to defendant. He had given no consideration for the note.

Buchanan (with him *Tennant*), for the defendant (now plaintiff in reconvention) maintained that the defendant was the legal holder of the note, and as such had a perfect right to sue thereon in reconvention. The transfer, regard being had to the nature of the document, was as perfect as could

1874.
Feb. 19.
„ 28.
Beukes vs.Steyn.

be given. A promissory note was properly transferred by indorsement. *Story on Prom. Notes*, § 120. The maker of the note could relieve himself of liability only by a payment to defendant, the holder of the note. A payment to Le Grange, even though he had endorsed the note away without consideration, would not be sufficient. *Milnes* vs. *Dawson*, 5, *Exch.*, 948. The indorsee of an overdue bill had a right to sue thereon. *Oulds* vs. *Harrison*, 10, *Exch.*, 572. As to consideration, it was not necessary that any should pass between the indorser and indorsee; it was sufficient if consideration had passed between the maker and payee. *Byles on Bills*, 8th ed., p. 124; *Story on Prom. Notes*, § 190.

Cur. adv. vult.

Posteà (February 28),

DE VILLIERS, C.J., in giving judgment, after stating the facts given above, said :—The question which this Court has now to decide is a pure question of law, viz., whether the defendant, as the holder of the note which is indorsed in blank by the payee, for which the defendant gave no value, and which he obtained merely for the purpose of collection, is entitled to sustain his claim in reconvention against the maker of the note. By the Roman Dutch law, in order to pass a valid title to a promissory note or bill of exchange to the indorsee or holder it was essential that the indorsement should be expressed to be for value received, and that the name of the person to whose order it was payable should be mentioned. *Van der Linden*, in his Institutes on the Law of Holland (Eng. Transl., p. 679), says : "In order to render such an indorsement sufficient to transfer the right in the bill it is necessary that the indorser acknowledge thereby to have received the value, for example as follows: Pay for me to N. N. value received, or 'value in account.' When these words are not inserted, the indorsement contains nothing more than a mere order to the person therein named, or indorsee, to receive payment of the bill, as the mandatory of the indorser, and to be accountable to him for it. Such an indorsee is therefore merely authorized to receive the amount of the bill, but not to bring an action on it in case of non-payment." *Heineccius* (*de Camb.* c. 2, § 11), on this subject, says : "Nec minus notari meretur. leges cambiales tantum non omnes ob innumeras fraudes prohibere cessiones, quae solo subscripto nomine fiunt, ac proinde vocantur 'indossamenta in blanco.' Ex his ne actio quidem datur, nisi ante praesentationem nomen indossatarii ab indossante inscriptum sit." *Pothier* indeed (in his Treatise on Bills of

Exchange, chap. 3, § 10), goes so far as to assert that "indorsements in blank are prohibited by the common law of all countries, so that no action can arise therefrom unless the blank be filled up." Whatever the common law of other countries may be, it is well known that the laws of England and the United States have never recognized the continental doctrine, but have always given full effect to indorsements in blank without an acknowledgment from the indorser of having received value for the same. In *Story on Bills of Exchange* (§ 224) it is laid down that every party indorsing a bill, either in blank or in full, and without restriction or qualification, thereby passes the interest and property in the bill to the indorsee, if he takes it for value. The invariable practice of the Supreme Court of this Colony, so far as I have been able to trace it, has been to follow the more liberal doctrine of the English law (*vide inter alia Muller* vs. *Redelinghuys and Van Reenen*, 1, *Menzies*, 41 ; *Levicks and Sherman* vs. *Eksteen*, 1, *Menzies*, 49 ; *Truter* vs. *Heyns*, 1, *Menzies*, 49). But in giving the holder of a bill or note by blank indorsement the right to recover thereon, the Court appears to have proceeded on the presumption that he is a *bonâ fide* holder for value, and that the object of the indorsement was to pass the property to the indorsee. (*Cf. Story on Promissory Notes*, § 196.) When therefore this presumption is rebutted by the evidence of the holder himself to the effect that he "never gave a penny for the promissory note," and that there was nothing due to him thereon "except as a professional man," it would, I think, be a serious departure not only from the forms but from the principles of the law of Holland to hold that, notwithstanding such admission, he is entitled, in his own name and on his own behalf, to recover the amount of the note from the maker. In the present case the defendant was sued for a debt incurred by him individually, and he claimed in the same action to recover from the plaintiff the amount due to Le Grange. If he had merely put in the note and proved the signatures of the maker and indorser, the presumption would have been that he was a *bonâ fide* holder for value, and he would have been entitled as *procurator in rem suam* to sustain his claim in reconvention. (See *Sande, de actionum cessione, c* 10, § 12). But his own evidence entirely put an end to the presumption raised by the fact of his being in possession of the note, and proved that he was merely a *procurator in rem alienam*. It is therefore impossible for me to come to any other conclusion than that the claim in reconvention cannot be sustained, and that absolution from the instance ought to be given in respect thereof, with costs for the plaintiff.

1874.
Feb. 19.
„ 28.
Beukes vs. Steyn.

DENYSSEN, J., said the only difficulty he found arose from the fact that the issues upon which the case rested had not been sufficiently pleaded. There should have been a special plea of want of consideration, and that defendant was not the legal holder of the note. But, as the case was before them, that point could not now be raised. He, therefore, concurred with the Chief Justice.

FITZPATRICK, J., also concurred. He said there was no such thing as a claim in reconvention in English law, but under the bankruptcy acts mutual credits were allowed. It had been decided that where an agent had a bill indorsed to him in his capacity of agent; and he bought articles from the bankrupt for the purpose of setting them off as a mutual credit against the bill, the set off was not allowed.

Judgment for plaintiff (defendant in reconvention), absolution from the instance, with costs.

[Plaintiff's Attorney, DU PREEZ.
Defendants' Attorneys, FAIRBRIDGE & ARDERNE.]

GAU vs. McDONALD.

Diamond Venture.—Construction of Agreement.—Claims.

An Agreement between plaintiffs and defendant, by which defendant bound himself, in consideration of a certain sum of money paid to him by plaintiffs, to proceed to the Diamond-fields, and at his individual expense and risk to organise certain working parties, and, on shares, for a period of six months, "to dig for diamonds and all other precious stones;" and further, "to devote his services for the benefit of the second contracting parties [the plaintiffs], as far as relates to superintending, procuring claims, and all other things necessary for the proper working of the companies aforesaid, to the greatest benefit of the second contracting as well as himself," HELD,—to be an agreement to account for all diamonds and precious stones found during the period stipulated for; but not such as to give plaintiffs any right, at the end of the six months, to an account of the value of the claims obtained by the defendant for the purposes of the agreement.

Feb. 27.
„ 28.
Gau vs.
McDonald.

This action was originally brought in the Eastern Districts Court; but, after hearing the evidence, the Judges of that Court not agreeing, it was, by consent, removed to the Supreme Court for argument and decision.

It appeared that in May, 1871, the defendant, H. H. McDonald, of the one part, and eight other persons of the second part, all residing in the district of Queen's Town, entered into an agreement, in which it was stated that " H. H. McDonald agrees, on his own responsibility, and at his own expense, to provide four parties, each party to consist of at least one European and four natives, for the purpose of proceeding to the Diamond-fields, to dig for diamonds and all other precious stones ; and further agrees to devote his services for the benefit of the second contracting parties, as far as relates to superintending, procuring claims, and all things necessary for the proper working of the companies aforesaid, to the greatest benefit of the second contracting as well as himself. This agreement to be in force for six months from the time that H. H. McDonald, and the working parties before mentioned, shall have arrived at the Diamond-fields, and shall have commenced work on some claim or claims. H. H. McDonald further agrees that the four parties aforesaid shall be properly fed, clothed, equipped, and in every respect provided for at his own cost, so that anything not herein mentioned shall be considered to the benefit of the second contracting parties." The agreement also stated that all the diamonds and other precious stones found by each and several of the parties, as well as by H. H. McDonald himself, were to be realised, and one-half the proceeds were to go to H. H. McDonald, and the other half to the second contracting parties, in proportion to the shares or capital subscribed by them. The second contracting parties were to pay to H. H. McDonald, in proportion to the shares allotted to them, the sum of £480 in all ; each such shareholder, saving the said H. H. McDonald, to be " liable to the extent of his share, or the value thereof, and no further."

The defendant commenced working on the 8th June, 1871. At this time the New Rush was not known, and people did not then consider so much the value of claims as the value of the diamonds discovered. The New Rush disclosed a new state of things, and claims there became of great value. Defendant, who was at that time working at Old De Beer's, where claims were comparatively worthless, was among the first to go to the New Rush. According to the rule in force at the fields at that time, no person was allowed to have more than two claims in his own name, so defendant secured ten claims, two in his own name and two in the names of each of the four Europeans with his working parties. He also got other claims for his friends. Nothing was paid for these claims, which turned out to be very valuable. A licence to work had to be taken out every month for each claim ; and if a claim was left unworked for

1874.
Feb. 27.
„ 28.
Gau vs.
McDonald.

longer than eight days, it was liable to be "jumped," or taken possession of by any other digger. The question arose as to whom these claims belonged at the expiration of the six months mentioned in the agreement. They were valued at that time to be worth £30,000. Plaintiffs claimed them as belonging to the company; defendant considered they were his individual property. Hence this action, which was brought for an account of all land, claims, goods, cattle, stock, and plant, procured or obtained during the continuance of the said agreement for the purpose of carrying out the same; and of all moneys received by the defendant in respect of any such land, claims, goods, cattle, stock, or plant sold or disposed of by him during the continuance of the said agreement; and of all diamonds and other precious stones, and the proceeds thereof not already accounted for.

It was admitted by plaintiffs' counsel that all finds of diamonds, &c., had been duly accounted for; and that the question at issue now was whether the claims belonged to defendant, or whether he was bound to account for them to the parties to the agreement of the second part.

Originally H. H. McDonald was sole defendant, and three only out of the eight persons of the second part plaintiffs. None of the others were parties to the action, as they had waived their right. An exception of non-joinder having been taken in the Court below, all the parties had been ordered to intervene, and were now before the Court.

The records having been read,

Jacobs, A.G. (with him *Buchanan*), for the plaintiffs, stated this was a question of construction of the agreement. He submitted two points for consideration; first, did the agreement—impliedly or expressly—include these claims? secondly, if it did not—if it was a *casus omissus*—what were the rights of the parties under the agreement? He contended that the agreement was sufficiently wide to include the claims. By it the defendant agreed to devote his services for the purpose, *inter alia*, of "procuring claims," and of working the company "to the greatest benefit of the second contracting parties as well as himself." Defendant might say this "procuring claims" was simply for the purpose of working them, and not for the purpose of benefiting the company by them. The agreement might have been so construed had the word "provide" been used instead of "procure." But "procuring claims" must be interpreted as procuring them for the company; besides which the agreement provided that anything doubtful therein "shall be considered to the benefit of the second contracting parties." The circumstances of the time must be considered as explaining what was probably the intention of the parties. The capital raised was small, as it was never expected or thought of that claims would have to be bought. These claims were an excrescence, like the good will of a business, and must be treated as part of the partnership property.

[DE VILLIERS, C.J.—There is no community of profit and loss between defendant and the company. He is not a partner, but an agent for a special purpose.]

. As far as the profits were concerned defendant was a partner, but as concerning the management and stipulation of services he was an agent. The parties were not partners as between themselves (*Lindley on Partnership, p.* 26); they were more in the position of joint-venturers. An agent or servant, acting as such, procuring property, could not keep it for his own benefit. Whatever was added to the property of the company, or obtained by means thereof, belonged to the concern. *Lindley, p.* 646. If land was acquired as an accessory to a trade, and treated as such, it formed part of the common stock of the company. *Lindley, p.* 654. The same principle applied to a good will of a business, which could hardly be said to be in existence, or perhaps in contemplation of the parties at the time of entering into the partnership. It was now settled that the good will of a partnership was the property of the firm. *Lindley, pp.* 648, 843. This company was a joint-venture, one party supplying his services, and the other supplying the money. Persons who agree to share the profits of an adventure, to the expenses of which they contributed, were *primâ facie* partners, although they stipulated they would not be liable beyond the sums they subscribed. *Lindley, p.* 23.

Cole (with him *Reitz*), for the defendant, submitted that the only way to arrive at a true solution of the question was to look at the agreement itself, and see what was the object of the parties. That object was simply this: to search and dig for diamonds and other precious stones for a period of six months, and to divide the diamonds, &c., so found between the parties in certain proportions. The distinction drawn by the Attorney-General between "provide" and "procure" did not touch the question. These expressions were interchangeable as far as this contract was concerned, for without claims it was impossible to carry out the agreement. If the defendant had leased these claims for six months, with the option of purchasing them at the end of that time, and had during the six months honestly worked them, he would have performed his agreement by accounting for the diamonds found; the company could not then say the right of purchase was theirs also. These

1874.
Feb. 27.
„ 28.
Gau vs.
McDonald.

claims were not of the same nature as leases, nor did they give any right to the ground; they were only rights to search for diamonds under certain conditions. It was in evidence that if a claim was left unworked for eight days it might be "jumped," and all further right to it would be gone. The undertaking was to work for six months. There was nothing in the agreement to compel the defendant to stay in the claims one day beyond the six months, so as to preserve any right to them. A good will of a business was totally different from a claim. A good will grew out of the thing, and the more the business increased the more the value of the good will increased; but the more a claim was worked the less valuable it became. As to the defendant being a servant of the plaintiffs, all he agreed to do was to put certain parties to work and to superintend them for six months. What he did beyond that and after that period was beside the purposes of the company altogether. There was no doubt that by the terms of the contract the defendant was bound to provide claims for the six months, at whatever cost it might have been to himself. But supposing he had bought the whole farm on which the fields were, as some other gentlemen had been fortunate enough to do, could the plaintiffs have claimed that the whole farm should be handed over to them at the end of the contracted time? Clearly they could not. Property used for partnership purposes even was not necessarily partnership property. It by no means followed that persons who were partners by virtue of their participation in profits were entitled as such to that which produced those profits. *Lindley*, p. 649.

Jacobs, A.G., in reply, quoted *Lindley*, p. 650, that if there be no express agreement, attention must be paid to the source whence the property was obtained, and the purpose for which it was acquired. As to renewing the leases, it had been decided more than once that if one partner obtained a renewal of a lease of partnership property, he would not be allowed to treat such renewed lease as his own. *Lindley*, p. 595.

Cur. adv. vult.

Posteà (February 28),

De Villiers, C.J., in giving judgment, said:—In order to arrive at a decision in this case the Court can only look at the agreement. This speaks of "procuring" claims; and the Attorney-General, in arguing, laid great stress on this term; and to show that a difference was meant, quoted a previous part of the agreement where the word "provide" is used. To my mind, however, the word "procuring" here has no other meaning than "providing" claims. Supposing the defendant, at the time the agreement was entered into, already possessed claims, and he then went to the fields, he would have been clearly within the terms of the agreement if he had worked those claims. Again, the Attorney-General laid great stress also on the words that defendant was to devote his services "to the greatest benefit of the second contracting party as well as himself." But this meant no more than that the defendant was to consider the benefit of all parties in whatever he did; that he was not to go to places where claims were worked out, or where there were no diamonds at all. The agreement, moreover, provides that the working parties should be properly clothed and provided for at defendant's expense, so that anything not therein mentioned "shall be considered to the benefit of the second contracting parties." The meaning of that is simply this—that the second contracting parties should be at no expense at all, that all the expenses should be at the risk of the defendant. This agreement appears to have been drawn by a person who conceived himself to be a lawyer; and he introduced here and there some legal terms without knowing what they meant. If he had used more ordinary language it would have been better. The agreement amounts to this: Defendant says to the other parties, "You provide this money, £480, and I will go to the fields. You provide that, and you shall not be liable for a penny more, and I will provide claims, plant, labour, and everything required, and will send you all the diamonds I find to be sold, and the proceeds divided." If the defendant provides claims for working such an agreement as that, he surely does not provide those claims for the purposes of a partnership. It really means this—that defendant was to provide everything, but whatever he provided belonged to himself. All he is responsible for is to look for the best claims, and do his utmost to find the greatest number of diamonds. The Attorney-General maintained that defendant was a kind of managing partner; and that whatever profits were made by him, must inure to the benefit of the whole partnership; but even if a partnership were established in this case, it does not necessarily follow that the matter or thing which produces the profits should be partnership property. According to *Lindley, p.* 694, as quoted by Mr. Cole, it was clearly laid down that a partnership might exist in the profits, but without entitling the partners to that which produces those profits. I find a similar doctrine in *Pothier de Société, p.* 5, and in *Story on Partnership*, section 29. If there did exist a partner-

1874.
Feb. 27.
„ 28.

Gau vs.
McDonald.

ship in this case (which I am not inclined to admit, because one of the essentials of a partnership—community of profit and loss—is wanting), it does not follow *ex necessitate rei* that the defendant should be bound to account for the claims. Supposing the claims had fallen in, as had recently occurred at the fields, who would have been at the loss? Clearly the plaintiffs would not have considered themselves liable, and the loss would have had to be borne by the defendant; and if he was to bear that risk, he was also entitled to have the benefit. Then, said the Attorney-General, if defendant was not a partner he was an agent, and being in a fiduciary relationship, whatever profits he made accrued to his principals. I do not deny that as a general principle of law; but it is also clear that the parties might by a special contract alter (as they appear to have done in this case) the relation which the law would otherwise impose on them. This being my view of the contract, if the defendant has accounted for all the diamonds found during the six months, he has done all that he was required to do. It has been admitted that he has accounted for all these diamonds; but I think it would be better if a consent or admission paper to that effect be put in. The Attorney-General has argued that this was a *casus omissus*. But this argument cuts both ways; for if the defendant had thought or had an idea that claims would have become so valuable, he would have required a much larger capital than was paid him. I think, therefore, as it is admitted that defendant has accounted for the diamonds, he cannot now be called upon to account for these claims.

DENYSSEN, J., and FITZPATRICK, J., concurred.

Judgment accordingly for defendant, with costs.

[Plaintiffs' Attorneys, FAIRBRIDGE & ARDERNE.]
[Defendant's Attorney, VAN ZYL.]

IN RE WILHELMINA MILLER.

One-half of an inheritance allowed to be paid to a wife, married in community of property, her husband being absent from the Colony and supposed to be dead.

Feb. 28.

In re Wilhelmina Miller.

Jacobs, A.G., presented a petition from Mrs. Wilhelmina Miller, which stated that petitioner was married in 1861, in community of property, to James Miller, and that subsequently she had removed with her husband to Banda Orientale, on the Brazilian frontier. That in June, 1871, in consequence of the disturbed state of the country, her husband directed petitioner to return to this Colony with her children, promising to follow as soon as possible. That since then petitioner had neither seen nor heard anything of her husband, and she believed he must be dead. That petitioner had become entitled to an inheritance of £285, out of her late father's estate; and that having to support herself and children by her own exertions, she was in very straitened circumstances. She therefore prayed that the Court would order either that the capital sum of the inheritance might be paid to her, or that it might be invested by the Master, and the interest, and from time to time portions of the capital, be paid to her as she might require it.

1874.
Feb. 28.

In re Wilhelmina Miller.

The Court made an order, directing the payment of one half the inheritance to the petitioner, the balance remaining in the hands of the Master, to be administered in the ordinary way.

[Applicant's Attorneys, FAIRBRIDGE & ARDERNE.]

[Note :—See also *In re Nelson*, 6 Buch. S. C. Rep., p. 130 ; *In re Storey*, 3 Buch, E. D. C. Rep., p. 150.]

MAGISTRATES' REVIEWED CASES.

A conviction for obtaining money under false pretences, against a prisoner who had sold wood to one person, and then afterwards sold and delivered the same wood to another person, quashed.

1874.
Jan. 12.
Feb. 2.

DE VILLIERS, C.J., said a case had come before him as Judge of the week, in which one Booysen was charged with obtaining money by false pretences. The facts of the case appeared to be that the prisoner had sold and delivered a quantity of wood to one person, and afterwards sold and delivered some wood (supposed to be the same) to another person. If any crime had been committed it was theft, and not obtaining money by false pretences. As the evidence was not clear, he wished the Attorney-General to argue the case for the Crown, and some other member of the bar on behalf of the prisoner. Meanwhile the prisoner would be released on finding bail to the satisfaction of the magistrate in the sum of £50, and his own recognizance for £50.

Posteà (February 2),—His Lordship stated, that as the Attorney-General was of opinion that the conviction could not be sustained; and, as upon the evidence, it appeared to the Court to be wrong, the release of the prisoner had been ordered, and the conviction quashed.

SUPREME COURT REPORTS.

1874.

PART II.

QUEEN *vs.* BREDA.

Ord. No. 40, Sec. 51.—Application for Bail in case of Murder.

The Court, where a person is charged with a Capital Offence, will not discuss the evidence taken at the preliminary examination for the purpose of ascertaining whether or not innocence may be fairly presumed, so as to admit to Bail under Sec. 51, of Ord. No. 40.* This would be taking upon the Court the functions of the Jury.

1874.
March 25.

Queen *vs.* Breda.

The Court (DE VILLIERS, C.J., and FITZPATRICK, J.) sat specially to hear an application made under sec. 51, of Ord. No. 40, to admit to bail D. G. van Breda, of Ratel River, in the Division of Bredasdorp, at present confined in the gaol of Bredasdorp upon a charge of the wilful murder of his late wife.

The petition of the applicant set forth that the death of petitioner's wife took place three years ago, in March, 1871. That within a month after her death a Commission of Inquiry was appointed by the Government, and that under such Commission all the facts connected with her death were fully elicited before Mr. M. L. Neethling, Justice of the Peace, and satisfied him that the death of petitioner's wife was the result of a most unfortunate accident alone. That in consequence of the report made by the said Mr. Neethling of the facts so elicited before him, no steps what-

* *Sed Vide* Act No. 17, 1874, sec. 7.

ever were taken against petitioner, nor any charge made against him in respect to the death of his said wife. That in the month of October last, petitioner was charged by one of his female servants with assault, in having struck her, and that the charge was subsequently dealt with by the Resident Magistrate of Bredasdorp, and petitioner was fined the sum of ten shillings sterling for such an assault. That the said female servant, from motives of revenge, and with the intention of bringing disgrace and trouble on petitioner, made statements to the Magistrate, and afterwards to other people, to induce them to believe that petitioner was guilty of the murder of his said wife, and had confessed his guilt. That although such statements were utterly false and without foundation, the Government thought proper to order that the charge just made should be investigated by the Magistrate at Bredasdorp. That a preliminary examination before the said Resident Magistrate was accordingly taken and lasted for many days, a great number of witnesses being produced in support of the accusation, and a few on behalf of the defence. That not one witness was produced whose evidence tended to criminate petitioner whose character would bear investigation; and that most of these witnesses were shown either to have feelings of animosity against petitioner or to have been instigated to say what they did by the aforesaid female servant. That, on the other hand, the witnesses produced by the petitioner were persons against whose character nothing could be said, and whose testimony conclusively and fully established his innocence. That petitioner was nevertheless committed for trial by the Resident Magistrate on the charge of wilful murder, and was now detained in the gaol of Bredasdorp as a prisoner on such charge.

The 51st section of Ordinance No. 40, above referred to, enacts:—" The Supreme Court has power to bail in all cases whatever, whether capital or not, where innocence may be fairly presumed, and in every case where the charge is not alleged with sufficient certainty."

Cole, in support of the petition, urged that the construction to be put on this 51st section was, that if any evidence whatever was adduced from which innocence might fairly be presumed, the prisoner should be admitted to bail. The section ought not to be construed as meaning that if the prisoner was admitted to bail, it was an expression by the Court of an opinion on the evidence that the prisoner should ultimately be acquitted. Such could not have been the intention of the legislature, as it would amount to this, that where the Attorney-General persisted in indicting a man who was innocent, that then such prisoner was to apply to the Court for bail. The section did not say that innocence "must be," but that it "may be" presumed. If strong evidence was brought on the part of the Crown against a prisoner, and this evidence stood uncontradicted, then there could be no presumption of innocence. But if the prisoner met the charge at once, and brought evidence which, if believed, would establish a presumption in his favour, that was a case which came under the 51st section. The Court were not called upon to declare that they did not believe the evidence for the Crown, but simply to say if there was evidence from which, taken alone, innocence might be presumed. The prisoner had produced such evidence, and should therefore be admitted to bail.

Jacobs, A.G., for the Crown, opposed the application. If it was granted it would be an expression of the opinion of the Court on the case. That was the view taken by the Eastern Districts Court in a case where an application similar to this one had been made to them. The Court could not come to a conclusion without hearing and weighing the evidence.

De Villiers, C.J., said if they allowed the prisoner out on bail, it was virtually expressing an opinion that he was innocent; whilst in allowing him to remain in gaol they expressed no opinion whatever, and did not prejudge the case. In *Buchanan's Reports*, 1869, p. 179, was mentioned the case of the *Queen* vs. *Scheepers*, which came before this Court, where a question arose under the Ordinance as to a person being justified in shooting upon reasonable suspicion of guilt. The Court there came to the conclusion that the law was against the prisoner, and refused to allow bail, and this without going into the evidence at all. *Roscoe* laid down that the law presumed a man to be innocent till the contrary be proved, though evidence, if it was such as would convince a reasonable man, was sufficient to rebut this presumption. If, therefore, there was any evidence in this case, however small, tending to show that the prisoner was guilty of murder, the Court could not go into it. The Court could not take upon itself the duties of the jury, and decide whether upon the evidence innocence might or might not be presumed.

Fitzpatrick, J., concurred.

Application for bail accordingly refused.

JOHNSON AND OTHERS *vs.* EXECUTORS OF ROUX.

Will: Construction of Bequest.—Parol evidence, when admissible.

*In a notarial Mutual Will, where the testators provided that a sum of money should be set apart after their death, from the interest of which a monthly payment was to be made to two servants for their sustenance and maintenance "for the faithful services rendered by them to the appearers, while only after the death of both these persons" the said sum should "devolve upon THEIR children,"—*HELD: *that the reversion was in favour of the children of the testators, and not of the children of the legatees.*

1874.
May 19.

Johnson and
others vs. Exe-
cutors of Roux.

The plaintiffs, who were the children, or representatives of the children, of Abel van de Kaap and Abraham van de Kaap, sued the executors of the late Mr. and Mrs. Paul Roux, senior, in an action to amend the liquidation and distribution account filed in their estate.

The declaration stated that the said Mr. and Mrs. Roux in their lifetime executed a joint will, wherein, amongst other matters not necessary to be set out, it was declared: —" In the second place the appearers declare it to be their will and desire that after the death of the first dying a sum of £800 shall be set apart from the joint estate, which amount shall be put out at interest under mortgage of immovable property, with further will and desire that after the death of the survivor out of the interest to each of their servants named Abel van de Kaap and Abraham van de Kaap, monthly the sum of ten shillings sterling shall have to be handed over for their sustenance and maintenance, for the faithful services rendered by them to the appearers, while only after the death of both these persons the capital, together with the accumulated interest, shall have to devolve upon *their* then living children, and on the predecease of one or more of them to their lawful descendants *per stirpes.*" (The will was in the Dutch language, and the above was a translation of the passage in issue.) Upon this clause the plaintiffs claimed the sum of £800 and accumulated interest thereon, as being due to them as the children of the said Abel van de Kaap and Abraham van de Kaap.

The defendant pleaded the general issue.

Hodges, for the plaintiff, contended that the will clearly indicated that the capital sum named was, after the death of Abel and Abraham van de Kaap, to go to their children. This was the plain grammatical construction of the words used.

Jacobs, A.G. (with him *Maasdorp*), for the defendants, maintained that the intention of the testators was that the money should go to their (the appearers) children after the death of the two servants, for whose personal sustenance only provision was made. He proposed to call parol evidence, which, from the surrounding circumstances at the time the will was made, would show this was the intention of the testators. In support of his right to call such evidence, he quoted the case of *Charter* vs. *Charter*, 2, L. R., *Probate*, 1871, p. 317.

1874.
May 19.
——
Johnson and others *vs.* Executors of Roux.

Hodges objected, on the ground that an ambiguity must be apparent on the face of the will before parol evidence could be admitted, and there was no such ambiguity in this case. This doctrine was sustained in *Caffin* vs. *Heurtley's Executors*, 1, *Menz.*, 181. The meaning of the words used in the will must be taken, and not the intention of the testators. *Wigram*, pp. 8, 10. The word "theirs" in the will was the relative pronoun of its antecedent "these persons," and not of "the appearers." In the construction of wills relative pronouns cannot be shifted. *Castledon* vs. *Turner*, 1, *Jarman*, 346.

The Court (DENYSSEN and FITZPATRICK, J.J.), considered there was no necessity in this case for extrinsic evidence.

DENYSSEN, J., said he found no difficulty whatever in the construction of this will. He himself knew as a fact it was a very common practice among the inhabitants of this Colony to make provision after their death for the support and maintenance of such of their servants as had been faithful during their lifetime. This will provided that for the faithful services of these two persons they should be allowed ten shillings per month as long as they lived. This provision was expressly stated to be for the faithful services of these persons. A sum of money was set apart to provide for their sustenance and maintenance, and during their lifetime the testators directed the capital was not to be touched; and it was only after the death of these two servants that the sum so set apart was to return again to the estate of the testator and testatrix. This was evidently the intention of the will.

FITZPATRICK, J., concurred. All through the will, which was a notarial one, the "appearers" was the dominant word; and by reading the clause, omitting the parenthetical sentence, the intention of the testators became quite clear.

Judgment accordingly for defendants.

[Plaintiffs' Attorney, MOORE.]
[Defendants' Attorney, WESSEL.]

BELLINGHAM AND ANOTHER *vs.* BLOOMMETJE.

Trespass : Compensation for Buildings erected bonâ fide.

*Where a person has bonâ fide built upon land not his own,
he is entitled to compensation for useful expenses incurred by him to the extent to which the value of the
land has been enhanced by the building ; and he cannot
be compelled to relinquish possession of such buildings
until such compensation has been paid or tendered to
him.*

1874.
May 19.
„ 21.
Bellingham and
another *vs.*
Bloommetje.

This was an appeal from a judgment given by Mr.
Justice Dwyer, at the Circuit Court held at Uitenhage, on
the 20th October last.

The plaintiffs brought this action to eject the defendant
from a portion of the farm Adolphus Kraal, of which they
had become proprietors. They complained that the defendant, who was a lessee of certain Crown lands adjoining
the said farm, had trespassed on the said farm, and without
leave or license of the plaintiffs or of the former owners,
had made a certain dam and erected certain buildings
thereon, which said dam and buildings, though often warned
that they were upon the plaintiffs' property, the defendant persisted in using and occupying as his own. The
plaintiffs further avowed that for the sake of peace they
had tendered the defendant £50 sterling as a reasonable
compensation for the materials used by the defendant in the
aforesaid constructions.

The defendant pleaded the general issue ; and then
specially, that in January, 1871, he constructed a house
and dam on a portion of the farm Adolphus Kraal, in the
belief that such portion formed part of land held by him on
lease from the Crown. And further, that the price and
value of the materials employed in the construction of the
house and dam, together with the value of the labour necessary for the construction of the same, and the wages of the
workmen employed thereon, amounted to the sum of
£203 17s., upon payment of which sum the defendant had
always been and still was ready and willing and offered to
deliver up possession.

The plaintiff replied generally.

From the records it did not appear that any evidence
was led by the plaintiff. For the defendant several witnesses were called. It was not clear whether or not the
defendant had been warned as to the actual boundary line
of the farm before he commenced building. The value of
the erections was not accurately stated, but was put down

by one witness at £150. Judgment was given in the Court below for plaintiff with costs. Mr. Justice Dwyer's note appended to the pleadings stated that it was evident from the statement of the defendant himself that there had been some difficulty about ascertaining the boundary when defendant was making the dam, and that counsel had stated the defendant had received compensation from Government for being misled as to the boundary line. His Lordship considered that all through defendant had notice of a dispute as to the actual boundary, and should have exercised more caution; but as he had acted in defiance of positive intimation he was not entitled to recover compensation.

1874.
May 19.
., 21.

Bellingham and
another vs.
Bloommetje,

From this judgment the defendant appealed.

Jacobs, A.G., for the appellant, urged that as it was a fact that defendant had built on plaintiff's land, whether he had done so *malá fide* or *boná fide*, he would still be entitled to recover something. The *quantum* might depend on whether or not he had notice or knew that he was trespassing. If he had acted *boná fide* he was entitled to all useful outlay, but if *malá fide* then to all necessary expenses. There was nothing in the evidence to justify the judge in having come to the conclusion that there had been *mala fides*. But even if there had been *malá fides*, all the authorities agreed that the defendant was entitled to some compensation, the only question was as to the amount. He quoted *Van Leeuwen's Cen. For.*, 2, 11, 7, and 8; *Groene. ad Inst.*, 2, 1, 30; *Voet*, 6, 1, 13; *Dig.*, 41, 1, 7, 12; *Groene. ad Cod.*, 3, 32, 5; *Story on Eq.*, 1237 n.

Cole, for the respondents, admitted that the only question now to be decided was whether the defendant, who had committed a trespass, was entitled to compensation for the amount he had expended. He contended the defendant had acted *malá fide* in building as he had done; and that being so, by the civil law he had no claim. The evidence was not very explicit, but from what there was, and from the remarks of the learned judge who presided at the trial, it was clear the defendant had not acted in good faith. He referred to *Grot.*, 2, 10, 8; *Van de Keessel, Ths.* 212, 213, 214.

Jacobs, A. G., replied.

Cur. adv. vult.

Posteà (May 21),

DE VILLIERS, C.J., in giving judgment, after reciting the pleadings, said:—It is common cause that the appellant constructed a house and a dam on the respondents' land

1874.
May 19.
„ 21.

Bellingham and
another vs.
Bloommetje.

without their permission; but the parties do not agree as to the value of the construction, or as to the outlay incurred in respect thereof, nor do they agree upon the question whether or not the appellant, in undertaking and carrying out the works, acted in good faith and in the belief that the land formed part of the leased Crown land. In regard to the value of the works, I am of opinion that the sum of £150 may be taken as a fair estimate of the extent to which the value of the respondents' land has been enhanced by the works. It is true that the appellant, in his evidence, puts his expenses as high as £200, but he is supported to the extent of only £150 by the testimony of Brehm; and moreover, it is the permanent increase in the value of the land to the owner, and not the mere outlay of the trespasser, which should guide the Court in deciding upon the value of the works. In regard to the question of the appellant's *bona* or *mala fides* in occupying and building on the respondents' land, the evidence, as it stands, is not such as to lead me irresistibly to the conclusion that he acted in bad faith, and in the absence of such evidence or of any proof that the boundaries of the respondents' land were indicated, as they ought to have been, by visible beacons, I am of opinion that the appellant had not sufficient reasons to believe he was building on another man's ground, but that he was the *bonâ fide* occupier of the land. Such being my view, it becomes unnecessary to decide upon the distinction strongly urged from the bar between the case of a *bonâ fide* occupier and the case of a *malâ fide* occupier building on land not his own. All the Roman-Dutch authorities are agreed that, where a *bonâ fide* occupier has built upon land belonging to another he is entitled to compensation for the useful expenses incurred by him, that is to say, for the expenses to the extent to which the value of the land has been enhanced by the building, and that he cannot be compelled to relinquish possession of such building until such compensation has been tendered or paid to him. (*Vide inter alia, Voet,* 6, 1, 36; *Groene. ad Inst.,* 2, 1, 30; *Grotius,* 2, 10, 8, *Schorer's note*). As to a *malâ fide* possessor, there is no doubt that, under the ancient Roman law, a person who built on land which he knew, or had reason to know, did not belong to him, lost all property in the materials, and was considered to have voluntarily alienated them. Such was the law as laid down by *Gaius* and followed by *Justinian* in one passage of the *Institutes* (2, 1, 30), and in one passage of the *Digest* (4, 11, 7, § 12); but there are passages in the *Digest* (5, 3, 38), and the *Code* (3, 33, 2 and 5), which are quite inconsistent with this doctrine. The first writer on Roman-Dutch Law, who denied this doctrine so far as Holland was concerned, was Groenewegen, who says (*ad Inst.*, 2, 1, 30) that inasmuch as legal penalties depriving persons of their rights have been abolished in practice, and as it is not just or equitable that any one should be enriched to the injury of another, it was held in his time that a person who has knowingly built on land belonging to another does not forfeit the price of the materials and the wages of the workmen, but is entitled to claim by an exception the right to retain the land for the amount of useful expenses, or even to bring an action for such expenses; and, he adds, that by the law of France of that day, although the right of retention did not exist, the right of bringing an action for the expenses was fully recognised. After *Groenewegen*, we find *Van Leeuwen*, (*Cens. For.*, 1, 2, 11, 7 and 8), *Voet* (6, 1, 36), and *Schorer* (*Notes to Grotius*, 2, 10, § 9), adopting his views to their fullest extent. On the other hand *Grotius* (2, 10, 8), who wrote before these writers, and *Van der Keessel* (*Th.* 214), who wrote after them, maintained that a *malâ fide* possessor has no redress, except for the necessary expenses. No explanation is given as to the meaning of the term " necessary " expenses, but as it seems to be used throughout in contradistinction to the term useful expenses (*utiles impensæ*) it can, I apprehend, only refer to expenses incurred on works which are absolutely necessary for the protection or preservation of the property. It would therefore be impossible to reconcile the conflicting authorities on the point under consideration, but considering the high respect which this Court has always paid to the opinion of *Groenewegen*, *Voet*, and *Van Leeuwen*, it is not too much to say that the weight of authority is in favour of the right of even a *malâ fide* possessor to compensation for useful expenses. It would follow that, even if the Court below was right in treating the appellant as a *malâ fide* possessor, he would still, according to very eminent authority, be entitled to an allowance of all expenses which have enhanced the value of the farm Adolphus Kraal, so far as such increased value exists. But, holding as I do, that there is no proof of *malâ fides* on the part of the appellant, it is unnecessary for the decision of the present case to express a decided opinion on this point. Under all the circumstances of the case, 1 am of opinion that the judgment appealed from erred in granting an unconditional decree of ejectment, and in ordering the appellant to pay the cost of the respondents, and that the following judgment should be substituted in its place: "That the defendant to quit possession of the farm Adolphus Kraal and of every part thereof upon payment to him by or on behalf of the plaintiff of the sum of

1874.
May 19.
„ 21.

Bellingham and another vs. Bloommetje.

1874.
May 19.
„ 21.

Bellingham and
another vs.
Bloommetje.

£150, and that the defendant be perpetually interdicted from thereafter trespassing on the said farm or any part thereof, and that each party do bear his own costs of this action." Considering that the respondent by his declaration offered to pay far less and the appellant by his plea claimed far more than what I conceive to be the amount of reasonable compensation, I am of opinion that each party should bear his own costs of this appeal as well as of the original action.

DENYSSEN and FITZPATRICK, J.J., concurred.

Appeal accordingly allowed.

[Appellant's Attorney, VAN ZYL.
Respondents' Attorneys, REID & NEPHEW.]

SINCLAIR vs. MEINTJES.

Ante-nuptial Contract : Trustee under, removed

A trustee under an ante-nuptial contract removed, after due notice, upon petition of the surviving widow, on the grounds of insolvency and departure from the Colony with intent permanently to reside abroad.

1874.
May 21.

Sinclair vs.
Meintjes.

Jacobs, A.G., applied on behalf of Mrs. C. E. Sinclair, widow of the late D. M. Sinclair, for an order removing the respondent from his office as one of the trustees under an ante-nuptial contract executed by the said late D. M. Sinclair and the applicant, by reason of respondent having surrendered his estate as insolvent, and being still an uncertificated insolvent; and also by reason of having, since his appointment under the said ante-nuptial contract, removed from the Colony to, and now residing permanently at Pretoria, in the South African Republic. He also applied for the appointment of the Graaff-Reinet Board of Executors as trustee in respondent's stead. Mrs. Sinclair's petition disclosed that two trustees had been appointed by the aforesaid ante-nuptial contract, one of whom had since died, and the respondent was the other. Mr. Sinclair had before his death appointed the Graaff-Reinet Board of Executors his executors testamentary. It was necessary that a trustee should be appointed for the purposes of the settlement under the ante-nuptial contract.

The respondent did not appear, but it was shown he had been served personally with notice of this application, and had stated he had no objection thereto or to the appointment of the Graaff-Reinet Board of Executors in his stead.

Order granted as prayed.

[Applicant's Attorney, VAN ZYL.]

Louw *vs.* Louw.

Restitution of Conjugal Rights.—Intervention.—Curator
ad litem to Children.

In an action by the husband for the restitution of conjugal
rights, collusion being alleged, the Court, on the applica-
tion of the defendant's brother, appointed him curator
ad litem to the minor children, with permission to such
curator to intervene as co-defendant.

Jacobs, A.G., on behalf of J. J. van Wyk, brother to
the defendant, prayed for leave to intervene as co-defendant
in an action for restitution of conjugal rights brought by the
plaintiff J. A. Louw, against his wife M. A. S. Louw (born
Van Wyk). Applicant alleged that the proceedings had been
instituted for the purpose of obtaining a divorce, and that
there had been a collusive arrangement between the plaintiff
and defendant. He also charged the plaintiff with adultery.
As there were minor children, counsel suggested that the
applicant might be appointed their *curator.*

Buchanan, for the plaintiff, opposed. The action was for
restitution of conjugal rights, a matter affecting only
plaintiff and defendant. The applicant had no interest in
the case which would warrant his being allowed to intervene.
Van der Linden, p. 419. The father was the natural
guardian of the children, and the Court should not appoint
a *curator* to them without his consent, or at least without
giving him notice. In the notice of motion nothing whatever was said as to appointment of a *curator* for the
children.

The Court appointed the applicant *curator ad litem* to the
children, with leave to intervene as co-defendant.

> [Applicant's Attorney, J. Horak de Villiers.]
> [Plaintiff's Attorney, Van Zyl.]

1874.
May 15.
„ 21.

Louw *vs.* Lonw.

Dodds *vs.* Baray.

Magistrate's Court Fees.

The fee payable to an Agent in the Court of the Resident
Magistrate is part of the costs of the cause.

This was an appeal from a judgment given by the
Resident Magistrate of Robertson on the 16th February,
1874.

It appeared from the records in the Court below, that
the plaintiff sued defendant for £3 19s. 5d., on an account

1874.
May 21.
——
Dodds *vs.* Baray.

1874.
May 21.
———
Dodds *vs.* Baray.
for goods sold and delivered. On the day of hearing, the defendant, by his agent, appeared and admitted the debt, but pleaded first a tender of the amount sued for, £3 19s. 5d., without costs on the ground that no formal demand had been made upon the defendant; secondly, if the first plea be disallowed, that he had tendered £3 19s. 5d., and amount of Court costs and stamps, 4s. 9d., refusing to pay the sum of 10s. 6d., agent's fee, by virtue of section 39, of Act No. 20, 1856, which amount of £4 4s. 2d. he again tendered into Court. There was a third plea of partnership between the plaintiff and his agent, but on explanation being given this was withdrawn. The plaintiff's agent called evidence and clearly proved repeated demands before action brought. There was no evidence offered by the defendant to prove any tender. The Magistrate overruled the first plea, and gave judgment for plaintiff for £4 4s. 2d., each party to pay his own costs. The plaintiff thereupon appealed.

Buchanan, for the appellant, stated the main question at issue was whether the defendant was not bound to pay plaintiff's agent's fee as being part of the costs. This was the only remuneration allowed the agent, and was payable to him for his services in the case whether he appeared in Court or not. The Magistrate's judgment was not sustainable, because without any cause to warrant the exercise of his discretion as to costs, he had refused to allow the costs of plaintiff's agent, though at the same time he awarded the plaintiff the costs he had incurred in Court fees.

The Court reversed the decision of the Magistrate as far as it related to the costs, and gave the appellant his costs in the Court below as well as on appeal.

[Appellant's Attorneys, REID & NEPHEW.]

CURATOR AD LITEM OF LETTERSTEDT *vs.* EXECUTORS OF LETTERSTEDT.

Curator ad litem to Minor out of jurisdiction.—pleading: exception non-qualificatæ.

1874.
May 26.
June 4.
———
Curator *ad litem* of Letterstedt *vs.* Executors of Letterstedt.
The Board of Executors, in their capacity as the surviving executors testamentary of the late Jacob Letterstedt, were sued by Charles Aiken Fairbridge, in his capacity as the curator *ad litem* of the minor Lydia Corinna Doligny Letterstedt, in an action for the amendment of certain

1874.
May 26.
June 4.

Curator *ad litem*
of Letterstedt *vs.*
Executors of
Letterstedt.

accounts relative to J. Letterstedt's estate, and for the refund of certain charges.

Plaintiff's declaration, after reciting the will of the late J. Letterstedt, stated *inter alia* that the testator died on or about the 18th March, 1862, leaving him surviving his wife, Lydia Letterstedt, and one child, the said L. C. D. Letterstedt, then of the age of nine years or thereabouts. It also stated that by the said will the testator appointed Messrs. Malmsten, S. G. Letterstedt, and Hildebrand, guardians of his said daughter during her minority, with power to the surviving or continuing guardian or guardians to appoint new guardians in the place of one dying, resigning, or becoming incapable of acting. That the guardians so appointed, after the death of the testator, accepted the guardianship. That S. G. Letterstedt having died in 1864, Count von Platen, pursuant to a codicil, took his place. That Hildebrand having resigned in April, 1872, Malmsten and Von Platen appointed the said Lydia Letterstedt, who was then married to M. de Jouvencil, to be co-guardian with them, and afterwards resigned their guardianship, leaving Madame de Jouvencil sole guardian, who on the 3rd March, 1873, assumed the said Fairbridge as guardian; but as all the guardians (except Fairbridge) were aliens, residing in Sweden, and had never been confirmed as guardians, Fairbridge was, by order of Court of the 26th February, 1874, appointed curator *ad litem* to the said minor L. C. D. Letterstedt, and as such was the proper person to sue in this action.

To this declaration the defendants proposed the exception of non-qualification, on the grounds: first, that the said L. C. D. Letterstedt, at the date of the making of the order of Court appointing Fairbridge her curator *ad litem*, was, and still is, beyond the jurisdiction of the Court, as would more fully appear from the petition upon which the said order was granted; second, that the said L. C. D. Letterstedt was of the full age of twenty-one years, and that the plaintiff Fairbridge had therefore no right or title in law to institute and prosecute this action; and third, that the plaintiff in his alleged capacity was not the proper person to institute and prosecute this action, inasmuch as that the said L. C. D. Letterstedt, to whom the plaintiff claimed to be curator *ad litem*, was not made a party to the action, assisted if need be by her said curator *ad litem*; and further that if the said L. C. D. Letterstedt was not competent to sue, her guardians were the proper persons to institute any suit or action on her behalf, and that by the declaration it appeared that Madame de Jouvencil was a co-guardian with the plaintiff of the said L. C. D. Letterstedt, and that the

1874.
May 26.
June 4.

Curator *ad litem*
of Letterstedt vs.
Executors of
Letterstedt.

said Madame de Jouvencil was residing beyond the jurisdiction of the Court, and had not been joined with the plaintiff in this action, and did not appear to have granted consent or authority to the institution of the proceedings in this cause.

The plaintiff answered that the exception of non-qualification was not good or sufficient to prevent his having and maintaining his action against the defendants; and he further denied that the said L. C. D. Letterstedt was of full age at the commencement of this suit.

This day (May 26th), the above exceptions were set down for argument. *Buchanan* (with him *Jones*), for the defendants, contended that as it had been decided no valid appointment could be made of tutors dative to a minor out of the Colony and beyond the jurisdiction of the Court, on the same principle no valid appointment could be made of a curator *ad litem* to an absentee. (*Tutors of Voget* vs. *Executors of Voget*, 3, *Menz.*, 79; *Westlake's Private and International Law*, 385; 3, *Burge*, 938.) As the plaintiff had been appointed curator in consequence of the minority of the ward, the ward having attained majority the plaintiff's authority had now ceased, according to the maxim *cessante causâ cessat effectus.* As the ward was now of full age she should be joined in the action, otherwise the decision of the Court might bind the defendant, but would not protect him hereafter against an action by the ward.

Jacobs, A.G. (with him *Cole*), for the plaintiffs, asked that the exceptions should be overruled. It did not appear on record that the ward was of age. As a fact she was under twenty-one when the action was commenced, and it was a question whether either by her domicile or the terms of the will she would come of age before .twenty-five. The appointment of plaintiff as curator *ad litem* had not been opposed at the time the order of Court was granted, although notice of the application had been given to defendant. Nothing had been submitted to induce the Court to cancel that order, or to show that it had not full power to clothe the plaintiff with the authority conferred.

Cur. adv. vult.

Posteà (June 4), the Court (Denyssen, J., and Fitzpatrick, J.), overruled the exceptions with costs.

Denyssen, J., said, that by the will of the late J. Letterstedt it appeared that the executors were bound to render from time to time accounts of their administration to the guardians of the minor. These guardians wished to institute an action to discuss these accounts, but seeing a difficulty owing to their residence abroad, the plaintiff, who had been assumed as co-guardian, applied to this Court for the purpose either of having his appointment as guardian confirmed, or otherwise that he should be appointed curator *ad litem* on behalf of the minor. Of this application he gave notice to the defendant. The Court made an order appointing the plaintiff curator *ad litem* of the minor, "with power to institute any action which he may be advised on behalf of the said minor," against the defendant as the surviving executor of Letterstedt's estate. On this order the plaintiff commenced proceedings and filed the declaration which had been excepted to. The first exception was, that at the date of making this order the minor was out of the jurisdiction of the Court. Now as this action had been commenced under the authority of the order of Court, it was rather too late now to except to the declaration on this ground. But it was a bad exception, as the jurisdiction of the Court to appoint a curator existed *ratione bonorum* as well as *ratione domicilii*. (3, *Burge*, 1,005), *Voet*, 25, 5, 2, confirmed this. The second exception involved a question of fact, and that could not be decided on exception. The third exception was also bad. *Grotius*, 1, 8, 4, laid down that legal proceedings must be conducted in the name of the guardians, without the ward being made a party. *Van der Linden*, p. 105, stated that the power of guardians consisted in general in assisting and representing the ward in all transactions concerning him, and especially in appearing for him in law. With regard to the remaining part of the exception, that the guardians were the proper persons to sue, it had been shown that they were unable to do so being foreigners and not having been confirmed by the Court. But even by the Roman law the Court might sometimes nominate curators for special purposes to persons having no guardians. The same principle was recognised in our local Act, for the Court had power to appoint a curator *ad litem* as well as a guardian for general purposes. And it would appear from remarks in *Kent's Commentaries* that guardians or curators appointed for special purposes might sue, even where an ordinary guardian could not.

FITZPATRICK, J., concurred.

[Plaintiff's Attorney, ARDERNE.
Defendants' Attorneys, REID & NEPHEW.]

1874.
May 26.
June 4.

Curator *ad litem* of Letterstedt *vs.* Executors of Letterstedt.

WEHMEYER vs. SWEMMER, TRUSTEE OF HEYNS.

Insolvency.—Trustee: execution against de bonis propriis, refused on motion.

A writ of execution against a trustee of an insolvent estate, personally, will not be granted on motion, for the amount of a writ obtained against him nomine officii, to which writ a return of nulla bona was made.

*1874.
June 4.

Wehmeyer vs.
Swemmer, Trustee of Heyns.

Jacobs, A.G., for the applicant, moved for a writ of execution to issue, commanding the sheriff to cause to be made of the goods and chattels of the respondent individually, the sum of £19 16s. 7d., being costs recovered by sentence of the Supreme Court on the 27th November, 1873, against the respondent in his capacity as sole trustee of the insolvent estate of the late M. S. Heyns, and for which sum a writ had issued against the respondent in his said capacity, to which a return of *nulla bona* had been made ; and also to cause to be made the sum of £30 14s. 3d., being the amount paid by the applicant in satisfaction of a judgment obtained against him by the respondent in his capacity as trustee in the Resident Magistrate's Court of George, under promise of restitution in case the magistrate's judgment should be reversed, as had been done on appeal. [For report of case, see *Buch. Reports*, 1873, p. 96.]

The receipt given by the respondent for the £30 14s. 3d., did not state any condition, nor was the usual bond *de restituendo* ever executed.

Buchanan, for the respondent, objected, as the effect of the application, if granted, would be to obtain a judgment by means of a motion instead of by action.

The Court refused the application. The insolvent ordinance allowed a trustee to bring an action *nomine officii*. If there had been *mala fides* on the part of the trustee sufficient to render him liable individually, he should be proceeded against by action. Costs refused.

[Applicant's Attorney, DE KORTE.
Respondent's Attorney, C. C. DE VILLIERS.]

NELSON AND MEURANT vs. QUIN AND Co.

Interdict.—Libel : publication of.—Property in Letters.

An application for an interdict restraining the publication of certain private letters, which had been produced at a judicial inquiry, there being no allegation that the publication would entail irreparable damage, refused.

SEMBLE,—*Where the writer of a letter has allowed it to pass out of his possession without restriction as to its circulation, he has no right on which to found an application for an interdict to restrain the publication of such letter.*

Notice had been served calling upon the respondents, the publishers of the *Fort Beaufort Advocate,* to show cause why a certain interdict granted by Mr. Justice Dwyer, of the Eastern Districts Court, on the 22nd May, 1874, should not be continued and made perpetual against the respondents and all parties whomsoever in this Colony, with costs against the respondents.

1874.
June 4.
„ 11.

Nelson & Meurant
vs. Quin & Co.

It appeared that on the 16th of December, 1873, Mr. Justice Smith granted a decree by which it was ordered that the respondents and all other parties whatsoever " be restrained from publishing in the *Fort Beaufort Advocate,* or in any other way whatsoever, certain three original letters written by Richard William Nelson to Louis Henry Meurant [the applicants], dated respectively the 9th, 19th, and 26th September, 1873, pending the result of an inquiry lately held before Messrs. Campbell and Hugo, and of certain legal proceedings in which one William Ewing was charged with the theft of these letters." On the 28th of February, 1874, the interdict was extended by Mr. Justice Dwyer until the 23rd of May, 1874, and on the 22nd of May the learned Judge extended the same until the 6th of June ; the then applicant, Nelson, undertaking to serve notice on the respondents forthwith that the Supreme Court would be moved during the present term to make the interdict perpetual.

The affidavits of R. W. Nelson, in support of the motion, and of John Quin, in reply, were put in and read. The facts deposed to therein will be found below in the judgment of the Chief Justice.

Cole, in support of the motion, maintained that the applicant Nelson, as the writer of the letters, had a right of property therein, of which right he could not be deprived without his consent. Having this right he was justified in applying for an interdict to prevent it being infringed. (*Pope* vs. *Curl,* 2, *Atkyns,* 342. *Addison on Torts,* 3rd ed., p. 1,026.) The mere fact of letters being produced at a trial, or even the reading of portions of them in open Court, did not confer on any one a right to publish them against the wish of the writer.

Buchanan, for the respondents, contended that the authorities quoted referred to cases where the copyright had been endangered, and not to the publication by a newspaper

1874.
June 4.
„ 11.
Nelson & Meu-
rant
vs. Quin & Co.

of evidence given and read out in open Court. Anyone publishing a faithful report of judicial proceedings was protected both civilly and criminally, although individuals might suffer therefrom. (*Starkie on Libel*, 709.) The original interdict was granted pending certain investigations which had now terminated. The respondents had done nothing prejudicial to any right belonging to the applicants; and from the affidavits it did not appear there was any well-grounded apprehension that any such act would be done by them. (*Vide v. d. Linden*, p. 441.) The letters had been published by others, and this application was to restrain those persons, who were not before the Court, and not the respondents.

Cole replied. The paragraph in respondents' paper plainly indicated an intention to publish the letters. So did the advertisement, which, though it was alleged to have been inserted for Ewing, did not appear to bear his signature or give any reference to him or any one else.

Cur. adv. vult.

Posteà (June 11),

DE VILLIERS, C.J., in giving judgment, said : As the original interdict was only granted pending certain inquiries, and as those inquiries have long since been concluded, I would have found great difficulty, upon the present notice of motion, in deciding the real question at issue between the parties, if the affidavits and arguments of counsel on both sides had not treated the present motion as a substantial application to restrain the respondents absolutely and unconditionally from publishing the letters in question. The further question, whether persons other than the respondents should or should not be interdicted from publishing the letters, cannot be considered in the present case, for, without a previous edictal citation, this Court has no power to make an order binding on persons who are not parties or privies to a cause. The facts of the case are briefly as follows : On the 9th, 19th, and 26th of September last respectively, Mr. Nelson, of Graham's Town, wrote certain letters to Mr. Meurant, of Fort Beaufort, and, in some unexplained way, these letters came into the possession of Wm. Ewing, of Fort Beaufort, who produced them before a commission which had been appointed by the Government to make an official inquiry into certain charges brought against Mr. Meurant as Civil Commissioner and Resident Magistrate of Fort Beaufort. Thereupon a charge of theft of the letters was made against Ewing, and as Mr. Meurant was so directly concerned in the matter, the preliminary examination was taken on the 9th December, 1873, before Mr. Van der Riet, J.P., who after hearing witnesses, dismissed the case, and refused to commit the defendant for trial, and it does not appear that any further criminal proceedings were taken against him. In the course of the preliminary examination the letters in question were produced as evidence by Mr. Hugo, one of the commissioners, but it is not quite clear that these letters or any portion of them were read in court. Mr. Quin, indeed, in his affidavit, swears that portions were publicly read, but as he makes this statement upon information received from others and not from his own knowledge, little weight can be attached to it. On the 13th December, 1873, a report of the evidence so taken was published in the *Fort Beaufort Advocate*, and in the same number appeared the following paragraph :—" We have not space this week for the letters alluded to in this case, and upon which a charge of theft was preferred against Mr. Ewing." Thereupon the applicants, concluding from this notice, not, I think, unreasonably, that the respondents, who are the publishers and proprietors of the paper, intended to publish the letters, applied for the first interdict, which was granted by Mr. Justice Smith, but, notwithstanding such interdict, the following advertisement was published in the *Fort Beaufort Advocate* of the 21st February, 1874 :—" Fort Beaufort Commission.—In the press, and will shortly be published, the whole of the evidence (with appendices) of the Commission appointed by Government to inquire into matters connected with and arising out of certain letters, signed ' Cosmopolite,' ' John Puffadder, senior,' ' Jantje Aasvogel,' published in the *Eastern Star* newspaper. As only a limited number will be printed, parties requiring copies of this interesting work are recommended to make early application." Mr. Quin says that since the deposit of the judge's order, he never gave the applicants any reason for believing that he intended to publish the letters, and that the advertisement was sent to him by Mr. Ewing for publication in the ordinary course of business ; but as the advertisement does not purport to be signed by Ewing or by any one else it might fairly lead the reader to presume that it issued from the publishers themselves. If, therefore, sufficient legal grounds can be shown for restraining a threatened publication of the letters, I do not think that the respondents' disclaimer would, in the face of the advertisement, be of any avail to them ; and this seems to have been the view taken by Mr. Justice Dwyer, who on the 28th February granted an order extending the first interdict. There is no affidavit from Mr. Meurant to explain how he

1874.
June 4.
„ 11.

Nelson & Meurant
vs. Quin & Co.

50

1874.
June 4.
,, 11.

Nelson & Meu-
rant
vs. Quin & Co.

lost possession of the letters, or from Mr. Ewing to explain how he got possession of them. Mr. Nelson swears that Ewing obtained them unlawfully, but he does not give the facts on which he founds this opinion, and the decision of the Court at the preliminary examination, so far as it goes, is in Ewing's favour. The letters having been produced as evidence before the Magistrate, this Court may fairly presume, nay, is bound to presume, in the absence of evidence to the contrary, that the respondents, in becoming cognizant of their contents, were not privy to any impropriety on the part of Ewing. I do not mean to say that if the letters contained any defamatory matter, the mere fact of their being produced in court, not for the purpose of being read but as the *corpus delicti* in question, would justify any one in publishing them; but I do think that the production of the documents in open court may be allowed to explain the knowledge of their contents on the part of persons other than the sender and receiver. There is no allegation in Nelson's affidavit that the publication of the letters would cause any loss, damage, injury, trouble, or even inconvenience to himself, or to Mr. Meurant, or to any one else, or that there existed any contract between himself and Meurant that they should never be published. The main ground on which he relies in his affidavit is, that these letters are private and confidential; but he does not state that, on the face of them, or of the cover enclosing them, they purport to be private and confidential. This Court would, as it strikes me, extend its interference beyond that which, according to the decided cases, has ever been actually exercised by the English Courts of Equity, if on such slender grounds it were to grant an interdict to restrain the publication. *Story*, in his work on *Equity Jurisprudence* (§ 944, § 496, *et seq.*), argues against the morality of publishing private letters, unless in cases where it is necessary to the proper vindication of the rights or conduct of the party against unjust claims or injurious imputations; and he points out that there are cases in which injunctions have been granted to restrain the publication of letters, even when they could not be considered in the light of literary compositions; but it will be found that in each of these cases there were special grounds, independently of the mere privacy of the communication, which called for the interposition of a Court of Equity. Indeed, the learned counsel for the applicants entirely abandoned the grounds taken up in Nelson's affidavit, and he rested the claim for an interdict solely on the ground of the sender's right of property in the contents of the letters; and until I had an opportunity of consulting the authorities, this was the only point on which I entertained any doubt during the argument. In order to make good Mr. Cole's contention, it would be necessary for him to show that, by the law of this Colony, every person has a clear and undoubted right of property in his own compositions, to the extent of being entitled to prevent every one else from multiplying copies of such compositions, whether they be of a purely literary character or not, and whether they have been communicated to others or not. No authority from the civil law bearing on this point has been cited in the argument, nor have I been able to find any but the most remote references to it. Cicero, in one of his speeches (*Oratio Philip.*, 2, *c.* 4), speaks of the practice of publishing private letters as a breach of good manners and an offence against common decency, and as calculated to put an end to all familiar correspondence between friends ; but he does not condemn the practice as illegal, on the contrary, he rather seems to assume that it is not illegal. Indeed, I am not aware that his own consent, or that of his heirs, was obtained to the publication of all his letters to Atticus and other friends, or that any attempt was ever made to restrain their publication, although some of them were of such a nature that no one can suppose he wished or intended them to be published. In *Justinian's Institutes* (2, 1, 33), it is said that, "If Titius has written a poem, a history, or a speech on your paper or parchment, you, and not Titius, are the owner of the written paper." *Voet* (41, 1, 26), *Groenewegen* (*ad Inst.*, 2, 1, 33), and *Grotius* (*Introduction*, 2, 8, 3), hold that this doctrine does not obtain in the law of Holland, but not one of them refers to the case of a person multiplying copies of a composition which has come to his knowledge. In the absence of civil law authority it is proper that this Court should refer to the decisions of the Courts of Great Britain with a view to ascertain whether the right now in question is there recognised as existing independently of statute, and, if so, on what grounds its existence is based. In the great case of *Boosey* vs. *Jeffreys*, decided in the House of Lords, the much-vexed question of common law right to literary property was raised, and after taking the opinions of the judges—among whom a great diversity of opinion existed,—the Law Lords (Cranworth, Brougham, and St. Leonards) held that copyright did not exist at common law and was entirely a creature of statute. As the reasons given for this view by Chief Baron Pollock throw a useful light upon the subject now before us, I shall quote a few short passages from his opinion (*H. of L. Cas.*, vol. 4, p. 936). "The ground," he says, "taken by the learned counsel for the defendant in error has been that an

1874.
June 4.
„ 11.

Nelson & Meu-
rant
vs. Quin & Co.

author has the same property in his composition, being his own creation or work, as a man has in any physical object, produced by his personal labour. If such a property exists at common law, it must commence with the act of composition or creation itself, and must, as it seems to me, be independent of its being reduced into writing. If it is the author's property, he may give or withhold it as he pleases ; he may communicate it to the public with a liberal or a niggardly hand, or withhold it altogether. And the same principle must be applicable to every other creation, invention, or discovery, as well as a poem, a history, or any other literary production. It must apply to every other offspring of man's imagination, wit, or labour; to discoveries in science, in the arts and manufactures, in national history; in short, to whatever belongs to human life. An ode, composed and recited by an ancient bard at a public festival, is as much the creation of his genius, and is published by the recitation, though not in the same degree as the poem of a modern author printed and sold in Paternoster-row. The speech of the orator, the sermon of the preacher, the lecture of the professor, have no greater claim to protection, and to be the foundation of exclusive property and right than the labours of the man of science, the invention of the mechanic, the discovery of the physician or empiric, or, indeed, the successful efforts of anyone in any department of human knowledge or practice. And it is difficult to say where, in principle, this is to stop. Why is it to be confined to the larger and graver labours of the understanding ? Why does it not apply to a well-told anecdote or a witty reply, so as to forbid the repetition without the permission of the author ? And, carried to its utmost extent, it would at length descend to lower and meaner subjects, and include the conjuror or the grimace of a clown." Lord Brougham, in his judgment, maintains that an author, before publication, has the undisputable right to his manuscript, that he may withhold or communicate it, and communicating may limit the number of persons to whom it is imparted, and impose such restrictions as he pleases upon their use of it; but that, when once he has published it or communicated it to others without any conditions or restrictions, he cannot at law prevent the persons to whom he gave or sold his paper, whether written or printed, from making their own use of it. He adds the following remarks :—" There is nothing in the thoughts of a person resembling the substance to which an incorporeal hereditament is related. They are of too unsubstantial, too evanescent a nature, their expression of language, in whatever manner, is too fleeting to be the subject of proprietary rights. *Volat irrevocabile verbum,* whether borne on the wings of the wind or the press, and the supposed owner instantly loses all control over them. When the period is demanded at which the property vests, we are generally referred to the moment of publication. But that is the moment when the hold of the proprietor ceases. He has produced the thought and given it utterance, and *eo instanti* it escapes his grasp." The only case to which we were referred by the counsel for the applicants in support of his argument is that of *Pope* vs. *Curl* (2, *Atkyns*, p. 342), decided by Lord Hardwicke in 1741. In that case a motion was made on behalf of Curl, the bookseller, to dissolve an injunction which Pope (the poet) had obtained against his selling a book entitled, " Letters from Swift, Pope, and others." These letters, having been formed into a volume, had been published in Ireland, and an attempt was now made to republish them in England. The first question raised was whether letters are within the intention of 8, Anne, c. 19, being " An Act for the encouragement of learning, by vesting the copies of printed books in the authors or purchasers of such copies," and the Lord Chancellor held that letters are within such intention. And here I may parenthetically remark that it was suggested by Mr. Cole, I hardly think seriously, that the rights claimed by the applicants, if not existing at common law, were conferred by our Colonial Copyright Act of 1873 (No. 2, of 1873). By the first and second sections of that Act the duration of the copyright in every book, published after the passing of the Act, is fixed, and by the 9th section the word " book " is construed " to mean and include every volume, part or division of a volume, pamphlet, sheet of letter-press, sheet of music, and map, chart, or plan separately published." There is a wide distinction between a book of letters published as the literary production of eminent writers, and an ordinary letter written without a view to publication, and in fact never published. The former would fall under the general appellation of books, whilst the latter could by no latitude of construction be embraced by the interpretation clause of Act 2, of 1873. But to return to the case before Lord Hardwicke. Another objection having been made by the defendant's counsel, that where a man receives a letter it is in the nature of a gift to the receiver, the Lord Chancellor gave his opinion, " That it is only a special property in the receiver; possibly the property of the paper may belong to him ; but this does not give a licence to any person whatever to publish them to the world, for at most the receiver has only a joint property with the writer." That case was followed by *Thompson* vs. *Stanhope* (*Amb.* 737), and *A—* vs. *Eaton* (quoted 2, *Ves. &*

1874.
June 4.
„ 11.
Nelson & Meurant
vs. Quin & Co.

1874.
June 4.
„ 11.

Nelson & Men-
rant
vs. Quin & Co.

B., p. 27). In the latter case letters were represented to have been written by an elderly lady of a nature that made it very important to prevent the publication; there was a contract not to publish them but to deliver them up for valuable consideration, and a sum of money paid to the defendant, who now threatened to publish them in violation of good faith and contract; and Lord Eldon granted an injunction to restrain the publication. The next case to which I shall refer is that of *Lord Percival* vs. *Phipps* (2, *Ves. & B.*, p. 19). In that case an application was made to Sir Thomas Plumer, Vice-Chancellor, to dissolve an injunction granted by the Lord Chancellor, by which the defendant (Phipps) had been restrained from publishing the plaintiff's private letters, alleged to have been obtained from an agent to whom they were sent in confidence. The defendant, by his answer, avowed his object in publishing them in a newspaper, of which he was proprietor, to be, not for profit, but the vindication of his character from the imputation of giving false intelligence, publicly cast upon him by the plaintiff. The Vice-Chancellor, in giving judgment, made the following remarks :—" This is the naked case of a bill to prevent the publication of private letters ; not stating the nature, subject, or occasion of them, or that they were intended to be sold as a literary work for profit, or are of any value to the plaintiff. Upon such a case it is not necessary to determine the general questions how far a Court of Equity will interpose to protect the interests of the author of private letters. The interposition of the Court in this instance certainly is not a consequence of the cases that were cited " (including the case of *Pope* vs. *Curl*) ; " upon which I shall merely observe that though the form of familiar letters might not prevent their approaching the character of a literary work, every private letter, upon any subject, to any person, is not to be described as a literary work to be protected upon the principle of copyright. The ordinary use of correspondence by letters is to carry on the intercourse of life between persons at a distance from each other, in the prosecution of commercial or other business, which it would be very extraordinary to describe as a literary work in which the writers have a copyright. Another class is the correspondence between friends or relations upon their private concerns ; and it is not necessary here to determine how far such letters, falling into the hands of executors, &c., could be made public in a way that must frequently be very injurious to the feelings of individuals. I do not mean to say *that* would afford a ground for a Court of Equity to interpose to prevent a breach of that sort of confidence, in-

1874.
June 4.
„ 11.

Nelson & Meu-
rant
vs. Quin & Co.

dependent of contract and property." The next case of which I have been able to find a full report is that of *Gee* vs. *Pritchard* (2, *Swanst.*, p. 402–427). There letters written by the plaintiff to the defendant had been returned by the defendant with a declaration that he did not consider himself entitled to retain them; but it appears that he had kept copies of them without the knowledge of the plaintiff, and upon his threatening to publish them, the Lord Chancellor (Eldon) restrained the publication, though represented by the defendant as necessary for the vindication of his character. He held that the defendant, by returning the letters to the writers, had renounced the right of publication ; at the same time he professed grave doubts relative to the jurisdiction of the Chancery Courts over the publication of letters, but, acting on the principle that if he found doctrines settled for forty years together he would not unsettle them, he refused to dissolve the injunction. In none of the English decided cases which I have found, does the right of property in the letters constitute the sole ground for restraining their publication by injunction. In most of them pecuniary loss to the authors was apprehended; in others the publication would amount to a breach of contract, express or implied; and in the last quoted case the receiver, by returning the letters to the writer, was held to have renounced his right of publishing them. But even if there had been English cases in which the right of property *per se* was the ground of decision, I think that this Court, bearing in mind the doubts entertained by Lord Eldon in a case admitting of far less doubt than the present, should hesitate before it establishes in this Colony a precedent fraught with the most mischievous consequences. If once the principle be established that a person may obtain an injunction to restrain the publication of his letters on the mere ground of his right of property therein, where are we to stop ? If the absolute right contended for exists, it would equally apply to letters and all other documents produced and read in open court; and, however necessary they may be for the proper apprehension or elucidation of the case, it would be competent to the author or writer to apply to the Court to restrain the publishers of newspapers and even of law reports from publishing such letters or documents. When we remember how often the result of a trial depends on the contents of a single letter, and how many cases hinge on the construction of a letter or other document, it is easy to conceive to what an extent the publicity of proceedings in courts of justice could be interfered with by such a state of the law. No doubt, in many cases the publication of such proceedings may be to the disadvantage of the particular

1874.
June 4.
,, 11.
Nelson & Meu-
raut
vs. Quin & Co.
individual concerned, but the general advantage to the country in having them made public more than counter-balances the individual hardship. In conclusion, let me observe that it is one of the first requisites to the granting of an interdict upon motion that there should exist a clear and undoubted right which is threatened with violation, the only exception to this rule occurring in case the act or thing against which the interdict is sought be of such a nature that, unless the application be granted, irreparable damage to the applicants would ensue. Holding, as I do, that the rights contended for on their behalf have not been estab-lished, and finding, as I do, that there is no allegation in any of the affidavits that the publication of the letters in question would entail irreparable damage on the applicants, I am of opinion, after the most careful and anxious con-sideration of the whole case, that the motion for a perpetual interdict ought to be refused with costs.

DENYSSEN, J.—I am of the same opinion, that the inter-dict granted by Mr. Justice Dwyer should be dissolved. I think the principle which is acted upon by the Supreme Court, and has always been acted upon, has been so often referred to and so clearly laid down, that it is not necessary for me to go into all the matters which have been noticed in the able judgment of the Chief Justice. *Van der Linden* has laid it down that three things are necessary before an interdict should be granted. "First, there must be a clear right on the part of the complainant. If this right which he conceives himself to have is not well founded, then it is manifest that the other party ought not to be disturbed by an injunction. If this right be of a doubtful nature, then the question is unfit to be decided in this summary way, on an application for an injunction, before a full investigation of the merits." There has not been one Roman Dutch Law authority referred to, to show a clear right on the part of the applicants. A number of cases have been referred to in the English authorities. I am always prepared to treat with great respect the opinions of the judges in England, but it is also clear in looking over these cases referred to, that there are great doubts at the present moment as to the rights of authors; some of the judges maintaining that copyright exists at common law, while others held it was created by statute. But at all events in this case it has not been shown there is any clear right on the part of the applicants. *Van der Linden* goes on:—"If, however, the act or thing against which the injunction is sought be of that nature that the proceeding in it would cause irreparable damage to the complainant, whilst, on the other hand, the stopping or suspending it for a time would not be attended with equal prejudice to the other party, the injunction in such cases should be granted, and an opportunity afforded to the complainant to establish his right (which in all cases ought to be apparent in his favour), by a regular and more complete judicial investigation." There has been no reference or any allegation made in which anything has been said about an irreparable damage arising to the applicants. The second requisite is " a thing actually done by the party to be restrained prejudicial to our right, or a well grounded apprehension on our part that such an act will be done by him." I have already mentioned that it has not been shown that any clear right exists, so that there can be no injury done to such a right. Then there must be an apprehension of an act to be " done by him." There is no evidence of such apprehension. On the contrary, Quin, against whom the injunction is prayed, positively swears, that the advertisement relied on by the applicant was inserted in the *Fort Beaufort Advocate* for Mr. Ewing in the ordinary course of business, and that he does not intend at present to publish the letters. If he had not given Mr. Ewing's name as the person for whom the advertisement was inserted, it might have raised an inference against him, but it was not so. Under these circumstances I cannot understand how there can be any well grounded fear that any act will be done by Quin which should be restrained. The third requisite is, that without this aid of injunction the party complaining would be remediless. This, too, has not been shown. I therefore agree with the decision of the Chief Justice.

FITZPATRICK, J., concurred.

Application refused accordingly, with costs.

[Applicants' Attorneys, REID & NEPHEWS.]
[Respondents' Attorney, VAN ZYL.]

GHISLIN *vs.* SYSTER.

Ejectment.—Act No. 20, 1856, sec. 10.—Magistrate's Judgment quashed.

Leave granted to bring judgment under review after the time for noting appeal had expired.

This was an ex-parte application on behalf of the above defendant for an order on the Magistrate of Stellenbosch to send the records in the case Ghislin *vs.* Syster, tried before him on the 28th August, 1873, to the Registrar of the Court, so that the same might be re-

1874.
June 4.
„ 11.

Nelson & Meurant
vs. Quin & Co.

1874.
June 2.
„ 13.

Ghislin *vs.*
Syster.

viewed, and the proceedings quashed should they be found to have been irregular or illegal. Applicant's petition set forth that he had been sued by the plaintiff, in an action to eject him from a certain house then in applicant's occupation. That at the trial he had appeared in person and pleaded that the house belonged to one Du Toit, and not to the plaintiff. That the Magistrate after hearing plaintiff's evidence, granted the ejectment, which was enforced on the 23rd September. That being a poor man, and having no professional assistance at the hearing, applicant was not acquainted with the law of appeal, or the time within which an appeal should have been noted. That he was anxious to bring an action for damages against the said Ghislin, but was advised by counsel that so long as the Magistrate's judgment remained undisturbed it would be a good answer to any such action. That applicant was further advised that the Magistrate had no legal right or authority to entertain the case after it had been pleaded that the property belonged to a person other than the plaintiff. That as the time for appealing against the said judgment had passed, defendant would be without redress for the wrongs suffered by him, unless the Court, in the exercise of its powers of review, took the case into consideration, and directed that the whole proceedings therein be quashed as irregular and illegal. The contents of the petition were verified by affidavit. There were also further affidavits sworn to by the defendant, and by Du Toit, in which it was stated that the house in question never belonged to or was ever in the possession of Ghislin, and that at the trial the Magistrate refused to hear any evidence on behalf of the defendant.

Cole, for the appellant, urged that in accordance with Act No. 20, 1856, sec. 10, as soon as the title to the ownership of the property was questioned, the Magistrate ought not to have proceeded to hear the case. This was more an application for review than for an appeal, as the irregularities complained of would not appear on the records. In the case of *Smith* vs. *Pinto, Buch. Reports,* 1868, p. 105, leave had been given to appeal after the time fixed for noting had expired.

The Court granted an order directing the Magistrate to transmit the records to the Registrar, and further ordered that the plaintiff, Ghislin, upon due service, do show cause, if any, on the last day of term, why the proceedings in the Court below should not be quashed. It was also directed that a copy of this order and of the petition and affidavits be served on the Magistrate.

Posted (June 13), the records having been sent up,

1874.
June 2.
„ 13.
Ghislin *vs.*
Syster.

Cole moved that the proceedings in the Court below be reviewed, and the Magistrate's judgment quashed on account of the irregularities above stated.

Buchanan, for Ghislin, the plaintiff below, stated it could not be denied evidence which had been tendered at the trial by the applicant had been refused by the Magistrate. He suggested that the case should be referred back with an order on the Magistrate to hear the evidence tendered. As to costs, he urged that they should not be given against Ghislin, as it had not been through any default of his that they had been incurred ; but rather that the Magistrate should be ordered to pay them as a penalty for his improper conduct.

DE VILLIERS, C.J., said this application could not be considered as one in the nature of an appeal, and therefore this Court was not restricted from entertaining it by the lapse of the time in which appeals were directed to be noted. It was rather an application for the review of the Magistrate's proceedings on the grounds of irregularity. There had been most extraordinary procedure on the part of the Magistrate, and the proceedings must be quashed with costs. The case could not be referred back as suggested by counsel, as there was already a judgment in existence. The plaintiff would not be barred from bringing a fresh action, if so advised. Costs would not be given against the Magistrate as there had been no allegation of *mala fides* on his part.

Application accordingly granted with costs.

[Appellant's Attorney, DICKSON.]
[Respondent's Attorney, BLORE.]

ALEXANDER *vs.* PERRY.

Contract of Service.—Nudum Pactum.

The breach of a contract of service for which no consideration is given, does not afford ground of action.

Edwin C. Perry was summoned to appear before the Resident Magistrate of Cape Town, to show why he should not be adjudged to pay to Messrs. L. Alexander & Co. the sum of £20, as and for damages sustained by reason that the said Perry did, at Cape Town, on or about the 7th June, 1873, make, execute, and enter into a certain written contract, whereby the said Perry engaged and agreed to

1874.
June 13.

Alexander
vs. Perry.

serve the said Alexander & Co. in the capacity of book-keeper, until three months' notice be given or received; and in breach and violation of the said agreement, and without giving or receiving the notice agreed upon, the said Perry on the 13th December, 1873, departed from and left the service of the said Alexander & Co.

The written contract referred to in the summons was as follows:—"Messrs. L. Alexander & Co. on the one part hereby engage Mr. Edwin Charles Perry as book-keeper, &c., and Mr. E. C. Perry on the other part agrees to accept the engagement as above, to commence from the 15th June, 1873. It is hereby provided that three months' notice shall be given by either party in the event of this engagement being cancelled."

The record stated:—" Defendant excepts to the action on the ground that the contract is void for want of consider-ation; and puts in copy of document upon which the action is founded.

"Plaintiff considers the objection invalid, as it is not essential to insert the consideration in the contract, when both parties agreed to the consideration, wages, or salary, and signed the agreement upon which the claim is founded; and further that defendant did actually for a term fulfil the agreement, and which he broke by leaving without notice.

"Exception sustained with costs."

From this decision the plaintiffs appealed.

Cole, for the appellants, contended that the exception to the summons was bad. It was, in fact, an exception not to the summons, but to a document put in by the defendant. Admitting that by the Roman law an agreement without *causa, i.e.,* consideration, gave no right of action, yet it was not necessary that the consideration should be expressed in writing, even although the contract itself be written, provided it be proved in point of fact to exist. (*Story on Contracts,* sec. 428.) The exception in this case was not that there was no right of action because there was no consideration given, but that the contract was void because it did not express con-sideration.

Jacobs, A.G., for the respondent, supported the exception. He argued that no declaration on a contract was good unless it disclosed consideration on the face of it. (*Chitty on Pleadings,* 7th ed., vol. 1, p. 299. *Fremlin* vs. *Hamilton,* 8, *Exch.,* p. 308.) No consideration was alleged in the summons in this case. The way in which the exception was taken might make it appear to have been an exception only to the contract, but substantially it was an exception to the action, and was so considered by the Magistrate. By English law the consideration must appear from the instrument itself; and parol evidence would not be allowed to supply the deficiency. (*Smith on Contracts*, p. 52.)

Cole, in reply, cited *Van der Keessel*, Th. 484.

DE VILLIERS, C.J. :—The exception ought to be sustained. The form of the exception did not put the matter properly before the Court, but substantially it was an exception to the summons on the ground that the contract referred to therein was void for want of consideration. There was no allegation of consideration in the summons. Whatever might be the general law of Holland, as to whether an action could be brought on a contract made without consideration—and on this point there was some difference among the different writers—still there could be no doubt that a contract for one person to serve another required consideration to sustain it. *Van der Linden*, p. 190, and *Van der Keessel*, two of the latest authorities, both seem to hold that some consideration is necessary to support a contract, and it was only natural that the law should not enable a person to enforce a contract for which there had been no consideration at all. My own opinion is in favour of requiring consideration. This seemed to be the law also in Ceylon. (*Vide Thompson's Law of Ceylon*, p. 322.) *Voet*, it is true, affirmed that the Roman doctrine *ex nudo pacto non oritur actio* did not apply to the law of Holland, and states (2, 14, 9,) that on this point *Van Leeuwen* is in error, having confused *pacta nuda* with a stipulation or caution which required the *causa debiti* to be expressed. The opinion of so learned an authority as *Voet* deserved and always was received in this Court as deserving great weight, still the authorities on the whole inclined to the side of consideration being required.

DENYSSEN, J.—I am of a different opinion, and think that the exception should be overruled. I am not prepared at this moment to enter upon the discussion of the very important question whether or not consideration is necessary to sustain a contract. But that was not the question raised by the exception. If the summons was bad, the exception should have been to it, and the grounds of exception stated. The exception was not taken to the summons. It is worded as to the action on the ground that the contract was void for want of consideration. Here was the Court below virtually deciding on an exception that the contract was void for want of consideration, an important question this Court was not now prepared to settle. The Court below had virtually determined that want of consideration in a contract vitiated the contract. This was the effect

1874.
June 13
———
Alexander
vs. Perry.

of the decision. Both the summons and the exception are bad, and the case ought rather to be referred back to the Magistrate for the purpose of commencing proceedings *de novo.*

FITZPATRICK, J.—It is well known that the practice and the feeling of the country is that there should be consideration for a contract. The Magistrate would be right in deciding as he had done until it should be judicially settled that no such consideration was necessary. I am of opinion that no man should be bound by a contract unless he received a *quid pro quo.* The consideration might be very slight, but there should be something to sustain a contract. I therefore support the view taken by the Chief Justice.

Appeal accordingly dismissed with costs.

[Appellant's Attorney, MOORE.
Respondent's Attorneys, FAIRBRIDGE & ARDERNE.]

MAGISTRATES' REVIEWED CASES.

GAOL ORDINANCE, No. 24, 1847, SEC. 12.

*An order to put a prisoner in irons must not form part of the
Magistrate's sentence.*

DE VILLIERS, C.J., said the case had come before him,
as judge of the week, of the *Queen* vs. *Piet Williams*, in
which the prisoner was charged with a contravention of
section 12, of Ordinance No. 24, of 1847, the Gaol Ordinance. The Magistrate had found the prisoner guilty and
had sentenced him to three months' imprisonment, after the
expiration of the previous sentence, and to be placed in leg
irons. The Magistrate had the power by the Gaol Ordinance
under certain circumstances to give an order for a prisoner
to be secured in irons, but that order should not form part of
his sentence. So much of the sentence, therefore, must be
quashed.

1874.
April 13.

MASTERS AND SERVANTS' ACT, 1856.

Indenture.

*A Magistrate has no power to sentence a prisoner on his trial
for theft to be indentured as an apprentice.*

DE VILLIERS, C.J., said that among the cases which had
come before him as judge of the week, was one of the
Queen vs. *Jan and Booy*, charged with stealing a cow.
Both prisoners pleaded guilty, and Jan was sentenced to
twelve months' imprisonment, and Booy to receive fifteen
cuts with the cane, and to be indentured to some fit person
till his eighteenth year, he being then thirteen years old.
This latter sentence was a most extraordinary one, and if
once its legality were established, there was no knowing to
what treatment such apprentices might be subjected. The
Magistrate had the power in certain cases to indenture an
apprentice, but he must go through certain forms set forth
in the Masters and Servants' Act of 1856, and he had no
power to make it part of the sentence. That part of the
sentence about the indenturing must be struck out.

1874.
June 11.

FINE.

Where a prisoner convicted of theft is sentenced to pay a fine the Magistrate must fix the amount. An order to pay in stock, without ascertaining the value, is bad.

1874.
June 11.

DE VILLIERS, C.J., said a case had come before him of the *Queen* vs. *Jantje Zwartboy*, in which the prisoner was charged with stealing a goat, but no evidence was adduced as to the value. The sentence was fifteen lashes, and to pay two goats, twice the value of that stolen. This was a very rough and ready kind of justice, for it did not appear of what value the two goats were to be. They might be scabby ones that were to be given in exchange for a valuable goat, or, on the other hand, the goat stolen might have been scabby, and the prisoner might have but two valuable angora goats of far greater value. The case must therefore be remitted to the Magistrate to ascertain the value of the goat stolen, and to fix the amount of the fine.

DE VILLIERS, C.J., mentioned another case in which a similar sentence had been passed. This also must be remitted back to the Magistrate for the same reasons.

SUPREME COURT REPORTS.

1874·

PART III.

TRUSTEES OF STRATFORD *vs.* MOSENTHAL & Co.

Ord. No. 3, 1846, secs. 84, 88.

Insolvency : Undue preference.—Contemplation of sequestration.

The delivery of assets by a debtor in difficulties and unable to meet his liabilities, shortly before the sequestration of his estate, to a creditor, is not such an undue preference in favour of such creditor as to be null and void under the 84th section of the Insolvent Ordinance, where such delivery was not made in contemplation of sequestration.

This was an appeal from a judgment of the Circuit Court for Port Elizabeth, delivered by Mr. Justice Smith, on the 1st May last, in an action in which the appellants were the plaintiffs and the respondents were the defendants.

The plaintiffs, in their capacity as the trustees of the insolvent estate of Stratford, sued the defendants, carrying on business at Port Elizabeth as merchants, to recover the respective sums of £1,173 7s. 2d., and £245 2s. 6d. The declaration set forth that Stratford, who formerly carried on the business of a wool-washer and dealer in wool at Uitenhage, had his estate sequestrated as insolvent on the 23rd October, 1872. That before the sequestration of the said estate, to wit, on or about the 11th September, 1872, the defendants, who were then creditors to an amount of nearly £2,000, upon promissory notes of Stratford's not yet due, purchased from Stratford, and the said Stratford sold to them, a quantity of wool at and for the sum of £1,173 7s. 2d., which amount the defendants claimed to set off, and did,

1874.
June 13.
July 13.

Trustees of
Stratford *vs,*
Mosenthal & Co.

1874.
June 13.
July 13.

Trustees of
Stratford *vs.*
Mosenthal & Co.

with the concurrence of the said Stratford, set off against the aforesaid amount of £2,000; the said Stratford at the date of such sale, contemplating the sequestration of his estate as insolvent, and intending thereby to prefer the defendants over and before his other creditors. Wherefore, and by reason of the 84th section of Ordinance No. 3, of 1846, the plaintiffs claimed that the set-off made in consequence of such sale was an undue preference, and null and void, and they prayed that it might be so declared, and that the defendants should be condemned to pay the said amount of £1,173 7s. 2d., with interest thereon, to the plaintiffs for the benefit of the insolvent estate; and further, that under section 88 of the said Ordinance No. 3, of 1846, the defendants might be declared to have forfeited their right to prove the amount of such undue preference upon the insolvent estate on the ground that such undue preference was received by the defendants by or through a collusive agreement, mutual understanding, or common consent between the defendants and the insolvent, the one to give and the other to get such undue preference. The declaration further set forth, that on or about the 22nd September, 1872, a further quantity of wool was sold by Stratford to the defendants for £2,824 6s. 1d.; that at the time of the sale the said last mentioned wool had been pledged by Stratford to the London and South African Bank for £2,579 3s. 6d., and the defendants, on making the purchase, promised and' undertook not only to pay off of such pledge, but also to pay into the said bank to Stratford's credit the balance of the purchase price, to wit, the sum of £245 2s. 6d., but that, in breach of such promise and undertaking, the defendants retained such last-mentioned sum in their own hands, and claimed to set it off and did set it off against the debt owing to them by Stratford, the defendants well knowing at the time that Stratford contemplated the sequestration of his estate as insolvent. Wherefore the plaintiffs prayed that the defendants might be condemned to pay to them, for the benefit of the insolvent estate, the said sum of £245 6s. 1d., together with interest and costs of suit, &c.

The defendants pleaded the general issue.

The notes of the evidence adduced at the trial in the Court below were very brief, but the material facts proved appeared to be the following :—Stratford, for some time before his insolvency, carried on an extensive wool-washing establishment at Uitenhage, and had large dealings besides as a buyer and seller of wool. Among his clients were the respondents, merchants at Port Elizabeth, who not only supplied him with orders for the washing of their wool, but also from time to time either purchased wool from him or sold wool to him, and sometimes shipped wool on his account. 1874.
June 13.
July 13.
Trustees of
Stratford vs.
Mosenthal & Co. About the 25th of August, 1872, one Weston, at Stratford's request, had an interview with Louis Bramson, a partner in the respondent's firm, and after telling him that Stratford had heavy payments to meet, solicited the assistance of that firm, but it was not quite clear what the nature of the assistance asked for was. Upon Bramson expressing a wish to know the state of Stratford's affairs, Weston gave him an approximate estimate of Stratford's assets and liabilities, which showed an excess of liabilities to the extent of £700. Against this deficiency, however, was to be allowed the value of certain improvements on Stratford's property which seemed to have been omitted in the computation of assets, as well as a balance then owing to him by the London and South African Bank; but it did not appear whether such additional assets fell short of or exceeded the sum of £700. The result of the interview was that Bramson made no direct promise of assistance, but said he wished to see a statement of Stratford's affairs on paper, and if it should be found satisfactory, assistance to the extent of two or three thousand pounds would be given. Bramson added that this sum would very soon be "washed out," i.e., that it would be paid off by means of Stratford's earnings for washing the respondent's wool. On the 11th September, Bramson, having large orders for wool from the Continent, went to Stratford's establishment at Uitenhage and purchased on behalf of his firm 50 bales of wool (being the only wool belonging to Stratford that was unpledged) for the sum of £1,173 7s. 2d. At the same time Stratford told Bramson that he had about 100 bales of wool lying at Port Elizabeth and pledged to the Bank, and the latter said that he would examine it. On this day (September 11th) a promissory note, made by Stratford in favour of the respondents, fell due, and was paid in the ordinary course by the Bank where it was payable, and the effect of this payment was to overdraw Stratford's account at the Bank. At this time the respondents held two other promissory notes, made by Stratford in their favour, viz., one for £1,333 0s. 3d., falling due on the 15th September, and the other for £444 14s. 5d., falling due on the 19th September. It appeared that upon the conclusion of the sale of the 11th September, Bramson proposed to Stratford that the price of the wool should be set off against Stratford's notes as they fell due, and that this proposal was tacitly assented to by Stratford. It appeared, also, that it is one of the customary terms of wool sales at Port Elizabeth that the price should be paid in cash on delivery. On the 16th December, the respondents sent to Stratford a statement of his account up to that date, which

F 2

showed a balance in his favour of £9 10s., this balance being arrived at by deducting the sum of £1.333 0s. 3d. (amount of promissory note, due September 16th) from the sum total of the washing amount for August (£169 3s. 1d.) and the purchase price of the wool £1,173 7s. 2d. On the 19th September the respondents wrote the following letter to Stratford :—" Dear Sir,—The present serves to inform you that your acceptance of £444 14s. 5d., which fell due this day, and is made payable at the London and South African Bank, was duly presented at that institution, but not honoured. With the view of rendering you every assistance, we are willing to let the amount go against your washing accounts, and you can pay us by instalments." On the 22nd September, Stratford, being at Port Elizabeth, sold to the respondents the wool that was pledged at the Bank, for the price of £2,824 6s. 1d. the engagement being that this sum was to be paid into the Bank to the credit of Stratford. On the following day the respondents released the wool by paying to the Bank the amount for which the same had been pledged, viz., £2,579 3s. 7d., and retired Stratford's notes for that amount; but having been informed that Stratford was in difficulties, and apprehending that he would not be in a position to wash any more wool so as to pay off the note due on the 19th September, they refused to pay the balance of £245 2s. 6d. into the Bank, but retained the same to meet that note. On the 23rd of October, Stratford's estate was placed under sequestration, and on the 13th of January of the following year the appellants were appointed trustees of his insolvent estate.

Judgment was given for defendants with costs. From this decision the plaintiffs appealed. Mr. Justice Smith in his reasons for his judgment said :—" I think it is not a case of undue preference at all. If any action is maintainable, it should have been for the sum of £245, due to the insolvent under contract. The Bank are the real parties injured by the breach of agreement, but they were not privy to it."

Cole (with him *Ross-Johnson*) for the plaintiffs and appellants, contended that the circumstances attending the sale of the wool by Stratford to defendants clearly showed that an undue preference had been given them; and that at the time of the transaction Stratford must be taken to have had in contemplation the surrender of his estate. The delivery of this wool to defendants was the act that brought the transaction under the 84th section of the Insolvent Ordinance. Counsel relied on the principles laid down Lord by Justice Knight Bruce in the case of *Smith* vs. *Carpenter*, 12, *Moore*, *P.C.C*, 101 ; *Buch*, 1869, p. 206 ; and by the Supreme

Court in *Daneel's Trustees* vs. *Van der Byl* (reported in *Cape Argus*, July 2, 1861).

Jacobs, A.G. (with him *Maasdorp*), for the defendants and respondents, replied that the cases cited by the other side could not now be taken as settling the law as to what was contemplation of insolvency, as these cases had been overruled by later decisions. The true doctrine was to be found in *Paterson's* case (*Thurburn* vs. *Steward*, 3, L.R., P.C.C., 518). Contemplation of insolvency was now considered a question of fact, and as this was therefore an appeal from a decision of a judge on a question of fact, this Court should not, except on very strong grounds shown, disturb the judgment of the Court below. (*Kent* vs. *Ogilvie, Buch*, 1869, p. 9.) From *Pocock's Trustees* vs. *Harris's Executors, Buch.*, 1869, p. 153, it appeared that the insolvency must be in contemplation at the time of giving the preference. The onus of proving this was on the plaintiff. The evidence in this case tended to the conclusion that the business carried on by Stratford was a living, going concern at the date of the transaction in question. Defendants had gained no advantage over the other creditors of Stratford beyond what was legitimately due to them for their vigilance.

Cole and *Ross-Johnson* replied.

Cur. adv. vult.

Posteà (July 13), the Court gave judgment affirming the decision of the Circuit Court.

De Villiers, C.J. :—The objects of the present action, as stated in the summons, are—Firstly, to recover on behalf, of the insolvent estate the sum of £1,173 7s. 2d., being the price of the wool sold on the 11th September, as an undue preference under the 84th section 'of the Insolvent Ordinance. Secondly, to have it declared that the respondents have, under the 88th section of the same Ordinance, forfeited their right to prove the amount of the undue preference on the insolvent estate. And thirdly, to recover the sum of £245 2s. 6d. as having been retained by the respondents in breach of their promise and undertaking to pay the same into the bank. The decision of the learned judge presiding at the Circuit Court was in favour of the respondents on all the counts. The first count of the summons is open to the objection that it does not distinctly specify the transaction which is impeached as an undue preference. It alleges that the insolvent intended by the *sale* of the wool to prefer the respondents before his other creditors, but it proceeds to pray that the *set off* made in consequence of such sale may be declared an undue preference. It will be found, however, that the 84th section of Ordinance 6, of 1843, does not mention either a sale or a set off as a transaction capable of being set aside as an undue preference. Upon my pointing out this difficulty to the appellants' counsel, he said that the transaction which they complain of is the *delivery* of the wool to the respondents, and he quoted the case of *Trustees of Daneel* vs. *Van der Byl* (reported in *Cape Argus*, July 2nd, 1861), as one in which the declaration had been framed in similar terms, and no objection taken thereto, either by the Court, or by the defendants. The difficulty in the present case is, that there is no evidence as to the date of the delivery, the examination in the Circuit Court having been confined to the day of the sale. We may assume, however, for the purposes of this case, that the delivery took place on the day of the sale, and, as no objection was taken by the respondents' counsel to the form of summons, I shall proceed to inquire whether there is sufficient evidence before the Court to justify the conclusion that the insolvent on that day contemplated the sequestration of his estate as insolvent, and intended by the sale and delivery of the wool to prefer the respondents directly or indirectly before his other creditors. That Stratford was then already in difficulties and could not meet his liabilities and that Bramson knew it there can be no doubt, for this is sworn to by the insolvent and not denied by Bramson. Indeed, from the admission paper put in it appears that at the time when Stratford took over the wool-washing establishment his liabilities exceeded his assets by £1,445; the deficiency being at that time greater than what Weston represented it to be in August, 1872. But it is equally clear that Stratford all along entertained sanguine hopes that his difficulties would be removed; hopes which were strengthened after the sale by Bramson's promise on behalf of the respondents to alleviate his difficulties; hopes which cannot be deemed ill-founded when we bear in mind the nature of his business, that of wool-washing being described by Weston as "very successful," and that of wool buying and selling as " not very unsuccessful." In this respect the present case materially differs from that of *Smith* vs. *Carpenter* (12, *Moore*, *P.C.C.*, p. 101), which was strongly relied upon by the appellants' counsel; for there all the circumstances of the case, including the insolvents' position in life, the nature of their business (that of bakers), and the nature of the impeached transaction (viz., passing a mortgage bond in security of an existing debt) led the Privy Council irresistibly to the conclusion that the insolvents were at the date of the bond, in a state of deep and hopeless insolvency, and intended to prefer the defendants before their other creditors. In the case of *Pocock's Trustees* vs. *Executors of Harris* (*Buch.* 1869, p. 157), where the transaction challenged was a security alleged to have been given in contemplation of insolvency, the late Chief Justice made the following very apposite remarks: "The period," he said, "which the Court has resorted to for solving the question of contemplation of sequestration has been that at which the debtor gave the security the subject of the challenge. The Court has not, even as to that period, resorted to a dry estimate of the assets and liabilities of the debtor as if the estate were already dead through the effect of sequestration. It has looked at the business of the debtor as a living, going one, and inquired whether at the date of giving the security challenged there could have been in the minds of the insolvents any reasonable probability that the business could continue to have that character after having given the security. If the Court could see such a probability it has not felt itself justified in finding that the debtor contemplated sequestration when he gave the security challenged." And in the latest and most authoritative decision upon the construction of the 84th section of the Insolvent Ordinance, *Thurburn* vs. *Steward* (3, *L. R.*, *P.C.C.*, p. 518), Lord Cairns, in delivering the judgment of the Privy Council, said, that "the mere fact that the whole of his (the insolvent's) property would not be sufficient to pay the whole of his debts is not sufficient" to prove contemplation of sequestration; and further on he remarked that "the words 'contemplating sequestration' have received, by the construction put upon them, the meaning that the tribunal judging of the fact must be satisfied that payment was made in the view of and in the expectation of a supervening bankruptcy, and in order to disturb what would be the proper distribution of assets under that bankruptcy." It is worthy of remark in the present case, that Stratford was greatly pleased at Bramson's coming to Uitenhage, for he hoped thus to obtain a better price than at Port Elizabeth, a matter about which he would be comparatively indifferent if at that time he was expecting a supervening insolvency, and desired to disturb the proper distribution of his assets. The conclusion which I have arrived at on this part of the case, is that there is not sufficient evidence to prove that either the sale or the delivery was made in contemplation of sequestration, or with the intention to prefer the respondents before the other creditors of the insolvent. This view of the case renders it unnecessary for me to discuss the important question (which has not, however, been raised either in the pleadings or in the arguments from the bar) whether the transaction now sought to be impeached is protected by

1874.
June 13,
July 13.

Trustees of
Stratford vs.
Mosenthal & Co.

1874.
Juue 13.
July 13.

Trustees of
Stratford vs.
Mosenthal & Co.

the 86th section of the Insolvent Ordinance, which provides that where the transaction has taken place in the usual and ordinary course of trade or business, it shall be held to have taken place *bonâ fide*, and without an intention to prefer, although the insolvent at the time contemplated the sequestration of his estate; and that in every such case it shall be necessary for the trustee, seeking to set the same aside, to show the existence of some collusive arrangement, mutual understanding, or common consent between the insolvent and the creditor, the one to give and the other to get a preference over the other creditors, under colour of a transaction in the usual and ordinary course of trade or business. It follows as a necessary consequence of the views I have expressed upon the first count, that in my opinion the claim for a forfeiture under the 88th section of the Ordinance cannot be sustained. It is not easy to understand the precise nature of the third count of the summons, whether the sum of £245 2s. 6d. is claimed as damages for the respondents' breach of contract, or on the ground of their knowledge that the insolvent contemplated the sequestration of his estate. The creditor's knowledge of the insolvent's contemplation of insolvency is not mentioned in the Insolvent Ordinance as a ground for avoiding any payment made to him by the insolvent, nor has any authority from the common law of this Colony been cited in support of such a proposition. The appellant's counsel in his argument relied entirely upon the respondents' breach of contract in not paying to the London and South African Bank the whole of the purchase price of the wool bought by them on the 22nd September, as sufficient to entitle him to recover the sum claimed. Now, it would appear from Bramson's evidence that if the money had been paid to the Bank according to the agreement, the Bank, and not the insolvent, would have had the benefit of the payment. If this statement be correct it is difficult to see how the trustees, in the absence of any actual loss to the estate, can maintain the present action; but as the proofs of debt and other records in insolvency are not before the Court, it is impossible to ascertain the correctness of Bramson's statement, or to make it a ground for decision in the present case. In the view, however, which I take of the case it really is immaterial whether the balance of £245 2s. 6d. had been made payable at the Bank or to the insolvent himself. In either case there would exist mutual debts between the insolvent and the respondents upon which compensation could by law be pleaded by the respondents, and, under the 28th section of the Insolvent Ordinance, they would be entitled to demand that, in the due course of administering the insolvent estate, their own claim should be set against that of the insolvent, and that they should be allowed to prove (as they have in fact done) for the balance still due to them. The result is that in my opinion the judgment of the Circuit Court ought to be affirmed on all the counts, with costs.

1874.
June 13.
July 13.

Trustees of
Stratford vs.
Mosenthal & Co.

DENYSSEN, J., after reciting the pleadings and facts of the case, said :—The question as to what constituted an undue preference under the 84th section of the Insolvent Ordinance has been frequently considered by this Court, and among its records many decisions will be found upon it. The appeal to the Privy Council in the case of *Smith* vs. *Carpenter* was considered finally to have settled it, and upon that judgment the case of *Trustees of Daneel* vs. *Van der Byl* was decided by this Court, and not appealed from, whereas the judgment in the case of *Thurburn* vs. *Stewart* was again appealed from, and a judgment delivered differing to some extent from the judgment of the Privy Council in the former appeal, and which more or less unsettled that question again. The 84th section of the Insolvent Ordinance, No. 6, 1843, provides that every alienation, transfer, cession, delivery, mortgage, or pledge of any goods or effects, movable or immovable, personal or real, and every payment made by any insolvent to any creditor, such insolvent at the time " contemplating the sequestration either voluntary or otherwise of his estate, and intending thereby to prefer directly or indirectly such creditor before his other creditors, shall be deemed to be an undue preference," and is declared null and void. Now upon the construction of the words " contemplating the sequestration of his estate," the Judicial Committee in *Carpenter* vs. *Smith* say, " We are of opinion, notwithstanding what Messrs. Taylor have deposed, and notwithstanding their probable ignorance of book-keeping and want of skill in matters of accounts," that the question whether they were conscious when the bond was executed that they were in a state of deep and hopeless insolvency must be answered in the affirmative, and they " must be taken to have known when the bond was authorised to be, and when it was executed, that public and avowed insolvency and a sequestration were impending, and substantially inevitable." Upon which judgment the Supreme Court (Chief Justice Bell and Justice Watermeyer), in the case of the *Trustees of Daneel* vs. *Van der Byl* laid down as a rule for the reading of the 84th section, that " when the circumstances of the debtor are such, that sequestration was actually impending and substantially inevitable, as in the case of the transactions challenged, he must be taken to have contemplated sequestration, whatever may have been passing in his own mind." In the case, however, of *Thurburn* vs. *Steward* the Judicial

Committee held, that "the mere insolvency of the person making the payment is insufficient. The mere fact that at the time of the payment the whole of the property would not be sufficient to pay the whole of the debt is not sufficient. It is a circumstance, an ingredient in the case, to be considered with all the other circumstances of the case. The payment must be made in contemplation of sequestration. The words 'contemplating sequestration,' are words on which, perhaps, some criticisms may well be bestowed, but they have received, by the construction put upon them, the meaning that the tribunal, judging of the fact, must be satisfied that the payment was made in the view and in the expectation of a supervening bankruptcy, and in order to disturb what would be the proper distribution of assets under that bankruptcy." Now I cannot help remarking that there is some conflict in these several judgments; what in the case of *Thurburn* vs. *Steward* is only an ingredient to be considered with other circumstances, in order to determine whether sequestration has been contemplated, is sufficient, according to the judgments of Chief Justice Bell and Mr. Justice Watermeyer, in *Trustees of Daneel* vs. *Van der Byl*, supported by the judgment on appeal in the case of *Carpenter* vs. *Smith*, to constitute such contemplation of sequestration. In this case, however, no difficulty arises, for whatever judgment be adopted, the result would be the same. It is admitted that when the wool-washing business was taken over by Stratford from Appleby in 1871, there existed a deficiency. No doubt, according to the books, in the month of September, in the same year when the transactions now challenged took place, Stratford was in difficulties; but these difficulties do not appear to have been insuperable so as to render the sequestration of his estate actually impending and substantially inevitable. No books have been produced in support of any such state of affairs, nor was there any balance-sheet or account to justify such a statement. On the contrary, according to Mr. Weston, Stratford's assets, immediately before the 17th September, were more than sufficient to meet his liabilities, and there is no reason to doubt that with the assistance he expected, he would be able to tide over the difficulties which then existed. Such being my view of this part of the case, the question of intending unduly to prefer him has not to be considered; but it is as well to remark, that when Bramson called at the wool-washing establishment Stratford was glad to see him, for he thought he would get a better price. This is one of the motives which led to the transaction, as well as the promise of Bramson to alleviate the difficulties of Stratford, and the proposal to depart from the usual practice of paying cash on delivery did not originate with the debtor, but with the creditor, the debtor acquiescing. The declaration also refers to the 88th section of the Ordinance; but with reference to collusive arrangements between debtor and creditor, and the effect of it, after what has been above said, that question does not now arise. The only other question requiring to be referred to is that raised in the second count of the declaration, respecting the balance of £245 2s. 6d. remaining after payment to the Bank of the amount for which the wool had been pledged, and which balance the defendant agreed and undertook to pay into the Bank for account of Stratford, but which, in breach of his agreement and undertaking, Bramson retained in his hands for setting it off against a balance due to them. This alleged breach of contract at common law has to my mind been improperly mixed up with the claim of setting aside a transaction on the ground of undue preference, under the provisions of the Ordinance No. 6, 1843; and what the contemplation of sequestration has to do with this breach of contract I am at a loss to discover. But it appears to me that the plaintiffs in this case cannot claim to be placed in a better position than the creditors would have been had the money been paid, according to agreement, to the Bank; for, as a creditor, the Bank would have claimed the right to apply this balance towards liquidating the debt due by Stratford, while the creditors generally would have derived no benefit, and under those circumstances I do not think the Court should interfere under the form of the action in the matter.

FITZPATRICK, J., also agreed that the judgment of the Circuit Judge must be sustained. With regard to conflicting decisions which had been referred to, they could be explained as being progressive interpretations of a rather loosely framed law. As these interpretations progressed they became more and more liberal. The last was the one given by Lord CAIRNS, a Judge of whose eminent ability there could be no doubt.

Appeal accordingly dismissed with costs.

1874.
June 13.
July 13.

Trustees of
Stratford *vs.*
Mosenthal & Co.

EITZEN AND CO. *vs.* VAN LAUN.

Civil Imprisonment.—Salary: what proportion allowed to petitioning creditor.

Where a defendant against whom civil imprisonment had been decreed, was in receipt of a salary of £80 per annum, the Court, under the circumstances of the case, stayed execution of the decree on the payment of £2 per month.

The defendant in this case, who had been a diamond broker carrying on business at Kimberley, had been entrusted by the plaintiffs with two diamonds for sale. On the 15th January last his canvas house in which he resided was cut open and entered during the night, and the diamonds stolen. He afterwards gave a written paper to plaintiffs in which he undertook to refund to them the sum of £127 10s., as the value of the two stones. Defendant removed to Cape Town. Plaintiffs obtained provisional sentence on the document, and took out execution. A return of *nulla bona* was made to the writ, and on this return on the 13th April last a decree of civil imprisonment was obtained against him by the plaintiffs. The decree had not yet been executed.

Buchanan, for the defendant, now applied, on notice, for an order staying execution, pending the payment by defendant of £1 per month. It was stated that the defendant was utterly without means, but had just obtained a situation as clerk in the railway department at a salary of £80 per annum, out of which he had himself, wife, and child to support. The Court had on previous occasions stayed the execution of a decree of civil imprisonment on condition of periodical payments being made. (*Blake* vs. *Barrow, Dickson and Co.* vs. *Rogers, Sutherland* vs. *Bird,* 3, *Menz.,* p. 152, *et seq.*)

Jacobs, A.G., for the plaintiffs, opposed.

The Court ordered execution to be stayed during the payment by defendant of £2 per month, with liberty to plaintiffs to apply to have the payments increased should the defendant at any time be in better circumstances; also with liberty to apply for immediate execution should plaintiff deem fit. Costs of the motion to be added to the debt.

[Plaintiffs' Attorney, MOORE.
Defendant's Attorney, I. HORAK DE VILLIERS.]

POULTNEY *vs.* VAN SANTEN.

Interdict.—Passage Money.

Writ granted, attaching proceeds of the sale of a vessel which had been abandoned (though not abandoned in consequence of being unseaworthy and not fit for repairs), pending an

*action by a passenger for damages arising from non-com-
pletion of the voyage.*

The applicant and one R. P. Wheatley, in the month of April last, being then in Buenos Ayres, took their passage in the Dutch bark *Catharina Maria* for New-castle, in New South Wales, for which passage they jointly paid to respondent, the master of the vessel, the sum of £36. The vessel sailed on the 5th April, and on the 2nd May put into Simon's Bay for repairs; and having been surveyed, was, on the 19th June, declared unseaworthy or was abandoned, and was afterwards sold. The applicant and Wheatley requested that they might be sent on to Newcastle at the ship's expense, or their passage money refunded. This the respondent refused to do. The applicant on the 23rd June obtained a rule *nisi* returnable this day, attaching the proceeds of the sale of the ship and appurtenances to abide the result of an action which had been instituted by him against the respondent for specific performance of the contract of passage, or for the damages for the breach thereof.

1874.
July 13.

Poultney *vs.* Van
Santen.

Several affidavits were read. The respondent averred that his vessel was thoroughly repaired at Buenos Ayres, and was tight, staunch and strong when he left that port; that meeting with a severe storm rendered it necessary for him to put into Simon's Bay. That the vessel was there surveyed, and certain repairs were recommended ; that tenders were invited for effecting these repairs, but as the expenses to be incurred were of such an amount as would not be beneficial to the interest of all concerned, he abandoned the vessel to be sold for account of whom it might concern. That the vessel being Dutch, and her voyage having been interrupted for a cause without the fault of the master or owners, according to the Dutch commercial code, they were not liable for any damages ; but that to secure a settlement he had, on the 26th June, tendered the applicant £10 sterling, with costs up to that day, but the tender had been refused. The applicant, in reply, averred that the vessel was only temporarily repaired above the water lines at Buenos Ayres ; and that the gale spoken of was only an ordinary one, and would not have seriously injured any vessel in a tight, staunch, and seaworthy state. In a counter affidavit the respondent stated the vessel was thoroughly repaired at Buenos Ayres, as appeared from the certificate of the local agent of the Veritas International Classification of Vessels Association. The affidavit of J. M. Hoets stated that he, and the other surveyors of the vessel at Simon's Town, after several surveys held, recommended certain repairs to be made,

1874.
July 13.

Poultney *vs.* Van
Santen.

but finding subsequently from the tenders offered that
it would be more beneficial to abandon the vessel, the
surveyors recommended her to be abandoned, as was thereafter accordingly done, but not in consequence of the vessel
being unseaworthy and not fit for repairs.

Jacobs, A.G., for the applicant, now moved to have the
rule *nisi* made absolute. He urged that this was not the
proper time to decide the questions of law arising out of
this case. An action had been instituted by the applicant
on two grounds,—the first was for breach of contract of
passage, and to this the respondent had in effect answered
not that the vessel had been totally lost, but that it did
not suit him to carry out his contract, because the repairs
required were too expensive. The second cause of action
was that the vessel was unseaworthy when she left Buenos
Ayres, and therefore the applicant was entitled to damages
for breach of an implied warranty.

Cole, for the respondent, opposed the motion, and contended that the respondent was not liable to any claim. He
admitted that if the vessel had left Buenos Ayres in an
unseaworthy condition, and the master was aware of it, then
he would be liable on an implied warranty; but the affidavit
and certificate showed this was not the case. As to the
other ground of action, the leading case of *Gillan* vs. *Simpkin*,
4, *Campbell*, 241, laid down the principle that if the passage
had been commenced, and before it was concluded the vessel
was lost, the passenger could not recover any portion of the
passage money paid by him in advance; but on the other
hand, if the passage money was to be paid at the conclusion
of the voyage, and the vessel was lost before the voyage
was ended, the owner had no claim against the passenger
even for a portion of the money in proportion to the
distance completed.

DE VILLIERS, C.J., said the authority cited referred to
where the vessel was wrecked. It was not necessary now
to express any opinion as to the right of the applicant to
the damages claimed by him, nor to dispute the law
contended for on his behalf, that, as the master of a Dutch
vessel, if he were obliged by causes beyond his control to
abandon his vessel, he would not be bound to convey his
passengers to their destination or to pay damages for not so
doing. Mr. Hoet's affidavit, in which he said that the
vessel was abandoned "not in consequence of her being
unseaworthy and not fit for repairs," was sufficient to justify
further inquiry as to the causes which led to the abandon-
ment. By refusing the application the Court would

virtually put it out of the applicant's power to establish any right to which he considered himself entitled; whereas by continuing the interdict for a short time longer no injury beyond some slight inconvenience would be done to the respondent, and at the same time the question of the applicant's right to damages would remain wholly undecided.

DENYSSEN, J., and FITZPATRICK, J., concurred.

Rule made absolute accordingly with costs; attachment to issue against the proceeds of the sale of the vessel to the amount of £100.

[Applicant's Attorneys, FAIRBRIDGE & ARDERNE.
Respondent's Attorneys, REDELINGHUYS & WESSELS.]

PUTNAM vs. REDFIELD.

Partnership.—Receiver.

The Court (DE VILLIERS, C.J., diss.,) under the special circumstances of this case, on the application of one of the partners, appointed a receiver to realise the assets and liquidate the affairs of the partnership concern.

This was an application to make absolute a rule *nisi* granted in chambers on the 16th ultimo, by Mr. Justice Denyssen, at the instance of Charles Hammond Putnam, one of the partners of the firm of C. H. Putnam & Co., to interdict Louis H. Redfield, the other partner in the said firm, from receiving, and the master and agents of the barque *Killarney* from delivering, any of the goods, wares, and merchandise shipped on board the said barque, consigned to the said Putnam & Co., pending the appointment of a receiver to receive and dispose of the said goods on account of whom it might concern.

Applicant's affidavit, on which the rule had been granted, set forth, that in the month of April last the respondent, with whom applicant had become intimate by living in the same lodging house in New York, recommended that applicant should set up business in East London, in this Colony, as an importer of American manufactures, and said that 2,000 dollars American,—(about £400 sterling) would suffice to start with, and offered to advance 500 dollars. That applicant resolved on carrying out the suggestion, and a friend, Mr. Mills, offered to lend 1,500 dollars on applicant's own note of hand, secured by his life policy, which was done. That applicant then proceeded to make purchases. That just before the first purchase was

1874.
August 1.

Putnam vs. Red-
field.

concluded, respondent proposed he should join applicant, and go with him to Africa, and they ultimately agreed to go into partnership on equal terms. That goods were bought and ordered to be shipped on board the *Killarney*, bound for Algoa Bay *viâ* Table Bay. That in the meantime respondent and applicant had resolved on establishing themselves in Cape Town, and thereupon had trade cards printed as C. H. Putnam & Co. That partnership promissory notes were passed for the invoices of goods purchased, applicant signing some and respondent others, excepting for an invoice of billiard tables, for which respondent said he himself would settle, and some show cases for which applicant paid cash. That it was then arranged that applicant was to leave New York on the 25th of April for England, there to take a passage for the Cape ; and that respondent was to follow, as he required time to settle his private affairs. That the night before applicant's departure respondent drew up articles of partnership, by which respondent was empowered to dissolve the partnership upon giving ten days' notice, and that in such an event respondent was to have the liquidation of the partnership assets. That, having the most implicit confidence in respondent, and as respondent had stated applicant might rely on it that respondent would at all times act fairly and rightly by him, applicant made no demur, but signed the articles. That after he had paid for the show cases, a few articles for himself and his passage to England, applicant had about £200 in hand. That about an hour before applicant's leaving New York respondent suggested he should leave £100 with respondent, one reason assigned being that he had to pay the premium on the policy of life assurance. That applicant gave respondent £90, in two bills of exchange of £40 and £50 respectively. That applicant left New York on the 25th April, arrived in England on the 5th May, left again on the 20th, and arrived in Cape Town on Sunday, the 21st June. That respondent, had arrived in Cape Town the day before, and sent to applicant's hotel at two o'clock on the afternoon of the 21st to inform him of the fact. That as applicant was about going to visit Constantia with some friends, he sent back word to say he would call on respondent the first thing the following day. That early the next morning respondent sent to applicant, stating he wanted certain bills of lading and invoices which were in his possession, as respondent was going to the Customs House about the goods. That applicant gave the documents at once to respondent's messenger, and after breakfast called at respondent's hotel, but did not find him in. That applicant called again at three o'clock, when he found respondent sitting on the stoep talking to a

1874.
August 1.

Putnam *vs.* Red-
field.

stranger. That applicant held out his hand, when respondent pretended not to know him, and then rose and walked up the street with his companion, saying he was engaged at that moment but would see applicant in two or three minutes. That respondent returned to the hotel in about half an hour, said he was still engaged, walked hastily through the hotel, went out at the back door, jumped into a cab, and drove away. That applicant, therefore, wrote him a note demanding an explanation. That in the evening applicant received a notice of dissolution of partnership, as provided by the articles of agreement. That applicant's attorneys wrote to respondent, stating that as applicant distrusted his motives, and suspected that respondent's conduct was not actuated by good faith, he called upon him to consent to the appointment of a receiver. That no reply was received to this letter. That applicant verily believed that respondent meditated a fraud upon him, and that applicant and the creditors of C. H. Putnam & Co. would be defrauded of their just claims if respondent be not interdicted from dealing with the partnership property. That the value of the goods on board the *Killarney* was about £1,500 sterling, and that applicant was willing and desired that a receiver be appointed to dispose of them on account of the partnership creditors.

Cole, for the respondent, opposed the motion. He put in respondent's affidavit, which contradicted that of the applicant. It stated further that although the applicant had agreed to proceed direct to Cape Town, instead of so doing he remained in London for a longer period than was necessary, living in a manner far beyond his means, and made away with the balance of the money in his possession. That by the deed of agreement above mentioned, it was provided " That the said partnership should be terminable and dissolvable upon the written notice of the said Redfield to the said Putnam of ten days, and in such event the said Redfield should have full and sole control of all assets of the firm, and should make liquidation and settlement of all debts due by and to the said firm." That under the circumstances, and finding that applicant had not arrived in Cape Town before him, but, as respondent had discovered, lived in a most extravagant manner, and far beyond the sum that was necessary, at the Langham Hotel in London, and that of the money advanced by Mr. Mills the applicant had spent about 1,000 dollars, and being extremely dissatisfied with the conduct of the applicant, in whose integrity, veracity, and discretion he had lost all confidence, and foreseeing that a continuance of the business must lead

1874.
August 1.

Putnam vs. Red-
field.

to the ruin of the firm, respondent gave ten days' notice under the agreement that the partnership would be terminated at the end of that period. That the allegation of the applicant that respondent meditated fraud, was entirely false and without foundation, but that respondent intended to act in a fair and *bonâ fide* manner in accordance with the provisions of the agreement of partnership. That the applicant did not contribute a single dollar of cash or credit out of any means of his own for the goods bought, and that every one of the creditors fully understood this, and looked entirely to the respondent; and in every purchase respondent together with Mills were known as the only parties having any pecuniary responsibility. That a large proportion of the goods were unsalable here, and it was desirable to re-ship some to New York, and that therefore a loss must ensue on the shipment. That applicant was well aware that respondent was in possession of a large amount of property in New York, and was in receipt of nearly 1,200 dollars per month rental; and that applicant well knew the social position and standing of respondent in New York, and that he was perfectly good and responsible.

Jacobs, A.G., for the applicant, put in answering affidavits. Applicant deposed that it was true his own personal means were very small, and that he had been assisted by his friends; and that his sense of obligation to those friends and his desire to see that they suffered no loss constituted the grounds of this application. That while in London he did reside at the Langham Hotel, which was the chief resort of Americans in London, and that he was recommended to this hotel in the presence of the respondent, but applicant denied having spent 1,000 dollars there, or 500 dollars in New York, his outfit having cost only 150 dollars. That applicant never disputed the respondent's right to terminate the partnership at ten days' notice, but that he felt the most profound distrust of the honesty and good faith of the respondent. That as the assets of the partnership were purchased on credit or with borrowed capital, applicant was desirous that some disinterested person be appointed receiver, with power to sell the assets, pay the creditors, and divide the balance (if any) between the partners. Further, that since the interdict was granted respondent had sold an invoice of jewellery which had been bought on the partnership account, and would have received the proceeds but for a notice served on the auctioneers.

[DE VILLIERS, C.J.—The applicant chooses to make a contract by which he places it in respondent's power to dissolve the partnership on ten days' notice, and moreover constitutes the respondent the liquidating partner. How can the Court go behind that contract?]

The Court would interfere should the managing partner act illegally, or in breach of the trust reposed in him. (*Kerr on Injunctions*, p. 168.) There was reason to believe Redfield intended to make improper use of his power.

DE VILLIERS, C.J.:—That is mere suspicion. The parties have entered into a contract by which full power is given to Redfield to put an end to the partnership. The wording of the articles gives him as wide a power as any words can do. The articles provide "that the said partnership is to continue for one year from this date, unless sooner dissolved as hereinafter stated." Then further on, "that the said partnership is terminable and dissolvable upon the written notice of the said Redfield to the said Putnam, of ten days, and in such event the said Redfield is to have full and sole control of all the assets of the firm," and is to make liquidation and settlement of all debts, paying to Putnam one half of the residue. It seems pretty clear that Mills, who advanced the money to Putnam, was well aware of this contract. I do not say that if there was clear proof of the contemplation of fraud that the Court would not interfere, but I think, with a contract in these terms, a strong case requires first to be proved. It was intended that Putnam was to make as much speed as possible to this Colony. Redfield, who left New York after him, arrives here, and finding Putnam not here, and learning also about the money that was expended, seems to have been annoyed, and in a fit of temper puts an end to the partnership. I cannot say he acted very fairly in the matter, without at all events making some inquiry or hearing any explanation, but that is not the question. It is not whether Putnam has done wrong, but whether there is such misconduct or fraud on the part of Redfield as to induce this Court to interfere. As I said before, to my mind there is not sufficient proof of fraud or misconduct. It was certainly strange conduct on Redfield's part to avoid Putnam, but he seems to have been excessively annoyed, and being annoyed it is quite possible he might prefer avoiding him to having an interview. He may also have been annoyed at Putnam's preferring to go on a pleasure trip instead of coming to see a man who had made himself liable for him. This may have added to his annoyance; but whether or not Redfield only exercises a power expressly given him by the articles. Even under the English law it is perfectly clear that gross misconduct or fraud is required before the Court will interfere (*Lindley on Partnership*, 1,008, 1,017); and no authority to the contrary has been shown to exist in our law. This application proposes to take out of Redfield's hands the power he has under the contract. I do not think that should be done, and I cannot agree to establish a precedent in favour of such a proceeding. I am of opinion, therefore, that the application should be refused.

DENYSSEN, J.—I am sorry I cannot agree with the Chief Justice. The application for the rule *nisi* was made to me in Chambers, and the impression made upon me on reading the papers then was very strong, and nothing I have heard to-day has modified the impression I then formed. It appeared to me that at New York it was Putnam who first consulted Redfield about entering into business at the Cape, and that Redfield forced himself on Putnam. That was my impression. Putnam contributed through his friends three times as much as Redfield. It was agreed that Putnam should start first, and that Redfield should follow in about fourteen days. The contract, written by Redfield, was prepared only the evening before Putnam's departure. I am not satisfied as to the reason of its being delayed so late. It may have been for the purpose of preventing the friends of Putnam from making themselves acquainted with it. There is no evidence to satisfy me that Putnam had incurred any unnecessary expenses in New York, nor is there satisfactory evidence of unusual delay in London. But what takes place here? Redfield arrives the day before Putnam. Immediately on his arrival he makes out the notice for the dissolution of partnership. He first, however, sends for the invoices of the goods, and they are delivered up to him. Putnam gives up the invoices without suspecting anything, and when he tries to find Redfield, Redfield does all he can to avoid him; and subsequently Redfield disposes of some jewellery, part of the partnership assets, notwithstanding the interdict. Redfield said nothing to Putnam about his being annoyed, that he considered Putnam had been extravagant, or that the market was such as to render a winding-up expedient; and it was no doubt his intention to dispose of all of the goods when he got them under his sole control. Under these circumstances, I see nothing to induce me to change the opinion I formed at first, that a receiver should be appointed to dispose of the partnership property, and distribute the proceeds in the way provided for in the contract.

FITZPATRICK, J.—I regret that the judgment of the Court upon so important a question is not unanimous, since it would then have carried much more weight. I regret it also for another reason, for I must by my judgment do what

is a disagreeable duty to perform, namely, throw an imputation on the moral character of one of the litigants. Not
only has the misconduct of one of the partners occasioned
loss, but it indicates a prospect of further loss. I consider
that after Redfield's behaviour, if Putnam allows him to
wind up the partnership affairs under his sole and exclusive
control, he will be imperilling his own interests and living
in a fool's paradise. It was his duty to his creditors as well
as to himself to have the respondent's sinister intentions
nipt in the bud; and the appointment of a disinterested
person will secure the honest realization and distribution of
the proceeds of the assets of the partnership.

1874.
Augus
Putnam *f.Red-
field.

Rule made absolute accordingly, with costs; and Mr. A.
S. Peabody appointed receiver in terms of the notice of
motion.

[Applicant's Attorneys, FAIRBRIDGE & ARDERNE.]
[Respondent's Attorneys, REID & NEPHEW.]

GERTENBACH & BELLEW vs. MOSENTHAL.

*Arrest: personal.—Rule of Court, No. 8.—Warrant of
Attorney.*

*An application for process to issue against a defendant about
to leave the Colony, refused, as the requirements of the
8th Rule of Court, as to the filing of Warrant of Attorney
with the Registrar, had not been complied with.*

SEMBLE,—*Proof that the Warrant had been filed in the
Eastern Districts Court would be sufficient.*

This was an application, on behalf of the plaintiffs, for an
order to compel the defendant, who was about to leave the
Colony, to fix his *domicilium citandi et executandi* within the
Colony, and to find sufficient security to abide the result of
an action now pending in the Eastern Districts Court.

1874.
August 11.

Gertenbach &
Bellew vs.
Mosenthal.

Cole, for the applicants, put in the affidavit of their local
attorney, stating the circumstances of the case, and the
grounds on which he believed the defendant intended to
leave the Colony. It further stated that this application had
been first made to the Eastern Districts Court, but owing to
a difference of opinion on the part of the Judges, no order
had been made.

Jacobs, A.G., for the respondent, read answering affidavits,
and contended that the requirements of the 8th Rule of
Court had not been complied with, more particularly as to
filing with the Registrar a warrant to sue, signed by the
plaintiffs.

1874.
August 11.

Gertenbach &
Bellew vs.
Mosenthal.

The Court (DE VILLIERS, C.J., and DENYSSEN, J.), in
the absence of the warrant required by Rule No. 8, refused
the application, but without costs.

DE VILLIERS, C.J., remarked, that if it had been clearly
proved that the warrant had been filed in the Eastern
Districts Court, this Court might then probably have
entertained the application.

[Applicants' Attorneys, REID & NEPHEW.
[Respondent's Attorneys, FAIRBRIDGE & ARDERNE.]

FICK vs. WATERMEYER.

Injury: literal.—Privileged communication.—Publication.

A letter written by defendant to his father-in-law, reflecting
on the plaintiff, who was engaged to be married to a lady,
a connection of defendant's, in consequence of which
letter the intended marriage was broken off, HELD (DE
VILLIERS, C.J., diss.), *to be a privileged communication.*

1874.
August 11.
„   12.

Fick vs. Water-
meyer.

This was an action for £1,000 damages, stated in the
declaration to have been sustained by reason of the defendant, on the 6th December, 1873, at Graaff-Reinet,
contriving and maliciously intending to injure the plaintiff
in his good name, fame, credit, and reputation, having in a
certain letter addressed and sent by him to, and received by,
one John Gerard Cloete, of Wynberg, falsely and maliciously written and published of and concerning the plaintiff
the words following:—" We hear here that a Mr. Fick
(meaning the plaintiff), commonly known among his compeers as 'Freek Fick,' is to be married to Miss Dreyer, a
daughter of Mr. Frederick Dreyer (to whom the plaintiff
was then engaged to be married). Whatever the fellow
(meaning the plaintiff) made himself out to be in Cape
Town, he must have grossly misrepresented himself to have
brought about this engagement. If he (meaning the
plaintiff) were a man earning an honest living, or with any
prospect of doing so, I would not write on the subject,
although he (meaning the plaintiff) is a bird out of a bad
nest, but of all the brood he (meaning the plaintiff) is the
worst, and I think it my duty to try and warn the unfortunate young lady (meaning the said Miss Dreyer) before it
is too late, even if she were no connection of ours, that she
is throwing herself upon the tender mercies of a good-for-
nothing blackguard (meaning the plaintiff). The money he
inherited from his father, who got it together by canteen
keeping and other more questionable ways, will soon be
done for, if not at an end already. I hear his (meaning the

plaintiff's) scheme is to sell off here and move to Cape Town. That means loaf on poor Dreyer, who, I suppose, can hardly support himself. If you (meaning the said Cloete) can do anything to prevent this match (meaning the marriage between the plaintiff and the said Miss Dreyer), I think you ought to do it. I know if I were in Cape Town I should see Mr. D. (meaning Dreyer), and, as the saying is, call a spade a spade. The last time this Fick (meaning the plaintiff) did anything in the shape of business was at the Diamond-fields, whence he (meaning the plaintiff) fled under an assumed name, having been found smuggling and tampering with diggers' Kafirs for diamonds." By means of the committing of which said grievances by the defendant the plaintiff had been and was greatly injured in his good name, credit, and reputation, and brought into public scandal and disgrace, and the engagement between him and the said Miss Dreyer was broken off, notwithstanding that the plaintiff had been put to great expense in and about furnishing a house and otherwise, which expenses had become wholly lost to the plaintiff, and whereby the plaintiff was also otherwise injured and damnified.

The defendant pleaded the general issue.

Jacobs, A.G. (with him *Buchanan*), for the plaintiff, called evidence to show that the letter in question was in defendant's handwriting, that the letter had been addressed to and received by Mr. Cloete, that it had by him been given to Mr. Dreyer, and that it had afterwards been sent by Miss Dreyer to the plaintiff. Defendant was Mr. Cloete's son-in-law, and by marriage cousin to Miss Dreyer. The plaintiff himself stated that his engagement had been broken off in consequence of the letter; that he had spent about £600 in furnishing his house at Graaff-Reinet so as to be ready to receive his bride; and that he had been much annoyed and ridiculed by his friends. He also stated that none of the imputations contained in the letter were true. He had received all his letters and presents back, with the exception of £40 he had made Miss Dreyer a present of to buy her outfit.

Counsel for defendant cross-examined the plaintiff closely as to most of the charges made against him, but he denied every imputation contained in the letter.

Plaintiff then closed his case.

Cole (with him *Tennant*), for the defendant. applied for absolution from the instance on the ground that no publication of the letter by the defendant had been proved. He cited *De Lettre* vs. *Kiener*, 3, *Menz.*, 12.

Jacobs, A.G., opposed, and quoted *Starkie on Slander and Libel*, p. 424.

1874.
August 11.
„ 12.

Fick *vs.* Water-
meyer.

Absolution refused.

For the defence were called—

John Frederick Dreyer, who stated that after he had
been shown defendant's letter he had made inquiries among
his relations at Graaff-Reinet, and in consequence of their
replies and of the letter itself the engagement between his
daughter and the plaintiff had been broken off.

Petrus G. J. Watermeyer, the defendant, who stated that
when he wrote the letter to his father-in-law, he did so *bonâ
fide*, believing its contents to be true. In cross-examination
he said he still believed the contents to be true, and that he
would not withdraw a single line of the letter.

Defendant then closed his case.

Jacobs, A.G., for the plaintiff, briefly summed up on the
evidence, remarking that any defence on the ground of the
letter being a privileged communication had been blown to
the winds by the line of conduct pursued by the other side,
and by the repetition of the defamation by the defendant
while under examination. The plaintiff had courted a full
investigation, but not a single allegation against him had
been attempted to be proved.

Cole, for the defendant, contended that the close relationship of the parties between whom the letter had passed, and
the fact that the defendant had acted *bonâ fide,* made it a
privileged communication; and the defendant therefore
should not be subject to an action for libel. (*Harrison* vs. *Bush,* 25, *L. J., Q. B.,* 25; *Addison on Torts,
3rd edition,* p. 775; *Todd* vs. *Hawkins,* 8. *C. & P.,*
888). Where a communication was *primâ facie* a privileged
one, it was necessary for the plaintiff to prove malice in fact
before the defendant could be made liable. In this case no
malice had been proved. (*Bromage* vs. *Prosser,* 4, *B. & C.,*
247; *Addison on Torts,* p. 770; *Taylor* vs. *Hawkins,* 16,
Q. B., 308.)

Jacobs, A.G., for the plaintiff, replied. The letter itself
and defendant's subsequent conduct were conclusive evidence
of malice. Defendant said he still adhered to his allegations, but he had not pleaded justification, though truth
would have been a good plea. The leading case of *Harrison*
vs. *Bush,* 25, *L. J., Q. B.,* 25, fixed the legal canon as to
privileged communications to be where the party communicating had an interest or duty. The defendant in this
case had no such interest or duty as would protect him. The
case of *Todd* vs. *Hawkins,* cited on the other side, was the
strongest case yet decided, and there the letter was written
by the defendant to his mother, who was about to be married.
Even if the letter was *primâ facie* a privileged communication, evidence of express malice would take it out of the

privilege. (*Roscoe*, p. 515.) Express malice need not be proved by express evidence, but might be collected from the document itself. (*Fryer* vs. *Kinnersley*, 33, L. J., C. P., 96.) The imputations made not having been retracted aggravated the injury and called for increased damages. (*Simpson* vs. *Robinson*, 12, Q. B., 513 ; *Bailey* vs. *Abercrombie*, 3, *Menz.*, 33.)

Cur. ad. vult.

Postea (August 12th),

DE VILLIERS, C.J., in giving judgment, said :—In this case the plaintiff, who resides at Graaff-Reinet, claims £1,000 damages from the defendant, also a resident at Graaff-Reinet, for an alleged libel published by the defendant, the terms of which are contained in a letter dated 6th December, 1873 (given above). No justification has been pleaded, nor has any been proved. No fact has been proved to support the statements contained in the letter, and therefore I am bound to assume that these facts could not have been proved, and that the plaintiff's character is not so bad as it is made out to be by the letter. I may be right or wrong in this assumption, but this Court can only take judicial notice of what is brought in evidence before it; and the legal presumption is in favour of a man's good character until the contrary is proved. Every man also is entitled to have his character vindicated quite as much as he is entitled to have his life and property protected. As a rule, in every case in which a man's reputation is assailed by another there must be good and strong reasons for the attack made. No doubt there are certain exceptions to this. By the Roman law the *animus injuriandi* is of the essence of the libel ; but where the words used are themselves libellous, it lies on the defendant to show there was no *animus injuriandi*. All the authorities quoted in this case were from the English law. Useful as these were in giving the Court some assistance by analogy, it would have been better if some authorities had been referred to from the Roman-Dutch law. *Voet*, 47, 10, 20, lays down that it is a good defence on the part of the person sued for libel that there is an absence of the *animus injuriandi ;* and this must be gathered from the circumstances, nor can it be otherwise established than from the words themselves. Therefore, if the words uttered admit of a double meaning they must be interpreted in favour of their not being libellous. There is also a passage in the *Code*, 9, 35, 5, to which *Voet* refers :— *Si non convicii consilio te aliquid injuriosum dixisse probare*

1874.
August 11.
„ 12.

Fiek *vs.* Water-
meyer.

potes, fides veri a calumnia te defendit. The English law does not presume *animus injuriandi* where there is a privileged communication, and I have no doubt the same doctrine would apply here. It is, therefore, important to consider whether or not this letter is a privileged communication. In my opinion it is not. I can understand a privileged communication by a person standing in *loco parentis;* by a father writing to his child; as in the case quoted yesterday of a son-in-law warning his mother-in-law; but I should be very sorry to extend this to a letter written to a cousin. To my mind a cousin does not stand in that relationship to justify a person aspersing the character of another unless he is prepared to prove the truth of his assertions. *Todd* vs. *Hawkins* is the strongest case which has been recorded in the English Courts, and there the writer of the confidential communication was the son-in-law. There was no case in which a privileged communication had been recognized as between cousins. Assuming that the statements in the letter were false, it behoved Watermeyer to have inquired into their truth, and unless he was prepared in this Court to establish their truth, he was not justified in writing what he did. And even if the letter was a privileged communication, it went far beyond what a privileged communication ought to do. If Watermeyer's intention was to warn his friends against what he believed was an undesirable match, he could have done so in a very different manner. In the first place, why did he write to his father-in-law at all, unless his intention was that the letter should be shown to others? He might have written to Mr. Dreyer and told him to make certain inquiries. As to the allegation that the plaintiff came from a bad family, if that had stood alone I should have hesitated to say it was a libel, for the defendant might be anxious that his cousin should not marry into a family he thought beneath him. But the defendant seems to have gone out of his way to asperse the plaintiff's character. He writes of him as "usually known among his compeers as Freek Fick," and speaks of "whatever the fellow may have made himself out to be." The words of the letter throughout show animus. The plaintiff was accused of having fled from the Fields under an assumed name, having been found smuggling and tampering with the diggers' Kafirs for diamonds. The counsel for the defendant remarked that it was difficult to plead justification to a letter of this kind, but here was an assertion of a fact capable of being proved. If the defendant could not prove it he ought not to have said it. Even then, if this letter is a privileged communication, I should hesitate before deciding that there was not sufficient proof of malice on the face of it to justify the Court in giving judgment for the plaintiff. As to the damages, the object of the plaintiff seems principally to be to vindicate his character, for no real damage has been proved. This is not a case for heavy damages, and I think the ends of justice would be satisfied by a verdict for plaintiff for £50 and costs.

1874.
August 11.
,, 12.

Fick *vs.* Watermeyer.

DENYSSEN, J.—What has to be decided by the Court is simply this : Is the letter a privileged communication or is it not ; and if it is, was the defendant influenced by malice in writing from Graaff-Reinet to his father-in-law here, or did he do so *bonâ fide;* and had he sufficient interest in the proposed marriage of his cousin ? I am of opinion that this is a privileged communication. As to malice, it appears to me, although I consider the letter extravagant and to abound in vulgarity, that there is nothing to show that the defendant was influenced by malice. In writing from Graaff-Reinet he had very likely adopted some expressions which might be common there. He did not, however, do so for a malicious purpose, but to prevent a marriage between the plaintiff and a young lady connected with him by marriage. I fail to find any malice on his part. And with reference to the question of interest I think the case quite clear. Here is a gentleman married to a cousin of the young lady, and he writes to his own father-in-law for the purpose of warning the lady against an engagement with one of whose conduct he did not approve. It appears to me from a consideration of all the authorities that the defendant's conduct was perfectly justifiable. I think judgment ought, therefore, to be for defendant.

FITZPATRICK, J.—I regret that I differ from the Chief Justice not only as to the malice, but on the more important question of privilege or no privilege. I consider that the defendant had not only a duty to discharge, but had an interest in the matter as grave as it was great. The defendant was married to a first cousin of the young lady's, and a first cousin is a close relationship. The family of the young lady had a perfect right and a bounden duty to inquire into the antecedents, character, and conduct of the gentleman who proposed to form an alliance with them. If Mr. Watermeyer honestly and *bonâ fide* believed, though he could not prove it, that this young gentleman was a man without fixed employment or principles, or that he came from a family that were objectionable, as for instance a family that were going down in the world, it might be perhaps from ill luck, or that it was a ne'er-do-well family, he was entitled and bound to tell his father-in-law that such were the opinions entertained by the public in the town

1874.
August 11.
„ 12.

Fick *vs.* Water-
meyer.

where he was well known, many hundred miles away fror
the residence of the father and of the lady whose affection
he had gained. I think it was both his privilege and hi
interest, if he *bonâ fide* believed the damaging reports whicl
prevailed at Graaff-Reinet, to take steps to communicat
them to some members of his family. It is not easy t
define the limits of this privilege or interest, but it woul
be doing a great injury to society to say that every hones
bonâ fide opinion as to the desirability of an aspirant for
lady's hand was not a privileged communication. It is
privileged communication to warn a person against th
character of a servant, unless you can prove malice ; an
malice in such a case cannot be inferred. In Lord Camp
bell's judgment, referred to in the course of the argument
it was laid down that if the communication was privilegec
the plaintiff must give evidence of malice; and if ther
was no such evidence given the judge ought to direct
non-suit. If the occasion of giving a servant's character i
sufficient to repel the presumption of malice, I think givin;
an opinion to the head of a family into which a gentlemai
wished to marry was a much stronger occasion. If I ai
correct in that, is there any proof of malice? There i
none except what can be drawn from the language o
phraseology of the letter. I agree with Mr. Justic
Denyssen that the letter does not commend itself. Th
style is bad, and it is full of vague general abuse. It woul
have been more becoming if the defendant had expressec
himself differently : and I must say I agree with th
Attorney-General that the style of the cross-examinatioi
is to be condemned. But taking everything into considera
tion, I do not consider there is sufficient proof that ther
was actual malice operating on the mind of Watermeye
when he wrote this letter ; and I think he honestly believec
in the substantiality of the imputations which had been cas
upon the plaintiff. I sympathise with the plaintiff in hi
having to submit to these insinuations being made agains
his character without any attempt being made to prove them
but I feel constrained to give my opinion that this letter wa
a privileged communication. I therefore agree with m:
brother Denyssen that judgment must be for the defen
dant ; but in consequence of the way in which the plaintii
has been treated I would not give costs.

Judgment accordingly for the defendant, without costs.

STIGANT *vs.* THE TOWN COUNCIL OF CAPE TOWN.

Election of Councillors.

Where, at an annual election of Town Councillors, the official
public notice by advertisement required that nominations
of candidates were to be sent in "On or before Mon-
day, the 21st July" (the 21st July in reality being a
Tuesday), and the notice was afterwards corrected to
" Monday, the 20th July," and persons had been misled
thereby, and sent in nominations on the 21st July, which
nominations were rejected by the Town Council, and the
election ordered to proceed between those persons only who
had been nominated on or before the 20th July, HELD—
that the persons nominated on the 21st July were entitled
to be placed on the list of candidates together with those
nominated up to and on the 20th July.

The respondents had been called upon to show cause why
they should not be interdicted from proceeding with the
election of Councillors for the Town Council of the Municipality of Cape Town, by reason :—First, that the notice
calling for the nomination of candidates for seats in the Town
Council for the ensuing year fixed a day of the week and
date of the month which did not correspond. Second, that
the said Town Council had refused to entertain certain
nominations of candidates for seats in the Town Council for
the ensuing year, sent in on the date of the month mentioned
in the said notice. Third, that the Town Council
had violated and neglected the provisions of section 31,
of Act No 1, of 1861. And also to show cause why
all the proceedings had and taken by the said Town
Council for the nomination and election of Councillors for
the ensuing year should not be declared illegal and null and
void, and a new nomination and election ordered in its
stead.

Jacobs, A.G., for the applicant, put in his affidavit, which
stated that the provisions of the 31st section of the Act No.
1, of 1856, relative to the framing and posting of annual lists
of householders, had not been complied with. Further, that
on the 26th June, 3rd, 7th, and 14th July, 1874. a notice
appeared in the *Gazette*, dated the 25th June, 1874, pur-
porting to be by order of the Town Council, calling upon
the householders of the several districts to nominate in
writing " on or before Monday, the 21st proximo (meaning
thereby the 21st July), at 12 o'clock noon, three candidates
for each of the said districts." That on the 27th and 30th

1874.
August 13.

Stigant *vs.* The
Town Council of
Cape Town.

1874.
August 13.

Stigant *vs.* The
Town Council of
Cape Town.

June, a similar notice appeared in the *Standard and Mai*
That in the *Gazette* of the 17th July the notice was altere
to " the 20th proximo." That in the *Standard and Mail* c
the 9th July, the words " 21st proximo," were altered to th
" 21st instant ; " and in the issue of the 16th July to " th
20th July." That the former notices were erroneous, a
Monday was the 20th July. That naming the 21st Jul
had the effect of misleading and did mislead the applican
That applicant had been nominated as a candidate to repre
sent several districts, and such nominations were sent in to th
Secretary to the Municipality before noon on the 21st July
but they, together with certain nominations of other person
were rejected by the Town Council, on the ground that al
nominations should be sent in before noon on the previou
day, the 20th July. That notice had been given by th
Town Council to proceed to the election of Town Councillor
on Monday, the 17th August, which election, if not inter
dicted, would take place and be carried out upon the lis
of candidates sent in on the 20th July, thus excludin
the applicant and others from the opportunity of bein
elected.

Cole, for the respondents, read answering affidavits deny
ing several of the allegations made by the applicant, bu
admitting the fact of the error in the date given in the notice
which error was corrected as soon as discovered. It wa
also averred that the nominations accepted and recorded o
Monday, the 20th July, for the several districts were i
each instance for the full number of Councillors to be elected
and in some cases for more than the number.

The Court declared that the nominations sent in o
Tuesday, the 21st July, were good and valid nominations
and ordered amended lists of candidates be at once publishe
in the *Gazette* and *Standard and Mail.* The election t
proceed on the day fixed, all the candidates nominate
to be eligible. Respondents to pay costs.

[Applicant's Attorney, C. C. DE VILLIERS.
Respondents' Attorneys, FAIRBRIDGE & ARDERNE.]

REDELINGHUYS AND OTHERS vs. SILBERBAUER.

Interdict.—Nuisance.

An injunction against proceeding with the erection of a steam engine and flour mill in Cape Town, refused, no clear case being made out that a sensible injury to health and property, and to the general comfort of the neighbourhood, would result therefrom.

This was an application for an injunction to restrain the respondent from proceeding with the erection of a steam engine and mill for grinding flour, &c., in a store recently purchased by him, situated in St. George's Street, Cape Town, adjoining the properties of the applicants, on the grounds, amongst others, that it would materially interfere with the health and ordinary comforts of the applicants, and would, moreover, seriously injure and deteriorate in value the properties adjoining the said projected steam mill, or in its immediate neighbourhood, by the great and incessant vibration and noise it would produce and by the smoke, soot, and vapour that would be emitted.

1874.
August 13.

Redelinghuys &
Others vs.
Silberbauer.

In support of the application were read a number of affidavits, including some deposed to by medical men, by engineers, and by persons resident in the neighbourhood of other steam mills in other parts of Cape Town, to show that a steam mill was a nuisance to adjoining proprietors.

For the respondent directly contradictory affidavits, also from professional men and from others, were put in. The respondent stated further that owing to the adoption of new improvements the steam engine and mill in question would, in fact, not create any nuisance.

Jacobs, A.G. (with him *Buchanan*), for the applicants, submitted that though the engine had not yet been erected, and no nuisance was actually in existence, still it was competent for the Court to grant an injunction, where it was satisfied a nuisance would inevitably result. The affidavits showed that similar erections in other parts of the city were nuisances. (*Kerr on Injunctions*, pp. 339, 349, 350, 361, and 363; *Erskine's Institutes*, p. 194; *V. d. Linden*, p. 441.)

The Court, without calling on *Cole* to reply, refused the application with costs.

DE VILLIERS, C.J., said there was no doubt the Court had power to interfere if a clear case had been made out that there would result a sensible injury to health and property and to the general comfort of the neighbourhood, but no such clear case was now before the Court.

[Applicants' Attorney, WESSELS.
Respondent's Attorneys, REID & NEPHEW.]

GIFFORD *vs.* TABLE BAY DOCK AND BREAKWATER MANAGEMENT COMMISSION.

[The " China."]

Patent Slip.—Negligence.—Master: authority of, to sue fo
injury to vessel.—Pleading.

The defendants, a Board vested with the control of a Paten
Slip, held liable for the negligence of the person entrustec
by them with the direction of the Slip and with th
superintendence of the taking up of vessels thereon.

A Master of a vessel has sufficient authority to sue for damage.
for loss occasioned by the wrongful acts of defendants oi
their servants.

Objection to the title of a Master of a vessel to sue in thi.
Colony on behalf of his owners residing abroad, should b
taken on exception, and not under the general issue.

1874.
August 27.
„   28,
„   29.
„   31.
September 1.

Gifford *vs.* Table Bay Dock and Breakwater Management Commission.

This was an action for damages. The declaration set forth that the plaintiff was the master and was lawfully in command of the barque *China*, of New Bedford, Mass., a vessel of the value of £3,500, bound on a whaling voyage, but then in the Alfred Dock of Table Bay. That the defendants, in their capacity as Commissioners, had the care, direction, and management of a certain patent slip situated in and being part of the said Alfred Dock. That it became expedient to put and take the *China* upon the said patent slip for the purpose of effecting certain repairs. That in consideration of the sum of £137 12s. 6d. agreed on the 10th July to be paid by plaintiff to defendants, the defendants undertook and engaged to haul or take up the *China* on the said patent slip. That thereafter, on the 29th July, the *China* was taken charge of by one Christopher Robertson, a person by the defendants employed and entrusted with the duties connected with the hauling or taking up vessels on the said patent slip. That the plaintiff surrendered the command of the *China* to Robertson, and ordered his officers and men to obey the commands of Robertson. That in executing the several orders of Robertson the said officers and men were assisted by others in the service of defendants. That Robertson, acting as aforesaid, not regarding his duty, and whilst the *China* was being hauled and taken on the said patent slip, negligently, carelessly, unskilfully, and improperly slipped or attempted to slip the said barque, so that owing to his negligence, carelessness, want of skill, and improper conduct, the *China* fell off the cradle of the patent slip and thereby became a total wreck, to the loss and damage of the plaintiff in the said sum of £3,500 sterling. That the plaintiff had sustained further loss to the amount of £1,000 from loss of voyage and other earnings. Wherefore he prayed judgment for the said sum of £3,500, and for the sum of £1,000 as and for damages sustained as aforesaid, tendering to make delivery and yield possession of the hull of the said vessel with her masts, spars, &c., on payment of the said damages.

1874.
August 27.
„   28.
„   29.
„   31.
September 1.

Gifford vs. Table
Bay Dock and
Breakwater
Management
Commission.

The defendants pleaded, first, the general issue. Secondly, that they did not undertake or engage to haul up the vessel as in the declaration mentioned. Thirdly, that the vessel was not taken charge of by Robertson for or on behalf of the defendants or with their authority; and that the vessel was not, at the time it sustained the injuries complained of, in the charge, control, care, or custody, or under the command of the defendants or their agents. Fourthly, that at the time the vessel was hauled and taken up on the slip the defendants hauled and took up certain vessels upon the said slip upon certain terms and conditions only, amongst others upon condition that the defendants should not be liable for any damages which might happen to any vessel in taking up the same upon the slip; and that the plaintiff or his agent, well knowing the premises, had the vessel hauled and taken up on the slip, and thereby became bound by the said terms and conditions. Fifthly, that the vessel was taken up on the slip upon the terms and conditions that the defendants should not be liable for any consequences of any damage which might happen in taking the said vessel up on the slip. Sixthly, that before and at the time the vessel was taken up on the slip, the plaintiff represented to the defendants that there were only a few empty casks and certain other things not of any weight between the decks of the said vessel; and that the defendants, relying upon these representations, took the vessel up on the slip; but that in fact there were at the time about 60 tons weight of things between decks, and that had the defendants known of the said weight they would not have taken the vessel on the slip as they did; and that the said excess of weight caused or materially contributed to the injury sustained by the vessel, and that therefore the plaintiff was not entitled to recover in this action.

The replication was general.

Cole (with him Buchanan), for the plaintiff, after putting in letter of demand and other correspondence, led the following evidence :—

Henry Wilson.—I am the Harbour and Dock Master of Table Bay. Among other things under the management of defendants is the patent slip. Christopher Robertson has charge of the slip, and takes up the vessels thereon and launches them. No one but himself, as far as I remember,

H

1874.
August 27.
„   28.
„   29.
„   31.
September 1.

Gifford vs. Table
Bay Dock and
Breakwater
Management
Commission.

has had charge of the slip. Robertson is a master shipwright, and carries on a business of his own in Cape Town.

Daniel Louis Gifford.—I am plaintiff. I was the master of the barque *China*, of 367 tons, belonging to the port of New Bedford, U.S., bound on a whaling voyage to the South Seas. We put into Table Bay on the 28th June for the purpose of sending home oil and for repairs. I discharged my cargo of oil to send home. It took some weeks doing. I engaged Robertson to do the repairs, and he was on board and about the ship from day to day. I spoke to him on two or three different occasions about going on the slip. About the 20th July I determined to have my vessel hauled up. Afterwards I went with Mr. Peabody (my agent) to the Harbour Board's office (defendants'). We saw Mr. Thwaits, the chief clerk. My agent told him I had come to see when the *China* could be taken on the slip. Thwaits said the *Namaqua* was then on the slip, but we could go on when she came off. We went again to Thwaits about a week or ten days after. Thwaits then said the slip would be ready about the first of the next week. This was on a Wednesday or Thursday. Nothing whatever was said about conditions on which vessels were taken on the slip. I heard about the price charged. On the Friday or Saturday after, Robertson told me the *Namaqua* was off the slip, and there would be a chance for the *China* to go on. I said I would be ready on Monday. When Monday came Robertson came on board and said the ship was too much down by the stern. I had some cargo in the lower hold moved midships to remedy this. Robertson came on board on Tuesday, but the weather was not favourable. He looked over the ship then to see how she was trimmed. I can't say if he saw the hold on Tuesday, but he had been down into it the week before. No more cargo was put in after he had seen the hold. He passed through between decks into the hold. About twenty casks were taken off the upper deck and put between decks so as to clear the ship for working. We had about 150 barrels of water between decks. Robertson recommended these barrels to be started, which was done. This was for the purpose of lighting the ship, not because she was top-heavy. The yards had been removed, and there was nothing but the lower masts standing. The anchors were taken out and put into a lighter, and the cables run down to the hold. On Tuesday afternoon I took Robertson on board to see if the vessel was right for going on the slip. He pronounced her in every way all right. I never before this had had a vessel on a slip. About eleven o'clock on Wednesday morning Robertson came on board. He made no remark about the ship. He dined with me about half-past twelve.

I said I had to go on shore on urgent business, and asked if
he wanted anything or if I should remain. He said no,
if he wanted anything he could call on my mate. Before
leaving I gave orders for my officers and crew to act under
Robertson's orders. I left and returned about three o'clock,
when I found the *China* capsized and stove in. That
evening at his shipyard I asked Robertson about the accident.
He could assign no reason for it. I never saw Mr. Saunders,
the Secretary to the Board, till the morning after the accident.
I saw him afterwards at Mr. Peabody's office, when he had a
printed form with him. The *China* was fifty-four or fifty-
five years old, American built, of live oak, and in very good
condition. She was fitted out for a four years' voyage. The
voyage so far had been successful. I value the *China* at
25,000 dollars (£5,000). I have a share in the profits of the
voyage. I do not know if the *China* was insured. Robertson sent in a tender for the repairs. He did not tender to
take the vessel on the slip. He told me he was the man
who took up vessels on the slip. I cannot say if he said anything about the Harbour Board. Before the accident I
never heard directly or indirectly of any terms or conditions
on which vessels were slipped. I don't remember Robertson
asking what I had on board. I did not tell him I had only
some empty casks and a few shooks between decks. He did
not tell me that if there was anything between decks it might
cause an accident. I had altogether between fourteen and
fifteen tons between decks (articles specified). There were
seventy-one tons by weight in the whole ship.

Frederick Cushman Swaine.—I was chief officer of the
China. I saw Robertson on board several times. He said
the vessel wanted to be raised more by the stern. That was
done. Robertson was on board on Tuesday and expressed
himself satisfied. On Wednesday Captain Gifford told me
before he went on shore to do whatever Robertson ordered.
I did so. Drysel, the diver, came with about ten men, and
Robertson told him to take charge forward and he would
take charge aft. The vessel was placed on the cradle, and
we hauled the two forward blocks taut, and then the two
middle ones. The two after blocks were not in my presence
hauled at all. Robertson gave the orders to the men on
board. He then went on shore with his men, and I began
clearing up the decks. The vessel was coming out of the
water gradually all the time. Robertson was watching her
from the shore. He left her twenty minutes or half an hour
before she capsized. The vessel had a little list to starboard
as she came out of the water. I did not call out to Robertson about it, as it could be seen from the shore. I think the
list caused the capsize. It threw the strain all on one side.

1874.
August 27.
„ 28.
„ 29.
„ 31.
September 1.

Gifford *vs.* Table
Bay Dock and
Breakwater
Management
Commission.

1874.
August 27.
„ 28
„ 29
„ 31.
September 1.

Gifford vs. Table
Bay Dock and
Breakwater
Management
Commission.

If the blocks had been properly secured she could not have
listed. She might have had a little list before she went on
the slip, but if so it was very little. There were about fifteen
tons between decks, and from fifty to sixty tons in the hold.
If Robertson had complained there was nothing to prevent
it being taken out. Robertson had several opportunities
for seeing what was on board. I did not notice any list
before the blocks were hauled under the vessel. There was
one of Robertson's men in a boat feeling with an oar if the
blocks were hauled taut. The wind had breezed up about
noon that day and then died away. The vessel went over
all at once. We heard no crack or noise of anything giving
way.

Giles Peleg Slocum.—I was third mate on board the
China. The list of articles between decks as stated by the
captain is correct. Robertson was between decks and in the
hold several times. He measured the ship from inside pre
paratory to going on the slip. I was on board and saw a
list in the ship after they began to haul her up on the slip
I had not seen any list before that time. I will swear there
was nothing between decks besides what is mentioned in the
list except a small cannon. The after blocks of the slip
were not hauled taut that I know of. The forward and
middle blocks were hauled taut and properly secured.
saw the list about twenty minutes before the accident. No
repairs were going on in the hold or between decks.

Thomas Kehoe.—I am a master mariner and now work a
a rigger. I was on board the day before the accident. The
China had nothing standing above her lower masts. After
the accident I was employed by the captain to discharge
the cargo. I took out from between decks about thirty ton
estimated by weight and measurement together. By weigh
alone I should say there were sixteen or seventeen tons.
took out of the lower hold about sixty tons weight at the
outside. The *China* was anything but top-heavy for going
on the slip. I recollect the *Gondola,* a ship about twenty o
thirty tons larger than the *China,* being taken up on the slip
with top-mast and top-mast yards standing. The *E. &*
Lemon, a vessel about the same size as the *China,* was taken
up with several hundred tons of sugar in the lower hold.
am well acquainted with the working of slips, and know well
what they ought to be. I attribute the accident to some
fault in the blocks or in the tackle. If there had been
list it might have caused a block to give way, in consequence
of the weight of the vessel being thrown on the blocks.
was employed on a slip in Nova Scotia, of which my father
was superintendent. The blocks used there are differently
made from those used here. I am certain about the quantit

1874.
August 27.
„ 28.
„ 29.
„ 31.
September 1.

Gifford vs. Table
Bay Dock and
Breakwater
Management
Commission.

of cargo on board. I had about fourteen men at work getting it out, and I was present all the time with the exception of my meal hours.

Henry Wilson, recalled.—Captain Perry and myself were employed by the Harbour Board to inquire into the cause of the accident. I received instructions, I presume, as an officer of the Board. We sent in our report.

Cole called for the report, notice to produce having been given. He quoted *Pothier on Ob.*, vol. 2, p. 144.

Jacobs, A.G., objected that a report made by an officer of a Board to such Board was not evidence. He further declined to produce the document, and in support of his right to do so cited *Taylor on Ev.*, sec. 410.

Witness continued.—It was a favourable day for taking up the ship. The wind was not strong enough to blow over a vessel properly secured on the cradle. I think the cause of the accident must have been some fault in the blocking, combined with the list the ship had, and the gusts of wind coming on the vessel's quarter throwing such a strain on the block caused the rope to give way, the block consequently receded, the block having too sharp an angle. Considering that all the top hamper was down, the amount of cargo on board was not sufficient to have capsized the vessel. There might be no danger in taking up a vessel with a slight list, but if the list was more than slight the vessel ought to be launched and put upright on the cradle. I have seen the *China* since she has been cut up, and estimate her value at £6 a ton. I hand a copy of the Dock Regulations (containing particulars of charges for use of slip) by the authority of the Board to every vessel coming to this port. Generally the cargo is in the lower hold when a ship is taken on the slip. If a ship had sixty tons between decks and nothing in the lower hold, I don't think any man would attempt to take her up in that condition. Very little gives a vessel a list, especially if she has a fine floor like the *China* had. With a fine floor more precaution should be taken. The *China* had a camber in her keel. They have taken up several ships with camber on the slip. I think the camber had something to do with the capsize. The diver might have discovered the camber. Robertson is generally very careful. When there is a camber it is usually provided for in fitting the cradle. The fine bottom of the ship can be ascertained from inside, and can be provided against by putting more blocks. The Harbour Board pay Robertson.

Captain Hoets.—I have assisted at slipping a good many vessels at the Simon's Town patent slip. I surveyed the *China* after her arrival at this port. There was nothing to render her unfit to go on the slip. A camber is very com-

1874.
August 27.
„ 28.
„ 29.
„ 31.
September :.

Gifford vs. Table
Bay Dock and
Breakwater
Management
Commission.

mon in vessels. Its existence can be ascertained by the diver. The blocks on the cradle as a matter of course ought to be arranged to meet the camber. A vessel having sixty tons of cargo in the lower hold, and sixteen or seventeen tons or even sixty tons between decks, with all the top hamper down, would be in a fit condition to go on the slip. The fine bottom would only require more caution, not necessarily incapacitate a vessel from being taken up. I attribute the accident to something wrong with the blocks on the cradle. The *China* was a fine, sound, old vessel. I would put the ship down as worth £2,500 without whaling gear. The amount of cargo on board a vessel is not of so much consequence as how it is distributed. A vessel of 360 tons, with sixty or eighty tons in the lower hold, can safely be taken upon the slip with forty tons between decks. If I was going to take a vessel on the slip and found too much between decks, I would ask to have it discharged. The blocks are built to fit the model of the ship, not the cargo on board. This was not a very crank ship, nor do I consider the camber she had a dangerous one. When a ship has a list the best thing is to launch her again. The accident may have occurred without the fault of any one. Ships ought to be insured against risks of this sort. There are certain policies in which risk of shipping is insured against. I have not examined the cradle or blocks. I should make myself acquainted with what cargo was on board before I attempted to slip a vessel. Either the blocks or a rope gave way, or the weight of the vessel, increased by the puff of wind, must have proved too great a strain on the arms of the cradle.

Alfred Symonds Peabody.—My firm were agents for the *China*. Saunders, the Secretary of the Board, came to my office the morning after the accident with a printed form for the captain or myself to sign. He said it was ready for signature and should have been signed before the ship was taken up, and that Robertson was not authorised to put the *China* on the slip, as he ought to have waited for orders from the Board's office. I have been agent for several vessels which have been put on the slip, and know that the Board have usually asked us to sign conditions. I did not tell the captain of these conditions. The last vessel we had on the slip was a year and a half ago. Of the two conditions produced, my partner, I see, signed one and the captain of the ship the other. My attention was in no way called to these conditions when we went to the Board's office. I know from general knowledge that Robertson put the vessels on the slip. We paid the charge to the Board.

George Thompson spoke of two occasions when vessels with 350 and 450 tons of cargo on board had been taken up on the slip. The captains signed the conditions on both these occasions.

The plaintiff then closed his case.

1874.
August 27.
„   28.
„   29.
„   31.
September 1.

Gifford *vs.* Table Bay Dock and Breakwater Management Commission.

Jacobs, A.G., applied for absolution from the instance, on the ground, first, that the plaintiff had not proved any interest in the vessel to authorize him to bring this action. The plaintiff was only master of the vessel, not a part owner, and had no authority to sue from the owners.

The Court refused the motion, as this objection ought to have been raised on exception.

Jacobs, A.G., again applied for absolution, on the grounds that no liability on the part of the defendants had been proved; and that the defendants being Commissioners appointed by Act of Parliament, they were not personally liable, and there was no property against which execution could issue if judgment was given against them in their corporate capacity. He cited the Act No. 22, 1872, and *Addison on Torts,* p. 730.

Cole argued against the application, and quoted *Hall vs. Smith,* 2, *Bing.,* 158.

Absolution refused.

For the defendants were then called :—

Frederick Fishenden.—I am Admiralty Clerk of the Works, in charge of the naval works at the Cape. I examined the slip yesterday, and found it damaged by the *China* falling over, but otherwise it is in serviceable condition, and fit to take up a ship three times the tonnage of the *China.* I have had experience of slips for a number of years at different naval stations. I never before saw a vessel capsized on a slip.

James Murison.—I am one of the members of the Harbour Board, the defendants. Robertson ordinarily gave directions for vessels to go on the slip. The parties who wish vessels taken up apply to the Secretary. He has a proper office. Robertson has no authority to enter into any arrangements. He is paid separately for each job. He is supposed to see the conditions are signed before he takes a ship up. There are no standing rules prohibiting him from taking up a vessel until the conditions are signed, but there are no orders authorizing him to do so before. He is not otherwise employed by the Harbour Board except to work the slip, and in this he is considered one of the most experienced men in the colony. After the accident I examined the ship and the cradle. The vessel was on the centre of cradle as straight as possible. There was nothing wrong with the arms or blocks on the port side. On the starboard

1874.
August 27.
„   28.
„   29.
„   31.
September 1.

Gifford vs. Table
Bay Dock and
Breakwater
Management
Commission.

side, on which the vessel was lying, the two fore arms of the cradle were broken. I could not see the bilge blocks or that side, as the vessel was on top of them. The slip was ordered from Scotland, and was to be capable of taking up a vessel of 1,400 tons. The orders to Robinson were, when a vessel of that size or larger was to be taken up, to clear everything out of her except what might be required for trimming the vessel. I don't think these instructions are in writing, but they are clearly understood. I was a master mariner and am able to form my own idea of the cause of the accident. The *China* was of remarkable build, very short and high; and on account of being short she only took three arms on each side, in fact, the third had little power, so she must have rested mainly on the two fore arms. She was so fine aft that the after blocks had very little power on her. Being a high-heeled ship, the blocks should have been half way up the vessel. In place of that these blocks were all below, and the *China* was like a castle on them. The blocks might have been made to go higher, but not much. Extra arms are sometimes fixed when they take up the steamers. The *China* was about 100 feet long and 20 feet deep, and is an old vessel. The accident was caused, I think, by the *China* with the list she had pressing hard on the two blocks, and a puff of wind listing her over further sent the loose cargo between decks to one side and thus added to the weight, and this broke the outer railing of the cradle, and so the vessel came down. With a vessel of this description there should have been 100 tons in the hold and not a ton between decks. After the accident I gave directions at once to the Secretary to have everything between decks weighed, as I was sure that was the cause of the accident. I consider the *China*, as she lay before going on the slip, worth £1,200. It is always understood that the conditions must be signed, but there is no notice posted at the Board's office to that effect. If the Secretary cannot be found, I suppose some of the clerks can make arrangements. Thwaits is one of the clerks, and has an office next to Saunders. Supposing they had been signed, Robertson could certainly have done all that he has done in this case. I think it is the Secretary who is to blame for their not being signed. Most certainly there is an instruction not to take up a vessel on the slip until the conditions are signed. I can't say it is in writing, or that there is a minute of the Commissioners to that effect. The *China* was a very peculiarly built ship, and should have been very carefully taken charge of, and carefully trimmed. It is Robertson's duty to ascertain what cargo a vessel has on board before taking her up on the slip. If I was in Robertson's place I should trim the ship to suit the slip. I mean I would move the cargo from one part to another. I should know she wanted trimming by the draught of water fore and aft. I never knew of a case before this one, of a vessel being taken up without the conditions being signed. If Robertson knew there was only fifty tons in the hold and even thirty tons between decks, it was gross neglect in him to attempt to take up the vessel in that state. When going into the hold Robertson would have an opportunity of seeing what was between decks. The build of the *China* is such that it would be wrong to take her on the slip with anything between decks. More arms could have been put to the slip if it was thought necessary. This might have increased the vessel's chance of safety.

1874.
August 27.
,, 28.
,, 29.
,, 31.
September 1.

Gifford *vs.* Table Bay Dock and Breakwater Management Commission.

John Saunders.—I am the Secretary of the Harbour Board. Robertson receives an intimation from me of any application to put a vessel on the slip. He trims the vessel, and when ready informs me, and then I take care to see that the conditions are signed. Robertson receives no definite instructions before the conditions are signed. The diver, the engine-driver, and boatswain are servants of the Board, and are under Robertson's instructions when he is taking up vessels on the slip. All the other labourers are supplied and paid by Robertson, and Robertson is paid by the Board a certain price per ton for each vessel taken up. (Copy of agreement between the Board and Robertson put in.) I know nothing of the *China* being taken up. In consequence of what Thwaits told me I made a memorandum in my diary of the application, and was expecting to be informed by Robertson or the agent of the vessel when the *China* was ready. I heard nothing more till informed of the accident. I called afterwards to ask Peabody to sign the conditions, and told him the ship should not have been taken up until they were signed had I known of it. (Conditions put in.) There have been one or two instances of small craft going on the slip without the signing of the conditions, but the engagement to take them up upon those conditions had previously been agreed to by the captain or the agent. The slip is very profitable, and pays a large percentage on the outlay. On the occasions when no conditions were signed the charges went into the funds of the Board in the ordinary way.

Henry Thwaits.—I am clerk in the office of the Table Bay Dock Commissioners, the defen'ants. About five weeks before the accident, Peabody and the captain called and said they had come to see about getting the *China* taken up on the slip. I told them the Secretary was engaged, and they left without saying anything more. I told them the

1874.
August 27.
„ 28.
„ 29.
„ 31.
September 1.

Gifford vs. Table
Bay Dock and
Breakwater
Management
Commission.

Namaqua was on the slip, and that they might go on after she came off. I was not the right person to make the arrangements. They are made by the Secretary. I did not tell them so.

Christopher Robertson.—I am a master shipwright carrying on business at the Dock Road. I am employed by the Board to slip vessels for them. I called at the office before taking up the *China* to see the Secretary, but he being engaged, I asked Thwaits what ship was next on turn. He told me the *China*. I had several times spoken to the captain about it, as my firm was engaged by him to do the repairs required. I had told the captain I had the management of the slip. He asked me the charge, and I told him, and also that he had to apply to the Board for permission, and to get at the office all necessary information, and that they would let me know when to take up his vessel. During the time Captain Gifford was transhipping his cargo I saw him several times about going on the slip. I spoke to him about the draught of water I wanted the ship to have, and he said he would bring her up to it. The captain and mate told me there was some of the cargo left on board. The day before taking the *China* up, I found they were putting a lot of water into empty casks in the lower hold. Previous to this the captain had told me he could not get the vessel up to the draught I wanted, and that he was afraid to take any more out of her as she was crank. I asked why he was putting the water into the lower hold, and he said it was to stiffen the vessel. I told him I could not allow it, and it was taken out. I said it was impossible for the ship to be crank with all the top hamper off her. As to the stability of the vessel, I am dependent on the captain. From what the captain told me I calculated he had about twenty-three tons of cargo in the hold. He told me he had only a few empty barrels and some shooks between decks, nothing of any weight. About five days before taking up the vessel I went down to the lower hold to measure the ship for the purpose of preparing the slip blocks. I did not go between decks, as they were all lumbered up with casks. A diver is usually sent down to measure the depth of the vessel and thickness of keel. Drysel, a diver of great experience, was the man employed for this. The *China* was an extraordinarily deep ship, and had a very deep keel, measuring twenty-one inches. She also had a camber. This camber could not be discovered before slipping. The diver could not have discovered it. The arms on the cradle are twenty feet apart. There is no provision for putting extra arms between the present ones, and the effect of putting more arms would be detrimental to the cradle, because the cradle is composed the

most part of wood, and even as it is now we are obliged to
load it heavily with iron to keep it down. The blocks used
were properly shaped, and could not have been made higher.
The ship had a list to starboard before we put her on the
slip. She took the cradle fair in the centre, and we first
hauled in the starboard fore block to get her upright and
take out the list. All the six blocks were properly hauled
in. When I left the vessel she had no list. During the
time the vessel was coming out of the water the wind was
puffy. Everything was going on all right when suddenly
she fell over. I was on the quay at the time. The blocks
were then half way out of the water and fitted well. The
vessel had not come to the stage when she ceased to be waterborne altogether. The side rail and three arms of the slip
were broken, but whether this was from the concussion or
not I cannot say. The slip was in a proper condition, and
perfectly fit to take up a ship three or four times as large as
the *China.* The cradle is always kept in good repair, and all
the ropes, &c., are good. The accident, I think, was caused
by the top weight, the extraordinary deepness, and the
peculiar build of the ship. The camber also had something
to do with it. The captain deceived me as to the weight
between decks. I saw some casks there, but whether they
were full or empty I don't know. I thought the captain
was a gentleman, and so took his word. Had I known he
had cargo between decks I would have had it all taken out.
I never took a vessel up yet with a cargo between decks.
I have taken up about 100 vessels on the slip. When I saw
Thwaits he said nothing about the conditions being unsigned.
Previous to this I have taken vessels up on the slip without
being told the conditions were signed. After I had measured the vessel, I knew of her shape and depth. It is
impossible for the diver to take a line and find out the
camber under water. It is not the rule to ask the captain if
his ship has a camber. Every wooden ship has more or less
of a camber. I consider a camber of little consequence. I
did not know of the cargo between decks when the Court of
Inquiry sat, so did not then account for the accident in that
way. I value the *China* as worth between £1,200 and
£1,400 to the owners, without whaling gear.

William Drysel.—I have had a good deal of experience as
a diver during the last thirteen or fourteen years. I examined
the *China.* I could not find out a camber under water, and
never heard of it being done. I assisted in slipping the
China. There was a slight list before she came on the slip,
which we righted. At the time Robertson and I left the
vessel she had no list. Had there been a dangerous list I certainly would have noticed it. The vessel was properly blocked.

1874.
August 27.
„ 28.
„ 29.
„ 31.
September 1.

Gifford vs. Table
Bay Dock and
Breakwater
Management
Commission.

1874.
August 27.
,, 28.
,, 29.
,, 31.
September 1.

Gifford *vs.* Table
Bay Dock and
Breakwater
Management
Commission.

George William Onions.—I am a civil engineer, and hav
had considerable experience in connection with slips. Ther
should never be any cargo allowed to remain between deck:
Sails and the like might be stowed between decks; they ar
not called cargo. I have seen the slip. The arms of th
cradle are certainly not long enough. The longer the arm
the more they can be elevated, and the better the blocks ca
be made to fit the ship. I never before this knew of a vesse
being capsized. It is scarcely possible for a ship to capsiz
if proper care is used, that is if she is properly blocked. If
vessel had a list of more than three degrees she certainly ough
not to be taken up. Blocks twenty feet apart, in the case o
a ship like the *China*, would be too far apart. The block
ought not to have been more than ten feet apart. Befor
the cradle was let down extra arms could have been fixed.

William Cook.—I am Assistant Dock Master, and am
master mariner, and have had some experience with th
working of slips. The arms are generally from fifteen t
twenty feet apart. I don't think I have seen them less o
more than this distance apart. I saw the slipping of th
China. I superintended the hauling of the vessel from he
berth to the slipways, and then handed her over to Rober
son. She had a list to starboard before she was put on th
cradle, but this I think was taken out in blocking her. Afte
the accident I ascertained what cargo was in the vesse
Between decks there were 61½ tons, and in the lower hol
51¾ tons. A ship with that proportion of weight betwee
decks was not properly trimmed to go on the slip, nor woul
it have been safe to have gone to sea or even to sail acros
the bay. The weather was gusty and puffy all th
while the vessel was being taken up. I cannot accour
for the accident unless some of the starboard blocks had bee
let go by mistake on board, or that a rope had broken. Th
ropes were perfectly sound before the vessel went on th
slip. The list the vessel had was probably about thre
degrees, but I think it was thoroughly rectified. I think th
weight of the wind assisted in sending the ship over.
would not have taken the captain's word for where the carg
was if I had been responsible, but would have satisfie
myself. The arms and outer rails of the cradle were pe
fectly sound and good before the accident. I consider th
China worth £6 10s. a ton, about £2,400, as an ordinai
merchant ship.

John Smith.—I remember the *China* being slipped.
tried the blocks on both sides, and found them to fit close
and properly hauled taut. The next day I went on boa
and found one of the block ropes let go. The other rop
were all secured.

James E. King.—I am wharfinger in defendants' employ. I weighed the greater portion of the things which came out of the *China*, and the list put in is correct. The defendants then closed their case.

1874.
August 27.
,, 28,
,, 29.
,, 31.
September 1.

Gifford *vs.* Table Bay Dock and Breakwater Management Commission.

Cole, for the plaintiff, summed up on the evidence, and urged that plaintiff's case had been amply made out, while the defendants' various pleas had altogether failed. As to the conditions, even if they had been signed, they would not have relieved the defendants from liability for damages resulting from negligence. This liability was not removed in consequence of their being a Board instead of individuals. (*Mersey Dock and Harbour Board* vs. *Gibbs*, 1, *L.R.*, *H.L.C.* 93.)

Jacobs, A.G., for the defendants, contended that the Harbour Board, even if they were rightly made the defendants, were not liable unless negligence was proved. The onus of proof of this was on the plaintiff, and though some evidence had been led it was not sufficient. The plaintiff must moreover be considered bound by the conditions, for it was shown that his agent, Peabody, was aware of their existence, and that the Board required them to be signed before vessels were taken on the slip. The real cause of the accident had not been made apparent, but it most probably arose from a combination of causes beyond the defendants' control, added to the contributory negligence and misleading statements of the plaintiff himself. If negligence gave the foundation to the action, then Robertson, who was not the servant or agent of the Board at all, but merely a sub-contractor, was the proper person to be sued. As to the amount of damages, the amount claimed was far in advance of the actual value of the vessel. The plaintiff was not entitled to damages resulting from loss of prospective profits. He cited *Moffat* vs. *Bateman, L.R.*, 3, *P.C. App.*, 122; *Great Western Railway Co. of Canada* vs. *Braid*, 1, *Moore's P.C.*, n.s., 101; *Hammack* vs. *White*, 31, *L.J.*, *C.P.*, n.s., 129; *Scott* vs. *London and St. Katherine's Dock Co.*, 34, *L.J.*, *Exch.*, 220; *Smith* vs. *Great Eastern Railway Co.*, 2, *L.R.*, *C.P.*, 11; *Fowler* vs. *Locke*, 7, *L.R.*, *C.P.* 286; *Simson* vs. *General Omnibus Co.*, 8, *L.R.*, *C.P.*, 392; *Pole* vs. *Leask*, 33, *L.J.*, *Ch.*, n.s., 155; *Rapson* vs. *Cubitt*, 9. *M. & W.*, 710; *Cuthbertson* vs. *Parsons*, 12, *C.B.*, 304; *Steel* vs. *South Eastern Railway Co.*, 16, *C.B.*, 550; *Murray* vs. *Currie*, 6, *L.R.*, *C.P.*, 24; *Broom's Com. L.*, 696; *Reed* vs. *Fairbanks*, 22, *L.J.*, *C.P.*, 206.

Cole replied.

DE VILLIERS, C. J., in giving judgment, said :—This is an action brought by the master of the American bark *China* against the Table Bay Dock and Breakwater Commissioners

1874.
August 27.
„ 28.
„ 29.
„ 31.
September 1.

Gifford *vs.* Table
Bay Dock and
Breakwater
Management
Commission.

to recover the sum of £3,500 as and for the value of the vessel at the time when she was injured, through the alleged negligence of the defendants or their servants, and the further sum of £1,000 as and for damages said to have been sustained by the plaintiff from loss of voyage and earnings. The first plea on the record consists of a general denial of the allegations of fact and conclusions of law contained in the declaration, and under this plea, the defendants' counsel, after the evidence of the plaintiff had been concluded but before the defendants' evidence was commenced, asked for absolution from the instance, and contended (1) that the plaintiff had not proved sufficient interest in the ship to entitle him to maintain the action; (2) that there was no evidence to show that Robertson, through whose alleged negligence the vessel was damaged and destroyed, was a servant of the defendants, or acted by their directions in taking her on the slip; and (3) that even if Robertson had been proved to be the defendants' servant, acting within the scope of his employment, they cannot—as a body acting gratuitously for the public — be held answerable for his negligence, and that the funds in their hands as Commissioners cannot be made available for the payment of damages caused by Robertson's negligence. These objections were over-ruled by the Court after very little argument from the bar, and the application for absolution from the instance was refused. Before proceeding, however, to the main grounds of defence, it may be useful to consider these preliminary objections and the reasons why they could not, in the opinion of the Court, be sustained. The first objection, that the plaintiff's interest in the vessel as her master is not sufficient to entitle him to bring this action, is inconsistent with the principles of the Roman-Dutch law and with the practice of this Court. (See *Voet* 14, 1, 1; *Voet* 3, 3, 14 *et seq.*) Even in England, where the right of an agent or *procurator* to bring an action in his own name on behalf of his principal is not recognised, it appears to have been held that the master may bring an action of trespass against a wrongdoer (*Maude and Pollock on Merchant Shipping*, 3rd ed., p. 82). The second objection having been raised by some of the special pleas, may be more conveniently considered hereafter. In support of his third objection the Attorney-General quoted the case *Hall* vs. *Smith* (2 *Bing.*, 156), where it was held that "no action can be maintained against a man acting gratuitously for the public for the consequence of any act which he is authorized to do, and which, as far as he is concerned, is done with due care and attention; and that such a person is not answerable for the negligent execution of an order properly given." In that case the plaintiff sought to

render the defendants, the commissioners for paving Birming-
ham, personally liable for negligence of the contractors
employed by them to make a sewer; whereas, in the present
case, the action is brought against the defendants, not in
their individual, but in their corporate capacity. It seems
doubtful whether the case of *Hall* vs. *Smith* would be sustained in Westminster Hall at the present day. *Manley
Smith*, in his work on *Master and Servant* (3rd ed., p. 308),
says, that the case of *Hall* vs. *Smith* must now be considered
as over-ruled in so far as it can be taken to lay down any
doctrine as to the non-liability of such bodies for acts done
by their officers. The case is commented upon by Mr.
Justice Blackburn in an elaborate opinion, delivered by him
to the House of Lords, as the joint opinion of himself and
all the Judges who heard the argument before that House
in the case of *Mersey Dock and Harbour Board* vs. *Gibbs,
L. R.*, 1, *App. Cases*, 93. In the latter case it was held by
the House of Lords, affirming the decision of the Exchequer
Chamber, but reversing that of the Court of Exchequer,
that the appellants, being the occupiers of the Docks, and
entitled to levy tolls from those who use the Docks, were
liable to the same responsibilities as would attach on them if
they were the absolute owners occupying and using them for
their own profit. "It would be a strange distinction," said
the Lord Chancellor (Lord Cranworth), "to persons coming
with their ships to different ports of this country, that, in
some ports if they sustain damage by the negligence of those
who have the management of the docks, they will be entitled
to compensation, and in others they will not; such a distinction arising, not from any visible difference in the docks
themselves, but from some municipal difference in the constitution of the bodies by whom the docks are managed."
And Mr. Justice Blackburn, in the opinion already mentioned, says that the proper rule of construction of statutes
creating bodies as trustees for public purposes is that "*in
the absence of something to show a contrary intention*, the
Legislature intends that the body, the creature of the statute,
shall have the same duties, and that its funds shall be rendered liable to the same liabilities as the general law would
impose on a private person doing the same things." It was
said by the Attorney-General that if judgment should be
given against the defendants there would be no property
against which execution could issue, but according to the
English authorities on this point, which are well summed
up by *Addison on Torts*, 4th ed., p. 740, the right to proceed
against such bodies exists whether they have or have not
funds at their disposal; though if there would be no funds
there may be a difficulty in the way of the plaintiff getting

1874.
August 27.
„   28.
„   29.
„   31.
September 1.

Gifford vs. Table
Bay Dock and
Breakwater
Management
Commission.

1874.
August 27.
„ 28.
„ 29.
„ 31.
September 1.

Gifford vs Table
Bay Dock and
Breakwater
Management
Commission.

his damages. These principles agree in the main with thos
which have always guided this Court in cases where publi
bodies, such as Municipalities* and Divisional Councils,† hav(
been sued for damages caused by the negligence of thei
servants. I am bound to add, that as the first and thir(
objections clearly appear upon the face of the declaration
they ought properly to have been taken by exceptions, an(
not raised under the general issue after the evidence fo
the plaintiff had been concluded. The great question in thi
case appears to me to be whether or not Robinson was guilt
of ordinary negligence in the manner in which he took u]
or attempted to take up the *China* on the slip on the day o
the misfortune which befell her. But before I consider thi
question, it will be desirable to dispose of three importan
issues raised by the defendants in their five special pleas
viz. : Did Robertson, in slipping the *China,* act as th(
defendants' servant ? Assuming that he did, was it on con
dition that the defendants should not be liable for any con
sequences of any damages which might happen to the vesse
in taking her on the slip ? And did the plaintiff by his ow
acts or conduct contribute to the injury sustained by th(
vessel ? The first of these questions is answered by th(
defendants in the negative. They say in effect that Robert
son had no authority to take any vessel on the slip until h(
received instructions to that effect from the Secretary, an(
that in the case of the *China* no such instructions had bee(
given. They do not, however, deny, nor, in the face of thei
own written agreement with Robertson, and their ow(
written instructions to the dockmaster, could they deny, tha
he is the person entrusted by them with the duty of superin
tending the slipping of all vessels. According to Captai(
Wilson, who is himself the dockmaster, no one beside
Robertson has had the management of the slip since it ha
been at work ; he puts vessels on the slip and launches them
and is considered at the dock as the recognized authorit
on matters relating to the slip. According to Mr. Thwait(
the clerk to Mr. Saunders (the Secretary), the master of th(
China and Mr. Peabody, his agent, called at the Secretary'
office some weeks before the day of the attempt of slippin(
her, and asked to see the Secretary ; Thwaits said that th
Secretary was engaged, and asked if he could do anything fo
them ; Mr. Peabody replied that he merely called in t
engage the slip for the *China,* and Thwaits said that th
Namaqua was on the list and that the *China* might go o
after the *Namaqua.* Then what is the effect of Mr. Robert

* See *Municipality of Port Elizabeth* vs. *Nightingale,* on appeal t
Supreme Court, Jan. 12, 1856.
† See *Morkel* vs. *Divisional Council of Paarl,* Supreme Court, Feb., 187(

son's own evidence? Previously to the 24th of July he had had several conversations with Captain Gifford about slipping the *China*, and had told him that he (Robertson) had the management of the slip. On the 24th of July he called at the Harbour Board Office to see the Secretary, and upon being told by Mr. Thwaits that the Secretary was engaged, he asked what ship was next in turn, as he was bound to launch the *Namaqua* on the following day; whereupon Thwaits told him that the next ship was to be the *China*, and he replied that the *China* was ready to go on the slip on the following Monday, that is the 27th of July. Captain Murison, in cross-examination, said that if the Secretary of the Board could not be found, one of the clerks could make the arrangements for taking a vessel on the slip, and that Mr. Thwaits is one of the clerks, having his office next door to that of Mr. Saunders. It is moreover in evidence that the slipway was cleared for the *China* by the assistant dock-master (Captain Cook) by the direction of Robertson, and that in slipping the *China* Mr. Robertson was assisted by Mr. Drysel, the diver of the Board, and by other servants of the Board. Taking all these facts together, I am of opinion that Robertson, in attempting to slip the *China*, acted as a servant of the defendants, and within the scope of his authority as slip superintendent, and that the plea denying his authority cannot be sustained. It has been urged, however, by the Attorney-General that Robertson was no more than a sub-contractor under the defendants for slipping vessels, and that, on the authority of the case of *Rapson* vs. *Cubitt*, 9 *M. & W.*, 710, they cannot be held liable for his negligence. If it had been shown that the defendants had parted with the whole control of the work of slipping vessels, there would be great force in the argument, but the evidence does not bear out this view. The instructions to the dock-master provide that the patent slip shall be "under the supervision of the dockmaster, and that Smith, of the diving gang occasionally employed there, be appointed to take charge of the ropes and other plant and materials belonging to it; that the slipping and launching of vessels remain as heretofore under the sole *direction* of Mr. C. Robertson, the dockmaster rendering such assistance as may be required." And the written agreement with Robertson is headed as follows :—"Terms upon which the Harbour Board have agreed with Mr. C. Robertson to undertake the *superintendence* of slipping vessels on the patent slip, with the aid of a diver." (See also *Randleson* vs. *Murray*, 8, *Ad. & E.*, 109.) It is not quite clear, moreover, that the distinction between the case of a contractor and a servant would be recognised by the Roman-Dutch Law. In the *Digest*, 19, 2, 25, § 7,

1874.
August 27.
„ 28.
„ 29.
„ 31.
September 1.

Gifford vs. Table Bay Dock and Breakwater Management Commission.

1874.
August 27.
„ 28.
„ 29.
„ 31.
September 1.

Gifford *vs.* Table
Bay Dock and
Breakwater
Management
Commission.

it is said :—" *Qui columnam transportandam conduxit, si*
dum tollitur, aut portatur, aut reponitur, fracta sit, ita id per
culum præstat, si qua ipsius eorumque quorum opera uteretu
culpa acciderit. Culpa autem abest, si omnia facta sunt, qu
diligentissimus quisque observaturus fuisset." If I am corre
in these views, it would follow that, if negligence on the part
Robertson can be proved, the defendants will be liable. Th
law on this subject is thus broadly stated by *Story on Agenc*
§§ 308, 452-456 :—The principal is liable to third persons fo
the torts, negligences, and other malfeasances or misfeasance
and omissions of his servant or agent in the course of h
employment, although the principal did not authorize c
justify or participate in, or indeed know of such misconduc
or even if he forbade the acts or disproved of them. " I
all such cases," he adds, " the rule applies *responde*
superior ; and it is founded upon public policy and cor
venience ; for in no other way could there be any safety t
third persons in their dealings either directly or indirectl
with him through the instrumentality of agents. I
every such case the principal holds out his agent as com
petent and fit to be trusted, and thereby in effect he warran
his fidelity and good conduct in all matters within the scop
of his agency." *Story* then proceeds to point out (§§ 458
461) that similar principles are recognised, though not wit
the same distinctness, by the Roman Law (see also *Pothie*
on Obligations, n.n. 121 and 453). The passage from th
Digest, which has already been quoted, clearly supports th
same view. But assuming that Robertson had the requisit
authority, the defendants next contend that one of the cor
ditions on which the *China* was taken on the slip was, the
they should not be liable for any damage which migt
happen to her in taking her on the slip. In support c
this view they say that the practice of the Board has alway
been not to allow vessels to be slipped until the master c
agent has signed certain conditions, of which the third run
as follows :—" The Harbour Board shall not be liable for th
consequences of any damage which may happen to the slip
and ship shall not be liable for any damage which may b
sustained by the slip or cradle, either in taking up or i
launching ;" but it is admitted that on some previous occasion
vessels had been taken up before the written conditions wer
signed. Then, it is said, that it was Robertson's duty not t
take the *China* on the slip until he saw that the conditions ha
been signed, but no resolution of the Board to that effect we
produced, nor any instructions to Mr. Robertson, nor
there any evidence of a public notice in the Secretary's offic
or elsewhere, warning persons who require the use of th
slip that the conditions must be signed before Robertson

authority begins. The dock regulations (framed under Act 22 of 1872), a copy of which is handed over to the master of every vessel entering the port, and which contained the scale of charges for the use of the slip, are silent as to such conditions. In the present case the conditions were not signed, but the defendants contend that the plaintiff should be placed in the same condition as if they had been signed. But on what principles of law or justice can such a contention be sustained? If there had been any previous understanding between the parties that the conditions should be signed, but through some mistake or inadvertence they were not signed, there would be some ground for holding that this Court, as a Court of Equity, should give no assistance to the plaintiff except subject to the conditions. But it is clear from the evidence that before the accident no mention of the conditions was made to the captain or his agent, either by Mr. Thwaits or by any one else connected with the Board. It is said, indeed, that Mr. Peabody had previously signed similar conditions, but his knowledge of what was done in other cases cannot be construed into a notice to the plaintiff that the signing of the conditions was necessary before his own vessel could be slipped. After the accident an attempt was made to obtain the plaintiff's signature, but as might have been anticipated he refused to sign any documents whereby his rights under the ordinary law might in any way have been lessened. Under all these circumstances I am of opinion that the question as to the defendants' liability ought to be decided independently of the conditions tendered for the plaintiff's signature. This view of the case renders it unnecessary for me to consider the question whether the defendants would under the conditions, even if they had been signed, be relieved from the consequences of gross, or even ordinary negligence on the part of their servants in the slipping of vessels. The plea that the plaintiff materially contributed to the injury by representing that there was nothing of any weight between decks, and allowing about sixty tons weight to remain there, has not, in my opinion, been supported by the evidence, and must therefore also fail. There is considerable discrepancy between the account given by Robertson and that of the plaintiff as to what was really said about the cargo; but the impression left upon me by Captain Gifford's evidence is that his version was substantially correct, and that Robertson's memory has failed him on this point. I now come to the real question at issue in this case, viz., whether Robertson has been guilty of such a degree of negligence as to render the defendants liable for the injuries sustained by the *China?* In considering this question, it will be un-

1874.
August 27.
„ 28.
„ 29.
„ 31.
September 1.

Gifford *vs.* Table Bay Dock and Breakwater Management Commission.

I 2

1874.
August 27.
„ 28.
„ 29.
„ 31.
September 1.

Gifford vs. Table
Bay Dock and
Breakwater
Management
Commission.

necessary to enter into the minute distinctions between tl
different kinds of negligence recognized by our law. It mɛ
be broadly laid down that where the contract of bailment
of mutual benefit, there ordinary diligence only is require
and as a consequence the bailee will be liable for ordinaɪ
negligence. (See *Voet*, 19, 2, 30; *Story on Bailmen*
§ 429.) Different things, however, may require veɪ
different care. The care required in building a commc
doorway is quite different from that required in raising
marble pillar, although both might come under the descriɪ
tion of ordinary care. It is observed by *Story on Bailmen*
§ 431, that "where skill as well as care is required in pe
forming the undertaking, if the party purports to haᴠ
skill in the business, and he undertakes for hire, he is boun
not only to ordinary care and diligence in securing and prɛ
serving the thing, but also to the exercise of due and ordinaɪ
skill in the employment of his art or business about it; o
in other words, he undertakes to perform it in a workmaɪ
like manner. In cases of this sort he must be understood t
have engaged to use a degree of diligence, and attentioɪ
and skill, adequate to the due performance of his undeɪ
taking. And if he has not the proper skill, *or, if having i
he omits to use it, or if he omits in other respects the propɛ
degree of diligence and attention required for the work*, he wiɪ
be responsible for the damages sustained thereby by hɪ
employer. The general maxim is: *Spondet peritiam artiᵢ
imperitia culpæ adnumeratur* (*Digest*, 50, 17, 132). It ɪ
the party's own fault, if he undertakes without havinɡ
sufficient skill, or if he applies less than the occasion requireɛ
And it has been well observed, that where a person is em
ployed in a work of skill, the employer buys both his labou
and his judgment." *Grotius* observes, in his *Introduction t
Dutch Jurisprudence* (3, 19, 11), that "the ignorance of an
art that the party undertakes, or a trifling imprudence iɪ
matters which can only be carried on with the greatest pru
dence, is considered as a neglect." To illustrate this doctrine
Ulpian observes (*Digest*, 19, 2, 9, § 5): "*Si quis vitulo
pascendos, vel sarciendum quid poliendumve conduxit, culpaɪ
eam præstare debere: et quod imperitia peccavit, culpam essɛ
quippe ut artifex conduxit.*" Now it cannot for one momen
be denied that Robertson was possessed of the requisite skil
for slipping vessels. The question, however, is, did he, iɪ
the case of the *China*, exercise that skill and use due anc
ordinary care? The slipping of a vessel appears to be ɪ
service which requires some skill, and very great care anc
attention to details. She should be so laden, balanced, anc
supported, as to be ready to meet every possible disturbinɡ
cause. For that purpose great care is taken before com-

mencing the operation to obtain correct information as to her length, breadth, and depth, the shape of her bottom and keel, the quantity of her cargo, and the way in which the cargo is distributed over different parts of her. Unless her shape is known, it is impossible properly to prepare the blocks which are to support her as soon as she ceases to be waterborne ; unless her length, breadth, and depth are known, it is impossible to say to what height the blocks ought to reach ; and unless her cargo is properly stowed all other precautions may prove useless. It is unnecessary here to describe the slip and cradle minutely. It is sufficient to observe that the cradle forms a movable bed for the ship to rest upon, and rests on wheels which move on slanting rails. In the centre of the cradle there is a long and stout beam, supported by a double set of wheels running on iron rails, and called the centre-piece. This centre-piece is connected with the outer beams on each side (called the outer rails) by cross-beams twenty feet apart, and these outer rails are supported by wheels running on iron rails. Between the cross-beams are the arms, also twenty feet apart, and extending outside the outer rails, and on these arms the blocks which serve to support and balance the vessel on each side travel in grooves. Each block consists of a number of wedge-like pieces of timber, which are united together by means of iron dogs. Great care seems to be required in preparing the blocks so as to make them suit the shape of the vessel, and in raising them no higher and no lower than her bilge. Captain Murison, one of the defendants, and a witness on their behalf, is of opinion that the blocks were not quite high enough to support the vessel properly, but Mr. Robertson does not agree with him, and says that if the blocks had been higher they would have reached above the bilge of the *China*, the effect of which would have been to lessen rather than strengthen the support which they afforded her. In this conflict of evidence between the defendants' own witnesses it is difficult for the Court to decide whether the misfortune was caused, or at all events facilitated, by the lowness of the blocks. But all the witnesses who were examined as to the distance of the blocks apart are agreed that it was quite possible to increase the number of arms and corresponding blocks, and by so doing to assist the existing blocks in supporting the vessel. Mr. Robertson indeed says that the addition of more blocks, by increasing the woodwork, would lighten the cradle in the water, but he admitted that this could be remedied by loading the centre-piece with more iron. Captain Murison says that on account of the *China* being so short she took only three of the arms on each side ; she must have rested mostly on the two forearms ; she was

1874.
August 27.
„ 28.
„ 29.
„ 31.
September 1.

Gifford *vs.* Table Bay Dock and Breakwater Management Commission.

1874.
August 27.
„ 28.
„ 29.
„ 31.
September 1.

Gifford vs. Table
Bay Dock and
Breakwater
Management
Commission.

so fine aft that the after block had very little power over he
and in answer to a question from the Court he said, that
more arms had been used her chances of safety would ha
been greatly increased. Mr. Onions, also a witness for t
defence, says that the blocks ought to be ten and not twen
feet apart. Now it is an important element in the prese
case that the shape and build of the *China* were such that th
could not fail to strike the attention of any one who kn
anything about ships. She was very short, and very dee
and had a very fine bottom ; in fact, she had just tho
peculiarities of shape which would necessitate every ava
able precaution in supporting and slipping her. Robertsc
moreover, swears that before he put her on the cradle t
captain had told him that she was a crank vessel, a rema
which he did not heed, but which ought certainly to ha
put him on his guard. It is impossible for me, with the
facts before the Court, to avoid the conclusion that Robe
son neglected to avail himself of those precautions whi
common prudence would dictate, and that among these pr
cautions that of providing additional arms and correspondi
blocks before launching the cradle was one of the mo
essential. It is quite possible that the accident would nev
have occurred if the weight of cargo between decks h
been less ; but if this be so, it is clear from the eviden
that it was part of Robertson's duty to see that the car
was properly distributed. Neither the captain nor the ma
had ever before witnessed the operation of slipping a vess
so that it could not be expected from them, without expre
directions from the slip-superintendent, that they should p
much attention to the state of the cargo. Robertson, on t
other hand, had successfully slipped about one hundr
vessels, and in the case of each of them had personally i
spected the cargo and observed the proportion in which
was distributed between the lower hold and between deck
Now his own evidence satisfies me that however careful
may have been— and, no doubt, has been—with other vesse
in this particular case he did not exercise that degree of ca
and diligence in regard to the state of the cargo which t
peculiar circumstances of the *China* required. In sayi
this I am by no means satisfied that the proportion of car
between decks to that in the lower hold was so great as t
defendants have attempted to make out. The cargo tak
out of the vessel was weighed after the whole of it had be
mixed together, and there is no evidence to show that t
memo. put in for the defendants gives accurately the quanti
of cargo that came from between decks as compared with th
of the lower hold. In regard to the list, about which
much has been said on both sides, one thing is clear, vi

that the vessel fell over on the side on which the list existed.
Captain Cook, the assistant dockmaster, says that immediately
before she went on the cradle the list was about three
degrees. This list was removed, or as the witnesses express
it, taken out, not by shifting the cargo, but by means of the
blocks which were intended to support her. It seems clear,
therefore, that if she was not made perfectly upright, there
would remain a greater degree of pressure on the starboard
than on the port blocks. It is quite possible, as urged by
the Attorney-General, that the disaster may be attributable,
not to any single cause, but to a combination of causes, such
as the effect of a gust of wind acting upon a top-heavy ship,
such ship having a list and having a camber in her keel, and
being insufficiently supported by the blocks; but it is quite
impossible for me to imagine any combination of causes
against some of which provisions could not have been made
by the exercise of ordinary care and skill. One of the
suggestions made on behalf of the defendants to account for
the misfortune is, that the forward starboard block rope,
which runs under the vessel and along the port side, and
ought to be properly secured on the port side, was let go
before the accident, and that the remaining blocks on the
starboard side were not sufficient to support the vessel. It
is said that on the day after the accident this rope was found
uninjured, but loosened, and that if it had been tight at the
time of the accident it must have been broken. If this rope
had not been properly secured, the strain on it at the time
of the accident might have loosened it. But those who use
this argument are in this dilemma, that either the crew on
board while the cradle was being hauled up were guilty of
the grossest misconduct or carelessness—which the Court
cannot without some evidence presume—or else Mr. Robertson himself neglected to secure the rope properly. Holding
as I do that there is evidence of actual negligence in this case,
it becomes unnecessary for me to consider at length the question whether the accident which befell the *China* was or was
not of such a nature as to raise a presumption of negligence,
and to throw the burden of the proof on the defendants to
repel the presumption of negligence. The weight of authority
appears to be in favour of an affirmative answer. The
Roman Law in some cases presumed negligence, and threw
the burden of disproving it on the defendant. Thus in the
Digest 19, 2, 13, § 6, it is said: " *Si fullo vestimenta polienda
acceparit, eaque mures roserint, ex locato tenetur : quia debuit
ab hac re cavere.*" So in England, when a railway and the
carriages in which the passengers are conveyed are under the
exclusive control of the company carrying the passengers, the
very fact of a train running off the line has been held to be

1874.
August 27.
„ 28.
„ 29.
„ 31.
September 1.

Gifford *vs.* Table
Bay Dock and
Breakwater
Management
Commission.

1874.
August 27.
„ 28.
„ 29.
„ 31.
September 1.

Gifford *vs.* Table Bay Dock and Breakwater Management Commission.

primâ facie proof of negligence on the part of such company or its officers, and throws upon them the burden of explaining how it happened, and of showing that it occurred without any fault or neglect of duty on their part (*Addison on Torts*, p. 402). In the case of the *Great Western Railway* vs. *Braid* (1 *Moore P. C. C., N. S.*, p. 101), the Privy Council held that when an injury is alleged to have arisen from the improper construction or maintenance of a railway, the fact of one of its embankments giving way will amount to *primâ facie* evidence of such insufficiency; and that this evidence may become conclusive in the absence of any proof on the part of the company to rebut it. In the case of *Scott* vs. *London and St. Katherine's Dock Company* (34 *L. J. N. S., Exch.*, p. 220), it was held by the Exchequer Chamber "that in an action for personal injury caused by the alleged neglect of the defendant, the plaintiff must adduce reasonable evidence of negligence to warrant the Judge in leaving the case to the jury; but that where the thing is shown to be under the management of the defendant or his servants, *and the accident is such as in the ordinary course of things does not happen* if those who have the management use proper care, it affords reasonable evidence, in the absence of explanation by the defendant, that the accident arose from want of care." This case was referred to and, it seems, approved of by the Privy Council in the case of *Moffat* vs. *Bateman* (*L.R.*, 3, *P.C. App.*, p. 122). Lastly, as to the amount of damages which should be awarded, I am of opinion that the sum of £2,500 would be a fair and liberal compensation to the owners for the loss of the vessel. The plaintiff estimates her value at twice this sum, and Captain Murison at half this sum, but in my opinion, the valuation of Captain Hoets, who is a disinterested, and at the same time a competent witness, is nearest the mark. No evidence has been given of the amount of damages sustained by loss of freight and earnings, and in the absence of such evidence, I fail to see how such damages can be awarded. The judgment of the Court will be for the plaintiff for the sum of £2,500 with costs; the plaintiff delivering up to the defendants the articles tendered in the declaration.

DENYSSEN, J.:—I am of opinion that the judgment of the Court should be entered for the plaintiff, and that the damages mentioned by the Chief Justice should be awarded to him for the loss he has suffered in this instance by the negligence of the defendants or their servants. I shall not go over all the ground that the Chief Justice has so ably gone over, but confine myself to a very few remarks to justify the opinion I entertain in regard to this case. As to the capacity in which Mr. Robertson appeared in this case various theories have been suggested for the defence, but I am satisfied in my own mind that he acted as a servant of the defendants, and that they are therefore bound by his acts. The captain and his agent went to the office of the Board, and there, in the absence of the Secretary, made an arrangement as to the slipping of this vessel. According to this arrangement, she was to be taken on in her turn after the *Namaqua* was launched. That arrangement having been made, she was ordered by Robertson to get ready for going up, and on Tuesday he was called upon by the captain to come down to the ship for the purpose of ascertaining whether or not she was in a fit state to go on the slip. Under the arrangements which had been made between Robertson and the Board, the harbour-master was to take his directions from Robertson, with whom rests the management and superintendence of vessels being slipped. He gave notice to the harbour-master to clear the slipway, which was done, and on the Wednesday morning arrangements were made for slipping. After dinner Robertson commenced taking the vessel on the slip, and there can be no doubt in my mind— indeed the various authorities quoted establish the point—that the capacity in which he acted was not that of sub-contractor, but that of a servant of the Harbour Board, who have the ownership of the slip. Having satisfied myself that this was the capacity in which he acted, the main question comes, did he, in carrying into effect his instructions, exhibit any negligence such as to render his superiors liable? The negligence first referred to was with regard to the cargo not being properly stowed, and I may here remark, that all the evidence to which reference has been made by the Chief Justice, and upon which the case has now to be decided, is evidence tendered on behalf of the defendants. Captain Murison, one of the principal witnesses for the defence, and on whose testimony I place very great confidence, says, that the *China* was a peculiarly built ship, requiring special care and precaution in going on the slip. Robertson, he said, had to see to the proper stowage of the cargo, and it is his duty before slipping a vessel to see what cargo she has on board. Further on he said, " I should trim a ship to suit the slip, and move the cargo from one part of the ship to the other; I would know whether she wanted trimming by the draught of water fore and aft. In trimming a ship he would have to observe what was in the hold. If Robertson had known there was only fifty tons in the lower hold and thirty tons between decks, it was gross neglect to take her on. From the build of the *China*, it would be wrong to take her on with anything between decks," and so on. This is the evidence of Captain Murison as regards the duty of Mr. Robertson, a servant of the Board, in

1874.
August 27.
„ 28.
„ 29.
„ 31.
September 1.

Gifford *vs.* Table
Bay Dock and
Breakwater
Management
Commission.

1874.
August 27.
„ 28.
„ 29.
„ 31.
September 1.

Gifford *vs.* Table Bay Dock and Breakwater Management Commission.

taking a vessel on the slip, but what does Mr. Robertson say himself? "I did not know what was in her." He had, however, been called upon the day before, to go and see whether she was fit to go on the slip, but although according to his evidence he had opportunities of going between decks and seeing the state of the vessel, he did not know about the cargo. Hence, there was not only negligence, but gross negligence on his part. Then the second cause assigned for the accident was the list on the starboard side. One side states that she had a list before going on the cradle, and the other when she came in contact with it, but to all intents and purposes the list existed, and according to Captain Cook, a witness for the defence, the list was at least three degrees. Mr. Onions, another witness for the defence, who has had considerable experience in the matter of slips, said that a list of three degrees was a dangerous one. But notwithstanding this, the vessel was taken on the slip. Then as to the state of the weather, Robertson states that in the morning it was blowing fresh from E.S.E., then it fell calm, but when the vessel was being taken up it became very gusty ; yet this ship, said to be very deep and short, and having a fine bottom, requiring particular care, was taken up with this puffy wind blowing, when she ought to have been re-launched and waited for a better opportunity. All these grounds were represented as showing great negligence, and being the cause of this vessel capsizing, namely, that the cargo was not properly stowed, that the list was a dangerous one, and that there was a very puffy wind blowing at the time. The vessel having been taken up under all these circumstances by Robertson, acting as the servant of the Board, they are clearly liable. It has been stated by Captain Murison and others that Mr. Robertson is usually a very careful man, as well as most competent for this service, and I am very willing to believe it. I also think that, having been so fortunate on every other occasion, he had too much confidence at this time, and neglected those precautions he should have taken. As to the value of the vessel, it has been differently stated, but under all the circumstances, I consider £2,500 to be fair and reasonable.

FITZPATRICK, J., concurred.

Judgment accordingly for plaintiff for £2,500, damages, and costs; the articles tendered in the declaration to be delivered to defendants.

[Plaintiff's Attorneys, FAIRBRIDGE & ARDERNE.]
[Defendants' Attorneys, REID & NEPHEW.]

MAGISTRATES' REVIEWED CASES.

MERCHANT SHIPPING ACT, 17 & 18 VICT., c. 104, ART. 243, SEC. 8.

Receiving with a guilty knowledge embezzled ship's stores, not an offence under the above section of the Merchant Shipping Act, but an offence punishable by the Magistrate under his ordinary jurisdiction.

Receiving stolen goods, without guilty knowledge, is no crime.

DE VILLIERS, C.J., said a case had come before him as Judge of the week, of *The Queen* vs. *Child and Harrison.* The prisoners had been charged, under section 8, of Art. 243, of 17 & 18 Vict., c. 104, with embezzlement of ship's stores. Child pleaded guilty. Harrison pleaded not guilty, but the verdict was " guilty of receiving one bottle," and the sentence one month's imprisonment with hard labour. Now receiving one bottle was no crime, but he supposed the Magistrate meant that he received it " with knowledge of the prisoner Child's embezzlement." If this was what was meant it ought to have been so expressed ; but even then His Lordship failed to see this could be a competent verdict upon a charge for a contravention of a particular section in which receiving with knowledge of the embezzlement is not mentioned as an offence. If the prisoner had committed the crime of receiving stolen goods knowing the same to have been stolen he could have been tried under the Magistrate's ordinary jurisdiction. Moreover, the evidence was not satisfactory that there was any knowledge on Harrison's part of Child's dishonesty. The Magistrate's sentence must therefore be quashed as far as regarded the prisoner Harrison.

1874.
July 13.

IMPRISONMENT IN THE HOUSE OF CORRECTION.

Ord. No. 10, 1844.

1874.
August 13.

FITZPATRICK, J., said a case had come before him as Judge of the week, from Springbok, in which all the proceedings seemed to be correct except the sentence. The Magistrate had sentenced the prisoner to six months' imprisonment in the House of Correction in Cape Town. His Lordship could not find any authority empowering the Magistrate to choose a distant place of imprisonment. Among the papers was a letter from the Attorney-General in which it was stated that the woman could be sent down to the House of Correction in Cape Town if there was no accommodation at Springbok, but this was merely an intimation on the part of the Government, and should not form any part of the sentence. The case must be sent back to the Magistrate.

Jacobs, A.G., said Ord. No. 10, 1844, gave the Governor the power to alter the place of imprisonment, but it did not confer any such power on the Magistrate.

NEW RULES OF COURT.

Provisional Days.—Edictal Citation.—Commissioners.

The following Rules and Orders for regulating the practice of the Supreme Court have been approved of by His Excellency the Governor, and were published in the *Gazette* of the 7th August, 1874, in accordance with the provisions of section 3, of Act No. 15, of 1867 :—

1. The 5th Rule of the 26th December, 1872, is hereby repealed, and in lieu thereof the following rule is substituted:—The Supreme Court will sit for the hearing of provisional cases and motions on the 12th of January, 12th of March, 12th of April, 12th of July, 12th of September, and 12th of October.

2. In every case where, under the practice heretofore existing in the Supreme Court, the process of Edictal Citation would be necessary for the purpose of citing or otherwise compelling the appearance of any person to answer any complaint or demand, it shall be competent for the plaintiff before suing out process to apply to the Supreme Court, or the Eastern Districts Court, as the case may be, by petition, for directions as to the mode of serving the summons in such case, and as to the time for the appearance of the defendant to such summons, and thereupon the Court shall, by its order, give such directions in the premises as it shall deem proper and necessary, having due regard to the distance from this Colony of the place where the defendant is or is believed to be residing and to the other circumstances of the case ; and such summons, as well as all subsequent notices, pleadings, writs, rules, or other process in such case, shall be served in such manner, and subject to such conditions, as the Court shall, in each particular case, direct: provided that in any case in which the service of such summons shall not have been made on the defendant personally, and the defendant shall not have entered appearance, such summons shall not be deemed to have been duly served unless the same shall have been published once at least in the *Government Gazette*, not less than one calendar month before the day fixed for the appearance of the defendant, and unless the Court shall be satisfied, by affidavit, that reasonable and proper efforts had been made to serve such summons on the defendant personally.

3. The appointment of Commissioners of the Supreme Court, to take affidavits or examine witnesses, in any place out of the Colony, shall be by a Commission to be issued, under the Seal of the Supreme Court, in the following form :—

" To A. B., Esq.
(Occupation and address),

" GREETING,—

" We, confiding to your knowledge and ability, have committed, and hereby commit, to you full power and authority as a Commissioner of this Court to examine witnesses in all cases in which, by any rule or order of this Court, such examination shall be committed to you, and to take affidavits in all suits depending in this Court.

" To have, enjoy, and exercise the said office of our Commissioner as aforesaid, and the power and authority as aforesaid, until this our Commission be revoked."

SUPREME COURT REPORTS.

1874.

PART IV.

KEYTER *vs.* CHAMPION.

Promissory Note.—Consideration.—Provisional Sentence.

Provisional sentence refused on a promissory note, the defence being that the note was given for the purchase price of a claim at the Diamond Fields, but that there had been a failure of consideration in consequence of the claim having been sold by the holder before the note became due.

Buchanan, for the plaintiff, prayed for provisional sentence on a promissory note for £551 10s., less £250 received on account.

1874.
Nov. 20

Keyter *vs.*
Champion.

Jacobs, A.G., opposed, and put in defendant's affidavit, in which it was averred that the note was given in settlement of the purchase price of a one-eighth share of a claim at the Diamond Fields, but that the claim had never been transferred to the defendant, the plaintiff remaining the registered holder as security for the note. That in defendant's absence from the Fields, the plaintiff, a month before the note became due, without any authority from the defendant, had sold the claim for £250, for which credit was now given.

There were no answering affidavits.

The Court considered this was not a case for provision. Costs to abide the result of the principal case.

[At the trial at bar the plaintiff recovered judgment for the amount claimed, with costs.]

⎡ Plaintiff's Attorney, VAN ZYL. ⎤
⎣ Defendant's Attorney, TREDGOLD. ⎦

EXECUTRIX OF HAUPT *vs.* JOONES.

Provisional Sentence.—Promissory Note.

Provisional sentence granted on a promissory note, where the defendant alleged he had paid the amount to the payee, since deceased, and whose executrix now sued, but had not received the note back, or taken a receipt for the money.

1874.
Nov. 20.
——
Executrix of
Haupt *vs.*
Joones.

Jacobs, A.G., for the widow and executrix dative of the estate of the late D. P. Haupt, prayed provisional sentence on a promissory note, dated the 25th June, 1873, for £72, signed by defendant in favour of D. P. Haupt, and payable on the 25th September, 1873.

Cole opposed, and read defendant's affidavit showing the circumstances under which the note was given, and also averring that defendant had paid Haupt the amount of the note about a month before it fell due, when Haupt told defendant he must call again for his note, which he, Haupt, would look for among his papers, he having no time to do so then. Further, that defendant shortly after started on a trading trip, and on his return he found Haupt seriously ill, from which illness he had never recovered.

Answering affidavits were put in, from which it appeared *inter alia* that the promissory note in question was found after Haupt's decease among other bills receivable, and that Haupt's cash book, which seemed to be well kept, contained no entry of the repayment of the £72.

The Court granted provisional sentence with costs, leaving it to defendant to make good his defence in the principal case.

[Plaintiff's Attorneys, FAIRBRIDGE & ARDERNE.]
[Defendant's Attorney, TREDGOLD.]

HOHENKIRK & CO. *vs.* REYNOLDS.

Wine and Spirit License.—Ord. No. 9, 1851, sec. 25.

A license to sell liquors on certain premises mentioned in the license does not authorise the holder of such license to send round for orders, and to deliver liquor so sold at places other than the premises mentioned in the license.

1874.
Nov. 21.
——
Hohenkirk & Co.
vs. Reynolds.

Messrs. Hohenkirk & Co., the present applicants, had been summoned to appear before the Resident Magistrate of Springbokfontein, on the 12th October last, to answer to a charge of having contravened section 25, of Ordinance No.

9, of 1851, in that, on the 25th of August, and at or near 1874.
Nov. 20. O'okiep, they wrongfully and unlawfully sold spirituous liquors at a place other than the premises mentioned in their Hohenkirk & Co.
vs. Reynolds. license. Mr. Coevorden, one of the partners of the firm of Hohenkirk & Co., appeared before the Magistrate, and being arraigned, pleaded not guilty. The evidence taken showed that Hohenkirk & Co. held a wine and spirit license to sell liquors at Springbok. That they were in the habit of sending their servant Hess with a cart to O'okiep. That Hess, while at O'okiep, frequently received orders and money for liquors, which orders and money he took to his employer at Springbok, and on his return to O'okiep, delivered the liquors to the persons from whom he had received the orders. That in this particular case one Janse gave Hess the money for three bottles of brandy in the morning, and received the brandy from him in the afternoon at O'okiep. The magistrate convicted, and inflicted a fine of £10. From this decision Hohenkirk & Co. now appealed.

Cole, for the appellant, maintained that the facts stated did not amount to a contravention of the Ordinance.

Jacobs, A.G., for the Crown, supported the conviction, and cited *Turner* vs. *Evans*, 22, *L.J.*, *Q.B.*, 412.

The Court sustained the conviction, holding that the sale of the brandy had been made and completed at O'okiep, a place at which the defendants were not authorized to sell.

(The question of the validity of a sentence against a firm was waived by counsel, it being stated that a decision was desired on the merits apart from any technical irregularity.)

[Appellants' Attorneys, FAIRBRIDGE & ARDERNE.]

DELIA vs. NEETHLING.

Injury : verbal.—Privileged Communication.

A member of a Licensing Board has no privilege such as may attach to a judicial capacity of protection for any statements made by him at a meeting of such Board.

A statement made by a member of a Licensing Board at a meeting of the Board, respecting an applicant for a license, is a privileged communication, so that express malice must be proved to sustain an action for damages for defamation founded on a statement so made.

1874.
Nov. 24.
,, 25.

This was an action for £200 damages for defamation. The declaration stated that before and at the time of the Delia vs.
Neethling.

K

speaking and publishing by the defendant of the words hereafter mentioned, the plaintiff carried on the trade of an hotel keeper and licensed dealer in wines and spirits at Stellenbosch, and was an applicant for the renewal of his license as such licensed dealer. That thereupon the defendant, well knowing the premises, and contriving and intending to injure the plaintiff in his good name, fame and credit, and in his said trade and business, and in order to prevent the plaintiff from getting a renewal of his said license upon such favourable terms as he then enjoyed, did, on the 18th March, 1874, and at Stellenbosch, wrongfully, unlawfully, falsely, and maliciously speak and publish of and concerning the plaintiff, and of and concerning him in his said trade and business, the false and malicious words following, that is to say: " Delia's (meaning the plaintiff's) hotel is improperly kept, and is a disgrace to the village (meaning Stellenbosch aforesaid). The place (meaning the said hotel) is a continued scene of drunkenness. He (meaning the plaintiff) is in the habit of selling after licensed hours;" whereby and by reason whereof the plaintiff's license was not renewed on such favourable terms as he then had and possessed, and the hours during which he was at liberty to sell wines and liquors were curtailed, and the plaintiff was otherwise greatly injured in his good name, credit, and reputation, and in his said trade and business, and had lost and been deprived of great gains and profits, and had been, and was otherwise injured and damnified.

The defendant pleaded the general issue.

Jacobs, A.G. (with him *Maasdorp*), for the plaintiff, proved that the words complained of had been spoken by defendant at a meeting of the Licensing Board for the division of Stellenbosch, of which Board the defendant was a member. That in the month of October previous defendant had uttered threats against plaintiff, to the effect that he would injure defendant at the meeting of the Licensing Board, if plaintiff did not vote for defendant at the election of members for the Legislative Council. That defendant did not vote for plaintiff; and that after the election the threats had been repeated. That defendant had offered a reward to a policeman to catch plaintiff selling after hours. That in the license granted to plaintiff the word "travellers" was defined to be persons residing beyond six miles from the seat of magistracy, which limitation had not been contained in the former license. That plaintiff had lost since March last, by the falling off in his trade, in consequence of this restriction, the sum of £209.

On plaintiff closing his case,

Buchanan (with him *Kotze*), for the defendant, applied for absolution from the instance, on the ground *inter alia*, that as the Licensing Board exercised judicial functions, no action would lie against a member of the Board for words uttered by him in the discharge of his duty, even though there was express malice. (*Voet*, 47, 10, 20, " *magistratus quoque;* " *Dig.*, 47, 10, 13, 6; *Starkie* (*3rd ed.*), *p.* 314; *Scott* vs. *Stansfield*, 37, *L.J.*, *Exch.*, 155; *Thomas* vs. *Churton*, 8, *Jur.*, *n.s.*, 795; *Kershaw* vs. *Bailey*, 1 *Exch.*, 743.)

Jacobs, *A.G.*, for the plaintiff, opposed, and contended that it was not clear by our law that even a judge was absolutely protected; but even if he was, the defendant did not come within any such privilege, for when he uttered the words complained of he was not acting in a judicial capacity. (*Floyd* vs. *Barter*, 12; *Coke*, *pt.* 13, *p.* 23; *Bowyer's Civil Law*, 276 ; *Inst.*, 4, 5, 1).

Buchanan, in reply, referred to the decisions in the notes to *Ashby* vs. *White*, *Smith's Leading Cases*, 5th ed., *p.* 259.

Absolution refused ; the Court, without deciding the point of law as to absolute privilege, holding that the defendant did not, in this case, act in such a judicial capacity as to bring him within the protection claimed.

The evidence for the defence was then led. The defendant denied having used any threats, or that he had been actuated by malice. Witnesses were called to show the manner in which plaintiff conducted his business, and that complaints had been made of irregularities to the police.

After hearing counsel on the merits,

DE VILLIERS, C.J., said there was no difference of opinion as to the law in this case. What was said by defendant was said upon a privileged occasion, and therefore for the plaintiff to succeed in this action he must show that the words were spoken falsely and maliciously. In his opinion the words complained of had been used *bon fide* in the discharge of a public duty, and not falsely and maliciously.

DENYSSEN, J., and FITZPATRICK, J., considered malice had been proved, and held, therefore, that judgment should be for plaintiff.

Judgment accordingly for plaintiff for £25 damages and costs.

[Plaintiff's Attorneys, CHRISTIE & DU PREEZ.]
[Defendant's Attorney, J. HORAK DE VILLIERS.]

LOUW *vs.* THE REGISTRAR OF DEEDS.

Bond : cancellation of.

The receipt of the amount and consent to the cancellation
of a bond, signed by the firm, held sufficient where the
bond had been passed in favour of "M.L., G.L., and
L.L., trading together under the style or firm of L.
Brothers."

The applicant, Louw, on the 3rd June last, passed and
executed a mortgage bond by which he declared himself
" to be really and lawfully indebted to, and on behalf of
Martin Lillienfield, Gustave Lillienfield, and Leopold
Lillienfield, trading together at Hope Town under the style
or firm of Lillienfield Brothers," in a sum of money arising
from, and being the amount of certain promissory notes
" due to the said firm of Lillienfield Brothers," which debt
had been taken over by him; and which applicant undertook to pay "unto the said firm of Lillienfield Brothers,
their order," &c. The amount having been paid, applicant
received his bond, endorsed :—

" Received the within amount, and we agree to the cancellation of this Bond.

(Signed) " Lillienfield Brothers.
" Hope Town, 6th October, 1874."

The bond, with this endorsement, was presented at the
Registry of Deeds, but the Registrar refused to cancel it
unless each of the partners individually signified their consent to the cancellation.

Cole, for the applicant, moved for an order to compel the
Registrar of Deeds to cancel the bond. He submitted that
as the bond was payable to the firm of Lillienfield Brothers,
or their order, the signature of the firm was sufficient to
authorize its cancellation. All the partners were not resident in the Colony, consequently each of their signatures
could not be obtained.

Jacobs, A.G., for the Registrar of Deeds, opposed ; and
read the affidavit of the Chief Clerk, which averred that in
refusing to cancel the bond, he was carrying out what had
always been the practice of the office in respect to the cancellation of bonds similar to the present; and that such
practice was expressly confirmed by the late Attorney-
General, Mr. Porter, who maintained that money invested
on mortgage of landed property by the partners of a firm

1874.
Dec. 3.

Louw *vs.* The
Registrar of
Deeds.

could not be considered as belonging to the ordinary mercantile transactions of such a firm; and that the signature and consent of every individual member of the firm was necessary to the cancellation of such a bond.

The Court held that the bond in this case, being payable to the firm, did not come within the rule contended for by the Registrar of Deeds, and granted the order for its cancellation as prayed.

[Applicant's Attorney, VAN ZYL.
Respondent's Attorneys, REID & NEPHEW.]

In re NEETHLING.

Contempt of Court.—Procedure.

A letter published in a newspaper containing undue reflections on a Judge of the Supreme Court in regard to his conduct in a suit which had been heard and determined, is a Contempt of Court which may be inquired into on summary process.

Words calculated to bring the administration of justice into contempt, though they do not amount to a libel on the Judge, constitute a Contempt of Court.

1874.
Dec. 3.
„ 4.
„ 8.

In re Neethling.

This matter rose out of the case of *Delia* vs *Neethling*, tried the early part of this term [*vide* page 129]. The defendant wrote a letter addressed to the Editor of the *Cape Argus,* which letter was published in the issue of that paper of the 3rd December. The defendant complained of the comments which had appeared in that journal, criticising the defendant's conduct in relation to the above suit. In the letter the following passage appeared :—" Had not Mr. Justice Fitzpatrick, with his wonted humour or abandon, given unrestrained license to his tongue, you would not have ventured to indulge in such intemperate language. You cannot plead the privilege of the Judge."

(December 3rd),—

DE VILLIERS, C.J., stated that the attention of the Court had been directed to the letter. As it contained so gross an attack upon a Judge of this Court in regard to what he had said in the discharge of his judicial duties, he would hand the matter over to the Attorney-General, leaving him to take such proceedings as he thought proper.

Postea (December 4th),—

Jacobs, A.G., on an affidavit, stating that the letter in question had been written by M. L. Neethling, J.H.'s son, and had been sent by him to the editor of the *Cape Argus* for publication, applied *ex parte* for an order of Court calling on the writer to appear peremptorily before the Court to answer for the contempt contained in the letter. This course had been adopted in *Skipworth's* case, and the cases of *Onslow* and *Whalley,* all in connection with the *Tichborne* trial (9, *L.R., Q.B.,* 219).

The Court granted the following order :—

" In the Supreme Court of the Colony of the Cape of Good Hope.
" Cape Town, Friday, the 4th day of December, 1874.
" The Queen
against
" The Honourable Marthinus Laurentius Neethling, J. H.'s son, Member of the Legislative Council, Respondent.
" Upon the motion of Her Majesty's Attorney-General for this Colony, and upon reading the affidavit of Patrick McLoughlin, Editor of the *Cape Argus* newspaper, sworn this day, and the documents annexed thereto,
" It is ordered that the above named Marthinus Laurentius Neethling do attend this Honourable Court on Tuesday, the eighth day of this present month of December, at ten in the forenoon, peremptorily to answer for a certain Contempt of Court committed by him, in having written and caused to be published in the *Cape Argus* newspaper, of the 3rd December instant, a certain letter signed by him, the said Marthinus Laurentius Neethling, dated Stellenbosch, 30th November, 1874; and to show cause, if any, why he should not be punished and dealt with as this Honourable Court shall think fit for the contempt aforesaid.

" By order of the Court,

" J. C. B. SERRURIER,
" Registrar of the Supreme Court."

Postea (December 8),—The order having been duly served, and Neethling being in Court,

Cole, for the respondent, took exception to the form of

proceeding adopted. He submitted that as this was a criminal offence, the respondent was entitled to be tried by a jury. It was unprecedented and unconstitutional to deal summarily with a case of this kind, where there was no necessity for so doing. In *Skipworth's*, and the other cases cited by the Attorney-General, there was a trial proceeding at the time; here the trial had ended. Moreover, the decisions in these cases had been seriously questioned by the profession. (*Vide Law Magazine*, February, 1873.) Counsel also argued that the words used did not amount to contempt of Court. The letter might be very improper, and the language used silly, but it was the language of an angry man smarting under the attacks of a newspaper, and could not bring the Court into contempt.

Jacobs, A.G., supported the procedure. It was clear that contempt committed when the Court was not sitting could be punished summarily, as well as contempt committed in its face and *sedente curiâ*. (2, *Pleas of the Crown*, p. 206; *Stephen's Blackstone's Commentaries*, p. 284; *McDermott's case*, 2, *L.R., P.C.*, 341; *In re Charlton*, 2, *Mylne & C.*, 216; *Ex parte Turner*, 3, *Mont., D., & De Gex.*, 523.)

The Court held that contempt of Court had been committed, and that it was punishable summarily.

DE VILLIERS, C.J.:—I do not think there is anything in the preliminary objection that has been taken, namely, that this is not a pending suit. The only authority quoted by Mr. Cole in support of his view, that there can be no contempt of Court except in a pending suit, is the opinion of the writer of an article in the *Law Magazine*. The author of that article may have very great weight as a writer as to what the law ought to be, but I think the opinions of Judges in the Court of Queen's Bench, and of the Privy Council, ought certainly to weigh against him. As to the second point the Court is satisfied that there has been a contempt of Court in this case. Mr. Cole in his argument has very fairly put this as a crucial test, whether the words are calculated to bring the administration of justice into contempt. Now, if in a serious case like that before the Court, namely, the case of *Delia* vs. *Neethling*, one of the Judges had "in a spirit of humour and abandon," as it is stated here, "given unrestrained license to his tongue," I do not know anything in the world more calculated to bring the administration of justice into contempt than such conduct on the part of a Judge; and for this simple reason I am of opinion that the words used amount to a contempt of Court. I do not think the test is whether the words would be a libel. In the case mentioned from British Guiana (*McDermott's* case) there was no libel upon the Judge, but there were words spoken of him calculated to bring the administration of justice into contempt. By this decision of the Court the freedom of criticising the judgments of Judges and the conduct of Judges, like that of anyone else, is not at all taken away. That freedom must always remain ; in fact it would be a sorry thing for this Colony or any other country if this freedom should ever be taken away. But I think in this case there has been exercised not a freedom, but a license, to use the words of Mr. Neethling himself; and when it comes to that, I think it is the duty of this Court to put a stop to it, and that in a peremptory manner.

DENYSSEN, J. :—I am of the same opinion. Although I do not see any objection to the preliminary objection which has been taken to the proceedings in this matter, I very much regret that another course has not been adopted with reference to what has now been declared to be a contempt of Court. Contempts of Court may be new—at least, I do not know of any instance since the constitution of this Court and the promulgation of the Charter of Justice; but it is an unquestionable right of the Court, and it is an inherent right, if anything is said or done to bring the Judges or the proceedings of the Court into contempt, to take notice of it by summary process, and if necessary to punish by fine or imprisonment, or both. I must not, however, be misunderstood. It is as unquestionably the right of the public to criticize fairly and honestly the proceedings of a Judge in Court, or the proceedings of the Court together, but in this case there has been an excess of that liberty, and not only an excess, but a very important excess. Therefore, I think it was not only necessary, but absolutely necessary for the Court, the custodian of its privileges, and bound to uphold its dignity and support its respect, that notice should be taken of what was said in the letter written by the defendant.

Cole :—Before judgment is passed I hope Your Lordships will allow me to say that all I have hitherto done has been done acting entirely in reference to my own opinion as counsel for the defendant. He placed his case in my hands, and at the time authorized me to present this apology to Your Lordships. I considered it my duty, as he was accused of a criminal offence, to have it judicially decided whether he was guilty or not. In so doing I hope I shall not prejudice my client in the least in the eyes of the Court. This is the apology Mr. Neethling has desired me to read :—

"**My** Lords,—In writing and publishing the letter complained of, I had but one object in view, to defend myself from the unjust aspersions of the *Argus*. I alluded to Judge Fitzpatrick indirectly, not with the purpose of holding His Lordship's judgment up to public criticism, but clearly with the view of exposing the insufficient grounds the Editor of the *Argus* had for his coarse comments upon the matter, an unprivileged journalist assuming the right of a privileged Judge on the Bench. When a man's honour is unexpectedly assailed, I respectfully submit he may be excused for not being particularly choice in his selection of language to express his strong feelings in such a moment of intense excitement, just as a person, when his life is unexpectedly endangered, may be pardoned for using a weapon in self-defence which in cooler moments he would consider inappropriate and even reprehensible. I beg to repudiate most emphatically the construction put upon the part of my letter in question, as being intentionally a reflection on the judgment of your Honourable Court or any member of it, or of having intended to commit myself to any act which may be considered as done in contempt of it. If Your Lordships should be of opinion that my language reflects improperly upon your Honourable Bench or any individual member of it, I can have no hesitation in urgently begging permission to apologise for having used such language, and to retract openly here any part of it which Your Lordships may consider unbecoming a gentleman towards our highest Colonial Civil Court, or derogatory to its dignity. In conclusion, may I be allowed to assure Your Lordships that my letter was exclusively intended to express my dissent from, and my dissatisfaction with, the remarks of the Editor of the *Argus* concerning this case, and with no other object.

1874.
Dec. 3.
" 4.
" 8.

In re Neethling.

"M. L. NEETHLING."

The Court, after hearing the above explanation, intimated that no order would be made.

The rule was accordingly discharged.

SMITH AND ANOTHER *vs.* KOTZE.

Insolvency.—Execution.—Ord. No. 6, 1843, sec. 127.

Writ of execution granted under the 127th section of the Insolvent Ordinance, against property acquired by an Insolvent subsequently to surrender, he not having obtained his rehabilitation.

138

Buchanan, for Smith, one of the trustees, and Mills, a creditor in the Insolvent Estate of L. J. D. Kotze, moved on a notice served on the insolvent to show cause why execution should not issue, in terms of the 127th section of the Insolvent Ordinance, against insolvent's goods and chattels for and in satisfaction of the deficiency existing in his estate, amounting, upon the liquidation account framed by the trustees, to the sum of £552 6s. 6d. sterling.

From the affidavits put in, it appeared that Kotze surrendered his estate as insolvent on the 5th February, 1868. That Smith proved claims to the amount of £57 3s. 2d., and Mills to the amount of £237 7s. That an account was framed by the trustees and confirmed by the Court on the 21st September, 1869. That the debts proved amounted in all to the sum of £552 6s. 6d., and the balance for distribution to £24; thus leaving a deficiency in the estate of £528 6s. 6d. That insolvent since his surrender had farmed very successfully for his own account, and had now valuable crops growing on the farm Uitkomst, leased by him. That an action was now pending against insolvent for ejectment, in which action insolvent had claimed £2,000 in reconvention as the value of improvements made by him. That the deficiency due Smith was £54 12s. 8d., and due Mills £217 7s. That insolvent was also possessed of certain mules, horses, stock, and a complete farming establishment.

Jacobs, A.G., for the respondent, opposed, and put in his affidavits showing that in consequence of the trustees of the insolvent estate having omitted to file the dividend receipts, he had been prevented from applying for his rehabilitation in November, 1872, when no objection was raised to his being rehabilitated. Further, that the greater part of the stock referred to had been purchased for account and in the name of respondent's children; and that what now belonged to respondent had been paid for by the earnings and the reward of his work and labour.

As respondent averred that this application was made so as to prejudice his defence in the action of ejectment above referred to, it was ordered to stand over until that action had been disposed of.

Postea (December 10),—

The Court granted the application, execution to issue for £250, and costs of the motion.

Applicants' Attorney, C. C. DE VILLIERS.
Respondent's Attorneys, BERRANGE & DE VILLIERS.

RAUBENHEIMER AND OTHERS *vs.* BLAND AND THE DIVISIONAL COUNCIL OF RIVERSDALE.

Act No. 4, 1865, sec. 13.—Member of Divisional Council : who is eligible to be elected as.

The uncontested election of a member of a Divisional Council annulled and declared void, on the ground that such member at the time of election was not a registered voter for the division under the Constitution Ordinance, and was not the registered owner of immovable property within the division assessed of the value of £500.

Notice had been served on respondents calling upon them to show cause why the election of Bland, the first-named respondent, as a member for District No. 1, of the Divisional Council of Riversdale, on the 16th July last, and notified in the *Gazette* of the 24th July, should not be declared null and void, by reason,—first, that the said Bland was not at the time of his election a registered voter under the Constitution Ordinance entitled to vote for the division of Riversdale ; and secondly, that he was not at such time the registered owner of immovable property situated in the said division, assessed for road purposes of the value of £500.

1874. Dec. 10.

Raubenheimer and Others *vs.* Bland and the Divisional Council of Riversdale.

The affidavit of applicants' attorney set forth that search had been made in the official registers, and that respondent Bland was found at the time of his election not to be a registered voter for the division of Riversdale, nor the registered owner of immovable property within that division of the value of £500. The affidavit of the applicant Raubenheimer stated that no notice inviting the nomination of a member for District No. 1 was ever posted up at any public place by the Civil Commissioner, and that for want of publicity the election of the respondent Bland was uncontested. That not being aware of the election, no objection was taken thereto by applicant at the meeting of the Divisional Council held on the 9th September, when Bland first took his seat ; but that at the special meeting of the Council held on the 7th October, he tendered a protest against the election on the grounds of non-qualification stated above, but that the Civil Commissioner, as chairman of the Council, refused to receive such protest.

For the respondents was put in an affidavit made by Bland, stating that he was formerly a resident in the division of Mossel Bay, in which district he was a registered voter, and a member of the Divisional Council ; that upon the 2nd May, 1873, he removed to Riversdale ; that upon

1874.
Dec. 10.

Raubenheimer
and Others *vs.*
Bland and the
Divisional Coun-
cil of Riversdale.

the 5th June he purchased immovable property to the
value of upwards of £500, of which transfer was effected
on the 18th September, 1874; that although possessing the
necessary qualification, he had no opportunity of registering
himself as a voter in the division of Riversdale until the
general registration of 1874. Also the affidavit of W. D
Rainier, clerk to the Civil Commissioner, stating that or
the vacancy occurring for District No. 1, a written notice
was posted up at the public offices at Riversdale, inviting
voters to nominate a candidate for the vacant seat, and that
a copy of the notice was published in the *Gazette* of the
19th June; that respondent Bland was the only candidate
nominated, and that he was accordingly declared duly
elected on the 17th July; and that no objections or pro-
tests were filed against the said nomination or election.

Cole, for the applicants, cited *Cane* vs. *Bergh and Mader,
Buch. Reports*, 1873, p. 102.

Jacobs, A.G, for the respondent Bland, showed cause, and
contended that this was not a case in which the Court had
power to interfere. The 25th section of Act No. 4, 1865,
provided that if no greater number of candidates were nominated than there were vacancies to be filled, the candidates
so nominated should be deemed to be duly elected. The 14th
section stated who were disqualified to be elected, and non-
registration was not there specified as a disqualification.
The respondent at the time of election was the possessor of
immovable property, though it was not transferred until
afterwards. The 49th section required that objections to
persons ineligible under the 14th section must be taken
within seven days after the election, while, in this instance,
no objection at all had been lodged. If this section did not
also provide for the objection of non-registration it was a
casus omissus, and there was no provision for its being
remedied. The 58th section showed how vacancies in the
Council would be created, but there was no authority given
to the Court to declare a vacancy.

Cole, in reply, referred to the difference in the wording
between the 47th section of the Constitution Ordinance,
and the 14th section of the Act No. 4, 1865. As to a
casual vacancy, that was provided for by the 59th section.

FITZPATRICK, J.—The 58th section refers to persons who
were duly qualified when elected, but who had since become
disqualified. In this case the person never was qualified,
and must be taken as if he had never been in existence.

DE VILLIERS, C.J.—It is clear that the voters are entitled
to be represented by persons properly qualified. Where
there is a right, and that right is infringed, there must be a

remedy. Where candidates are qualified under the 14th section a remedy is provided by the 49th section, but nothing is said as to disqualification under the 13th section. If, then, the voters have no remedy within the four corners of the Act, this Court should provide one. I am of opinion Bland was not qualified to be elected, and in this decision I am supported by the judgment already given in *Cane's* case. This election must be declared void *ab initio*.

1874.
Dec. 10.
—
Raubenheimer
and Others *vs.*
Bland and the
Divisional Coun-
cil of Riversdale.

Ordered accordingly, with costs against the respondent Bland.

[Applicants' Attorneys, CHRISTIE & DU PREEZ.
Respondents' Attorneys, FAIRBRIDGE & ARDERNE.]

OWEN *vs.* VIGORS, N.O.

Execution : payment of proceeds of into Court, and action brought to recover same stayed.

Where the Sheriff had, in execution of a writ, attached certain movables, which movables were subsequently claimed by a third person, and on obtaining an indemnity from the plaintiff, the Sheriff had proceeded to sell the attached goods, the Court allowed the proceeds of such sale to be paid into Court, and ordered an action instituted by the plaintiff against the Sheriff to recover the amount realised to be stayed, pending the result of a suit commenced by the alleged owner of the goods attached.

The Deputy-Sheriff of King William's Town had been directed to make a levy of the goods of one Sage, in execution of a sentence of the Eastern Districts Court in a suit in which Owen had been plaintiff, and the said Sage defendant. Under this writ a wagon and eight oxen were seized, but were immediately claimed on affidavit by one Devitt as his property. Owen instructed the Deputy-Sheriff to sell the goods, giving a personal indemnity to hold the Sheriff harmless. The Deputy-Sheriff sold, and realized £84 13s. 7d. Devitt thereupon commenced an action against the Sheriff for £150, the value of the wagon and oxen, and damages. The Sheriff gave notice of this to Owen, and called upon him to intervene, but without result. Owen also commenced an action against the Sheriff for the amount realised by the levy, and for £50 damages.

1874.
Dec. 10.
—
Owen *vs.* Vigors,
N.O.

Jacobs, A.G., for the defendant, now applied for an order

1874.
Dec. 10.

Owen vs. Vigors,
N.O.

attaching the sum of £84 13s. 7d., in defendant's hands pending the result of the action instituted by Devitt; and further restraining Owen from proceeding with the sui commenced by him.

Buchanan, for the plaintiff, opposed, urging that as Owen had given an indemnity he was entitled at once to receive the amount levied in execution of his writ.

The Court ordered the money realised to be paid into Court pending the result of the action brought by Devitt in the meantime, the action brought by Owen to be stayed Costs reserved.

[Applicant's Attorneys, REDLINGHUYS & WESSELS.]
[Respondent's Attorney, TREDGOLD.]

QUEEN vs. REIKERT.

Malicious Injury to Property.

The offence of malicious injury to property is a crime by the law of this Colony, and as such is punishable criminally.

1874.
Dec. 10.

Queen vs. Rei-
kert.

Simon Johan Reikert, an agriculturist, residing at Martha's Put, in the district of Victoria West, was tried at the Circuit Court for that district on the 5th October last on an indictment charging the crime of malicious injury to property, in having, on the said farm Martha's Put, shot killed and destroyed certain horses and cattle, the property of Thomas Hugo and others. The jury found a verdict of guilty, whereupon arrest of judgment was moved on the ground that the facts stated in the indictment did not amount in law to a crime. The presiding Judge [DE VILLIERS C.J.] overruled the objection, and passed sentence against the prisoner of a fine of £100, or in default twelve months imprisonment; but granted leave to the prisoner, if so advised, to bring His Lordship's decision under the review of the Supreme Court, saving to the Public Prosecutor all just exceptions.

Buchanan, for the prisoner, now moved to set aside the conviction as being incompetent, irregular, and contrary to law, and to have the judgment of the Circuit Court thereon vacated. He submitted that the crime of malicious injury to property was unknown either to the statute or common law of the Colony. Malicious injury was, at common law, merely a trespass, and had in England been rendered penal only by statute. There was no statute in this Colony rendering it penal, and the text writers referred to it only as entitling to pecuniary compensation. In this case the cattle had been shot by prisoner while straying on his own property. Though convictions had been obtained in the Supreme Court on indictments charging this offence, yet a crime could not be created by usage. (*Stephen's Com.*, 230; *Voet*, 9, 2, 12; *Inst.*, 4, 3, 1; *Dig.*, 9, 2, 1; *Groene. de. leg. ab.*, 1, 4, 3, 9.)

Jacobs, A.G., for the Crown, opposed. Since 1837, indictments had been laid and convictions obtained in this Colony for the crime of malicious injury to property. The common law of Scotland bore more similarity to our law than did that of England; and *Alison*, p. 448, stated that this crime was punishable at common law in Scotland. The definition of crime against property, in *Grotius*, 3, 37, 1, included a charge such as was laid in this case.

DE VILLIERS, C.J.—The only doubt I had at the trial arose from the fact that the horses were shot on prisoner's land. But the indictment charges the prisoner with having " wrongfully, unlawfully, and maliciously " shot them, and the jury found him guilty of this. As I stated then, I may now repeat, that as it had been the practice of the Supreme Court to treat this offence as a crime, I felt bound by their decision. Since then, in looking over the authorities I came upon *Mathæus de Crim.*, 2nd ed., p. 120. The conviction must therefore stand.

Application accordingly refused.

[Applicant's Attorney, PIERS.]

1874.
Dec. 10.
——
Queen *vs.* Reikert.

GOODISON *vs.* GOODISON.

Divorce.—Adultery.—Desertion.

The absence of the husband leaving the wife unprovided for, does not excuse the adultery of the wife, or afford a defence to an action for divorce.

This was an action for divorce on the ground of adultery, brought by the husband against his wife. The defendant pleaded the general issue, and then specially, that between the day of the celebration of the marriage, to wit, the 11th January, 1859, and the 4th March, 1865, the plaintiff was guilty of repeated acts of cruelty and neglect towards the

1874.
Dec. 15.
——
Goodison *vs.*
Goodison.

defendant, and left her constantly without any means of support. That on the said 4th March, 1865, the plaintiff took his departure from this Colony for Australia without making any sort of provision for the defendant or the children born of the marriage, thereby wilfully and maliciously, and without any lawful cause, deserting the defendant; and that from the day of such wilful and malicious desertion up to the present time, the plaintiff had never contributed in any way to the maintenance and support of the defendant and her aforesaid children, but had left them wholly destitute and unprovided for. Further, that during such wilful and malicious desertion, the plaintiff was in Australia convicted of forgery, and sentenced to imprisonment for five years. By reason whereof the plaintiff was estopped and debarred by his own acts from demanding a dissolution of the marriage.

The replication was general.

Buchanan, for the plaintiff, led evidence to prove the marriage and the adultery. Plaintiff admitted that he left the Colony in March, 1865, but asserted that it was with the defendant's knowledge and consent, defendant's mother undertaking to provide for her and the younger children during plaintiff's absence. The conviction in Australia was admitted, and also that plaintiff had not, after leaving the Colony, contributed towards defendant's support.

Cole, for the defendant, contended that plaintiff's conduct amounted to desertion, and that, even though the adultery had been proved, the plaintiff not coming to the Court with clean hands was not now entitled to ask for a divorce. But after reference to *Voet*, 24, 2, 7, he withdrew his contention.

The Court granted the decree as prayed.

[Plaintiff's Attorney, BUISSINNE.
Defendant's Attorneys, FAIRBRIDGE & ARDERNE.]

WALKER vs. EXECUTORS OF WALKER.

Will: execution.—Ord. No. 15, 1845, *sec.* 3.

A will written on four pages of a sheet, attested only at the end of the writing, set aside as informal, section 3, of Ordinance No. 15, of 1845, requiring that the testator and witnesses shall sign upon at least one side of every leaf upon which the instrument is written.

This was an action to set aside the will of the late Henry Walker, on the ground that the document having been written on more than one leaf of paper, namely, on two such leaves, and the attesting witnesses having signed their names at the end of the writing only, and not on one side at least of such leaves, the will was invalid. It was also prayed, as the plaintiff was the sole surviving brother of the deceased, and his nearest surviving relation, and as such the only person interested in the administration of his estate *ab intestato*, that the plaintiff might be declared sole heir *ab intestato*, and entitled to all deceased's estate and effects.

Cole, for the plaintiff, produced the will and proved his case.

Jacobs, A.G., for the executors, submitted to the judgment of the Court.

The Court ordered the will to be set aside as invalid; but refused to declare the plaintiff sole heir, leaving him to proceed as in an ordinary case of intestacy. Costs to come out of the estate.

[Plaintiff's Attorneys, REID & NEPHEW.
Defendants' Attorneys, FAIRBRIDGE & ARDERNE.]

1874.
Dec. 15.

Walker *vs.*
Executors o
Walker.

In re BASSON.

Insolvency.—Ord. No. 6, 1843, secs. 62 and 65.—Commissioner.—Order for examination.

The Court will not grant an order in general terms for the examination of persons before a Commissioner appointed under the Insolvent Ordinance. The persons to be examined must be indicated.

This was an application made on behalf of the trustee of the insolvent estate of Jan Hendrick Basson, of the division of Wodehouse, for the appointment of a Commissioner for the purpose of examining on oath the insolvent regarding his dealings and transactions, and also to examine one Wagenaar, "and such other person or persons as the trustee may deem necessary in the interest of the estate," with power to call upon such witnesses or any of them to produce any books, papers, deeds, writings, or other documents in his or their custody, which might appear necessary to the verification or disclosure of any of the insolvent's transactions.

Buchanan, for the trustee, read affidavits and report,

1874.
Dec. 17.

In re Basson.

showing that an investigation was desirable and had been requested by the creditors; and submitted that under the 62nd and 66th sections of the Insolvent Ordinance, it was not necessary to name the persons to be examined, but that the trustee should be empowered to call upon such parties as it might transpire could give any explanation on insolvent's dealings.

The Court refused to grant an order in general terms, but appointed a Commissioner to examine the insolvent and Wagenaar, who had been specially named.

[*Sed vide In re* BARKER, next case.]

[Applicant's Attorney, VAN ZYL.]

In re BARKER.

Ord. No. 6, 1843, *sec.* 65.—*Commissioner.*

The Court granted an order for the examination before a Commissioner appointed in terms of the Insolvent Ordinance, of " the clerks employed by the insolvent," without such clerks being specially named.

Jacobs, A.G., for certain creditors in the insolvent estate of Joseph Barker, applied in terms of Ordinance No. 6, 1843, for the appointment of a Commissioner, to examine James Scullard and H. P. Bennett, with whom the insolvent had had large transactions, and also to examine the clerks employed by the insolvent. Counsel submitted that this was not a general or roving commission, but that the persons to be examined, though not individually named, were sufficiently indicated.

The Court granted the order as prayed.

[Applicant's Attorneys, FAIRBRIDGE & ARDERNE.]

MACDONALD, N.O., *vs.* BRAMSON.

Appeal.—Charter of Justice, sec. 43.

For the purpose of deciding whether, under the 43rd section of the Charter of Justice, there is a right of appeal from the decision of a Circuit Court, the " sum or matter at

*issue " must be ascertaind by reference to the pleadings,
and not from the circumstances of the case as disclosed at
the trial.*

The defendant had been sued in the Circuit Court for the
district of Port Elizabeth, held in November last, by the
plaintiff in his capacity of tutor dative to certain minors, in
an action for the recovery of the sums of £90 for rent, and
£30 5s 5d. for rates and taxes, alleged to be due under the
provisions of a certain lease. The defendant pleaded, first,
the general issue; secondly, a set off of £86 7s. 3d. for costs
due by plaintiff in his said capacity to the defendant;
thirdly, a tender before action brought of £3 12s. 9d., the
balance between the set off and the claim of £90; fourthly,
a tender of £22 2s. 3d., part of the amount claimed for rent
and taxes. Judgment was given for the plaintiff for
£112 2s. 3d., and costs; being for full amount of £90
claimed as due for rent, and £22 2s. 3d. as tendered. The
presiding Judge refused to grant an appeal, which the defendant claimed to be entitled to as of right under the 43rd
section of the Charter of Justice, on the ground that although
the amount sued for and the amount for which judgment
was given exceeded £100, yet as the defendant had tendered
£3 12s. 9d. part of the rent, and £22 2s. 3d. part of the
rates and taxes demanded, the amount " at issue " was under
£100, and therefore there was no right of appeal.

1874.
Dec. 17.
———
Macdonald,
N.O., vs.
Bramson.

Ross-Johnson (with him *Upington*), for the defendant, now
moved for leave to appeal from the judgment of the Court
below, and submitted that from the pleadings the sum or
matter at issue, the defendant having pleaded the general
denial to plaintiff's claim, amounted to more than £100. In
the case of *Knight* vs. *Chabaud*, where damages were laid at
£500, an appeal was allowed, though only £50 were recovered; and in *Harris* vs. *Dreesman*, 23, *L.J., Exch.,* 210,
an appeal was held to lie from a County Court, the sum
claimed being above the limit, though the verdict was for an
amount under the limit.

Jacobs, A.G. (with him *Cole*), for the plaintiff, opposed, on
the ground that the issue to be tried was under £100.
Moreover no hardship was suffered by the defendant, for it
was competent to him to bring an action to recover the
amount he claimed to set off against plaintiff's demand. The
sum claimed in the declaration must not always be taken
as deciding the amount in issue. In the case of *McFarlane*
vs. *Leclaire,* 15, *Moore's P.C.C.,* 181, it was held that the
value of certain goods seized in execution of a judgment,

1874.
Dec. 17.

Macdonald,
N.O., vs.
Bramson.

and not the sum claimed and for which judgment was obtained, must be considered in deciding on the right to appeal. In *James* vs. *Lord Harry Vane*, 29, *L.J.*, *Q.B.*, 169, an action in which more than £20, the limit entitling to costs on the higher scale, was claimed, the defendant having paid £24 into Court, and the jury gave damages to the extent of £2 10s. in excess of the sum paid into Court, it was held that the costs should be taxed on the reduced scale. Deducting the amount tendered by the defendant in this case, the matter at issue was less than the £100 fixed as the limit by the 43rd section of the Charter.

Ross-Johnson replied.

The Court held the defendant entitled to an appeal as a matter of right, and it was therefore unnecessary to grant the leave now moved for. Costs of the application to abide the result of the appeal.

Applicant's Attorneys, FAIRBRIDGE & ARDERNE.
Respondent's Attorneys, REID & NEPHEW.

HOUGH vs. VAN DER MERWE.

Water rights of lower proprietors.—Public Stream.

In considering the uses to which the water of a public stream may be applied, a distinction must be made between the ordinary or primary use, and the extraordinary or secondary use of the water.

If the upper proprietor, in the enjoyment of his ordinary use, deprives the lower proprietors of their ordinary use, he would not be liable to them in an action; but if an upper proprietor, in the enjoyment of his extraordinary use, deprives the lower proprietors of their extraordinary use, he would be liable.

The owner of land by or through which a public stream flows, is entitled to divert a portion of the water for the purposes of irrigation, provided,—firstly: That he does not thereby deprive the lower proprietors of sufficient water for their cattle and for domestic purposes. Secondly: That he uses no more than a just and reasonable proportion of the water consistently with similar rights of irrigation in the lower proprietors (what constitutes a just and reasonable use is entirely a question of degree, dependent upon the circumstances of each particular case). And thirdly: That he returns the water to the public stream with no other loss than that which irrigation has caused.

Jacobus Nel van der Merwe and Schalk Willem Jacobus van der Merwe, the defendants in this suit, were summoned to answer Jacobus Petrus Hough, the plaintiff, in an action for the recovery of damages, and for other purposes.

1874.
Aug. 27.
Dec. 1.
„ 2.
„ 19.

Hough vs. Van der Merwe.

The plaintiff declared that at the time of the committing of the grievances complained of, the plaintiff was possessed of the farm Elandsvlei, in the Calvinia district, and the defendants were possessed of the farm Elandsdrift, situated above the plaintiff's farm. That by reason of such possession the plaintiff was entitled to the flow of a certain stream called the Groot Rivier, or Doorn Rivier, from the farm of the defendants through and over the farm of the plaintiff without the same being obstructed; yet the defendants, well-knowing the premises, in or about the month of January last, erected upon their farm a certain dam across the said stream or river, and kept the same so erected from the 23rd January until the 8th March, during all which time the water of the said stream or river was prevented from flowing through and over the plaintiff's farm as it of right ought to have done; whereby the plaintiff suffered damage to the amount of £75. And the plaintiff further complained that in the month of March last the defendants made or commenced to make a water-furrow or ditch across the bed of the said stream or river, whereby the water which ought of right to flow through and over the plaintiff's farm during certain months of the year had been and would be diverted from its usual and proper course and prevented from flowing down to, through, and over the plaintiff's farm as of right it ought to do. Wherefore the plaintiff prayed the Court to declare that he was entitled to have the water of the said stream or river flow through and over his said farm without being obstructed; and that the defendants be ordered to remove any dam or other obstruction, and be restrained by perpetual interdict from again erecting any dam or obstruction, or constructing any ditch or water-furrow, so as to interfere with the flow of the water to plaintiff's farm, or in any way interfering with the natural course and flow of the said stream or river; and that the defendants be adjudged to pay the sum of £75 as and for damages; and lastly, for such further and other relief as to the Court should seem meet, with costs.

The defendants excepted to the declaration as not disclosing any right of action accruing to the plaintiff.

This day (August 27),—

Buchanan, for the defendants, appeared to support the

1874.
Aug. 27.
Dec. 1.
„ 2.
„ 19.

Hough vs. Van
der Merwe.
exception, and contended that the fact of plaintiff possessing a farm situated on a stream below defendants' farm, was of itself not an allegation of a right sufficient to found an action.

Jacobs, A.G. (with him *Cole*), for the plaintiff, were heard contra.

Exception overruled, with costs.

. The defendants pleaded, first, the general issue ; and then specially traversed the plaintiff's right to the flow of the water of the said stream or river in manner and form as in the declaration alleged.

After taking the evidence (December 1, 2),—

Jacobs, A.G. (with him *Cole*), were heard for plaintiff; and *Buchanan* (with him *Tennant*) for the defendants. The facts proved are sufficiently set forth in the judgment below. In the argument the following authorities were cited by counsel :— *Dig.*, 43, 12, 1, 2; *Voet*, 43, 12; 43, 13; 2, *Bell's Com.*, 6th ed., p. 796 ; *Inst.*, 2, 1, 1; *Gaius* (Tompkins and Lemon's trans.), p. 209 ; *Addison on Torts*, 3rd ed., p. 57 ; *Vinnius in Inst.*, 2, 1, 1; *Retief* vs. *Louw*, decided 12th June, 1856 ;* *Grot.*, 2, 35, 14 & 15 ; *Erasmus* vs. *De Wet*, decided 16th Feb., 1867 ;* *Minor* vs. *Gilmour*, 12, *Moore's P.C.C.*, p. 156 ; *Dig.*, 8, 3, 17 ; 8, 5, 10 ; *Breda* vs. *Silberbauer*, 3, *L.R.*, *P.C.*, 99 ; *Chasemore* vs. *Richards*, 7, *H.L.C.*, 382—8 ; *Bell's Principles of the Law of Scotland*, 1,100, 1,104 ; 3, *Kent's Com.*, 11th ed., p. 560 ; *Domat*, 1, 8, 2, par. 11 ; *Bicket* vs. *Morris*, 1, *L.R.*, *Scotch Ap. C.* 47 ; 3, *Burge*, 417 ; *Mason* vs. *Hill*, 5, *B. & Ad.*, 1 ; *Acton* vs. *Blundell*, 12, *M. & W.*, 348 ; *Embrey* vs. *Owen* ; 6, *Exch.*, 368 ; *Gale on Easements*, 202, 289 ; *Angel on Watercourses*, 92, 93, 116, 119A, 129, 135 ; *Voet*, 8, 3, 6 ; 39, 3, 1 ; 3, *Burge*, 421 ; *Dreyer* vs. *Ireland*, decided 12th July, 1866 ;* *Broadbent* vs. *Ramsbotham*, 11, *Exch.*, 615.

Cur. adv. vult.

This day (December 19), the judgment of the Court was delivered by—

DE VILLIERS, C.J. :—This is an action brought by the owner of a farm called Elandsvlei against the owner of a farm called Elandsdrift for damages alleged to have been suffered by the plaintiff through the damming-up by the defendants of a stream called the Doorn River, and for an in-

* See Appendix to this Volume.

terdict to restrain the damming-up and diversion of the
water. It appears that the Doorn River takes its rise in the
Bokkeveld Mountains, and after flowing a very long distance,
partly over Crown land and partly over private land, it
reaches the farm Elandsdrift; and after passing this farm
and some intermediate Government land, it reaches the farm
Elandsvlei, through which it flows, and ultimately discharges
itself into the Oliphant's river some distance below. It
will be unnecessary, for the purpose of the present case, to
decide the question whether the Doorn River is a public or
a private stream, or whether the owner of land through
which a private stream runs is entitled to the use of all the
water flowing on to his land. It was contended, on behalf of
the plaintiff, that the Doorn River is a public stream, and
that the construction of the dam and the diversion of the
water amounted to an infringement of his rights as a lower
proprietor of land situated on the banks of a public stream,
and my judgment will proceed on the assumption that the
plaintiff is correct in his view that this is a public stream.
In regard to the dam, the declaration complains that in the
month of January, 1874, the defendants erected upon their
farm a certain dam across the said stream or river, and kept
and continued the same so erected for a long space of time,
to wit, from the 23rd of January, 1874, until the 8th of
March last past, during all which time the water was prevented from flowing through and over the said farm of the
plaintiff as it of right ought to have done, whereby the
plaintiff sustained damage to the amount of £75. But from
the evidence given in the case, it appears that a dam had
been constructed in the month of January, 1873, and that
the water did not cease to flow through the plaintiff's farm
until January, 1874, and that from March, 1874, in consequence of heavy rains which had fallen, the water again
flowed down freely to and through the plaintiff's farm.
There is considerable discrepancy in the evidence as to the
proportion of the water which the defendant allowed to flow
down in the bed of the river so long as the dam stood. According to the plaintiff's evidence, it was only one-half of
the water; according to the defendants' evidence five-sixths.
It is difficult, from the materials before the Court, to form a
decisive opinion upon the question whether, considering the
nature of the soil and country through which the stream
passes between the defendants' and the plaintiff's land, and
considering the drought which prevailed between January
and March, 1874, the water would have flowed freely to the
plaintiff's land during that period even if there had been no
dam at all. But it is quite unnecessary to decide this question in the present case for two reasons. In the first place,

1874.
Aug. 27.
Dec. 1.
„ 2.
„ 19.

Hough vs. Van
der Merwe.

1874.
Aug. 27.
. Dec. 1.
" 2.
" 19.

Hough vs. Van
der Merwe.

the declaration complains of a dam made in January, 1874,
whereas the only dam of which the existence on the defendants' farm has been proved was constructed in January,
1873. In the second place, the defendant has not, in fact,
asserted his right to maintain the dam, for as soon as he was
threatened with legal proceedings in February, 1873, he took
immediate steps to divert a portion of the water by means
of a furrow placed higher up than the dam in the bed of the
river, and allowed the water which was not caught in this
furrow to flow down freely over and through the dam.
Under these circumstances the Court is bound to dismiss
from its consideration the question of damages alleged to
have been sustained by the plaintiff owing to the construction of a dam in January, 1874. The really important question, which remains to be determined, is whether the plaintiff is entitled to a perpetual interdict to restrain the defendants from diverting any portion of the water by means of
the appliances which one of them has described in his
evidence. These appliances are as follow :—In the first place
a furrow has been cut through the left bank of the river, and
in the bed of the river to a distance of about three yards
from the right bank. It is not, however, the whole body of
the water caught by this furrow which is used by the defendants. The lower extremity of this furrow (which is a few
yards in length) is closed up by an embankment, and only so
much of the water is diverted from the stream as will flow
through an oblong aperture in the embankment of about nine
inches in length, and five inches in height. This aperture is
caused by a wooden sluice placed horizontally in the embankment. The water of the stream which does not flow
through this sluice is allowed to flow down in the bed of the
river towards the plaintiff's farm. The water which flows
through the sluice is led through the defendants' land in a
furrow (which after flowing some distance branches off into
two or three furrows), and is used by the defendants for domestic purposes and for the purpose of irrigating their culti-
vated lands. The defendant, Schalk van der Merwe, says
that so much of this water as is not used for these purposes
(which cannot, however, be of any considerable quantity) is
allowed to flow again into the Doorn River. The questions
we shall proceed to consider are the following :—Are the defendants entitled to divert a reasonable quantity of the water
for purposes of irrigation? If they are so entitled, have they
made an unreasonable use of their rights? The first of these
questions is as important as any that a Court of Justice
can be called upon to decide, and it is not a little singular
that in a country like this, where the value of water for the
purposes of irrigation is so immense, the question should

never have been authoritatively settled by the Supreme Court. According to *Justinian's Institutes* (2, 1, 1), the right to the use of flowing water (meaning, I apprehend, flowing water of a public stream) is common to all. "A river," said Lord Kames in the case of the *Magistrates of Linlithgow* vs. *Elphinstone* (3, *Kames' Decisions*, p. 331), "which is in perpetual motion is not naturally susceptible of appropriation; and were it susceptible, it would be greatly against the public interest that it should be suffered to be brought under private property. In general, by the laws of all polished nations, appropriation is authorised with respect to every subject that is best enjoyed separately; but barred with respect to every subject that is best enjoyed in common. Water is scattered over the face of the earth in rivers, lakes, &c., for the use of animals and vegetables. Water drawn from a river into vessels, or into ponds, becomes private property; but to admit of such property with respect to the river itself, considered as a complex body, would be inconsistent with the public interest, by putting it in the power of one man to lay waste a whole country." * * * "A river may be considered as the common property of the whole nation; but the law declares against separate property of the whole or part." * * * "A river is a subject composed of a trunk and branches. No individual can appropriate a river, or any branch of it; but every individual of the nation, those especially who have land adjoining, are entitled to use the water for their private purposes." In considering the uses to which the water of a public stream may be applied, we must distinguish between the ordinary or primary use and the extraordinary or secondary use of the water. The ordinary use is that which is required for the support of animal life, and, in the case of riparian proprietors, for domestic purposes; the extraordinary use is that which is required for any other purpose than those just mentioned. If the ordinary use is common to all the riparian proprietors, it would be manifestly unjust to allow the upper proprietor to make an extraordinary use of the water if he thereby deprives the lower proprietors of their ordinary use thereof. It is for this reason that the upper proprietor is not allowed to divert water for the purpose of irrigation if he thereby prevents the lower proprietors from having the enjoyment of the water for domestic purposes, or for watering their cattle. But if the extraordinary use by the upper proprietor would not deprive the lower proprietors of the ordinary use, it remains to be considered to what extent such extraordinary use will be permitted. If the ordinary use is common to all proprietors, it would seem that the extraordinary use must be equally so. The right to the ordinary use is derived from

1874.
Aug. 27.
Dec. 1.
„ 2.
„ 19.

Hough *vs.* Van der Merwe.

1874.
Aug. 27.
Dec. 1.
„ 2.
„ 19.
Hough vs. Van
der-Merwe.

necessity, the right to the extraordinary use from convenience. If, therefore, the upper proprietor, in the enjoyment
of his ordinary use, deprives the lower proprietors of their
ordinary use, he would not be liable to them in an action;
but if an upper proprietor in the enjoyment of his extraordinary use deprives the lower proprietors of their
extraordinary use, he would, according to the weight of
authority, be liable to them in an action. It is upon
this principle that the Emperors Antoninus and Verus
decided, in answering a case submitted to them by a
provincial magistrate, that water from a public river ought
to be divided for purposes of irrigation according to the
measure of possession of the riparian proprietors, but that no
diversion should be allowed if any injury is thereby done to
the remaining riparian proprietors. (*Digest*, 8, 3, 17.) *Voet*,
indeed, in one passage of his *Com.* (39, 3, 1) broadly lays
down the doctrine that a riparian proprietor, unless prohibited
by the Crown, may freely lead water out of a public river
which is neither itself navigable nor renders another navigable; but this passage would be inconsistent with other
passages in the same great work (for instance, *Voet*, 43, 13),
unless taken with the qualifications introduced by the
Emperors Antoninus and Verus. In *Domat's Public Law*
(1, 8, 2, 11) it is laid down that any riparian proprietor of
land on a brook may divert the water for the irrigation of
his meadows, "yet every one must use this liberty so as to
do no injustice to his neighbours who have a like want and
equal right." In the case of *Milner* vs. *Gilmour* (12,
Moore's P.C.C. 156), which was an appeal to the Privy
Council from Lower Canada, where the old French law
prevails, Lord Kingsdown says:—"By the general law
applicable to running streams, every riparian proprietor has
a right to what may be called the ordinary use of water
flowing past his land; for instance, to the reasonable use of
the water for domestic purposes and for his cattle, and this
without regard to the effect which such use may have in
case of a deficiency upon proprietors lower down the stream.
But, further, he has a right to the use of it for any purpose,
or what may be deemed the extraordinary use of it, provided
he does not thereby interfere with the rights of other proprietors either above or below him. Subject to this condition, he may dam up a stream for the purposes of a mill,
or divert the water for the purpose of irrigation. But he
has no right to intercept the regular flow of the stream if
he thereby interferes with the lawful use of the water by
other proprietors and inflicts on them a sensible injury." In
Kent's Commentaries (vol. 3, sec. 25) the law is thus
stated:—"The owner must so use and apply the water as to

work no material injury or annoyance to his neighbour be- 1874.
Aug. 27.
Dec. 1.
,, 2.
,, 19.

Hough vs. Van
der.Merwe.
low him, who has an equal right to the subsequent use of
the same water; nor can he, by dam or any obstruction,
cause the water injuriously to overflow the grounds and
springs of his neighbour above. Streams of water are intended for the use and comfort of man; and it would be unreasonable, and contrary to the universal sense of mankind,
to debar every riparian proprietor from the application of
the water to domestic, agricultural, and manufacturing purposes, providing the use of it be made under the limitations
which have been mentioned; and there will no doubt inevitably be, in the exercise of a perfect right to the use of
the water, some evaporation and decrease of it, and some
variations in the weight and velocity of the current. But
de minimis non curat lex, and a right of action by the proprietor below would not necessarily flow fron such consequences, but would depend upon the nature and extent of
the complaint or injury, and the manner of using the water.
All that the law requires of the party by or over whose land a
stream passes is, that he should use the water in a reasonable
manner, and so as not to destroy or render useless, or
materially diminish, or affect the application of the water by
the proprietors above or below on the stream. He must
not shut the gates of his dam and detain the water unreasonably, or let it off in unusual quantities, to the annoyance of
his neighbour. *Pothier* lays down the rule very strictly,
that the owner of the upper stream must not raise the water
by dams, so as to make it fall with more abundance and
rapidity than it would naturally do, and injure the proprietor below. But this rule must not be construed literally,
for that would be to deny all valuable use of the water to the
riparian proprietors. It must be subjected to the qualifications which have been mentioned, otherwise rivers and
streams of water would become utterly useless either for
agricultural or manufacturing purposes. The just and
equitable interest is given in the Roman Law: *Sic enim
debere quem meliorem agram suum facere ne vicini deteriorem
facint.*" This passage from Kent is cited with approval by
Baron Parke in the case of *Embrey* vs. *Owen* (6, Exch.,
370). The conclusion at which we have arrived is, that by
our law the owner of land by or through which a public
stream flows, is entitled to divert a portion of the water for
the purposes of irrigation, provided—1stly, That he does not
thereby deprive the lower proprietors of sufficient water for
their cattle and for domestic purposes. 2ndly, That he uses
no more than a just and reasonable proportion of the water
consistently with similar rights of irrigation in the lower proprietors; and 3rdly, That he returns it to the public stream

1874.
Aug. 27.
Dec. 1.
„ 2.
„ 19.

Hough vs. Van
der Merwe.

with no other loss than that which irrigation has caused. What constitutes a just and reasonable use of the water is entirely a question of degree which depends upon the circumstances of each particular case. In the present case we are satisfied that the diversion on the part of the defendants of a stream of water through the aperture already described does not deprive the plaintiff of sufficient water for his cattle and for domestic purposes. We are not satisfied that it is an unreasonable use of the water, or such as to prevent the plaintiff from irrigating his land to the same extent as the defendants irrigate theirs; and we see no reason to disbelieve the statement of one of the defendants that the waste water after irrigation is returned into the Doorn River. The plaintiff, in his evidence, admitted that since the construction of the furrow in question he has never suffered from want of water, but it is just possible, although not proved, that during very dry seasons his rights, such as have already been described, may be interfered with by the diversion complained of. In order, therefore, not to debar him from asserting such rights hereafter the Court will not pronounce judgment for the defendants, but absolve them from the instance with costs.

Absolution granted accordingly, with costs.

[Plaintiff's Attorney, TREDGOLD.
Defendants' Attorney, C. C. DE VILLIERS.]

TWENTYMAN & CO. vs. BUTLER.

Foreign Bill of Exchange.—Provisional Sentence.—Presentment.

Provisional sentence granted without protest of presentment and dishonour against the acceptor of an English Bill of Exchange, accepted payable at a specified banker's, such acceptance being a general acceptance by English Law.

1874.
Dec. 19.

Twentyman &
Co. vs. Butler.

Provisional sentence was prayed on the following foreign Bill of Exchange :—

"£28 10s.   Manchester, May 18th, 1870.

"Three months after date pay to the order of myself, the sum of twenty-eight pounds ten shillings, value received.
                    (Signed) John A. Wood.
"To Mr. E. Butler,
      Hampton House, Tothedown, Bristol.

"Accepted and payable at Messrs. Stuckey's Bank, Bristol.

1874.
Dec. 19.

Twentyman &
Co. vs. Butler.

(Signed)   Ephraim Butler.
(Endorsed)   John A. Wood.
"Pay Messrs. E. H. Twentyman & Co., of Cape Town.
(Signed)   John A. Wood."

Buchanan, for the plaintiff, could not produce protest of presentment at Stuckey's Bank, Bristol, where the bill was made payable, but cited *Byles on Bills*, p. 205, and *Story on Promissory Notes*, sec. 227, to show that as the acceptor had not added the words "and not otherwise or elsewhere," the acceptance, by statute 1 and 2 Geo. 4, ch. 78, was a general one, and therefore it was sufficient to demand payment from the acceptor, who was now in this Colony, and who had been personally served.

The defendant did not appear.

Provisional sentence as prayed.

[Plaintiff's Attorney, TREDGOLD.]

In re HONEY.

Attorney : admission of.—Proof of enrolment of Articles.— Rule No. 213.

The Court required the Registrar's Certificate to state the date of enrolment of Articles of Clerkship, filed in the office of the Registrar of the Eastern Districts Court, to prove that the requirements of the 213th Rule of Court had been complied with. Affidavits not sufficient proof of enrolment. [FITZPATRICK, J., *diss.*]

1874.
Dec. 19.

In re Honey.

This was an application on behalf of Jesse Spicer Honey, for an order, authorizing him to be admitted and enrolled as an Attorney of the Supreme Court. Applicant's petition, verified by his affidavit, stated that he was, on the 29th October, 1867, articled in due form of law to Thomas Hoskins Giddy, of King William's Town, an Attorney of the Court of the Eastern Districts of this Colony. That the articles of clerkship were, on the 13th December, 1867, duly and regularly filed in the office of the Registrar of that Court. That petitioner had duly served for the term of five consecutive years and upwards. That the said Giddy was by virtue of section 2, of Act No. 6, 1872, duly admitted an Attorney of the Supreme Court.

An affidavit sworn to by Mr. Giddy contained similar

averments. The Registrar of the Eastern Districts Court certified the copy of the articles produced to be ".a true copy of the original articles of agreement, filed in this office."

Jacobs, A.G., for the applicant, submitted that the requirements of Rule 213 had been met by the averments of the affidavits, showing the articles had been filed within three months of the date of execution; and cited *Chitty's Archbold* to show the practice in England.

The Court [FITZPATRICK, J., *diss.*] considered that the Registrar's certificate was the proper manner of proving the date of enrolment of the articles. The order for admission was, however, granted, but subject to the production of the certificate. The oaths to be taken before the Resident Magistrate of King William's Town.

[Applicant's Attorney, TREDGOLD.]

LETTERSTEDT *vs.* LETTERSTEDT'S EXECUTORS.

Legitimate Portion.

The legitimate portion to which a child is entitled out of the estate of the parent, must be left free and unencumbered, and cannot be subject to a condition postponing the date of payment. The value of the estate at the time of the death of the parent must be value taken for the purpose of computing the amount of the legitimate portion.

1874.
Dec. 10.
,, 19.

Letterstedt *vs.*
Letterstedt's
Executors.

This was an action instituted by Lydia Corinna Doligny Letterstedt to declare her entitled to the legitimate portion out of the estate of her father, the late Jacob Letterstedt, of whom the defendants were the executors.

The declaration set forth that plaintiff was the only child of the late J. Letterstedt, who departed this life on the 18th March, 1862, leaving a last will and testament dated the 12th May, 1861. That in and by the said last will, certain gifts, bequests, and legacies were given and bequeathed to the plaintiff, but that the payment of the same was postponed until the plaintiff should have attained the age of twenty-five years, and was burdened with certain trusts and conditions. That the plaintiff attained the age of twenty-one years on the 13th May, 1874, and that she thereupon became entitled to demand and receive at once, and free from the said trusts and conditions, her legitimate portion out of

1874.
Dec. 10.
„ 19.

Letterstedt *vs.*
Letterstedt's
Executors.

her father's estate, without thereby forfeiting her subsequent right to receive out of the residue of the estate the gifts and bequests named in the will. The plaintiff therefore prayed that she be declared entitled to demand and receive forthwith her legitimate portion, and that the defendants be ordered to render a proper account of the estate as the same now was, so as to ascertain the amount of such portion, and to pay over the amount so ascertained; further, that it be declared that the plaintiff would not, by demanding and receiving such legitimate portion, forfeit any of her rights to and in the several gifts, bequests, and legacies, given and bequeathed to her in and by the aforesaid last will; and lastly, for further or other relief.

The defendants pleaded, first, the general issue; and then specially that the said J. Letterstedt did, by his said last will in the declaration mentioned, bequeath to the plaintiff, in case she should attain the age of 25 years or marry under that age, the sum of £12,000; also the sum of £5,000 should she survive the wife of the testator, and if and when the plaintiff should attain the age of 25 years or marry under that age; further that the testator directed his executors to pay the sum of £1,000 annually for the maintenance and education of the plaintiff, which said annual payments had been duly made; and subject to the payment of several legacies and bequests in the said will contained that the testator bequeathed all the rest, residue, and remainder of his estate to the plaintiff if and when she should attain the age of 25 years or marry under that age, the same to be burthened with *fidei commissum* so that the plaintiff should enjoy only the interest, dividends, and annual income thereof, with remainder over as stated in the will. Wherefore the defendants submitted that the plaintiff was not now entitled to claim and receive her legitimate portion out of the estate of the said late J. Letterstedt; or otherwise, that should she be so entitled, that the aforesaid sums of £12,000, £5,000, and the annual payments of £1,000 should be taken and reckoned as part of the legitimate portion, and that the plaintiff was entitled to receive only such further sum as upon account being taken should appear to be due. And the defendants further submitted that if the plaintiff claimed and received her legitimate portion, she was not entitled also to claim and receive the interest, dividends, and annual income of the residue.

The replication was general.

The facts referred to in the pleadings were admitted. An inventory was put in, showing the value of the estate at the time of the late J. Letterstedt's death.

Jacobs, A.G. (with him *Cole*), for the plaintiff, submitted

1874.
Dec. 10.
,, 19.

Letterstedt vs.
Letterstedt's
Executors.

that it was clear by the law of the Colony that the legitimate portion must be left free and unencumbered; and that the testator having been silent on the point, the plaintiff was not obliged to forego the benefits conferred on her by the will, although she claimed her legitimate portion which had not been left to her under the will. Counsel cited *Voet,* 5, 2, 64; *Sandenbergh's case*, 2, *Menz.*, 427; *Trustees of Van Schoor* vs. *Gie* (reported in *Advertiser and Mail*, 1st September, 1858).

Buchanan (with him *Jones*), for the defendants, contended that a claim for the legitimate must be either by the *querula inofficiosi testamenti*, or by action *ad supplementum*. That this was an action to supplement gifts and not to set aside the will, and therefore the benefits granted by the will must be taken into consideration in estimating the amount of the legitimate. That the value of the estate at the time of the death of the testator, as shown by the inventory, and not the present value, must be taken as the basis upon which to reckon the amount of the legitimate. Further, that if the plaintiff claimed her legitimate she was bound to make up out of the residue of the estate the amount so claimed, and of which the *fidei commissaries* would be deprived. That in analogy to the equitable doctrine of satisfaction the legacies and other gifts contained in the will must be taken as *pro tanto* extinguishing the plaintiff's claim for her inheritance. (*Voet*, 5, 2, 51; *Van Leeuwen's Cen., For.*, 34, 17; *Thomson's Institutes of the Laws of Ceylon*, 238.)

Jacobs, A.G., for the plaintiff, in reply, cited *In re Wium*, 2, *Menz.*, 431; 4, *Burge*, 230.

Cur. adv. vult.

Posteà (December 19),—

The COURT held, that in accordance with the principle laid down by *Voet*, 5, 2, 63, the plaintiff was entitled to her legitimate portion unburdened and without the time of payment being postponed; and that the plaintiff did not, by claiming her portion, forfeit any benefit conferred upon her by the will. Further, that the value of the estate at the time of the death of the testator must be taken as the basis upon which to calculate this portion. That the plaintiff, having received an annual allowance, was not entitled to interest on the amount claimed by her.

Judgment for plaintiff accordingly, costs to come out of the estate.

[Plaintiff's Attorneys, FAIRBRIDGE & ARDERNE.]
[Defendants' Attorneys, REID & NEPHEW.   ]

REYNOLDS vs. WEINER.

House of Assembly.—Costs.—Constitution Ordinance, secs. 65, 66, and 68.

A member of the House of Assembly, whose return had been petitioned against on grounds relating to the proceedings at the election (but not affecting his personal qualification), held unable to recover at law from the unsuccessful petitioner the costs incurred in appearing by counsel and with witnesses before a select committee of the House of Assembly appointed to inquire into and report upon the statements of the petition.

The declaration in this case set forth that on the 24th February last the plaintiff was duly elected one of the members to represent the division of Worcester in the House of Assembly. That on the 28th May, the defendant, well knowing the premises, petitioned the House, alleging the plaintiff was not so duly elected, and praying the House to declare the plaintiff disqualified to be and disseated as such member. That in consequence of said petition a select committee was appointed by the House to investigate into and report upon the statements and allegations set forth therein. That said committee did so investigate, and on the 16th July reported to the House that the plaintiff had been duly elected, and was qualified and entitled to retain his seat. That in consequence of the said petition, the plaintiff necessarily incurred and was put to great costs, charges, and expenses in attending by his counsel and his witnesses the said investigation, to wit the sum of £60 3s. 1d. sterling. Which sum the plaintiff now claimed, and prayed that the defendant might be adjudged to pay.

The defendant pleaded the general issue.

Buchanan, for the plaintiff, cited the 65th and 66th sections of the Constitution Ordinance, which provided that when a petition had been presented against the property qualification of a member of the Legislative Council, and such petition had been dismissed, the member petitioned against was entitled to recover, in any competent Court, the costs and expenses incurred by him in his defence. The 68th section extended these two sections so that they should apply "to the inquiry of and determining of all questions of disqualification alleged against any member of the House of Assembly;" and also regulated the number and manner of selection of the select committee to be appointed to inquire

1874.
Dec. 19.

Reynolds *vs.* Weiner.

1874.
Dec. 19.

Reynolds *vs.*
Weiner.

into any petition. Under these sections plaintiff claimed to be entitled to recover the expenses incurred by him in defending his seat against the charges made by the defendant.

[DE VILLIERS, C.J. :—Was the committee in this case appointed in the manner prescribed by the Ordinance ?]

It was not, but that was a matter within the control only of the House ; and moreover any defect in the mode of election of the committee had been cured by the defendant having appeared before and submitted to its investigation.

Cole, for the defendant, maintained that the sections referred only to petitions against the qualification of the member. The petition in question attacked the mode and actual fact of the election, not the qualification of the sitting member.

The COURT held that the sections of the Ordinance cited had reference to petitions raising the question of qualification of persons elected, and not to those where the mode of election was in dispute. If the case did not come under the sections cited, common law did not apply, and the claim must therefore be dismissed.

Judgment accordingly for defendant, with costs.

[Plaintiff's Attorney, DE KORTE.
Defendant's Attorneys, FAIRBRIDGE & ARDERNE.]

MAGISTRATES' REVIEWED CASES.

Act No. 17, 1867, § 2.

Spare Diet.

A Magistrate has no power to order spare diet, where the prisoner has been sentenced to a period of imprisonment exceeding three months.

DE VILLIERS, C.J., said a case had come before him as Judge of the week, where a person named Oelsen had been tried under Act No. 17, 1867, and convicted. The Magistrate had passed sentence of six months' imprisonment, the first five months to be with hard labour, and in the last month to spare diet on eighteen days. The Act did not give the Magistrate power to order spare diet where the sentence was for a period exceeding three months. The sentence would therefore be amended by striking out the part relating to spare diet.

1874.
Dec. 15.

M 2

APPENDIX.

RETIEF *vs.* LOUW.

[Referred to in Hough *vs.* VAN DER MERWE, *ante, p.* 148.]

Water rights.—Perennial stream.—Private stream.

Per BELL, J.—*A perennial stream, not in strict propriety capable of receiving the name of a river, flowing through but rising above private land, does not belong absolutely to the proprietor of the land through which it flows, but all the proprietors of land throughout its course have each a common right in the use of the water. This use, at every stage of its exercise by any one of the proprietors, is limited by a consideration of the rights of the other proprietors.*

The use of water may be, 1st.—For the support of animal life. 2nd.—For the increase of vegetable life. 3rd.— For the promotion of mechanical appliances. If the upper proprietor require all the water for the support of life, the lower proprietors must submit. If there be more than sufficient water for this purpose, sufficient must be allowed to pass for the supply of animal demands of all the lower proprietors before the upper proprietor can use the water for irrigation. The proprietors are in succession entitled to use the water for agricultural purposes. Agricultural uses being supplied throughout the course of the stream, the proprietors are then entitled to apply the water to mechanical purposes. No proprietor is entitled to use the water without regard to the wants of the other proprietors. The extent to which any one proprietor is entitled to use the water will depend on the circumstances of each case.

Water rising on private land (erumpentem in suo), is the property of the owner of the land on which it takes its rise.

Per CLOETE, J.—*The water of certain weak springs rising above but descending directly on to the land of the plaintiff, and increased by the water of other weak springs rising on his land, which waters there become intermixed, and flow downwards in one and the same channel, belong to the class of private waters, and the right to their use differs in no way from any other private right.*

1855.
Dec. 12.
„ 13.
1856.
Jan. 12.

Retief vs. Louw.

This case was heard before BELL, J., and CLOETE, J., on the 12th and 13th December, 1855, *Denyssen* appearing for the plaintiff, and *Porter, A. G.,* (with him *C. J. Brand,* and *J. Brand*), for the defendant. The matters in issue and the evidence taken are sufficiently set forth in the judgments given below.

Cur. ad. vult.

Postea (January 12th, 1866), the following judgments were delivered:—

BELL, J.:—Van der Byl was proprietor of the place called Freethof. In 1814, he sold the lower half of this estate to Du Plessis, and by succession from him the title to it is now vested in the plaintiff Retief. In 1845, the remaining or upper half of the land became vested in Louw, the defendant. At the time that Van der Byl sold Lower Freethof to Du Plessis, and for some time previously, Van der Byl had been in use to pasture his cattle on land which lay still lower than Lower Freethof, but which had not, as yet, been granted by the Crown to any one. A stream of water, having its rise in the mountains behind the Paarl, ran successively through Upper Freethof and Lower Freethof, and then discharged itself on the Government ground, the pasturage of which was thereby rendered valuable. The deed by Van der Byl to Du Plessis in 1814, conveyed Lower Freethof as "certain piece of land," of which it gives the description and dimensions, and the conveyance is made under this express condition, however, that the proprietor of this piece of land shall be obliged to allow the water during the whole summer to run undisturbed in its old course, and that, besides his drink water, he shall be entitled to the water for his own use; twice a week to wit, Sundays and Wednesdays. The main question which has been raised by the parties, is in regard to the interpretation to be put upon these words,—whether they constitute a burden on the conveyance of Lower Freethof, in favour of Van der Byl, the continuing proprietor of Upper Freethof, and his successors, who are represented by the defendant,—or whether they create a servitude on Upper Freethof, in favour of the purchaser of Lower Freethof, and his successors, represented by the plaintiff; but beyond this there is a much more important question in regard to the rights of proprietors of land on a running stream to the water of the stream, independently of any special stipulation in their titles, which will have to be disposed of after the special question has been considered. Assuming that the clause I have quoted constitutes a servitude on Upper Freethof in favour of Lower Freethof, the plaintiff, by his declaration, alleges that from the year 1813, downwards, until the year 1854, the proprietors of Lower Freethof have, on Wednesdays and Sundays, had the undisturbed use of the water flowing unimpeded from Upper Freethof, the proprietors of Upper Freethof having "only on other days" used the water for irrigating that land, —that the defendant during the months of December, 1854, and thenceforth until April, 1855, dammed up the water in Upper Freethof, on Wednesdays and Sundays, and did not allow it to flow undisturbed to Lower Freethof. Upon these allegations, the declaration prays that the defendant may be interdicted from using the water " on the said days," and that the plaintiff may be declared to be entitled to the full use of the stream, " in accordance with the condition as aforesaid," and also by reason of his uninterrupted possession for upwards of one-third of a century. The declaration also prays for £50 damages. The defendant pleads the general issue, or a denial of all the plaintiff's allegations; and adds, as a claim in reconvention, that there was certain water taking its rise on the defendant's land, which the plaintiff's land was, by way of servitude, bound to receive, after the defendant should have made such use of it as he required; but that, from the beginning of 1855, the plaintiff had dammed " the said water " up at the point where their two lands joined, and by so doing had thrown it back on the vineyard of the defendant, to his injury and damage to the amount of £50. To this claim in reconvention the plaintiff pleaded the general issue, or a general denial. I shall not go minutely through the evidence which was led by the parties, but only give a summary of it. The witnesses of the plaintiff, Dantje, a servant of Van der Byl, and November, a servant of Du Plessis, established that sufficient water for drinking purposes had always passed from Upper Freethof, during every day of the week,—nay, that more than sufficient for that purpose had passed every day of the week,—but that on Wednesdays and Sundays the water ran much stronger (Dantje accounted for this by saying he had Van der Byl's orders not to use the water on these days), and that the strong running of the water was never stopped on a Sunday or a Wednesday. The other witnesses for the plaintiff were Rossouw and Hiebner, successive proprietors of Lower Freethof. Both of these gentlemen had been of opinion

1855.
Dec. 12.
„ 13.
1856.
Jan. 12.

Retief vs. Louw.

1855.
Dec. 12.
,, 13.
1856.
Jan. 12.

Retief vs. Louw.

that the condition of 1814 gave them a right to the water on Wednesdays and Sundays. In the time of the proprietorship of Rossouw, who was a good neighbour and a good "friend" of Louw, then the proprietor of Upper Freethof, when the water did not come down on a Wednesday or a Sunday, he sent up to Louw to say so. Louw either said "it had been forgotten to be turned on," or said pleasantly, "you are not so much in want of water, are you?" but he never denied Rossouw's right to have the water on Wednesdays and Sundays. In the time of Hiebner, the water once, in February, 1840, did not come down. Hiebner sent to Louw; Louw's son questioned Hiebner's right, whereupon Hiebner said, if that were his father's opinion, he would show him his right. The same thing occurred again in March, 1840. Hiebner wrote to Louw, and shortly afterwards he got a verbal answer, that he had inquired into the matter and was satisfied Hiebner had the right he claimed. After this, the water was never stopped on a Sunday or a Wednesday, though sometimes it was not so plentiful as the witness thought it ought to have been. Supposing the right claimed by the plaintiff to have been established by this evidence, the only evidence brought of interruption of the enjoyment was that of one witness, Onverwacht, that on one Sunday morning in February last, the water not coming down, he went up the watercourse, and found the water turned off into a pond at the defendant's stables. Upon this discovery the action was brought, without any communication with the defendant to ascertain the cause of the interruption, whether design, accident, or carelessness. The evidence for the defendant was given by three servants, two of Van der Byl's, and one of Louw's. According to them, there was no distinction in the use of water upon Upper Freethof between Wednesday and Sunday and any other day of the week; it was used alike upon all days of the week, except Sunday; upon which day the slaves of Van der Byl, who were numerous, and had each a piece of garden, were in use to irrigate their gardens, that is to say more water was used on Upper Freethof on Sunday than on other days. Miss Aling, a step-daughter of Van der Byl, who had lived with him on Upper Freethof, and managed that farm for her mother during two years after her stepfather's death, swore that there was no change so far as she knew in the use of the water after the sale of Lower Freethof to Du Plessis, although she did hear at one time something said by somebody about two days in the week on which the water should be allowed to go down to Du Plessis, and that, during the two years she managed, she used the water as she required it, without making any distinction

1855.
Dec. 12.
„ 13.
1856.
Jan. 12.

Retief vs. Louw.

between Wednesday and Sunday and any other day.
Petrus Neehaus, a nephew of Du Plessis, swore that he was
not aware and never heard of. any distinction of days as to
the use of water. Albert du Toit, brother-in-law of the
defendant, who lived on Freethof during Rossouw's proprietorship, swore that he never heard of stated days when
the water was to be used, though old Louw once told him
that Hiebner had written him on the subject of the water.
Such being the evidence, the plaintiff argued that the
clause in the deed of 1814, imported an obligation on Upper
Freethof in favour of Lower Freethof, and not *vice versâ* an
obligation upon Lower Freethof in favour of Upper Freethof, and that the obligation admitted of two constructions,
according to one of which he had a right to the whole water
of the stream upon Wednesdays and Sundays, without
any part of it having been used by defendant; and according to the other to the same unrestricted use of the water
upon five days of the week, leaving only two to the defendant.
I am of opinion that the plaintiff and his predecessors in
Lower Freethof have misapprehended the meaning of the
clause in question. It was intended, in my apprehension, to
impose an obligation upon the purchaser of Lower Freethof
and his successors, not to use the water which should descend from Upper Freethof for any other than drinking purposes during five days of the week (so that it might pass on
to the pasturage land lying beyond and lower than Lower
Freethof), leaving them a right to use it for any and every
purpose during the remaining two days, which are specified to
be Wednesday and Sunday. The conveyance is of " a certain piece of ground," and as a " condition " upon that conveyance it is declared, that " the proprietor of this piece of
land shall be obliged, &c." " This piece of land " is obviously
the " certain piece of land " which had been conveyed, for
no other piece of land had been mentioned, so as to form an
antecedent to the word " this." The " proprietor," then,
who is to be bound for the future, who, in the words of the
condition, " shall be obliged, &c.," must be " the purchaser "
who was to become " proprietor " by the conveyance ; and
who therefore could be laid under an obligation for the future
in regard to the land and the water, and not the vendor, or
person who was proprietor at the time of the conveyance,
who was, by the conveyance, to cease to be proprietor, and
so could not be laid under any obligation for the future, in
regard either to the land or the water. This appears to me
to be the natural construction of the language. To hold
that " the proprietor " meant the vendor, or Van der Byl,
would lead to the extraordinary construction contended for
alternatively by the plaintiff in the face of his own declara-

1865.
Dec. 12.
,, 13.
1856.
Jan. 12.

Retief *vs.* Louw.

tion, that the vendor, in the form of a condition annexed by him to a conveyance to a purchaser, imposed upon himself the restriction that he was not to have any water during five days of the week, which the nature of the transaction renders most improbable and incredible independently of the terms of the clause, and which, as observed, is in the face of the plaintiff's own declaration, which does not set up any such extravagant pretension, but confines itself to two days' water weekly. If I am right in this interpretation, then Du Plessis and his successors were to be obliged to allow "the water" to run undisturbed in its course during five days of the week, and besides his drink-water on these five days, which latter words were plainly intended, though omitted, he was to be entitled "to the water for his own use" twice a week, to wit, Wednesdays and Sundays. It is not necessary, therefore, for me to consider the evidence of either of the plaintiff's or of the defendant's witnesses in regard to the nature of the past possession of the water, further than is necessary for the disposal of the plaintiff's pretension to a right to the water by virtue of prescriptive possession. I shall defer giving this consideration of the evidence until after I have disposed of the rights of the parties in other respects. I come now to the other argument which was raised by the plaintiff, in regard to what it was he was thus to be entitled to. He argued that supposing he, and not the defendant, was the person bound to allow the water to pass during five days of the week, he would be the person entitled to have the use of the water on the remaining two days. That would be the necessary result of the interpretation I have put on the clause; but then he raised the further question, as to what was "the water" to which he was to be entitled on the two days? He argued that "the water" to which he was to be entitled on the two days, was not the water which he was bound to allow to pass during the five days—that is, such water as should come down from Upper Freethof after the defendant had made every use he chose of the stream, but the whole stream as it should have entered the upper part of Freethof without allowing the defendant to make use of any part of it during its passage through Upper Freethof, except for necessary purposes. As I am of opinion, however, as I have already expressed, that the clause in question, according to the form of its expression, which is a condition upon Du Plessis' conveyance, imposes an obligation upon Du Plessis and his successors, and does not confer any right upon them, I am further of opinion that as "the water" which they were to be allowed to pass free, was "the water," whatever might be its quantity, which came from Upper Freethof, less what Van der Byl and the defendant as his successors might use for drinking purposes, so "the water" to which they were "to be entitled" on the two days was, as on the five days, just such water as might come down from Upper Freethof. In other words, instead of having, as in ordinary cases, a right to use the stream that came from Upper Freethof for irrigation and such like purposes on every day of the week, Du Plessis was prohibited from exercising that right except on two days of the week,—Wednesdays and Sundays. The plaintiff will be "thus entitled" not by virtue of any expression in the clause in question; for though the clause does not use the expression "shall be entitled," yet that arises, not from any intention in the framer to confer a title on the plaintiff, but from the particular form which was adopted in framing what was intended to impose a restraint, and not to give a right. But for the clause, the plaintiff would have been entitled to the water every day of the week; but the clause in effect says :—he shall not have it for five days except for drinking purposes, but he shall be entitled to it, or shall not be restrained from his right to use it, for all purposes on the remaining two days of the week which a proprietor of land has in regard to a stream of water passing through his land, with respect to the portion of the stream which the proprietor of land higher up must allow to pass him. Still the question remains, what is the extent of these rights? It was boldly argued for the defendant that the proprietor of land on the upper part of a stream of water is under no obligation in regard to the use of the water to the proprietors of lands on the lower part of the stream,—that while those proprietors are bound to receive such part of the stream as he may allow to pass them, he is under no obligation to allow any part of it pass,—that, in short, the upper proprietor of a stream is sole owner of the water of the stream to use the whole or give away a part at his discretion. The result, then, if this construction be correct, is, that although the plaintiff has no right of any kind conferred on him by the clause in question, he has reserved to him by it all the rights on, and that even on Wednesday and Sunday, the two days on which the plaintiff's use of the water was to be unrestrained; the defendant might pass on to him much, little, or no water at all. This makes it necessary to determine the broad general question I have before referred to in regard to the rights of respective proprietors of land situated relatively higher and lower upon the course of a running perennial stream as to the use of the water of the stream.

The counsel for the defendant, in support of the very

1855.
Dec. 12.
„ 13.
1856.
Jan. 12.
Retief vs. Louw.

1855.
Dec. 12.
„ 13.
1856.
Jan. 12.
Retief vs. Louw.

startling doctrine raised by him in regard to the absolute right of an upper proprietor to the water of the stream, which, in certain forms of country, would be productive of the most ruinous consequences, did not refer the Court to any precedents in the decisions of Courts, or to any authority in text writers with the exception of a single passage in *Voet*, 8, 3, 6. The author is there treating of *aquæ ductus*, or the right of conveying water *per fundum* or *ex fundo alieno*, that is, through or from the land of another, which I may observe is not the right claimed either by the plaintiff or by the defendant. He says this right may be given not only to one but to several to be used at the same time, or on different days and hours, provided the course and the water be sufficient for all. If, the author says, the water to be conveyed has for a long time flowed from the upper to the lower land, a question is made whether the proprietor of the upper land can grant the right of conveying the water to a stranger in prejudice of the proprietor of the lower ground whom the water had hitherto benefited. To determine the special question whether a proprietor can grant to a stranger the servitude of *aquæ ductus* in prejudice of the proprietor of the lower ground, he says it must be seen how the water flowed to the lower ground, whether naturally or by a construction made on the upper ground. In the former case, *Voet* says, there is no reason why the proprietor of the upper ground should not retain to himself or grant to another the right of leading away from the lower land the water bursting out in his own land (*erumpentem in suo*), and therefore his own. And the reason he gives for this is, " as no prescription can here be conceived as being made by the proprietors of the lower grounds with a view to the water, but the upper proprietor has retained to himself the fullest power of action ; or if any servitude be in question, it consists in this, rather, that lower grounds must serve upper grounds by receiving the water which comes from them." The passage was referred to for the benefit of the last words in it, which were supposed to prove in regard to all water, whether surface water, or spring water rising on land, or whether a stream of water passing through but having its source beyond land, that the proprietor of land has, in regard to all these kinds of water alike, an unrestricted right of absolute property. It seems to me, however, that this special question suggested by *Voet*, and the answer he gives to it, has little bearing upon the question between the present parties, and will not at all warrant the argument that was raised upon it by the defendant. It applies to the case of a proprietor granting to a stranger the right of using water rising on the proprietor's own land, *erumpentem in suo*, and therefore his own, *atque adeo suam*, and still reserving to himself full liberty, *plenissimam libertatem*. It applies to a case in which servitude cannot be conceived, or, if any can be conceived, it would only be that servitude which attaches to low lying land of receiving the water which comes naturally, *naturaliter*, from higher land. In other words, the author is treating of the rights of persons to water which they could not have, but for the liberality of the owner of the contiguous and higher grounds in which the water has its source. That is a totally different case from the present, which regards the rights of parties having lands upon the course of a rivulet or perennial stream rising upon the ground of neither. In a country such as this, where the value of land is greatly dependent upon the facilities for obtaining water, there are few questions which can be conceived of greater magnitude or importance to the inhabitants, yet, singular to say, after making inquiry, I am not able to discover that any case upon the subject has ever been decided by this Court, or by its predecessors, or that there is any judicial authority on the subject beyond a dictum of that learned and much respected Judge, Mr. Justice Menzies, in a case which never ripened to a judgment. With regard to the text writers upon the law of Holland, their authority is very meagre upon the subject, as was indeed to be expected, water being in Holland rather a nuisance than an advantage. The passage in *Voet*, 8, 3, 6, to which I have before referred, is obviously derived from the *Dig.*, 39, 3, 1, 13, where it is said that the action *aquæ pluviæ arcendæ* is not competent to an inferior proprietor against a superior one, to prevent him sending down the water otherwise than it had been accustomed to flow, where the injury is produced by the nature of the ground. But, even in such a case, *i.e.*, where the injury is produced by the nature of the ground, the action is said to lie "only if the rain water, or the water which the rain increases, injures not naturally, but through artificial cause, unless these causes have been produced for the purpose of agriculture." In section 21, it is continued that the action will not lie if the effect of the structure has been only to prevent the water doing as much benefit as it used to do, for the application of the action is to cases where the water injures, "not where it does not benefit;" and in section 22, *Labeo* is said to have doubted whether the action would lie, even where the effect of the structure was to make the water reach the lower ground, and so to injure it, for which he gave the same reason as the passage in *Voet* concludes with, viz., because it always was the servitude of lower ground that it should receive water flowing by nature. This doctrine applies to *aquæ pluviæ*, or the water,

1855.
Dec. 12.
  „   13.
1856.
Jan. 12.

Retief *vs.* Louw.

1855.
Dec. 12.
„ 13.
1856.
Jan. 12.
Retief vs. Louw.

which, in the language of the 1st section of the same title of the
Digest, is said to fall from heaven, and is increased by the
showers, *quæ de cœlo cadit atque imbre excrescit.* The law
quoted, then, applies to the water which falls upon any
given land, and says that the owner of the property may
either retain such for his own use or give it to another; and
what he neither retains nor gives away, the proprietor of
the next lower ground must allow to flow on to his ground;
provided always the proprietor of the upper land has not
collected it artificially so as to make its discharge damage the
lower ground, unless such collection has been made for
agricultural purposes. This law, in short, says what common
sense enforces, that as from the very necessity of things
the water which falls from heaven and is not absorbed by
" the place beneath," must be allowed to find its way
somewhere, it must be allowed to take that course which
nature assigns it, viz., through ground having a lower level.
This law may apply to that water which was proved to
ooze out of the land of Upper Freethof, and which forms
the subject of the claim in reconvention by the defendant to
be afterwards noticed; but it cannot regulate the rights of
the parties in the stream—the perennial stream—which has
its origin not in Upper Freethof, but in the mountains above
it. It seems to me useless to look for the law on this subject
in the doctrine upon the servitude *aquæ ductus.* In the
first place, a prædeal servitude, in the language of the
Censura Forensis, 2, 14, 1, is " a right " constituted over the
property of another, whereby that other is forced to suffer
something on his property which is advantageous to the
other, or not to do something on his own property. Now it
cannot be said with any accuracy that the necessity under
which the proprietor of lower ground lies, either to receive
the surplus water from the upper land, or to allow a perennial running stream to pass through his land, is in virtue of
any "right" constituted, *quovis modo,* in favour of the
proprietor of the upper ground, it arises *ex necessitate rei*
from the nature of things as they existed before social rights
were known. Putting all things out of the question, the
water which falls from the heavens, if it be not absorbed by
the ground on which it falls, must pass in the way nature
has provided, and so must the water issuing from the bowels
of the earth. The obligation, therefore, upon the lower
ground, to receive the water from the upper ground, is not
of the nature of a servitude generally, though for convenience' sake it may be classed under the title servitude for
want of a more appropriate title; for servitude is a service
constituted by agreement, or *quasi* agreement, not *operatione
nature*; as little will the obligation come under the designa-

1855.
Dec. 12,
„ 13.
1856.
Jan. 12.

Retief vs. Louw.

tion of the special servitude *aquæ ductus.* The servitude *aquæ ductus,* in the language of the *Institutes,* 2, 3, 1, is *jus aquæ ducendæ per fundum alienum.* Voet says it is *jus aquæ ducendæ per fundum vel fundo alieno, sive ex capite sive ex alio quovis loco.* This servitude, he says, vanishes when the fountain, from which the •water comes, dries up; but it revives with. the water, although that should not take place within the time in which a right will be lost by prescription, because the right is not lost either by negligence or blame. In the *Censura Forensis aquæ ductus* is said to be the right of conveying water through the tenement of another, which is done by channels or ditches. Now it is obvious that a right to convey water from or through the land of another to your own land, is a totally different thing from an obligation, *vi naturæ,* to receive water from the land of another. The right to convey is in favour of the lower land; the obligation to receive is against it; but what is more, the obligation to receive the water can never cease but with the existing nature of things, however great the interval between the drying up of the water and its reflowing. As soon as the water begins to flow the lower ground must receive it *ex necessitate rei*—negligence, blame, or nonsesser can have no application to such a case. It seems to me, therefore, that only by a confusion of language and a misapplication of terms can this passage in *Voet,* which treats of the right of the proprietor of upper ground to lead away the water growing out of that ground from the lower ground, be applied to support the argument of the defendant, that he is entitled to use this perennial stream as he chooses, because the lower ground is under an obligation to receive the water, which, by the operation of nature, may be sent down to it from his upper ground. If there be law, then, upon the subject in question between the parties, it must be found elsewhere than under the title of servitude. In the *Institutes,* 2, 1, it is said some things are by the law of nature common, some are public; some belong to the community, some to nobody, and most to individuals; and further down " by natural law these things are common, the air, running water, and the sea;" again, all rivers and harbours are public; and in the *Digest,* 43, 20, it is said " water does not of right belong to any one." The water in the present case is "flowing water;" it does not rise in the defendant's land; it is not *erumpentem in suo,* in the words of *Voet,* and cannot, in his words, be said to be *adeo suam,* so that the defendant might either retain it to himself or give the right of leading it out to another. The stream may not in strict propriety be capable of receiving the name of a river, which in the language of the

1855.
Dec. 12.
„ 13.
1856.
Jan. 12.

Retief vs. Louw.

Institutes is said to be public, that is, what may be used by the public generally, *cuivis e populo*, without regard to the possession of land, but it is undoubtedly a rivulet or perennial stream, and as such is a "flowing water," which in the language of the *Institutes* is said to be "common," that is, common to the different persons entitled to use it, in respect of the land through which it . runs. In the *Censura Forensis*, 2, 1, 6, it is said, "common things are chiefly the air and the sea, which, on account of the common use that all have a right to by nature, cannot, by the law of nations, be divided : thus flowing, water, which, collected either from the rains or from veins in the earth, makes a perpetual current. These things, by nature itself as it were, are attributed to, and may be occupied by, any one, provided the common and promiscuous use is not injured, for without the use of air and water no one could live or breathe." This, in my opinion, destroys the right asserted by the defendant that the proprietor of land upon the upper part of a running stream is under no obligation to the proprietor of the lower lying land in regard to the use of the water ; but is entitled, if he choose, arbitrarily. to prevent any. part of the stream whatever reaching the lower land, whether for the preservation of life, the irrigation of land, or its application to manufacturing purposes. To that extent his argument must go, otherwise it entirely · fails, for *Voet*, the authority upon which he rests it, says, that the water of which he speaks is the water of the upper proprietor, which he may either retain to himself or give out to another, so as to prevent its reaching. the land of the lower proprietor, without a reservation of any portion of it for that lower proprietor; which may be true, and is true, if the water spoken of be the water arising on the upper proprietor's land, but cannot be true as to streams merely running through the upper proprietor's land but having their source beyond it, for as to these the. *Censura* says the occupation is subject to the proviso that the common use is not injured. In my . opinion, after considering the authorities to which I have referred, and others which would take too much space to mention here, the flowing perennial stream which takes its rise in the Paarl mountains, and after flowing a certain distance through a channel wrought by nature enters the lands of Upper Freethof, and flows through them in the same channel until it reaches the lands of Lower Freethof, is the common property of the proprietors of these two parcels of land, and of all the other proprietors of land lying on the course of the stream. If so, the only question which remains to be ascertained, is the nature and extent of the rights of these persons in the enjoyment of this common property. In the absence of any more direct authority in the Roman law or the Roman-Dutch law, I have turned to the law of Scotland, which, like the Roman-Dutch law, has the Roman law for its foundation, and in *Erskine's Institutes*, the greatest authority in that law, I find, in 2, 9, 13, this passage:—"The proprietor of both sides of a running water, though he be subjected to no servitude in favour of the inferior tenement, cannot alter its bed if the alteration should bring any real prejudice to the owner of that tenement;" for which the author refers to a case in *Morr*, 14,529; and in *Bell's Com.*, 6th ed., p. 796, the law is laid down to the same effect. So far as the Scotch law can be used as an authority it is destructive of the absolute right in the water asserted by the defendant for the proprietors of higher lands. I have also turned to the law of England, as far as my means would give access to it, and although England is a country very different from Holland as to its use of water, yet its law is by no means devoid of authority on this subject. Upon the maxim of the civil law, introduced into the English law, *cujus est solum ejus est usque ad cœlum*, there can be no doubt that the proprietor of a water-course is owner of the water which flows over the land, as distinguished from those who have no right in the land at all; but it is impossible to say that he is so in a question between the proprietor of the other lands on the course of the stream to the same extent and for the same purposes to which he is owner of the land itself. In 2nd *Roll. Abr.*, 142, it was found that an assise will be against an heir, if he refuse to amend an obstruction to the privilege of fishery; and in *Weld* vs. *Hornby*, 7, *East*, 195, the conversion of a brush-wear into a stone-wear was held to be a nuisance, because it obstructed the passage of fish higher up the stream. These authorities plainly show that the right to the water is limited, so far as regards fishing, to a use of it which shall not affect its use by others, within certain limits. But, moreover, the right to water is limited in this other respect, that the owner cannot divert its course,—*aqua currit et debet currere ut solebat. Shury* vs. *Piggot, Bulstr.*, 339, &c. Accordingly, in the *Year Books*, 32nd, ed. 3, fo. 8, it was adjudged that a stream of water which had been drawn away by the defendant from the course which it had been used to run, should be restored to its ancient channel; and there are many authorities to the same effect in the older law books. The right of the proprietor of the land over which a running stream flows to the water itself, seems to be of a mixed and innominate character, and to be hardly better than a usufructuary right. In *Williams* vs. *Morland*, 2, *B and C*

1855.
Dec. 12.
„ 13.
1856.
Jan. 12.

Retief *vs.* Louw.

1855.
Dec. 12.
„ 13.
1856.
Jan. 12.

Retief vs. Louw.

910, BAYLEY, J., said:—" Flowing water is originally *publici juris.* So soon as it is appropriated by an individual, his right is co-extensive with the beneficial use to which he appropriates it. Subject to that right all the rest of the water remains *publici juris.* The party who obtains a right to the exclusive enjoyment of the water does so in derogation of the primitive right of the public." HOLROYD, J.:— " Running water is not in its nature private property. At least it is private property no longer than it remains on the soil of the person claiming it. Before it came there, it clearly was not his property. It may perhaps become *quasi* the property of another before it comes upon his premises by reason of his having appropriated to himself the use of the water accustomed to flow through his lands before any other person had acquired a prior right to it." LITTLE-DALE, J.:—" The mere right to use the water does not give a party such a property in the new water constantly coming, as to make the diversion or obstruction of the water *per se* give him any right of action. All the king's subjects have a right to the use of flowing water, provided that in using it they do no injury to the rights already vested in another by the appropriation of the water. The cases which have occurred in England have regard to the water chiefly as a motive power. In *Bealey* vs. *Shaw,* 6, *East,* 208, it was laid down that every man is entitled to a stream of water without diminution or alteration. See also *Wright* vs. *Howard, Sim. and St.,* 203; and *Mason* vs. *Hill,* 3, *Ba. and Ad.,* 304; and in *Stears* vs. *Wood,* 7, *Moore,* 534, action was held to lie upon an allegation that water was not allowed to run to the plaintiff's mills at the proper and usual times and in sufficient quantity, as it had been accustomed. These authorities are equally destructive of the right asserted by the defendant either to allow a part or none of the water to pass to the plaintiff. But there are also authorities upon their right to use water for irrigating purposes, to the effect that the water of the stream may be so used, provided there be not a material diminution of the water—*Greenslade* vs. *Halliday,* 6, *Bing.* 379; *Strutt* vs. *Bovington,* 5, *Esp.,* 58; *Hall* vs. *Swift,* 6, *Scott,* 167; and in *Gale on Easements.* a non-suit of the plaintiff in an action, brought for the disturbance of a watercourse, was set aside by the Court, because it appeared that although the water, after being used for irrigation, was returned to its usual course, yet a portion was lost by irrigation and absorption.

These other authorities in the English law are also inconsistent with and destructive of the argument asserted for the defendant, that the proprietor of land through which a stream flows is absolute owner of the stream to all intents and purposes; though they perhaps go too far to be of use here, as they would go to show that neither the defendant nor the plaintiff could use the water to any extent for irrigation, as to which I shall observe by and by. I have also turned to the laws of America upon this subject. In that country water seems to be of much greater value than in the European states, for the cases upon the question of water rights are much more numerous and much more satisfactory in the American Courts than they are in the English Courts. The difficulty indeed is to make a selection from such a superabundance of valuable material. I shall therefore content myself with two out of a great number of cases, because they lay down such broad general principles as I think will go far to determine this case. In *Tyler* vs. *Wilkinson*, 4, *Mass.*, 401, Mr. Justice STOREY, than whom no greater legal authority upon general legal questions such as this case can be cited, lays down the law in these terms: "I do not mean to be understood as holding the doctrine that there can be no diminution whatever, and no obstruction or impediment whatsoever, by a riparian proprietor, in the use of the water as it flows; for that would be to deny any valuable use of it. There may be and there must be allowed of that which is common to all a reasonable use. The true test of the principle and extent of the use is, whether it is to the injury of the other proprietors or not. There may be a diminution in quantity, or a retardation or acceleration of the natural current indispensable for the general or valuable use of the water, perfectly consistent with the use of the common right. The diminution, retardation, or acceleration, not positively and sensibly injurious, by diminishing the value of the common right, is an implied element in the right of using the stream at all. The law here, as in many other cases, acts with a reasonable reference to public convenience and general good, and is not betrayed into a narrow strictness, subversive of common use, nor into an extravagant looseness which would destroy private rights."

In *Evans* vs. *Merriwether*, 3, *Scamm.* (*Ill.*) *R.*, 496, the Court laid down the law in these terms:—"Each riparian proprietor is bound to make such a use of running water as to do as little injury to those below him as is consistent with a valuable benefit to himself. The use must be a reasonable one. Now the question fairly arises, is that a reasonable use of running water by the upper proprietor by which the fluid is entirely consumed? To answer this question satisfactorily, it is proper to consider the wants in regard to the element of water. These wants are either natural or artificial. Natural are such as are absolutely necessary to be supplied in order to

1855.
Dec. 12.
" 13.
1856.
Jan. 12.

Retief *vs.* Louw.

1855.
Dec. 12.
,, 13.
1856.
Jan. 12.
Retief vs. Louw.

his existence. Artificial such only as, by applying them, his comforts and prosperity are increased. To quench thirst, and for household purposes, water is absolutely indispensable; he could live if water was not employed in irrigating lands, or in propelling his machinery. In countries differently situated from ours, with a hot and arid climate, water doubtless is indispensable to the cultivation of the soil, and in them water for irrigation would be a natural want. Here it might increase the products of the soil, but it is by no means essential, and cannot therefore be considered a natural want of man. So of manufactures, they promote the prosperity and comfort of mankind, but cannot be considered absolutely necessary to his existence." The law of France I find to be pretty much in consonance with the laws of the other countries to which I have referred. In *Domat's Public Law*, 1, 8, 2, 11, it is laid down that any riparian proprietor of land on a brook may divert the water for the irrigation of his meadows. "Yet everyone must use this liberty so as to do no injustice to his neighbours who have a like want and an equal right." As the laws of all these countries, Scotland, England, America, and France, have the civil law for their foundation, and upon this subject of land and water rights are not stinted or confined by any peculiar municipal regulations of these countries, arising out of the genius of their people or the particular frame of their government, but are founded upon the universal and immutable principles of sound reason and general justice,—the foundations of the laws of all countries, I believe I may say civilized or uncivilized,—I consider their authority as available for the decision of this case as if they were part and parcel of the Roman-Dutch law, which, strictly speaking, is the law of this colony. In the law of America and France the right to use running water for the purposes of irrigation is distinctly admitted in terms, and the law of America in particular recognizes irrigation as one of the natural and indispensable uses of water in an arid country. The law of England, on the contrary, while it recognizes the use of water for the uses of irrigation, limits the use to an immaterial diminution of the quantity of water,—this in arid countries would obviously make the use unavailable for any good purpose. The defect in the English authorities is to be ascribed to the peculiar climate of that country, in which draining rather than irrigation is generally required. But it is of little consequence, because the principle which in that law is the very foundation of the doctrine upon the natural and artificial uses to which the proprietors of land on running streams are confined in the use of their water, viz., the general good of all, must prevail to regulate the use of these streams in a country like this, in which, from the arid-

ness of the climate and soil, irrigation is, as the American
authorities recognize, one of the natural and indispensable
uses of water. Upon a review of all these authorities in
the Roman, Roman-Dutch, Scotch, English, American, and
French laws, to which I have felt it necessary to refer in a
case of such paramount importance to the land owners of this
Colony, I have come to the conclusion that the proprietors of
lands throughout the course of a perennial running stream of
water have each a common right in the use of that water,
which use, at every stage of its exercise by any one of the
proprietors, is limited by a consideration of the rights of the
other proprietors; and it seems to me that the uses to which
the proprietor of land lying on the upper part of a stream
may make of the water of the stream, is, from the very nature of things, to be classed in the following order: 1st, the
support of animal life; 2nd, the increase of vegetable life;
and 3rd, the promotion of mechanical appliances; and the enjoyment of any one of these uses would seem, also from the
very nature of things, to depend consecutively upon how far
it deprived the owners of the lower land of their enjoyment
of the water for the same purposes. If the upper proprietor
require all the water for the support of life, for human beings
and cattle upon his land—a very improbable case with regard to a perennial stream—the lower proprietors must submit; if the water be more than sufficient for such animal
demands, sufficient must be allowed to pass for the supply of
animal demands of all the proprietors lower down the stream
before the upper proprietor can be allowed to use the water
for the support of vegetable life, or to improve his lands by
irrigation. Again, the demands for the supply of animal
life being answered, the proprietor of the upper ground is
entitled to use the water for the purpose of vegetable life,—
he is entitled to water his land by irrigation or otherwise; so
are the proprietors of the lower grounds in succession entitled to use the water for agricultural purposes. Agricultural uses being supplied throughout the course of the
stream, and the natural use of the water being thus exhausted,
the proprietors are then entitled to apply the water to
mechanical purposes. But I apprehend that no proprietor on
any part of the stream is entitled to use the water for all
these three purposes, even consecutively in the order in
which I have mentioned them, or for any one of them,
recklessly and without any regard to the wants of those below and above him. The defendant has argued that the
plaintiff is not entitled to dam up the water at its entrance
into his land, so as to throw it back upon that of the defendant. The same legal principle which supports that argument will support the converse, that the defendant is not en-

1855.
Dec. 12.
„ 13.
1856.
Jan. 12.

Retief vs. Louw

titled so to use or divert the water as that no part of it shall reach the lower grounds to its detriment. In either case the maxim applies, *sic tuo utere ut alienum non lœdas.* They are both proprietors of the water, the common subject of all the proprietors in the line of its course, and each proprietor must use his right consistently with the common enjoyment by his co-proprietors. If I am right as to the consecutive uses to which water may be applied, it is possible to conceive many cases in which questions will arise as to the extent to which any one proprietor is entitled to use the water for any one of these purposes; but these questions will be easily solved by the application of the maxim to which I have just referred. No one can exercise his right *in invicem vicini,*—whenever he does that he is subject to challenge,—when he does so will depend on the circumstances of each case, and will be easily ascertainable. I am of opinion, therefore, that in this case, as there is no deficiency of water for all natural purposes, the defendant is entitled throughout the whole seven days of the week to use the water of the stream for drinking and irrigating purposes within reasonable limits. That the water which, after he has satisfied these objects, will pass to the land of the plaintiff, is the water which by the clause in his title the plaintiff is bound to allow to pass on the grounds lower than his, after he has abstracted from it water for drinking purposes, and that this is also the water which he is entitled to use for drinking or irrigation, also within reasonable bounds, upon the Wednesday and Sunday of every week. Such being my opinion of the construction to be put upon the clause in the title of the plaintiff, and of the rights of the parties in law generally, independently of any peculiarity of their titles, there still remains the question of prescriptive title to the water, without any abstraction from it by the defendant except for drinking purposes, by virtue of a possession to that extent averred to have existed for more than a quarter of a century. I am of opinion, however, that no such possession has been established by the evidence. Upon weighing the evidence for the two parties, I am decidedly of opinion that the preponderance is in favour of the evidence for the defendant; and that, although the plaintiff and his predecessors may from good neighbourhood and fellowship have got more water on Wednesdays and Sundays when they asked for it, on the supposition on their part that they were entitled to it on these days, yet, in fact, no such right was recognized by the defendant or his predecessors, or was ever enjoyed by the plaintiff. The case of the plaintiff, therefore, fails upon the point of prescription.

I have now disposed of all the questions which arise upon

the case raised by the plaintiff's action. But there still remains for disposal the case in re-convention raised by the
defendant. It appears that from the land of the defendant
water oozes out in several places, in quantities which in
summer make this water exceed the perennial mountain
stream ; but the evidence establishes that, both in summer
and in winter, they unite in one channel on the defendant's
land, and thence are discharged upon the plaintiff's land.
The complaint of the defendant is that the plaintiff has
dammed up this water, and thereby thrown it back upon
the defendant's lands, for which he makes his claim of
damage. The evidence, however, shows that before the
dam was made the water was always impeded by the road
itself, at that point where the dam is made, viz.—where the
road intersects the lands of the plaintiff and defendant, the
surface of the road having been always higher than the bottom of the watercourse. The dam was constructed in the
beginning of the present year, and a great deal of evidence
was led by both sides, more or less contradictory in its
nature, as to the effect produced by it, but there is one circumstance which to my mind disposed of the whole of the
case in re-convention. According to the witness Hiebner,
he made a new cut from the course of the stream in order to
convey water to his dwelling-house,—this cut commences
just at the dam,—it was made so long ago as 1839, on the
suggestion of Louw (one of the defendant's predecessors)
and has been in use ever since, that is, both before and since
the dam was made. Now the defendant's own witness, Du
Toit, swore that the water in this cut "ran very slowly—it
almost stands still." If that be the case, even after the dam
has been constructed, it proves in a way the defendant's
counsel could not answer when I put to him in the course of
the argument, that the dam cannot have altered the level of
the water materially, if it has in fact altered it at all. This
is confirmed by the defendant's own witnesses, who say that
the ground of his vineyard was wet before the dam was
made, and that if the water had overflowed the vineyard since the dam was made it did so before (two
years ago), and also in October last year, and that
though the dam when the sluice is down raises the
water only eight inches, the bottom of the culvert
under the road is about twelve inches lower than the surface
of the road as it existed formerly. The culvert has lowered
the stream therefore as it passes the road by twelve inches,
and the sluice raises it only eight inches—there has been a
lowering of the stream, therefore, by four inches. On the
whole, I am of opinion that the case in re-convention has
entirely failed, and that we would never have heard of it but

1855.
Dec. 12.
,, 13.
1856.
Jan. 12.

Retief vs. Louw.

for the question raised by the plaintiff in regard to his supposed right to the water of the stream on two days of the week. I think that the plaintiff is entitled to a declaration that he has a right to the use, on Wednesdays and Sundays in summer, of such water as the defendant, after all reasonable use of the stream for drinking and irrigation, shall allow to pass to his lands, to be used by the plaintiff in the same way, and that the plaintiff should be absolved from the instance of the claim in re-convention; but as the plaintiff by this declaration gets only what the defendant never denied to him, except in argument at the bar, I think he ought to pay the costs of the defendant, except such part of them as may have been occasioned by the claim in re-convention, and that the defendant should pay such of his costs as have been occasioned by that claim.

CLOETE, J.:—Not having had an opportunity of consulting my brother Judge upon the reasons and grounds upon which he has come to his conclusions, although concurring in the final judgment which has just been read, to reject the claim both in convention and re-convention, yet as great principles are involved in the decision of this case, and as I may not entirely concur in the grounds of my brother's judgment, I shall only observe that questions of this nature have been very fully argued and determined by the former Court of Justice; and also by this Court, in the case of Le Roux vs. Minnaar (at the Paarl) and of Cloete vs. de Wet (near Stellenbosch) where the principles of the Roman-Dutch law upon such questions were well considered, and in both of which I was engaged as counsel. I have therefore felt it my duty, not knowing exactly the grounds upon which my brother Judge has come to his conclusions, also to commit to paper the views which have brought my mind to a decision on this case, confining myself entirely to the principles of the Roman-Dutch law, which are to govern the decisions of this Court. [After reciting the pleadings, His Lordship continued:]—On the trial of this case many witnesses have been examined on both sides, and it might suffice, as at once disposing of this case, to state that the plaintiff has altogether failed to prove to my satisfaction that he has in any way been disturbed in the beneficial enjoyment of the water flowing down to his farm : the only approach to evidence on this point being contained in these words of the witness Onvervacht,—"In February last (1855) the water which is to come from the defendant's only ran half-a-day. I do not remember what day that was. On a Sunday morning the plaintiff sent me to the defendant's to ask why the water was kept up. I went up to the defendant's homestead, and saw the water running into a pond before the stable. I went back and told

1855.
Dec. 12.
„ 13.
1856.
Jan. 12.

Retief vs. Louw.

the plaintiff." This is all the evidence in the whole case on the part of the plaintiff to show a trespass or injury, while not a word is even hinted in all that evidence of any injury being sustained. In like manner the defendant has failed to show any injury for the act complained of by him; and on this ground, therefore, it also would be sufficient to state that the plaintiff has altogether failed to prove his case as to any injury sustained by him, and that the defendant has failed in like manner to prove his injury, so that on this point both the claims for damages set up by the plaintiff and by the defendant must be rejected. But the plaintiff has prayed for a further declaratory decree to establish his right to the water in question, and I conceive that it is fitting that we should not decline entering upon that question, as its decision may tend to settle the vexed question as to the use and right of water, which has ever been, and is still likely to be, an endless source of litigation in this country. To settle that question it is necessary to look minutely into the general aspect and relative positions of the farms of these litigants, and to declare the law as defined by the Roman-Dutch authorities on similar questions. First as to the position of these farms, and the character or legal definition of the waters on which they depend. It would appear from the plans laid before the Court, that on the rugged heights of the Paarl mountain certain weak springs arise, the waters of which descend directly on to the farm of the plaintiff; that these waters during the summer months at least yield but a scanty supply of water, but are fed or increased by some other weak springs arising in the lands of the plaintiff, which thus become intermixed and flow downwards in one and the same channel. Such waters are declared by the Civil law to belong to the class of private waters, *vide Digest*, lib. 43, tit. 12, the whole context of which lays down, that although water may not be diverted or obstructed in rivers whether by themselves navigable, or in other tributaries which flow into the first and thus render them fit for navigation, and which are denominated public streams, and over which the crown or the prætor exercised authority to restrain anyone: that yet as to private streams the right as to their use differs in no way from any other private right. *Digest*, lib. 43, tit. 12, sec. 4 :—" *Hoc interdictum ad flumina publica pertinet, si autem flumen privatum sit, cessabit interdictum, nihil enim differt a ceteris locis privatis flumen privatum ;*" and again, sec. 10 :—" *Quod in privato flumine factum est, perinde est, atque si in alio privato loco fiat.*" This distinction is followed by the law authorities in Holland, and firstly by *Grotius* in his *Introduction to the Roman-Dutch Law*, where (book 2, c. 35,

1855.
Dec. 12.
„ 13.
1856.
Jan. 12.

Retief vs. Louw

secs. 14, 15), he has these words,—" *Uit Heerenwateringen of Banwateringen mag iedereen op zyn grond leiden, voor zoo veel de Keuren zulks niet verbieden.*" These words are of great legal importance, as they have been expressly followed and adopted by *Van Leeuwen* in his *Censura Forensis*, lib. 2, c. 1, s. 9, and by *Voet* in his *Commentaries*, lib. 43, tit. 12, and yet they are terms which to many a Roman-Dutch student are not readily intelligible, from the mode adopted by this great author to avoid all words of a Latin or foreign origin, and to give to all his legal terms a strictly Saxon derivation. It is necessary, therefore, to ascertain what *Grotius* and those authors mean by the term "Heerenwateringen" and "Banwateringen," which they declare anyone may lead out, if not prohibited by express authority, I have referred for the meaning of this passage to the translation of *Grotius* recently made by *Herbert,* where the translator gives the words, "lakes and reservoirs," as intended by *Grotius,* but this is clearly vague and unintelligible, and does not convey the meaning of *Grotius.* By "Heerenwateringen" I have no doubt are meant all such running or stagnant waters upon which the nobles of Holland had still certain feudal rights, as fishing and the like, expressly thus declaring that the proprietors of such lands had yet the right to lead out such waters. The definition of "Banwateringen" is more difficult; the word "Ban," although known to the English, French, and Dutch laws, has become obsolete, or only applicable to other meanings than those to which the word originally applied. The word "Ban" in the French language referred to a proclamation by which the labouring class were liable to perform some feudal service, from thence "Convoquer le Ban ou L'Arriere Ban," which rights have, however, ceased to exist from the first sittings of the National Assembly in 1789 and following years, which for ever abolished all those feudal rights. The same meaning was attached in England anciently to this word, which applied to the "service in socage" (as it was called) by which the rural population was also liable to perform such personal services as might be required by the lord of the manor. In that sense, however, the word has become obsolete, and is now only applied to "Banns of Marriage." In like manner I find, from a valuable treatise on the law of Holland—for the perusal and reference to which I am indebted to my esteemed brother at the bar, Mr. Advocate Brand, sen.—(the *Jus Agrarium of Holland,* by Professor Trotz), that the word "Ban" anciently was used in Holland for calling out the rural population in villages and the country for keeping in repair the roads and watercourses, he giving at page 241, the distinct explanation of "Banmerken aan wegen en wateringen," *i.e.*, "Ban or compulsory work done to roads and watercourses." This authority thus completely explains the legal meaning of those obsolete terms, and establishes the principle that according to the ancient laws of Holland (in conformity with the rules of the Roman law), every proprietor of land has the right of leading out any waters (not being public streams), even from such streams as are subject to feudal rights, or such as require to be kept up by the "compulsory" labour of the working classes belonging to each community.

1855.
Dec. 12.
„ 13.
1856.
Jan. 12.

Retief *vs.* Louw.

That this principle is still maintained down to the last century throughout Holland, further appears from a valuable authority, to be found in the Dutch consultations of *Schrassert*, vol. 2, consult. 61, p. 407, which, from the importance of the case, I carefully translated for the information of the Bench when engaged in a case of a similar nature as the present one many years ago, which translation I have preserved, and which I shall therefore proceed to give in full as strongly illustrating the present question. The case there submitted to counsel was, whether a person through whose lands the waters flowed of a small stream flowing into the Zuider Zee, might erect a mill thereon without consulting the proprietors of lands situate lower down than his own ? These are the words of the consultation : "The question being submitted to the undersigned, ' whether a person possessed of lands on both banks of the Hierdenbeek, a stream flowing partly out of the fields and partly out of the several private ditches, and discharging itself into the Zuider Zee, might at once proceed to erect a paper mill upon that water, or whether the consent of other persons interested should be first required and called for ;' it appears to me under correction, that the solution of this question depends entirely whether this water is to be considered a public or private water. A *flumen publicum* is defined in our law to be *quod perenniter fluit, ac ad totum populum pertinet*; *privatum, quod æstate exarescit, et in privati dominio est, nec a cæteris locis privatis differt. Vide Voet, Comment., ad. tit. ff. de flumen.* Under the latter class (*privata flumina*) our law authorities also bring all such lesser streams of which lands are drained of their superfluous water, commonly called with us, ' beeken' (brooks), in Latin ' *rivi.*' which the *l.* 1, *s.* 1, *ff. de flumen*, explains to be ' *quod a flumine discernantur magnitudine et existimatione circumcolentium.*' As therefore the water here in question is not an open river, fit for navigation or other public purposes, but only a stream collected partly from the water of the fields, and partly from private ditches, it cannot be considered in any other light than as a brook, as it also has always been considered *existimatione circumcolentium,*

1855.
Dec. 12.
,, 13.
1856.
Jan. 12.

Retief vs. Louw.

and is therefore called a stream, deriving its name (the Hierden stream) from the village Hierden, along which it flows to the province of Harderwyk. Concerning such streams the law authorities lay down, as *Bartolus*, in his *Treatise de Insula*, in the following words :—'*Et alia parte, quod rivus, sive sit manufactus, ita ut per eum aqua ducatur ad utilitatem privati, sive accipiatur pro eo loco, per quem aqua naturaliter fluit, regulariter sit privatus, per l. 6, ff. fin. regundu, et pertineat ad eos, qui ex utraque parte prædia possident.*' The same principle is laid down by *Baldus* in *item lapilli, col. 2, ff. de rerum div. :* '*Quod omne flumen, quod arescit, vel pusillum aquæ in æstate continet, ut vix te laves, interdum ibi, dicatur privatum ; quia hoc non est aptum natum esse ad publicum bonum;*' which passage is directly applicable to this stream (the Hierden stream) which is known to dry up so much in the summer that only here and there a little water is collected in it from the private ditches flowing into it. So that I am of opinion that all law authorities concur in considering this stream as one of those in which a property is acquired by him who is possessed of lands on both its banks. It is further clear in law that every one can do what he likes upon his own : '*eo quod quilibet sit liber, rerum suarum moderator et arbiter,*' *l.* 21, *Cod. Mandat.* '*In specie quod quilibet in suo solo pro lubitu ædificare possit,*' as is to be found in *Struv., de ædificiis privatis, th.* 32. Without any consent being thereto required by supreme authority, as would be required in placing mills upon public waters, as this licence is granted not with regard to the mills, ·*cum molendina extruendi jus non sit de regalibus,*' but with regard to the water, '*eo quod flumina publica pertineant ad principem, et inter regalia numerentur; prout in terminis docet Sixtin. de Regalibus, l.* 2, *cap.* 3, *num.* 87. But on the other hand, the same author states, *eodem capite, num.* 45, '*in privatis fluminibus et aquis certum esse, libere et sine ulla auctoritate principis molendinum in illis ædificari posse, cum ea nihil ab aliis privatis differant. Neque enim princeps est dominus rerum particularium, quæ ad subditos spectant ; sed dominia talium rerum sunt apud singulos.*' *Vide Instit., s. singul., de rerum divisione. Bartolus in Prooem., ff. col.* 2. '*Ideoque frustra precibus a principe impetraretur, quod de jure et lege permissum est,*' *l. unic. cod. de Thesaur.* Which being the case, it follows that no citation or consent of any parties interested is required to place the mill, as no one upon the ground of any pretended interest could prevent any one from doing what he pleases upon his own. And in express terms several standard law authorities who have written on this subject declare that any one can construct a mill upon his water, even to the prejudice of another, who might have had a mill previously upon

1855.
Dec. 12.
,, 13.
1856.
Jan. 12.

Retief *vs.* Louw.

the same water. On these grounds I am of opinion that any one possessed of lands on both banks of the Hierden stream has a right within himself to erect a mill upon the same without applying for leave of the supreme authority, or citing the parties interested. And I do not know any statute, resolution, or local ordinance, exacting anything contrary to these principles. Wherefore, I see no ground for deviating from the concurring decision of the authorities and law commentators thereon." Having thus laid down these principles, it will be sufficiently easy to apply them to the present case. The little streamlets (the subject of the present action), whether first flowing from the Paarl mountain and descending into the defendant's land, or whether they arise on the lands of the defendant himself, are such weak springs only yielding a sufficiency of water as thus legally to constitute them private streams, wherewith, consequently, the defendant has the right to treat as he would with any other part of his private property. In my opinion, therefore, he might construct ponds or reservoirs, irrigate his lands with any part thereof, erect mills for his own or public use, or turn the same to any lawful or beneficial purpose, so long as he or those from whom he has derived his title have not restricted or limited that use by any servitude, either expressly covenanted, or by the free and undisturbed use of that water or any part thereof, during such a period of time as has conferred a right to others by a title of prescription. This, then, brings me to the consideration of the express title which the plaintiff has set up, viz., that he has acquired a right to the use of this water coming from the defendant by virtue of an express clause in the transfer of Van der Byl to his predecessor Du Plessis, in the deed of transfer of the 14th October, 1814, by which he became entitled to the daily use of drink-water, and also for the purpose of irrigation to the water for two days in each week, viz., on the Wednesdays and Sundays throughout the year. In support of this claim, the plaintiff has put in the original deed of transfer containing this clause :—" That the proprietor of this place shall be obliged to allow the water during the whole summer to run undisturbed in its old course, and that besides his drink-water he shall be entitled to the water for his own use twice a week, viz., Sundays and Wednesdays." This clause embraces three distinct servitudes,— (*a*) That the water shall flow undisturbed during the whole summer in its old course ; (*b*) That the proprietor of the lower farm, Du Plessis, now represented by the plaintiff, shall be entitled to his drink-water; (*c*) That he shall have a right to divert or irrigate his lands from this water-course two days in every week, viz., Sundays and Wednesdays. Now as re-

1855.
Dec. 12.
„ 13.
1856.
Jan. 12.
Retief *vs.* Louw.

gards the first part of this servitude, no question has been raised before the Court. The defendant's counsel only contended that this clause was inserted for the purpose of securing to the late Gert Van der Byl a right to have a quantity of water to irrigate a piece of land situate below that of Du Plessis, which at the time was Government land, but which he was occupying, and of which he subsequently acquired a grant; but this view I cannot take, as it is manifest that no right of servitude can be acquired except as an accessory to, or a burthen upon immovable property, over which the person imposing the servitude has a right of dominium. Gert Van der Byl, on the 14th October, 1814, had no dominion over this lower piece of Government land; he could not therefore lawfully impose a servitude on any land in favour of that over which he had no property, and therefore that part of the servitude cannot legally be construed as conferring such a right; but is therefore the whole of this clause to be considered as waste paper, and to be treated as a nonentity? I cannot come to that conclusion, but applying to the construction of this clause those rules which *Pothier* has so clearly laid down in his treaty on contracts I am of opinion that we must endeavour to give to this clause such construction as may be fairly judged most consistent with the then position of the parties, and the meaning they intended. "*In conventionibus contrahentium voluntas potius quam verba spectari placet.*" The second rule he lays down is :— "*Quoties in stipulationibus ambigua oratio est, commodissimum est id accipi quo res de qua agitur in tuto sit.*" The fourth rule is :— "*Semper in stipulationibus et in cæteris contractibus id sequimer quod actum est, aut si non appareat quid actum est, erit consequens ut id sequimur quod in regione in qua actum est frequentatur.*" And again in the fifth rule he lays down this principle :— "*In contractibus tacite veniunt ea quæ sunt moris et consuetudinis.*" In applying these rules to the custom and usage throughout the country, it must be known to every one acquainted with the physical aspect and cultivation of the soil in this Colony, that during this century (in particular) as population and agriculture have increased, proprietors of large farms (as in this case of Mr. G. Van der Byl) have sold off sections of land which they had not the means of cultivating; and a supply of water being the great desideratum, on those occasions the purchasers of the fractional parts invariably and necessarily stipulate for the use of a portion of water, without which their purchase would be utterly valueless. The proprietor of the entire estate (or the seller) then generally concedes or allows a limited supply of water to the purchaser, either by ensuring him the use on one or two days in the week, and sometimes even on a certain number of hours in the day, to enable him to maintain a garden, or for the family supply; and on this principle I could refer to numberless farms in and about Stellenbosch, the Paarl, and other places even near Cape Town, and throughout the whole Colony, where such divisions have been established, a common phraseology having been generally introduced that such or such a place has so many days, or so many hours' water, and the like. Now knowing that this principle prevailed throughout the Colony, that this is "*moris et consuetudinis*," I feel satisfied that Gert Van der Byl (the proprietor of the whole estate Vredenhof) at the sale of the lower part of his farm gave up, as it is called, two days' water to Du Plessis for irrigation, and a sufficiency of daily drink-water, and although many witnesses have been brought forward to show that Van der Byl did not inform them of this, which is very possible as a proprietor of the *fundus serviens* is not very likely to proclaim the existence of this servitude to every one, yet the evidence of the defendant himself, that of Miss Louena Aling, and that of F. G. Nieuwenhuis, satisfies my mind that Du Plessis immediately made use of such water by virtue of such a servitude; as he would and could not have had any extensive gardens such as are stated by Nieuwenhuis to have been upon that farm soon after its purchase. I entertain, therefore, no doubt but that Gert Van der Byl did, in the transfer of the 14th October, 1814, give to Du Plessis and the subsequent proprietors of this farm a right to claim daily drink-water and two days' water for irrigation a week, viz., on the Sundays and Wednesdays, and that consequently the defendant will be bound to allow to the plaintiff the beneficial enjoyment of those rights, and that an action will be against him if he wilfully obstructs the plaintiff in the enjoyment of that right, on which in a great measure the value of his farm depends; but, as I have said before, the plaintiff having failed to prove in this case that he has suffered any injury, or that the defendant had wilfully obstructed this enjoyment, I concur in the opinion already expressed on the Bench, that the plaintiff's claim must be rejected with costs. With regard also to the reconventional claim set up by the defendant, I am of opinion that the defendant has failed to show that he has sustained any damage by the act of the plaintiff, and indeed it is probable that this claim would not have been made except as a set-off to the action commenced against him. The defendant, however, at the trial brought forward many witnesses to show that the plaintiff has raised the level of the water-course, by which he leads the water to his lands in such a way as to damage his vineyard; but he has failed to satisfy me that his vineyard has been damaged,

1855.
Dec. 12.
„ 13.
1856.
Jan. 12.

Retief *vs.* Louw.

1855.
Dec. 12.
,, 13.
1856.
Jan. 12.
Retief vs. Louw.

or that he has sustained any injury by the back-water (as he terms it) produced by raising this water by means of a sluice. But I am further of opinion that the plaintiff has the full right to raise the water to such an extent as to ensure the irrigation of his lands, upon the principle of law that when a servitude has been conceded everything necessary to give effect to the enjoyment of that right must also be held to have been granted. And in this case it has been proved by evidence of Albert du Toit, that the plaintiff cannot bring the water to his house except at the spot where he has erected the sluice. The further evidence of the officers of the Municipality of the Paarl also satisfies my mind, that the plaintiff and the former proprietors of that farm had continuously during the last forty years exercised this right of water leading; that they obtained their water by means of a channel, which, flowing over the main road leading to the Paarl, is continued at so high a level so as to admit of an easy flow by being dammed up but a few inches, but that this channel over the main road having been since converted by the commissioners of the Municipality of the Paarl, of which the defendant was himself a member, into a culvert or under drain, in the formation of which the defendant, as such commissioner, was the chief director; that the floor of this culvert was so excavated as to sink this water-course to the depth of one foot and three inches below its former level; that it thus became absolutely necessary for the plaintiff to form a sluice or embankment by which the water was again restored to that former level, and that this sluice has been proved to be in the whole, of the height of one foot and eight inches, so that there is a flow of only five inches of water thus secured to the plaintiff, and the witness Du Toit says of only two inches at the only spot where such a diversion of this water can fitly be made. I am also of opinion that there is not a tittle of evidence to show that the defendant is injured by this back-water. The vineyard in which injury is said to have been sustained has been sworn to be apparently as healthy as the remainder, showing no symptoms of decay, but if this might at any time hereafter ensue, it is to be hoped that, these parties will find the means of boarding up or securing the banks on both sides of the vineyard at less expense than resorting to legal proceedings, which, independently of their cost, leave a sore and unfriendly feeling between neighbours, which I trust they both will avoid as only tending to their mutual annoyance and injury. On these several grounds I concur in simply rejecting the claim made to the plaintiff for damages, with costs, and also in rejecting the defendant's reconventional claim.

DREYER vs. IRELAND.

[Referred to in HOUGH vs. VAN DER MERWE, *ante*, p. 148.]

Water-rights.—Upper Proprietor.—Servitude.
Registration.—Prescription.

Per WATERMEYER, J.*—As a general rule, no servitude in*
favour of a lower proprietor existing, the upper proprietor
may use water flowing through his land in any way he
thinks proper.

A servitude of aquæductus granted in favour of an individual,
and distinct from any land, is a personal servitude, and
must cease with the usuary's life, and cannot be trans-
mitted to his heirs.

Where a servitude is not attached to land, the possessor of such
right is designated "usuarius." A usuarius cannot sell
or cede his right.

This case was tried before SIR WILLIAM HODGES, C.J., CLOETE, J., and WATERMEYER, J. The plaintiff's declaration set forth that a water-course, taking its rise from New-lands Spring, and from thence flowing down through the estate called the Brewery, situate at Wynberg, and from thence into an adjoining property called Palmboom, and finally discharging itself into the Liesbeek River, had existed for a long series of years; that in June, 1851, the executors of one Jacob Cloete, the owner of the property, transferred to Rudolph Cloete a portion of the same upon which there stood a water-mill, the wheel of which was turned by the water of the said stream, and after flowing past the mill ran downwards into the River Liesbeek; that there was no dam or other excavation in the bed of the stream at the time of the transfer, but that the mill had the use of the water as it ran and flowed, continuously and uninterruptedly. That by the conditions of sale set forth in the deed of transfer to Rudolph Cloete, it was provided "that the course of the stream or water-course called the mill-stream, should remain undisturbed and uninterrupted." That the said executors at about the same time sold to Zeederberg and Wicht the said stream or water-course, being the right to the water running and flowing therein, for £535, and that the conditions of sale were similar to those already mentioned in the sale to Rudolph Cloete. That the plaintiff afterwards purchased from Zeederberg and Wicht the said stream of water, and afterwards established a brewery upon

1866.
June 7.
" 8.
July 12.
——
Dreyer *vs.*
Ireland.

1866.
June 7.
„ 8.
July 12.

Dreyer vs.
Ireland.

land belonging to him, through which the said stream ran,
and that the water continued to flow after passing the mill
uninterruptedly and continuously. That Rudolph Cloete, in
October, 1864, sold and transferred the property acquired by
him to the defendant, who for some time allowed the water to
flow as it had at all times previously run, but that in April,
1866, he began to excavate a capacious dam or reservoir in
the bed of the water-course, the effect of which would be to
prevent the continuous flow of the water to the plaintiff's
brewery, to his serious loss and damage. Whereupon the
plaintiff prayed that the defendant might be required to remove the dam or reservoir, and by perpetual interdict be
prevented from doing anything whereby the constant and
uninterrupted flow of water might be hindered.

The defendant pleaded first, the general issue. Secondly,
that the conditions of sale under which the executors of
Jacob Cloete sold to Rudolph Cloete the portion of the place
called Palmboom, on which the said mill stood, were conditions upon which not only the said portion of the said place
was sold, but also divers other lots of the same place were
sold at the same time, and among such lots the right to the
use of the said water of the same stream below the point E
on the general plan was sold to the persons through whom
the plaintiff claims title thereto, and subject to the same
conditions, and the same conditions were contained, partly in
the deed of transfer of the 2nd June, 1851, and partly upon
the said general plan in the same deed referred to, whereon
the course of the said stream was traced. And that upon
the said plan were endorsed the following words:—"That
the course of the mill stream, marked A to E, shall remain
undisturbed and uninterrupted for the sole use of the mill on
lot 3, and that the purchaser of the stream below the point
E shall have the right of leading the same along its present
course, entitling him thereby to the private thoroughfare, or
along the dotted line E F G, or over any lots which from their
contiguity may enable the same to be effected without detriment to private rights." That before and after the said sale
and transfer, the owner for the time being of the mill had
been used, and of right accustomed, to restrain and keep back
the water of the stream until it should rise to a level higher
than it would flow at if left to its natural course, and while
so restrained all the water of the stream was by the said
mill-owners of right kept for a short period from flowing beyond the point at which the restriction was placed. In a
second special plea the defendant alleged that the making
of a dam or reservoir would not affect the plaintiff's rights
to use the water.

The replication took issue on these several pleas.

The judgment of the majority of the Court [Watermeyer, J. diss.], was, under the special circumstances of the case and the form of the pleadings, in favour of the plaintiff. (The authorities on the question of water-rights will be found cited by Watermeyer, J.)

1866.
June 7.
„ 8.
July 12.

Dreyer vs.
Ireland.

Sir William Hodges, C.J., delivered the judgment of the majority of the Court. After reciting the pleadings and stating that the averments they contained rased the principal points argued in the case, continued :—Witnesses were called for the purpose of showing the character of the works complained of by the plaintiff, which the defendant had been carrying on in the channel through which the water flowed to the mill. It was shown that the ancient channel was of irregular width ; that many trees and bushes were growing on its sides, whereby the water was absorbed in the heat of summer, and the quantity of water thereby diminished. It did not appear that the water was caused to flow by the defendant's new works at a lower level than it formerly did, but the width of the channel had been considerably increased and the trees and bushes removed. Some progress had also been made in lining the channel at its sides and bottom with stone. The works, as far as they had been carried, did not appear to form any part of an intended reservoir or dam, and it appears to me that all these works, so long as they are not used to pond or keep back the flowing water, are calculated to benefit the plaintiff, and not to injure him ; the larger the flow of the water, especially in the time of summer, the more advantageous it would be to the water supply of the plaintiff's brewery, and if the stream continued to flow continuously and without interruption in the usual and direct channel, the plaintiff could have had nothing to complain of. I am not by any means sure that the defendant did not contemplate, by the works complained of, to commence the formation of a dam or reservoir. If he did, then it appears to me that he would have contemplated the doing of an unlawful act, for the defendant, in support of the allegations in the first special plea that there had always been a right exercised by the owners of the defendant's mill to restrain and keep back the water of the stream until it should rise to a level higher than it would flow at if left to its natural course, has failed altogether. The former owner of the mill and his son, also some of their servants, and some of the witnesses called for the defendant also, proved to my satisfaction that no such restraints of the water had been exercised, and the weight of the evidence was on this point clearly in favour of the plaintiff, nor was the defendant more successful in showing that the allegation in the second special plea could be

O 2

1866.
June 7,
„ 8.
July 13.

Dreyer vs.
Ireland.

maintained, *i.e.*, that the effect of making a dam or reservoir would not be prejudicial to a continuous flow of water, although I observe that that allegation is cautiously stated in the plea, by alleging that it would not be calculated to prevent a continuous flow of water at all times, "in sufficient quantities for the use of the said plaintiff in his said brewery." The plaintiff is entitled to receive a continuous flow of the whole water at all times, after it has first served the purpose of the mill. This part of the case may be summed up by saying that although under the terms of the contract of sale the defendant was not bound to use the water in the same precise manner as it was used at the time of the sale, for if he were he could not avail himself of any improvements in the machinery of his mill, he could not, nevertheless, prejudice the right of the lower proprietor to have the water flowing in a continuous stream and in the ordinary course. He could, I think, clear out the channel and improve and widen it for the purpose of allowing the water to flow freely ; but he would not be justified in making a dam or reservoir, so as to keep the water back, and thus make the supply below intermittent and uncertain. There is another question to be disposed of. The defendant appears to have insisted on a right to deliver the water below the mill when the mill was not in motion, not in the most direct course, but by turning it off so as to enable it by a circuitous course to reach the point of delivery; but it appears to me that the general plan which was referred to in the conditions of sale makes this point quite clear in favour of the plaintiff. The conditions of sale refer to the general plan, and it is one of the conditions " that the course of the mill-stream marked A to E (on the plan) shall remain undisturbed and uninterrupted." Now the plan of the stream so marked and thus referred to shows that the stream was described as flowing in a direct and not in a circuitous course to the point E, and therefore, when the mill was not working, the defendant would be bound to throw it over the wheel by means of a trough or shoot, or by making a channel by the side of the stream, to lead it round the wheel so as to regain the water-course before it reached the point E. I have mentioned the general plan because it appears to me to have been incorporated with the contract made between the executors of Jacob Cloete and Rudolph Cloete. When reference is made in a contract to a plan, the rule is, that to the extent that the contract refers to the plan it is part of the contract, but not otherwise. Here the plan is referred to, and, on the authority of the *North British Railway Company* vs. *Todd* (12, C. *and Fin.*, 722), the plan in this case may be looked at for the purpose of ascertaining what the contract between the parties really was. But, in the course of the argument, great stress was laid by the learned counsel for the defendant upon a general question of very great importance. He contended that the plaintiff had failed to show a good title to the water running in the course of this mill-stream, after it had left the boundary of the defendant's property at the point E already referred to. As has been already mentioned, the mill-stream below the point E, as marked on the general plan, was sold by the executors of Jacob Cloete to Messrs. Zeederberg and Wicht on the 20th February, 1851. By the memorandum of purchase the executors declared that they had sold to these parties "the mill-stream of the place Palmboom below the point marked E on the general plan framed by the surveyor, Mr. L. Cloete, dated 10th of January, 1851, and the right of using it from there," for the sum of £535 sterling, on the following conditions and stipulations, as stated in the conditions of sale of lots 1 to 45 :—That the course of the said stream marked in the general plan above mentioned A B C D to E, shall remain undisturbed and uninterrupted. 2nd. That the purchasers of said stream from the point marked E, shall have the optional right of leading off the same to Liesbeek River, either through its present course, marked on the aforesaid plan by a blue streak along the space called in the plan private thoroughfare for the water-course, or through a course to be made at their own expense along the dotted line in the said plan, running over the border of lots 22 to 34, to Liesbeek River, and that they shall be entitled to the right of private thoroughfare along the said dotted line (E F G), or over any of the lots which may be contiguous to the optional water-course aforesaid. The plaintiff subsequently (on the 26th November, 1852) purchased these rights so granted to Zeederberg and Wicht, and received from them the following memorandum in writing :—" We do hereby cede and transfer to Mr. Dreyer all right in the foregoing memorandum (save and except a stream of water of one inch in diameter, which we do hereby reserve, and shall belong to us for our disposal), on the same conditions as in the foregoing memorandum. Value received without any responsibility." There was no evidence before us to show that the plaintiff had any other transfer made to him to secure his title to the water than the document I have already referred to, and it was contended on behalf of the defendant that plaintiff was not on that account entitled to bring the present action. But I must observe, in the first place, that is no special plea denying the plaintiff's right to claim the water in the stream, and if the defence be admissible under the general issue, then the defendant appears to me to be estopped, under the circumstances of this case, from taking

1866.
June 7.
„ 8.
July 12.

Dreyer vs.
Ireland.

1866.
June 7.
" 8.
July 12.
———
Dreyer vs.
Ireland.

this objection. Estoppel binds privies as well as parties. On Rudolph Cloete's transfer and conditions of sale the intention of the executors to sell the water when it should have left the point E on the plan was plainly announced, and it is not because the conveyancer, who transferred the right to the water to Zeederberg and Wicht, omitted to make transfer of the land over which the water passed from the point E to the Liesbeek River with the private thoroughfare adjoining it (all which still remains the property of the executors), that the defendant can be allowed to contend that the plaintiff has shown no strict title to the water. He is not, I think, entitled to ask this Court in the present state of his title for a perpetual injunction against the defendant, but he may maintain this suit for the disturbance of the stream. The effect of mere possession of easement or interest in the property of another, as affording presumptive evidence of right, is very powerful, and in respect of personal property the ordinary proof of title is the possession of it; and it has been held that the mere naked possession of land is *primâ facie* evidence of right against a mere stranger who can show no colour of title. It is possible that very nice questions may arise as to the precise interest in the water and the use of it, which the plaintiff has acquired by reason of the cession from Zeederberg and Wicht of their rights; but these questions do not, in my opinion, arise in this case. The defendant, as claiming through Rudolph Cloete, knew that the water, or the use of it, did not and was not intended to belong to him after it had once passed the point E on the general plan; and the plaintiff has proved a continual and uninterrupted use of the water, after passing over land still belonging to the original vendor, from the time of the sale to him by Zeederberg and Wicht, on the 26th November, 1852. Our verdict will therefore be in favour of the plaintiff for nominal damages, and the defendant will be interdicted from making any dam or reservoir or any other works which will prevent the water from flowing continuously in the course marked on the plan up to the point E; it being understood that when the mill is not working he may deliver the water over the wheel or by a channel formed by him by the side of the wheel, so as to bring it again into the stream before it reaches the point E. Under the circumstances we make no order as to costs, but each party must bear his own.

WATERMEYER, J., after stating the facts of the case, said :—I speak my views on the questions raised with diffidence, as my brethren hold, in part at least, different opinions. But it seems to me that no real servitude of any kind appears to have been thus created on the mill property. There must be, says *Burge*, following the *Institutes*, two properties,

1866.
June 7.
" "
July 12.

Dreyer v.
Ireland.

the one *cujus causâ servitus constituitur*, for the benefit of which the servitude is established, and the other on which the servitude is imposed (3,*Burge*, 400). Real servitudes are *jura quibus prædia prædiis serviunt*, rights of properties over properties, or diminution of rights of properties in favour of other properties. Especially in regard to the *jus aquæductus*, the right of leading *aqua viva*, flowing water, over the property of another, the rules are strict, for this twofold reason probably: the water is in one sense attached to the land on which it rises and over which it flows, and in another is common to all men immediately it ceases to flow over private property. It is less a subject of personal right than movables, which remain the property of those who have owned them wheresoever they go, or are carried. So clearly is water considered portion of land, that the right of conveying water over the land of another was originally confined to the purposes of irrigation. *Noodt*, 1., 8, tit. 3, says: *Causa ab initio fuit rigandi agri, quatenus ei erat opus, non ultra. Adeoque non potuit aqua duci ad quem personæ usum commoditatemve, ut pecoris causa vel amœnitatis, in prædia rustica vel urbana, nec magis potuit ducta cum alio communicari prædio aut alio prædii loco quam cui acquisitus esset aquæductus. Fundamentum regulæ erat: quod aquæductus non putabatur esse jus sive qualitas ipsius domini sed prædii, ideoque extra prædium ejusque necessitatem non intelligi.* Originally water was allowed to be led over another's land only for the purpose of irrigation, and no other. Accordingly this right of water passage over another's property could not exist for any personal use or convenience—whether for bringing down water for cattle or for purposes of personal enjoyment, either over *prædia rustica* or *urbana:* nor could the water so led over another's property be communicated to any other property, or any other part of the property than that for which the right of water passage had been acquired; because *aquæductus* was not considered to be a right or quality of the owner, but of the property which he owned, and therefore was not understood to exist except for the property and its necessity. *Noodt* proceeds to say that the strictness of the rule in later times (as we are aware) in regard to the leading of water over another's property, so as to confine it to the necessary uses of the dominant tenement, was by degrees modified; and that the *jus aquæductus* subsisted no longer *in necessitatem prædii*, but for all purposes *commoditatis et amœnitatis*, of comfort and enjoyment. of the owner of the *prædium*. But there must be a *prædium cui prædium servit*, or there is not a real servitude. *Voet*, 8, 1, 4, also repeats "that both a dominant property, to which a service is due, and a servient property which owes it, are necessary to the

1866.
June 7.
„ 8.
July 12.

Dreyer vs.
Ireland.

constitution or exercise of a prædial servitude," and he adds "such servitudes have no existence without these properties are dominant and servient." It seems unnecessary to pursue this further than to call attention to the strictness with which it has been found advisable to adhere to the legal principle in this respect in all modern legislation founded on the civil law. The Code Napoleon, the new Civil Code of Holland, and the Civil Code of Louisiana, all have the following section, which is even more strict than the Roman and old Dutch law :—" Proprietors have a right to establish on their estates, or in favour of their estates, such servitudes as they deem proper. Provided, nevertheless, that the services be not imposed on the person, or in favour of the person, but on an estate in favour of an estate : and provided, moreover, that such servitudes imply nothing contrary to public order." It seems plain that the condition in the transfer to Rudolph Cloete fails to constitute a real servitude *aquæductus*. The water shall flow down undisturbed, says the title, but there is no estate for the benefit of which it is to flow down. A servitude is constituted, if at all, in favour of the persons who might purchase the water below E, and this water separated and distinct from any land ; which could not take place at all according to the passage from the Codes to which I have last referred. But what did Zeederberg and Wicht buy from the Association according to the condition of 1851 and the memorandum of 1852, without any further act on the part of the vendors, if in law they made any purchase that can be recognised of this water? They professed to buy the mill-stream below the mill, and the right to use it from there. They bought no land, and how it was possible for an individual (I do not now speak of public rights of water) to buy any right in flowing water, except as attached to land, I cannot at present conceive. But however this may be, as regards the mill property they bought the right, or professed to buy the right, limiting the owner's use of a stream passing over his land to its passage over the mill-wheel only, and entitling them, for the benefit of no specified land, to an uninterrupted passage of the water to the point E. Thus they gained a certain right, preventing him, for their personal benefit, from using water which otherwise passing through his land, he might use as he thought fit. As a general rule, no servitude in favour of lower proprietor existing, the upper proprietor may use water flowing through his land in any way he thinks proper. As I believe I have shown, no real servitude was created. But I think our law is sufficiently favourable to the position of Wicht and Zeederberg to allow them to have gained a personal servitude on the mill property in their favour. Certainly the vendor intended to sell a real

servitude, and as far as the plaintiff is concerned, what he
required and thought he had bought and got, was a real
servitude in favour of his brewery; but this was not obtained
nor conveyed. *Voet*, 8, 1, 4, has the following passage:—
" I should not omit to add that it is not infrequent that a
servitude in its nature real, should be modified into a personal servitude." And this is effected when a right of
" going," or of " driving," of " pasture," of " drawing water "
is granted to a certain person, and does not pass to his heirs,
and then it is that Modestinus and Paulus have held that the
use of water is personal, and it is not transmitted to the
heirs of the *usuarius*. The references are to *Dig.*, 7, 8, 21.
*Usus aquæ personalis est, et ideo ad hæredem usuarii trans-
mitti non potest.* And 8, 3, 37: *Lucius Titius, Caio Seio
fratri, P. S. De aqua fluente in fontem quem pater meus in
isthmo instruxit, do concedoque tibi gratuito digitum sive ad
domum, quam in isthmo tenes, sive quocunque tandem volueris.
Quæro, an ex hac scriptura usus aquæ etiam ad heredes Caii
Seii pertineat? Paulus respondit, usum aquæ personalem ad
hæredem Seii, quasi usuarii, transmitti non posse.* This is
translated for the purpose of this case : there having been
sold or granted to Zeederberg and Wicht a right as regards
the mill property, that all the water shall flow undisturbed
to E, and then Zeederberg and Wicht should have the whole,
not in respect of any land, but to be used for whatever purposes they might please ; that which they have acquired,
and which the owner of the mill is bound to concede to them
—in the present state of the titles,—is a personal use of the
water, which personal use, like all other personal servitudes,
must cease with the usuary's life, and cannot be transmitted
to his heirs. Accordingly, *Wissenbach* (20, 8, 16) lays
down that although *ductus* is a *servitus prædii*, a personal
obligation of this nature might be constituted, *veluti si con-
cedens his verbis usus fuerit : Permitto tibi ex fonte meo aquam
ducere in domum tuam aut quocunque volueris. Qua con-
cessione non ad utilitatem alicujus prædii respexit, sed ad
personæ illius commodu duntaxat.* And in this sense
he says that an expression of Labeo's is to be understood when he speaks of a right of water passage being
capable of existence without a *fundus*, as a personal right
belonging to the individual and not capable of transmission.
The conclusion to which I arrive is that Wicht and Zeederberg can be looked upon as having bought only a life interest in this water, a *personalis usus aquæ*, to terminate at the
furthest on the death of the survivor of them, but possibly at
the death of the first dying of them, for then the *persona* of
the two who had bought jointly ceased to have any existence.
But if this be in law what Wicht and Zeederberg have pur-

1866.
June 7.
  " 8.
July 12.

Dreyer *vs.*
Ireland.

1866,
June 7,
,, 8.
June 7.

Dreyer vs.
Ireland.

chased, what is the position of the purchaser, Dreyer? I am extremely doubtful whether this personal right for the period of the purchaser's life, could be sold at all. Usufructs may be sold : it is in their nature that they should, for when a man has a right to the enjoyment of all the fruits, natural or civil, of a thing, while its substance is untouched, the most valuable fruits to him, especially in usufruct of money, may be the price he can obtain for his right. But as a universal rule, the "usuary," who has less than the usufructuary, cannot sell or cede his right. "A usuary," says the *Institutes* (2, 5, 1), "cannot let, or sell, or give gratuitously his right to another, while a usufructuary may." Now, throughout the authorities, where a right to water of this nature, *i.e.*, not attached to land is spoken of, the possessor of such a right is designated *usuarius*. It seems to me to have been the policy of the law not to encourage the confusion necessarily to be created by an endeavour to separate real rights from the land. And therefore personal rights of this nature on *prædia* appear to be placed in the category of the non-transferable. In this very instance, as I have before pointed out, the value of this to the plaintiff consists in his having used it as a real servitude in favour of his brewery. And such he plainly believed it to be. While thus compelled to express my opinion of Mr. Dreyer's present position, which is one of considerable hardship, I do not think it irremediable. All the parties to these different transactions are still living. If their attention had been directed to the fact, no doubt the Association, as executors of Cloete, would have made a real transfer to Zeederberg and Wicht, as could easily have been done, and then *pari passu* there would have been a distinct servitude in favour of a dominant *prædium* on R. Cloete's property. If as I think was intended at the time, it was desired that the purchasers of the water should, at the conclusion of the sale, point out for the benefit of which lots they wished to have the water, the conveyances could have been drawn out accordingly. As Dreyer plainly bought the water for the benefit of his land, it may be quite possible that in a suit properly brought with all the parties before it, the Court could declare that Dreyer was entitled to a real servitude in favour of his brewery property on Ireland's land, and the titles might be so amended. But before this is done, I do not see how the prayer of the declaration is to be granted. Certainly there could not be a perpetual interdict, where there is but a limited right even in Wicht and Zeederberg, and less than that, in my opinion, in the plaintiff. I regret that I am unable to see that Dreyer has a right of action in the terms of this declaration, and would have felt myself forced to absolve the defendant from the instance. It will

1866.
June 7.
„ 8.
July 12.

Dreyer vs.
Ireland.

be observed that I do not in any respect controvert the doctrine of estoppel. I look on Ireland as exactly in the same position as Rudolph Cloete, and subject to the same conditions. Nor do I dispute that mere possession is a good title against anyone who cannot show a better. But my difficulty is that the right to water flowing over Ireland's land does not appear to me to be, in the circumstances of this case, the subject of possession to Dreyer. But if I be right that the defendant has his title in the land without a distinct servitude, this is better than *quasi* possession of that which required a qualified title. If I accept the doctrine of my brethren that there is sufficient in Dreyer to give him a right to this action, then, as regards the facts and the use of the right, I perfectly agree with the views expressed by them.

In reference to a question of interest raised in the course of this discussion—that of the necessity of registration to the due constitution of a real servitude, except only in the case where it is constituted by prescription for the third of a century*, and the very slight value of personal agreement where there has been no due registration—it may be advisable to direct attention to a case decided by the Privy Council in appeal from the Supreme Court of British Guiana, in 1860. It is the case of *Steel and Another vs. Thompson*, in 13, *Moore's P.C. Reports*, p. 280. In October, 1826, there had been articles of agreement by which part of a sugar plantation in Essequibo was sold upon terms (*inter alia*) that a fresh water canal running across part of the plantation retained by the vendor as well as the part sold, should be for the joint use of the two plantations constituted out of the old one. This agreement was recorded in the Secretary's office. On the 16th November, transfer was effected *corum lege loci*, which in Guiana is before two Commissioners of the Court, of the plantation sold according to the forms in use there, which appear to be very nearly our own. Unfortunately, on this conveyance there was no actual mention of the use of the canal, which was situated on ground retained by the owner of the whole: though the conveyance to the purchaser stated that the transfer of the land, with the boundaries, &c., was effected " all agreeably to contract of sale and purchase recorded in the Secretary's office." After this —from 1826 to 1857—the canal was used for the benefit of both proprietors, notwithstanding change of proprietors: it was in fact the only means of conducting the shipping and navigation of the plantations. The proprietors of the two estates at the date of the proceedings had become proprietors on transfers following on execution sales—the one of the

---

* The period of prescription in this Colony in regard to servitudes upon or connected with immovable property is now fixed at thirty years. *Vide* Act No. 7, 1865, sec. 106.

1866.
June 7.
„ 8.
July 12.

Dreyer vs.
Ireland.

property alienated in 1826—in 1849; the other of the property retained in 1826—in 1854. In 1857 the latter placed an obstruction in the canal, so that it could not be used by the former. In the Supreme Court of Guiana it was contended for the owner of the part alienated in 1826, that the reference in the transfer of that year to the agreement of purchase and sale, registered in the secretary's office, by saying that the transfer was effected "all in accordance with the contract of sale and purchase," was in fact an incorporation of it, and thus the transfer conveyed the right of navigation of the canal. But the Court held that, notwithstanding this, the right of navigation that was intended to be sold by the agreement with the land, was not conveyed by the transfer. And the Privy Council affirmed the judgment. So that absence of due registration and conveyance of the servitude intended to be constituted in 1826 deprived the owner of the property of a privilege which it was believed had been secured, and this, although it had been enjoyed for thirty years and nine months. It is right that conveyancers should bear in mind the strong views of the law entertained by the Privy Council on the subject of conveyance of servitudes.

ERASMUS *vs.* DE WET.

[Referred to in HOUGH *vs.* VAN DER MERWE, *ante*, p. 142.]

Water-rights.—Upper Proprietor.—Private Stream.

Per WATERMEYER, J.—*The proprietor of an upper farm is entitled to the free use of water flowing through, and to a great extent rising upon, the upper farm, for the purposes of irrigation and increasing plantations, though such free use and new plantations may cause damage to lower proprietors.*

WATERMEYER, J., said:—This was a case heard at the Robertson Circuit, in October last, between Louw, Erasmus, and others, plaintiffs, and De Wet, defendant. I did not proceed to judgment, but made an order by which the judgment was to be delivered by me here in the Supreme Court, as if in the Circuit Court, *nunc pro tunc*. There was some doubt whether it was competent for me to make such an order, and so a consent paper was drawn up by counsel for the parties, by which it is provided, with reference to this order I had made, "that they consented to judgment being pronounced in the Supreme Court by Mr. Justice Watermeyer, and to its being valid and binding as if delivered in the Circuit Court of Robertson immediately after the trial of the case;" so that now there is no difficulty on this question. The case was brought by the brothers Erasmus, proprietors of a farm called "Wandsbeck," otherwise Onder Poesnel's River, division of Robertson, against De Wet, the proprietor of a farm called "Upper Poesnel's River." Between these two farms there is another called "De Fontein," occupied by the plaintiffs Erasmus, and the property of their mother. The action was brought against De Wet in consequence, as it was alleged, of certain acts of his in regard to the water of the Poesnel's River, which flows down through De Wet's farm, then through the farm Fontein, then to Wandsbeck, and through it when there is a sufficient quantity of water. By these acts it was alleged the plantations on Wandsbeck were seriously injured. It appears that of late, to a greater extent than before, cultivation has been going on on the farm Upper Poesnel's River, which is De Wet's and through his irrigation, to a greater extent than previously, on the south of the Poesnel's River. The allegation on the part of the plaintiffs is, that the farm Wandsbeck is of right entitled to the water of the Poesnel's River; that there has not been until lately any plantation to the south of the Poesnel's River on the farm Upper Poesnel's River, and that these new plantations caused considerable damage. I think that the plaintiffs are mistaken in their claim. The farm Wandsbeck has neither by right nor by prescription, nor in any other way of right, any claim by which the proprietors of the Upper Poesnel's River should be barred from the free use of the Poesnel's River for the purpose of irrigating and increasing their plantations. There are allegations in the declaration that for a series of years past the water had been used by the lower place, Wandsbeck, in the manner now claimed by the plaintiffs; but the evidence did not bear out these allegations at all. There was an allegation that the proprietor of the upper farm had never had a dam on the river for the purpose of irrigating to the south of the river; whereas it was proved in the case that for many years back there had been, though not to such an extent as now, cultivation to the south of the Poesnel's River upon that upper farm, to which objection is now made. What has been done upon the upper farm is nothing more than this: that this water flowing, and to a very great extent rising upon this upper farm, though not wholly (some of the water comes from beyond from certain mountains, some portion of the water rises from fountains on the upper farm, and some has its source just immediately beyond the boundary of the upper farm, all these come together), is used for irrigation on

1867.
Feb. 16.

Erasmus *vs.* De
Wet.

this upper farm without any reservation of any right
to the lower farms, although they have been in the
habit of using the water when it came down to them, which
sometimes was the case in summer, but certainly not always.
But the farm Wandsbeck is provided for, or intended to be
so, when its grant was made out; for it is distinctly stated
upon the title deed of Wandsbeck, in accordance with the
report of landdrosts before the grant of the farm, that when
the water of the Poesnel's River should not come down, when
it failed, then the farm Wandsbeck should be entitled to a
waterleading from the farm Fontein, which is situated between these two farms. If the claim of the plaintiff were
allowed, it would be utterly impossible to make any improve-
ment on the upper farm, which by right of its situation is entitled to the use, and the fee use, of such waters as may be
required for the purpose of irrigation, and as I have said before, there is no right upon the evidence, either by grant or
prescription, or any other way, that I can see, by which the
proprietors of Wandsbeck can claim that which they now
claim. Under these circumstances the judgment must be for
defendant, with costs. There is a claim (by the defendant)
in re-convention, against the plaintiff Erasmus, for having
broken a dam on the defendant's farm, made for the
purpose of irrigating a vineyard on the upper farm. This
claim in re-convention I think will entitle the upper proprietor to damages of 1s. Judgment is therefore generally
for the defendant, with the costs. I should have gone much
more fully into the authorities, but I am unable to do so just
now. [His Lordship was about embarking for England.] I
may add, that as this is a Circuit Court decision, if the parties
wish to appeal to the Supreme Court they have a right to
do so.*

---

* [No appeal was noted in this case.—ED.]

Lightning Source UK Ltd.
Milton Keynes UK
UKHW040807090120
356646UK00003B/810/P